Your Complete Forecast 2014 Horoscope

Your Complete Forecast
2014
Horoscope

BEJAN DARUWALLA

 Ranvir Books

First published in India in 2013 by Harper Element
An imprint of HarperCollins *Publishers*

Copyright © Bejan Daruwalla 2013

ISBN: 978-93-5116-073-1

2 4 6 8 10 9 7 5 3 1

Bejan Daruwalla asserts the moral right
to be identified as the author of this work.

HarperCollins *Publishers*
A-53, Sector 57, Noida, Uttar Pradesh 201301, India
77-85 Fulham Palace Road, London W6 8JB, United Kingdom
Hazelton Lanes, 55 Avenue Road, Suite 2900, Toronto, Ontario M5R 3L2
and 1995 Markham Road, Scarborough, Ontario M1B 5M8, Canada
25 Ryde Road, Pymble, Sydney, NSW 2073, Australia
31 View Road, Glenfield, Auckland 10, New Zealand
10 East 53rd Street, New York NY 10022, USA

Typeset in 11/14 Sabon
By Saanvi Graphics Noida

Printed and bound at
Thomson Press (India) Ltd.

Contents

Section II
Articles

A Disclaimer from Bejan

My regular and, I hope, new readers will be somewhat familiar with my style. I have published my horoscopes from 2010 onwards with a new publisher. However, I need to point out that the zodiac itself does not change. The qualities and the predictions for each sun sign are unchanged. Since the author/astrologer is also the same, the style and language are therefore bound to be similar to what was seen in earlier books. Any perceived similarities are merely coincidental. Moreover, forecasts for previous years no longer have any relevance, and copying from them would be an exercise in futility.

Foreword

Ancient Indian thought traditionally and historically quantifies long spells of time according to yugas, each of which is approximately twelve years. For example, the present era or yuga we are living in is considered to be the yuga of kali (Kalyug) in which all kinds of iniquities, sins, malpractices flourish. There is a reason for this little preamble. I wrote my books for my previous publishers for more than one 'yuga' – sixteen years or so. It was time for a change. Remember, great philosophers have said that change is the only constant in life. However, my changeover has resulted in some degree of acrimony and heartburn. Perhaps it was necessary to accomplish it. Whatever it may be, I hope that all these factors will not affect the loyalty of my regular readers or the interest of my new ones. Ultimately, you are the ones who matter. Now, having crossed eighty years of age, only the future of the world excites me. Before my eyes close and I go to meet my boss, Ganesha, I hope to predict world peace and compassion. That's all. I dedicate the new, changed version of my book not only to my Lord Ganesha, as always, but also to all my readers, both old and new, and hope you enjoy it. The content – astrology – is as old as time itself.

Bejan Daruwalla: New Milestones and Achievements

Ganesha says that the world-famous scientist Brian Cox predicts that our cosmos will one day shut down. It will be the end of all of us. Even if he is right, your Ganesha devotee sweetly replies:

> *'Everything will clang shut*
> *One night*
> *But a tiny spark of light*
> *Yours and mine*
> *Will sing and*
> *Dance through the night'*

Yes, this may probably be our greatest achievement. Reason? We will not go down fighting, screaming, shouting, hollering, raving at the cosmos. We will go down singing and dancing and sweetly fulfilled. We will be human and happy. That will be our greatest achievement. Dear Readers, you are free to agree or disagree.

My Lord and Master Ganesha says loud and clear, 'Love and serve Humanity and Mother Nature.' I see the future. Therefore, I am happy that my prediction about Vidyadham High School – which served very poor students, and which had closed down – reopening has now come true, thanks to Rohini Rao, Dr Usha Nair and others. It is of more value than the Best Astrologer 2013 Award conferred on me by the Russian Society of Cosmic Healers on 7 January 2013. My 2013 annual horoscope book was translated in the Russian language and was exhibited by the Russian Vice-Consul Dementiev at the Russian Centre, Mumbai.

Also, I have been included as one of the eleven persons in the book *Change Your Life*, published by Random House and Penguin. Being human, it gives me sweet satisfaction. I am now eighty-three (born on 11 July 1931). I also know that after a few years it will be somebody else who will help to change the world. I know that nothing lasts forever. But I also know how to enjoy the moment to the hilt. That is the secret of happiness. Other achievements, for whatever they are worth, include *Libas International*, Pakistan, *Outlook*, 5 November 2012; plaque for me and my son Nastur from *Dainik Bhaskar*, 26 December 2012; chief guest at the annual prize-giving ceremony of Maharana Mewar Educational Institution, Udaipur.

Bejan cares, Daruwalla dares. Therefore I am sticking my neck out again and saying that between July 2013 and July 2014 the seeds of lasting peace will be sown. I admit I may be wrong. But I must take a stand for humanity and peace. That is my karma and dharma. I am prepared to pay the price for it.

Let me conclude from my 2013 book: 'Bejan was on NDTV Profit, CNBC Awaz, TV 9, India TV and he made it absolutely clear that despite setbacks India will be the superpower of the twenty-first century and from July

2013 or so there will be an upturn for the world. In short, Bejan says that 27 June 2013 to 30 March 2025 will be the greatest period of evolution in human history. He is acknowledged as one of the 100 great astrologers in the last 1000 years in *The Millennium Book of Prophecy*, published by Harper Collins, USA.'

1. Awarded the highest degree of Vedic astrology, 'Jyotish MAHAHOPADHAYA' by the Federation of Indian Astrologers.

2. He was the astrologer in residence at Manila Hotel, Philippines.

3. Bejan featured on *Hard Talk India* on the BBC channel in August 1999.

4. On 10 December 2010, Bejan featured in 'The Job: Corporate Astrologer' in *The Financial Times*, London. The interviewer was Rhymer Rigby.

The Planets and Their Indications

MARS: Body, ego, brother, force, technical education, arrogance, anger, tamas (ignorance), blood, blood relatives. Energy produces power and power is Mars.

MERCURY: Buddhi, intelligence. The whole universe is covered by intelligence. Intelligence is essential for education, discretion, business dealings, and business acumen. Also younger siblings and friendship.

JUPITER: The Jeevatma, Jeevakaraka, preacher, guru, children, money and nobility.

SUKRA: Wife, Jeevakaraka for females, luxury, vehicles, bhoga or materialistic pleasures and learning.

SATURN: Karma, profession, lethargy, lazy, slow moving.

RAHU: Apasavya Karma, poison, pain, foreign, unethical things and materialism.

KETU: Binding, wiry, imprisonment, trying for mukti, rejection of materialistic pleasures.

(Rahu and Ketu are called destiny breakers while the moon is considered a destiny modifier.)

Aries

YEARLY FORECAST

Till 16 July 2014

Summary and Guidance

Ganesha says, till 16 July 2014, Jupiter will be in your fourth house. The results will be:

Home is the hunter from the hills
The sailor from the sea.

'A home away from home is also a home,' says Bejan.
Renovation, decoration, alteration, buying and selling of property are an integral part of the year for an Aries. Office and shop also come in this bracket. So do land and agriculture.

17 July 2014 to 11 August 2015

From 17 July 2014 to 11 August 2015, Jupiter will be in your fifth angle. Pleasure and profit, high-powered creativity, children, love, romance and freedom will be your destiny. Joy and delight will hug you. But during this period you should avoid all risky ventures, specially those that have to do with finances, investments, loans and funds. You should also take care of your health.

Dear readers, please understand that in astrology, the exact time and period is not clearly and completely defined. One major trend runs into another for 2–3 months. Therefore, one needs to take that into account. Like life, in astrology too, many events happen at the same time or in quick succession or rotation. Make allowances for it.

Ganesha says we are in the age of digital technology. That means everything is made simple, direct and easy to understand. If we take one look at it, we can follow it completely and cleanly.

Main Trend

Ganesha says, as we have already said at the very beginning, that the home will be the hub of attention. Strictly speaking, the year is all about property, be it house, home, office, godown, storehouse, warehouse, farmhouse, agricultural land or any other property. Together with it, I repeat what I said last year: astrology cannot be put into watertight compartments. The predictions are based only on your sun sign by Western astrology. Therefore, it does not include your horoscope, your moon sign, and other necessary details. I openly admit that it is not perfect. But as a guideline it should be reasonably correct for most of you. Therefore, do not use it as a crutch.

Saturn will be in Scorpio from 6 October 2012 to 23 December 2014. In simple terms, it means you have to take care of your bank account, joint finances, loans, credits, debts, funds and health. Luckily, Saturn and Jupiter will be in fine formation from 5 April 2013 to 15 July 2014. This will be mighty important for anything to do with house, home, loans, funds, property and family. This is how you can use astrology to your advantage. I am sure you do understand this very well, because Aries are quick and fast and grasp things easily. Haste is waste.

But Ganesha reminds us very strongly that this is not the whole story. From 17 July 2014 to 11 August 2015, Jupiter will be in your fifth angle according to Western astrology. The fifth angle stands for (a) forceful creativity, (b) progeny, (c) father, (d) mental ability, (e) learning, (f) scholarship, (g) character, (h) conception, (i) prosperity, (j) acquisitions through wife, (k) fascination (for women), (l) sharp wisdom, (m) discrimination and analytical skill, (n) capability, (o) devotion to gods, (p) means of earning, (q) official seal, (r) good or bad memory, (s) speculation, (t) humiliation, (u) authorship, (v) shruti (vedas), (w) smriti, (x) knowledge of mantras, (y) karmas of past lives, and (z) knowledge.

A poet has said, 'Give me life, life and still more life.' It means all the pleasures and pains of life, all the romance and freedom of love and laughter, and a heart big enough to embrace the whole world. I know that I am asking too much from the Aries. But Aries are intense and courageous and, therefore, you have the ability to give your best and cheer up the world. You have really strong shoulders and, as they say, you do carry the heaviest burden. Be proud of it. Enjoy yourself and do your duty. In other words, have your cake and eat it too. This is the greatest compliment I can pay you.

Saturn in Scorpio will be in bad formation with Jupiter in your fifth angle from 17 July 2014 to 11 August 2015. Therefore, during this period, be careful of all financial matters; dealing with loans, funds, joint finance, banks, trust, wills, codicils, and so on. Secondly, please also take good care of your health. I am saying this for your own good. I am sure that readers who have been following me for the last twenty years know very well that I have always said astrology is only a guideline. Nothing is final. Above all else, have faith in God and yourself. Believe me—that is my last word.

Journey and Communication

From 8 to 22 April, Mercury is in your own sign and it favours travel, trips, communication, contacts, hard work and matching results. Team work will give you the best results. The months of June, December and February during the period under review are also favourable for it. Make a note of it in your diary.

Health

As said earlier, Saturn could cause ill health. Hanuman is the lord of Saturn. If you believe in prayers, the mantras are? (i) Hum hanumantaye ramdutaye namah, (ii) Om praam preem proum sa sanaye namah. If you do not believe in prayer, I suggest charity. In any case, helping the poor, the weak and the forsaken is always good.

Love/Marriage

As said in the summary, love, marriage, children, romance will be more favourable from 17 July 2014 to 11 August 2015. Venus, the instigator of love and romance, will be in your sign from 3 to 28 May 2015. You will woo and coo as we say. Enjoy! August and to some extent October 2014, and February 2015 will be good for matters of the heart. Music and romance, good food and ambience/atmosphere go together.

Property

As said earlier, till 16 July 2014, all property matters will be highlighted. It should be very clear that land, building and construction take a lot of time and, therefore, this trend will continue for one or two years. I repeat: there are no clear, distinct, definite dates when one trend ends. Life is a continuous flow.

Job/Business/Loans/Funds/Investments

August and September 2014 will be mighty important for job and business. January 2015 will really be the springboard for job, business, commission and sales. In fact, all types of activity are focused in January itself.

Children/Entertainment

17 July 2014 to 11 August 2015 is specially meant for children, entertainment, films, music and all sorts of creative pursuits. Also, Venus in your sign from 3 to 28 May favours it. Yes, I admit your ventures and adventures could be a bit risky. But as we say, 'Nothing ventured, nothing gained.'

Trips and Ties

Trips and ties go together with journeys and communication. But ties are particularly emphasized in August and December 2014 and February and April 2015.

Publicity, Projects, Performance

Performance and projects mean much to you Aries. Mercury in your sign from 8 to 22 April 2015 and Venus in your sign from 3 to 28 May act as a spur to gain publicity and up your performance. I am trying to motivate you to give your best by showing you the chart of your favourable months. August 2014, and January, February and April 2015 should help you move forward at a fast and furious pace. Expect good results.

Happiness Quota

Strictly speaking, happiness is a personal equation and varies from person to person. But for Aries, performance, action and results matter greatly. Performance becomes an integral part of happiness. Romance and love add infinitely to joy and delight. Taking all these into active consideration for this period and Jupiter's stay in your fifth angle till 11 August 2015, my marks for you will be 77 per cent.

Monthly Round-up

January: up and about, hard work—you will be really ready to be on the go, be it home or office; February: fun and games, friendship and fraternity, gains and gaiety; March: too many things happening all together, see that you conserve your energy/vitality; April: month of progress, prosperity, pelf and getting things done; May: loans and funds and deals and transactions, buying/selling; June: assignments, communication, transport, ties, trips, relatives; July: home, house, family, shopping, renovation/decoration/alteration; August: trips, ceremonies, rites, fame and name, future plans; September: work, health, rewards, service, pets, projects, colleagues, promotion; October: love, marriage, lawsuits, relationships, travel, contracts, communication, enemies; November: joint finance, loans, funds, immigration, moving, shifting, capital formation, passion, sex; December: joy, publicity, travel, ceremony, functions, parties, invitations, import and export, collaboration, contacts, and happiness because of abundance.

Outer Planets

In Western astrology, Uranus, Neptune and Pluto are the outer planets. They also have their say in the destiny of human beings.

URANUS: Uranus, the planet of rebellion, is in your twelfth angle. This could mean court cases, separations, expenses, bad health, accidents and even isolation and hospitalization. Please do not panic. These are only the possibilities I have suggested. But astrology is a symphony and an orchestra. Other planets also play a part. My suggestion is to take it a bit easy in the months of March, July, October and April. The brighter side is that you will be into many welfare schemes and projects and will certainly help the poor and the weak. Remember, there are two sides to a sword. Finally, I say to you, in the name of Ganesha: 'Live long and prosper.' This is an old, wise saying.

NEPTUNE: Neptune will be in your sign in 2014. Neptune represents inspiration and hallucination. Your dreams will come true only if they are grounded in reality and practicality. But from 17 July 2014 to 11 August 2015, all creative pursuits, pleasures, enjoyments, films, music and dance give delight and also motivate the whole world. It is a grand time to show and manifest your undoubted talent and genius.

PLUTO: Pluto will be in your tenth angle and will activate you to give your best performance. Pluto means power. You must learn to use it wisely and well. The months for it will be January, April, October and July. Be reasonable and diplomatic. Remember that others too have feelings and ideas. Be patient and tolerant, though I know it is difficult for you.

Month by Month

January

The new moon is in Capricorn and you make headway as the new year begins. There are a few maudlin moments, ill health and domestic concerns, but you manage to overcome all. There are expenses and increased earning, so it balances out. The highlight of the period is clearly money. By the end of the month, there is new intensity in all that you do. There are expenses, aggression, temper tantrums, ego issues, passion, lust, love and bonding. This is a good period for those in stocks, housing, realty, pharmaceuticals, chemicals and insurance sectors. You also display a philanthropic streak. Ganesha is with you.

February

You make big money and sign new deals. Others join you as success breeds and attracts success. There are alumni meetings, new friends, social gatherings, family outings and a lot of outdoor activities. You will bond with elders, parents, in-laws, siblings and extended family in a very special way. Women, in particular, may get excessively emotional around this time. Leave the rest to Ganesha.

March

You are filled with new ideas, hopes, dreams and aspirations. New vistas open, and you are engulfed in the fragrance of success, happiness, friendship and love. There are meetings and many new associations. You hog the limelight. You are poised to achieve something of real value. You may activate hidden forces that may change your life. Ganesha is delighted.

April

This is a very significant period. Mercury is in Aries from 8 to 22 April. You have the Midas touch. There is career success, good health, love and joy. You set your sights high. You are filled with energy. You are aggressive, determined and mow down the opposition. There is health, wealth and happiness.

May

Your thinking is disciplined and your critical faculties are sharp. This is a great time for important business transactions. You are filled with zeal and vision; you cannot go wrong. There is a selflessness in your personal relationships. On the work front, there are new challenges, new associations and foreign travel. By the end of the month, there is a new awareness and sensitivity. Venus is in Aries from 3 to 28 May. Venus is another important planet and is of great significance. This is also an important phase. You take powerful strides and move ahead with speed, dexterity and purpose. Ganesha is happy for you. You look for new directions and there is a major upheaval in your life. Ganesha blesses you.

June

There are new opportunities and lady luck smiles. You are prudent with finances and save for a nest egg. There are powerful psychological energies at play and your life could change dramatically. There may be a break-up with your partner; if married, you will have to move several roadblocks to bring peace. There could be medical emergencies, and children will need attention. By the end of the month, there is tremendous intellectual and mental energy. There is success, rewards, awards, accolades and applause. There could even be new love. Ganesha is with you.

July

There is a lot on your plate now as you swerve from one emotion to another. There are expenses, moments of despair alternating with hope, joy, ecstasy, anger and so much more. You are grappling with many emotions. You may need to make fundamental changes in your life. This is a great time for people in media and those running big corporations. There are new relationships and new experiences. By the end of the month, there are windfalls and lucky breaks. There is raw passion, new love, even crazed lust. This is also a good time for those working with stocks, realty, construction, insurance, pharmaceuticals, journals and films. Ganesha blesses you.

August

You are inventive, health is good, love life is rocking, and the family is well settled. There are secret liaisons, temper tantrums, jealousy, anger, hate and possessiveness. You will have to cope with a lot of inner negativity. There is also the danger of burnout and ill health. You work on new projects and collaborations. Your pace is frenetic. There is stability, hard work and a new direction in your life. You win the admiration of your peers. Ganesha is delighted.

September

There could be altercations, needless disputes, irritability, emotionalism, rash action and hastiness. You are overly critical of people and could be prone to accidents too. There are maudlin moments that snare you. This is also a creative phase and those in the arts do well. You look at the larger issues of life. You want renown and celebrity status. This is a good time for all kinds of business negotiations. There are expenses and new love. Ganesha walks with you.

October

You are excited by parapsychology, psychic insights, nursing, healing, mantra, tantra and yantra. This is a soft, mellow and beautiful period when beauty, magic, love, romance and passion take over. Your faculties are stimulated and you are fascinated by the twists and turns of life around you. The tempo is brisk and you make plans and set about executing them. By the middle of the month, you are in an indulgent mood and spend time with friends and in comfort shopping. There could also be crazed love. This is a good time for financial enterprises, especially those involving foreign investments. Ganesha lends a helping hand.

November

You are in the throes of communication. You use every tool of modern technology. You are on every social networking site. You are alert, congenial and direct. There could be travel, outdoor sport, love and bonding. You are in a powerful creative space. You are drawn to the contemplative life and look deep within. By the end of the month, there are soft, tender moments. Those in love reach new heights of ecstasy. You are filled with love and bonhomie and it is contagious. Ganesha smiles.

December

You are particularly perceptive of the fine sensitivities of others. You apply balm on wounds, introspect and handle your own hurts. This is a period of inward growth. You are calm, balanced, rational, cool and detached; emotional issues are well handled. You glow in the limelight. There is love, money, significant progress in all areas of your life and, most importantly, you have evolved into a better human being. You enter the new year with renewed fire, gusto and zeal. Ganesha blesses you.

Months at a Glance

January

Be up and about, work hard; you will be really ready to be on the go, be it home or office.

February

Fun and games, friendship and fraternity, gains and gaiety.

March

Too many things happening all together; see that you conserve your energy/vitality.

April

Month of progress, prosperity, pelf and getting things done.

May

Loans and funds and deals and transactions, buying/selling.

June

Assignments, communication, transport, ties, trips, relatives.

July

Home, house, family, shopping, renovation/decoration/alteration.

August

Trips, ceremonies, rites, name and fame, future plans.

September

Work, health, rewards, service, pets, projects, colleagues, promotion.

October

Love, marriage, lawsuits, relationships, travel, contracts, communication, enemies.

November

Joint finance, loans, funds, immigration, moving, shifting, capital formation, passion, sex.

December

Joy, publicity, travel, ceremonies, functions, parties, invitations, import and export, collaboration, contacts, and happiness because of abundance.

Weekly Review (By the phases of the moon)

1 January: New Moon in Capricorn

Aries is symbolized by the ram. A ram's horn is part of a cornucopia, the 'horn of plenty', symbolizing abundance. The Aries are said to be leaders and pioneers. Aries is the first sign of the zodiac. It is an active, energetic sign. Generally, people born under this sign are direct, straightforward and uncomplicated. Famous Aries include Edgar Wallace, Ayrton Senna, Al Gore, René Descartes, Arnold Toynbee, Bob Woodward, Sir Charles Chaplin, David Lean, Eddie Murphy, the Sundance Kid, Wilbur Wright, Jackie Chan, Leonardo Da Vinci and Lady Gaga. The new moon is in Capricorn and you make headway as the new year begins. Well begun is half done and you are sitting pretty. You work hard and there is success. There are a few maudlin moments, ill health and domestic concerns, but you manage to overcome them with stamina and determination. If you had started on a new venture the previous year, there will be continued success. Ganesha wishes you well.

8 January: First Quarter in Aries

There is fire in the belly as you surge ahead. Nothing can stop you. There are expenses and increased earning and so it balances out. You make fancy purchases and may take an exotic holiday with family and friends. The highlight of the period is clearly money. You are busy with fiscal issues, partnerships, profitable alliances and business collaborations. You do well and make waves with sound judgement and uncanny moves. You are shrewd and cunning. You have love and bonding as well, since you spend time with friends and loved ones. Ganesha is with you as you surge ahead. If a child in the family has been unwell for long, there could be chances of recovery now. Elders will need attention. Those in social work or heading large organizations meet with success.

16 January: Full Moon in Cancer

There are emotional moments with loved ones. There could be a break-up of a relationship, and you are scathed by it. It will be a time to rethink your priorities and decide on a new course in life. There is continued work pressure along with the emotional upheaval and so there is a lot on your plate. You will have to deal with disparate issues without bringing your emotions into play, and that could be difficult. Rationality and balance take a back seat, and that could be your undoing. Ganesha holds your hand and guides you through the turbulent times. New windows will open up soon in your life and you just need to wait for the clouds to part. Endless possibilities will beckon, and you will be richer with the experience of loss. Now, demons and witches, fairies and ghouls are doing the tango with you. There are moments when you feel completely lost. Under all the bravado, you are like a tender leaf shivering in a tempest.

24 January: Last Quarter in Scorpio

There is new intensity in all that you do. At one level, there is work and its pressures calling out to you and on another, domestic demands are mounting. There are expenses, new people flit into your life in some guise or the other. Rebellion, aggression, temper tantrums, ego issues, passion, lust, love and bonding will keep you occupied. Yes, there is a lot on your plate. You may look at unethical options and revenge for perceived insults. Ganesha asks you to take a step back and let the phase pass. There is success, but it comes with a heavy price tag. Take to yoga and meditation, watch your diet and indulgences, and do not react negatively. There is money to be made but, alas, honey may take some time.

30 January: New Moon in Aquarius

Your mind is plagued by thoughts. You run helter-skelter in several directions without a clue. You are also in a creative phase and could indulge in extreme self-promotion which could backfire. This is also a good period for those in stocks, housing, realty, pharmaceuticals, chemicals and insurance sectors. You also display a philanthropic streak and help in old-age homes and work with the less privileged. There could be an addition to the family. You may also embark on a pilgrimage and seek out gods and goddesses. You are looking for deliverance. You look at relationships to save you and could be indiscreet in your affections. Finally, no one other than you can deliver yourself. That is a great learning, and Ganesha nods in complete agreement. Wherever we are and whoever we are with, we cannot run away from ourselves.

6 February: First Quarter in Taurus

'Nature does not hurry, yet everything is accomplished,' said Lao Tzu. Quite like nature, you accomplish a lot in this phase without scurrying around like a busy beaver. You make big money and sign new deals. Others join you as success breeds and attracts success. Colleagues and friends envy you as somehow you make all the right moves. You seem to be guided and goaded by a friendly magician, like Merlin. There is also love and passion and you are lost in the arms of Eros. There are alumni meetings, new friends, social gatherings, family outings and a lot of outdoor activities like picnics and treks. Ganesha is happy for you. You look for love and you get it. It is as simple as that.

14 February: Full Moon in Leo

This is a great time to surge ahead in all your dealings. There is stability, luck, hard work and all the right openings. You are the right person at the right place. You are like the cat with the cream. You lap it all up and are filled with gratitude. 'The measure of a man is what he does with power,' said Plato. You have the power now and it is up to you. You could become a domineering tyrant with ego burdens, or step out of line to help those less gifted. Money is in sharp focus as you revamp your finances. The thrust is on realty, loans, insurance, investments and other fiscal instruments. You may visit museums and attend plays, poetry and book readings. There are rewards and awards, money and honey, acclaim and applause. You live in abundance and attract it. Ganesha is thrilled.

22 February: Last Quarter in Sagittarius

There is a lot of movement now in every sense of the word. The focus, though, remains on strong family ties.

You will bond with elders, parents, in-laws, siblings and extended family in a very special way. You realize that you need their love and cannot live without it. This is not a weakness. Love reciprocated is a sign of strength and can be a pillar of support, propelling you to greater heights. Women in particular may get excessively emotional now and make several demands of their partners. I must add here that these are generalizations. I need a personal horoscope to be more accurate. You also have free will to work your way through life. These are nudges and signposts. Use them well. Leave the rest to Ganesha, like *I* always do. He knows best.

1 March: New Moon in Pisces

You are in a mild mood. You think of roses and petals and listen to ghazals, Jim Reeves and soft music. There are emotional issues to contend with but this is also an excellent time for working with others. You are assertive and make your point in no uncertain terms. You do not look for altercations but are clear that you do not like others stepping on your turf either. You are polite yet firm, and earn the respect of others. You are filled with new ideas, hopes, dreams and aspirations. Youngsters do exceptionally well, young adults find love and the elderly are in a state of peace and balance. New vistas open and you are engulfed in the fragrance of success, happiness, friendship and love. Ganesha smiles.

8 March: First Quarter in Gemini

You take time out and lock yourself up. You need me time to reorganize your life and seek a new direction. You are now keen to formulate new goals and follow them through. There are powerful ego energies at play and you want to work with them and not allow them to become burdensome. You are also a team player and realize that you have to carry others along to reach where you want to. You go out of your way to balance your interests with others. There is powerful energy working in your favour. There are meetings and many new associations. You hog the limelight and just love it. Ganesha is pleased. There are awards and accolades.

16 March: Full Moon in Virgo

You plough ahead with single-minded devotion to detail. You have an open mind and allow new currents into your life. There is a lot of learning and you are richer for it. You are able to listen to others and moderate your rather fanatical views. In the process, you are sought after and become the soul of the party. This is a powerful phase and Ganesha suggests that you use it well. There is stability in domestic affairs; children bring joy and elders seem happy and well settled. Of course, let me add that these are generalizations, gentle nudges and prods. More precision will require a personal horoscope.

24 March: Last Quarter in Capricorn

There is both work and fun. You spend time at home. You need the love and warmth of family. If you have been away for long, this is the time you crave for home food and the warmth of the fireplace, in a manner of speaking. Those who are in hostels and boarding schools come home for a while. You entertain in style and are the most sought after host. You feel content, and indulge. Enjoy, says Ganesha. I agree. Look at me. I just love my food and the good times. My middle name is indulgence. You may take the family on a holiday as all of you will bond like an old-fashioned Indian joint family without any hiccups. And that is saying a lot.

30 March: New Moon in Aries

You are filled with jet fuel as you scorch the stratosphere. The new moon is in Aries and it is imperative that you use the energies well. You are poised to achieve something of real value. You could activate hidden forces that could well change your life. 'The only person you are destined to become is the person you decide to become,' said Ralph Waldo Emerson. He is spot on. In this phase, you propel yourself towards a new you. There are new directions at work; there is expansion and growth. 'Let your highest aspiration organize your life,' said the Mother at Puducherry. You let that simple but powerful line take over your entire being. Ganesha is delighted. There is new love, lust, passion and deep bonding. You are on the threshold of new discoveries that could turn your life around.

7 April: First Quarter in Cancer

This is a very significant period. Mercury is in Aries from 8 to 22 April. Mercury, the mighty, all-powerful planet is in your sign now. It favours travels, meetings, conferences, interviews, trips, more brain power, contacts, communication, correspondence and contracts. Mercury has a special connection with the circuits of the brain. Chess, crossword and other such games belong to Mercury. Also, short-distance runners and spin bowlers are controlled by Mercury. Mercury, in short, is the ambassador and salesman of the zodiac. Mercury is the symbol of news, views, messages, interviews, contacts, communications, travel and transport, and gives an impetus to all of the above in the sun sign where it is deposited. This is also your birth period and the cumulative energies are powerful. 'Take the tide at the flood and it will lead to fortune,' said the Bard. You have the Midas touch. There is success in career, good health, love and joy. Ganesha is happy for you.

15 April: Full Moon in Libra

'Seek not to follow in the footsteps of men of old; seek what they sought,' said the poet Matsuo Basho. You set your sights high on what could be called unattainable. You are filled with energy and could go overboard in its expression. You are aggressive and determined and will stop at nothing to get what you want. You mow down the opposition and grind it to dust. You could well be General Rommel, the Desert Fox, in one of his famous campaigns. Ganesha feels that if you temper this aggression and ruthlessness, and replace it with the simple art of persuasion, there will be more value to your success. It is pointless to step on toes when you can avoid it. There are expenses as you spend without a thought. There is health, wealth and happiness. Unless your personal horoscope indicates otherwise, I should be spot on.

22 April: Last Quarter in Aquarius

There are maudlin moments. You go down memory lane and rake up old hurts like a vacuum cleaner picking up everything in its vicinity. This could be a critical time in your communication with others, particularly with loved ones. You could hurt them with your outbursts, and hurt yourself too in the process. Your emotions are at boiling point and will impede your rational mind. You could be subjective, irrational, moody, picky, and patently unreasonable. You alienate others, and no one can even fathom what you are going through, or what is going through you. Keep a low profile and let the moment pass as it will. Your mind and heart are in a state of flux at the moment. On the plus side are romance, socializing and fun times. The bag is mixed. Ganesha watches over you.

29 April: New Moon in Taurus

Venus is in Aries from 3 to 28 May. Venus is another important planet and is of great significance. This is an important phase. As often discussed, Venus is the planet for love, romance, sex, beauty and the good life. This is the planet of attraction, love, wealth, knowledge and prosperity. The compatibility of partners and the type of life an individual will lead is judged from the placement of Venus in the horoscope. As a planet, Venus is considered to be beneficial, feminine and gentle. Venus symbolizes the force of attraction in the universe. In human beings, this attractive force manifests as love and beauty. When Venus is well placed in the chart, there is love, art, beauty and all the goodies of life that make it worth living. Venus rules Libra and Taurus, though its role in every sign is important. Like other planets, it also has its transits. In Libra, Venus is aesthetic and cultured. In Taurus it is more earthy, materialistic and sensual. Venus rules the venous system, kidneys, urinary tract, throat, larynx, and is responsible for good looks. In short, Venus in Western astrology stands for comforts, arts, wealth, relationships, sex, decorations, luxuries and wealth. Along with it, the new moon is in Taurus. This is a propitious time for growth in all areas of your life. You take powerful strides and move ahead with speed, dexterity and purpose. You have just had the beneficial effects of Mercury. Take risks. Go for the jugular, in a manner of speaking. Let there be no full stops in your life. Ganesha is happy for you.

7 May: First Quarter in Leo

'It isn't what you have, or who you are, or where you are, or what you are doing that makes you happy or unhappy. It is what you think about,' said writer and lecturer Dale Carnegie. Right on! You are moving ahead with single-minded dedication. Your thinking is disciplined and your critical faculties are sharp. This is a great time for important business transactions. You are filled with zeal and vision and cannot go wrong unless otherwise indicated in a personal chart. Watch out for ego issues, though. You believe that you are right all the time and fire on all cylinders. There is substantial headway at work with windfalls and bushels of good fortune, but you rub others the wrong way in the pursuit of success and this doesn't bode well. What goes around, comes around. Ganesha watches over you.

14 May: Full Moon in Scorpio

You feel you are in love. There is selflessness in your personal relationships. You want to love and care for someone without expecting anything in return. This is a great space to be in as love, in most situations, needs to be reciprocated. You love 'until it hurts', as Mother Teresa said. The flip side is that you could feel that you are a martyr and may wear a halo for loving so selflessly. That will undo everything. On the work front, there are new challenges, and you meet them head-on. There could be new associations and foreign travel. New frontiers open up and you busy yourself with loans, funds, rent, leases, legacies and inheritances. Ganesha watches over you.

21 May: Last Quarter in Pisces

There are emotional moments. You travel down memory lane and look at your errors with a magnifying glass. Let it be. Nothing can be done about the past. You can be irrational and emotional in your dealings and lose perspective. You need emotional reassurance and may withdraw from unfamiliar situations. It may be a good idea to lie low till the phase passes. There is travel, and strong overseas links. You may team up with a foreigner who is completely different from you. It could be a work association and nothing more. You also find energy and solace in new philosophies, and look hard for a spiritual master. Ganesha is with you. What could be better?

28 May: New Moon in Gemini

There is confusion and uncertainty. Your thoughts are zooming away like a meteor that has lost its way. You are like a pup in unfamiliar territory without its leash. There is new awareness and sensitivity, and your ego drive is thankfully low. You look at understanding others and not at competition or confrontation. You are not assertive or aggressive. You look for new directions like the tributaries of a great river. You are looking for answers and self-expression. You want to tether yourself to higher realities. There is a major upheaval in your life as you discard all that does not work any more. Our lives are like trees in the jungle. They look separate on the surface but their roots meet under the earth. You need others for a kind of organic rejuvenation. No man is an island. You understand that well, but all your contacts are not touching your soul. Ganesha blesses you as you go about reinventing yourself.

5 June: First Quarter in Virgo

There are strong ego drives. If you are rich or famous, you identify with it. You feel that your richness in material terms is indicative of your worth. You get possessive about your belongings, which then become a yardstick for comparison. But the work front sees a lot of stability. There are new opportunities and lady luck smiles. You are prudent with finances and save for a nest egg. You know that the future is uncertain and anything can happen. So you count your pennies and make sound investments. Ganesha journeys with you as you roll up your sleeves, dirty your hands and get down to the business of earning a living in earnest.

13 June: Full Moon in Sagittarius

There is fire in your belly. You have an open mind and are willing to take risks. If there is a call for astronauts, you will be the first to apply. You look at extreme adventure sports and take undue risks. Watch out for accidents. Take the necessary precautions. There are powerful psychological energies at play and your life could change dramatically. You look at new opportunities to make money. The employed are in for promotions and raises. Those on their own sign big deals and expand their businesses furiously. Very little time is spent at home but you are aware of your responsibilities and priorities. It is not neglect. It is just that you are preoccupied with the work front. The summer is here and you are beating the intense heat with cold calculations for a better future. Ganesha blesses you.

19 June: Last Quarter in Pisces

The last quarter is in Pisces and there are maudlin moments. There are tears of joy and sorrow. You are like a puppet with regard to your emotions. You could be ultra-sensitive to the most innocuous remarks. You are quick-tempered and take every criticism personally and react forcefully, hurting yourself and others in the process. There could be trouble in paradise. There may be a break-up with your partner, and, if married, you will have to move several roadblocks to bring peace. There could be divorces and out-of-court settlements. There could be medical emergencies and children will need attention. Hand yourself over to Ganesha. He will protect you. Of course, these are generalizations and gentle prods. Astrology never compels. There are several other influences, including your free will.

27 June: New Moon in Cancer

You are buzzing away like a million beehives. There is tremendous intellectual and mental energy. You are able to accomplish a lot. You get success and rewards and awards, accolades and applause. Ego drives are high. You are the toast of the peer group. Your competitive drives are heightened and you feel that you are right and everyone else is wrong. You meet up with old friends and family. There could be festivities in the family, alumni meetings, and backslapping with old buddies whom you haven't met in a long time. You make new contacts and love it. Handle your emotions and all will be well, says Ganesha. There could even be new love. Every cloud has a silver lining.

5 July: First Quarter in Libra

'A healthy attitude is contagious. But don't wait to catch it from others; be a carrier.' I quote Tom Stoppard, the British playwright. There is a lot on your plate now as you swing from one emotion to another like a trapeze artist. There are expenses, moments of despair alternating with hope, joy, ecstasy, anger and so much more. You are grappling with many emotions. There are issues at home and in the office that need attention. Children are also a cause of anxiety. They may be leaving home or chasing dreams that you don't care about. There could be the much-talked-about generation gap where you don't seem to see eye to eye on anything or it could even be plain, simple misunderstandings. You may need to make fundamental changes in your life. You seek out gods and godmen, tantra, yantra and mantra. There may be health issues too, and you check out alternative therapies. You need to reinvent yourself. Ganesha is with you as you embark on overcoming new challenges.

12 July: Full Moon in Capricorn

You are moving ahead at full throttle. There is a lot to be done and deadlines to be met. This is a great time for media folk and those running big corporations. Time is flying and you realize that every moment is precious. The 'golden hour' is here and now. You realize that you are way behind the high benchmarks you have set for yourself and work like one possessed. There are distractions but you find the balance soon. There are new relationships and new experiences. You may look at remarriage, same-sex marriage if that is your proclivity, a live-in relationship or even single-parent adoption. These are mere indicators. Ganesha nods. Astrology never compels. There is a lot of strength in free will too. Never be fatalistic. I must also add that times are changing and we must be open to change.

19 July: Last Quarter in Aries

The last quarter is in Aries and you are firing on all cylinders. There could be foreign travel too. Domestic and work pressures will be heavy, but you cope with everything and do exceedingly well. You set new goals and reach for the stars. There are also ego issues and you may feel that you are infallible. You often feel this way and nothing could be further from the truth. There are new encounters and experiences. With every challenge surmounted you evolve and become more complete. Ganesha blesses you.

26 July: New Moon in Leo

You continue on the winning spree. You are like Jesse Owens, Mark Spitz and Nadia other spell variation Comăneci put together at the Olympics. There is luck too, and that is always a blessing. Ask Ganesha! There are windfalls and lucky breaks, and you make money and honey. There is raw passion, new love, even crazed lust. This is also a good time for those working with stocks, realty, construction, insurance, pharmaceuticals, journals and films. There are awards and rewards, accolades and applause. You love the limelight. You will do anything for it. And here it falls on your lap without an invite!

4 August: First Quarter in Scorpio

There is new intensity and you take on anyone and everyone like Attila the Hun. You ooze confidence. There is fire in your belly and in your soul. You send out strong vibrations and others pick it up without much effort. They see you cracking big deals and want to join you for a slice of your luck. You are inventive and think out of the box, and, despite the ego drives, manage to work well in groups. Health is good, love life is rocking and the family is well settled. You are making money and enjoying yourself. What more do you want, asks Ganesha. Any demand now is sheer greed, I add.

10 August: Full Moon in Aquarius

You continue on the growth trajectory but there are maudlin moments that derail you, and the superfast express train that you have become resembles a goods train chugging away on coal now. But this is short-lived. There are secret liaisons, temper tantrums, jealousy, anger, hate and possessiveness. You will have to cope with a lot of inner negativity, with bottled emotions nestling deep in your subconscious threatening to blow up in your face. There could be embarrassing moments too, like a fashion faux pas on the ramp. Ganesha is with you and that helps. There is also the danger of burnout and ill health.

17 August: Last Quarter in Taurus

The last quarter is in Taurus and there is strength and solidity in your affairs. There is hard work ahead and money to be made. The hurt, acrimony and negativity of the past is done and dusted. You work on new projects and collaborations. You have the stamina of a horse and forge ahead, leaving the competition far behind. Your pace is frenetic, planning is excellent and the future looks bright. You take time out for the family too. Ganesha is pleased.

25 August: New Moon in Virgo

You are on jet fuel. There is stability, hard work and a new direction in your life. You sign deals and run a comb through them. You are the cynosure of all eyes and win the admiration and approval of your peers. Ganesha is delighted. There are no trap doors and trip wires. Your ascent is as steady as the rising sun in a clear sky. You have worked hard and made sacrifices and the results speak for themselves. There is a new confidence and self-belief. Life is dancing and calling out to you to participate. You have already accepted the invitation!

2 September: First Quarter in Sagittarius

There is a Zen proverb which says, 'Holding on to anger is like grasping a hot coal with the intent of throwing it at someone else. You are the one getting burned.' In this phase there could be altercations, needless disputes, irritability, emotionalism, rash action and hastiness. You lose your cool and angry words fly out of your mouth. Words are like arrows. Once let loose, they can't be retrieved. You find people management difficult. Learn to let off steam without hurting others. You are overly critical of people and could be prone to accidents too. Take the necessary precautions, says Ganesha. To be forewarned is to be forearmed. These are nudges. Use your free will to your advantage. Along with all the business expansions are massive investment outlays. There are loans to be paid off and you could be cash-strapped, leading to increased stress. Ganesha is with you as you surmount all the challenges and come out better and stronger for it.

9 September: Full Moon in Pisces

'The secret of health for both mind and body is not to mourn for the past, not to worry about the future, or not to anticipate troubles, but to live in the present moment wisely and earnestly,' said the Buddha. There are maudlin moments that snare you. You live in various timeframes and lose the present as it slips out of your grasp. You mourn over opportunities missed in the past. This is also a creative phase and those in the arts do well. There could be indulgences and you could lose focus as you let your life drift like passing clouds. You could seek to pacify a troubled mind by indulging in some god or guru shopping. You may also work with the less fortunate and join some philanthropic organization. There are challenges on the home front too. Ganesha walks the tightrope with you.

16 September: Last Quarter in Gemini

'If you want others to be happy, practise compassion. If you want to be happy, practise compassion,' said the Dalai Lama. You are in a whirl, trying your best to tame your monkey mind. This is a good period for all kinds of mental work. You are attentive to detail and look for perfection in whatever you do. You could be overcritical and intolerant of the frailties of those around you. In the process, while you mow down the opposition, you also create enemies. There could be jealously and animosity. Ganesha blesses you. You have no time for the home, as you go about seeking your inner self and taming the demons that trouble you.

24 September: New Moon in Libra

You look at the larger issues of life. You want your life to be significant and not ordinary. You are ambitious and want to do big things. You want renown and celebrity status. You want to become a person to be reckoned with, to be counted. You have clarity and go for it. This is a good time for all kinds of business negotiations. You sign on the dotted line, and sign big! There are expenses and new love. A lot is happening in your life and you are in a twirl. Ganesha walks the walk and talks the talk with you. 'First you should know who is inside you, then the same god will show you who is inside others,' said Ramana Maharshi. Understand yourself. That is the key.

1 October: First Quarter in Capricorn

There is hard work ahead. There is also love, and you are grappling with all the things that have suddenly fallen on your plate. You could be in a pleasant mood in which you want to meet up with people, party and have fun. This is a creative phase and those in the arts do well. It is not that you want to waste your time, you just want to do different things to torch your appetite for the big leap ahead. It is the lull before the storm. You spend time with your partner or loved one and may take a well-deserved holiday. You are excited by parapsychology, psychic insights, nursing, healing, mantra, tantra and yantra. This is a soft, mellow and beautiful period when beauty, magic, love, romance and passion take over. You want to just be or chill, as the next generation would have it. Ganesha is happy for you.

8 October: Full Moon in Aries

The full moon is in Aries and you are raring to go. Your faculties are stimulated and you are fascinated by the twists and turns of life around you. You read the papers and watch television and feel that you live on a fascinating and crazed planet. The tempo is brisk and you make plans and set about executing them. Everything does not work according to plan, but that should be expected. There is success in the material realm but you also look for spiritual succour. You turn to yoga, meditation and alternative healing. Ganesha blesses you.

15 October: Last Quarter in Cancer

You spend time with the family. You want to be surrounded by love. You go out of your way to give and receive it. You could be reasonably undisciplined and may just lie back and allow life to take over, which is not a bad idea at all. You are in an indulgent mood and spend time with friends and in comfort shopping. There could also be crazed love. You feel that your partner is the ultimate in the world and you are ready to do anything for him or her. There is passion and also deep, profound love. You may even take the relationship to the next level. There is sharing, bonding and harmony. You are like a Cheshire cat with a stomachful of milk, purring away. Life is bliss. Ganesha is delighted.

23 October: New Moon in Scorpio

I quote Mahatma Gandhi, the Father of the Nation: 'The only devils in this world are those running around inside our own hearts, and that is where all our battles should be fought.' There is intensity in all that you do now. You want to change the world and a lot is on your plate, but you also feel contented and benevolent. You are at peace. You love being with people, and they love being with you. There are picnics, outings and jamborees. You have a great time. This is also a good time for financial enterprises, especially those involving foreign investments. There is also room for amorous activity. You are caught in the coils of passion and are quite helpless. It is an emotional phase. You could fall headlong for a poet, writer, painter, singer, or anyone who is soulful. There are expenses too, as you make luxury purchases. Ganesha watches over you.

31 October: First Quarter in Aquarius

Socrates said, 'Contentment is natural wealth, luxury is artificial poverty.' You are not concentrating on work or on making more money now. There has been enough of it over the last few months. You want to enjoy yourself and have a good time. You hang around with friends, party, take part in festivities, indulge in comfort shopping for what you don't need and may never use, and generally go with the ebb and flow of life. You look for love and allow maudlin thoughts to caress you. You want to stand on the mountain and scream your love for the person who matters most in your life. On the flip side, lending, borrowing, investing, buying and selling are important. Life rolls on as Ganesha lends a helping hand.

6 November: Full Moon in Taurus

William Shakespeare said, 'Our doubts are traitors, and make us lose the good we oft might win, by fearing to attempt.' In this phase, there is no dearth of attempts. You try everything in the book to get your way through.

There is stability and hard work. You display stamina and perseverance. You show camaraderie and togetherness, and also have fun with colleagues, peers, family and friends. This could be a fruitful period as your creative juices are overflowing. There is money and honey, lucrative deals, storybook romance, leisure and pleasure. Ganesha holds your hand and leads the way. You want name and fame, and indulge in a lot of self-promotion. Hype is the name of the game and so you are not really off the track. There could be international travel too, and you make new profitable associations.

14 November: Last Quarter in Leo

I quote Mark Twain here. He said, 'Our opinions do not really blossom into fruition until we have expressed them to someone else.' You are communicating effectively now. Your mental faculties are at their best and this is a great time for all kinds of negotiations. You use every tool of modern technology. You are on every social networking site. You are alert, congenial and direct. You are able to assert yourself without treading on toes. You earn the respect of your peer group. You are organized and your thought processes are well laid out. There is no confusion. There could be travel, outdoor sport, love and bonding. There are profitable business associations, and family life is good. There are expenses, and you live large. And why not? Ganesha is pleased.

22 November: New Moon in Sagittarius

According to psychologist Carl Jung, 'We are in this world but not of it. We are now able to observe ourselves from a different perspective. We are now capable to step out of our own mind, out of our own body and understand who we really are, to see things the way they are. We become the observer of our lives.' The world is changing rapidly. Technology and spirituality have opened new vistas. Gaia seems to be preparing for what Sri Aurobindo called the supramental man or the man of the higher consciousness. In this phase, your energies are optimized. You are in a powerful creative space. Life is calling and you are part of the tango. Ganesha is happy. You are also drawn to the contemplative life and look deep within yourself. You want answers for profound questions. There is free will and the magic of the cosmos. There are the stars and their interpretation. Life has many dimensions. Ask me. I have been doing charts for decades. I believe in science and in poetry. There are many questions which can never be answered.

29 November: First Quarter in Pisces

There are soft, tender moments. Those in love reach new heights of ecstasy. There is powerful bonding as your body and soul are set on fire by your love interest. You may take time off to cosy away in some secluded spot or you may hang out with friends or with your partner. The feeling is pleasant. You are in the mood for what I would call mellow excitement. You make an exciting and stimulating companion. You could also be spending time at home gardening and doing the cleaning or looking after the family and the pets. You are filled with love and bonhomie, and it is contagious. Ganesha smiles in happiness.

6 December: Full Moon in Gemini

'Forgive, O Lord, my little jokes on Thee and I'll forgive Thy great big one on me,' said Robert Frost. Human beings have an interesting relationship with the creator. There are more questions than answers. Freud and Jung and countless others have tried in vain to fully comprehend the mind of man in relation to the cosmos and its creator. I stick to Ganesha. It is simple, uncomplicated devotion. In this phase, you are particularly perceptive of the fine sensitivities of others. In the process, you are able to create an open, sympathetic atmosphere for the peer group to flourish. Your communication skills are heightened and you thrive in all aspects of life that involve networking. You apply balm on wounds, and introspect and handle your own hurts too. This is a period of inward growth. Friends will be lucky totems and bring good luck.

14 December: Last Quarter in Virgo

According to Henry Ford, 'Wealth, like happiness, is never attained when sought after directly. It comes as a by-product of providing a useful service.' You realize this well and incorporate it into your work. Those in the service industry win kudos. There is hard work, and money to be made. There are expenses too, but the bank balance is fine. Plug all leaks and you will be in a bullish phase. This is also a favourable time to party and be with friends. You are calm, balanced, rational, cool and detached, and so emotional issues are well handled. There are fun times and deep, intense bonding. You also spend time with the family, meet people, travel and ink profitable agreements. You are in the throes of activity. You glow in the limelight. Ganesha is delighted.

22 December: New Moon in Capricorn

Ramana Maharshi said, 'Your duty is to *be* and not be this or that.' This is profound and difficult. While you make big plans and set long-range goals, you also examine yourself closely. You see the larger picture and also see the minute details. There are abstractions and also foresight and planning. You do well in commercial transactions. You love meeting people and are most certainly not a solo player, that you have never been. There is love, money, significant progress in all areas of your life and, most importantly, you have evolved into a better human being. There are also accolades. The year is ending well, and Ganesha blesses you.

28 December: First Quarter in Aries

'Perfection is attained by slow degrees; she requires the hand of time,' said Voltaire. You are not in a hurry. You have seen the fruit of your sustained labour and you know that it takes time. The great poet Kabir has also said that everything happens at the right time, not before and not after. So did the Bard in his own way when he said, 'take the tide to fortune'. You could be impatient sometimes and this is human, but you are also aware of the sacrifices that are made to attain perfection, or even something of considerable value. Ganesha is happy for you. You barge into the new year with renewed fire, gusto and zeal. The cards are in your favour. What more do you want?

Key Dates
January
1*, 5–6, 9–11, 14*–19, 21–23, 27*–28.
Ganesha says loans, funds, income, pets, projects are all highlighted. Extra pressures in your work sphere could cause some health problems. Learn to relax more.

February

1*–2, 6*–7, 10*–16, 19*–20, 23*–25, 28–29.
Success, partnerships, also opposition, marriage, a journey with a stopover. Lots of activity this month, and in different spheres! You're truly busy!

March

1*, 4–5, 9*–14, 17*–18, 22–23, 27*–28.
Funds, buying/selling, property, investment, passion and sex are all highlighted. In my favourite phrase: money and honey. Be happy!

April

1–2, 4*–10, 13–15, 18*–20, 23*–24, 28*–29.
Ganesha says journey and ceremony, collaborations, overseas studies, contacts, contracts, children, joy, pilgrimage, romance are all there for you. You are reaching out in several ways and mostly fulfilling ones too.

May

3*–8, 11–12, 16*–17, 21*–22, 26*–27, 30*–31.
Tremendous hard work lies ahead. Take care of your health. Your profession, money for the family and from the father, progress as well as competition will be in the spotlight now. The health of parents, in-laws, or older relatives may not be up to the mark. Health issues are therefore not to be taken lightly.

June

3*–4, 7*–8, 11*–18, 21*–22, 26*–27, 30.
Entertainment, socializing, group activities, hobbies, and

functions make you happy and keep you busy. You show charisma as well as style, both at work and at play.

July

1*, 4–5, 9*–15, 19*–20, 23*–25, 28*–29.

A house move, office expenses, spiritual pursuits, parents and family, nursing and caring keep you more busy this month. Be loyal to your family. They are your best bet in life!

August

1*–6, 10*–11, 15*–16, 20*–21, 24–25, 28–29.

A great month, but do take care of your heath. Efforts, success, charisma, leadership to come; favours will be granted, says Ganesha! It was a long way to go!

September

1*–8, 11–13, 16–17, 20*–21, 24*–25, 29*–30.

Entertainment, food (hospitality), finance, family as well as buying/selling and new projects for you. You're doing well this month, since both work and play areas are greatly energized.

October

4*–5, 9*–10, 13*–18, 22*–23, 26–27, 31.

Travel, neighbours and the community, fine communication. You will be loved and respected. Ganesha says, one of the happiest months of the year! Make sure you do it full justice.

November

1*, 5–6, 9*–15, 18–19, 22*–24, 27*–29.

Journey and ceremony, contacts and contracts, renovation, decoration, buying and selling, parents, in-laws, therefore achievements. Home and family matters will be resolved only after a struggle, says Ganesha!

December

2*–4, 7*- 12, 15*–16, 20*–21, 24–26, 30–31.
Children, romance, gifts, holidays, joy, good news are Ganesha's gifts for you. He also says luck will be your companion. In short 'kiss and bliss' sums it up! A fine end to a fine year.

Taurus

YEARLY FORECAST

Till 16 July 2014

Summary and Guidance

Ganesha says a spurt, sprint and even splurge in communication is indicated in this period. 'Communication is a meeting of minds with different memories and habits. When minds meet, they don't just exchange facts; they transform them, reshape them, draw different implications from them, and engage in new trains of thought,' says Theodore Zeldin. Learn to reach out to people and places in a very organized, practical manner. You have the personality and the energy to impress and influence others. The five Cs—contacts, contracts, correspondence, communication and consciousness—will be predominant. They will decide your future. Remember these five Cs are your lifeline.

17 July 2014 to 11 August 2015

We all know that a man's home is his castle. But Alexander Chase says a man's house is his wife's castle. Ha! Ha! Your astrologer agrees with Alexander. A Taurean will do well to have a garden and grow vegetables, though I know that space is a problem for most of us. I understand only the rich can afford a big garden but ikebana, the Japanese art of flower arrangement (Japanese call it living flowers) would, I believe, suit you, artistic Taurean very well. I have often said that Taurus is a combination of beauty and utility. The formula is Taurus = beauty + utility. Also, many Taureans are great chefs and cooks. Tendulkar, a Taurean, told me that he loves good food. This is my personal observation over the years, and remember I will be eighty-three on 11 July. Renovation and decoration, buying and selling, a home away from home, a change of scenery and office or shop or godown shift, is possible. See that you control your expenses.

Main Trend

As said earlier, till 16 July 2014, travel and trips, communication and contracts will hold centre stage. Move fast, adapt quickly to changing situations. That is your key to success. From 17 July 2014 to 11 August 2015, your base of operation could well be your home or another office, or even another country. That means collaborations are Emphasized in 2014 and 2015. It may not be a completely easy year because Saturn, the planet of delay and difficulties, will be opposing your sun sign, but I know very well that you are extremely resolute, determined and tough. You are not only the bull in the china shop, you are also a bulldozer. Also, you can be generous, caring and loving. Yes, success can be yours and that is my last word.

Journey and Communication

Till 16 July 2014, as said at the very beginning, journey and communication will be all important. Also, from 23 April to 7 May, Mercury in your sign favours it. January is also its launch pad.

Health

I know very well that most Taureans are really strong. But till 25 July Mars could pose health problems related to back, throat, loins and private parts of the body. I suggest that you go in for a medical check-up if you feel like it. The choice is yours. December could usher in a few health problems for you, your servants and your pets.

Love/Marriage

Till 16 July 2014 there is a chance of love and marriage. You Taureans are, as a rule, practical and look at all sides before jumping into a marriage. Believe me, this will be excellent advice this year. Friendship is different from marriage and I suggest it strongly.

Property

As said earlier, all property matters will be highlighted from 17 July 2014 to 11 August 2015. But I must clarify that you cannot fit astrology into watertight compartments. One trend flows into the next one. The date and month is not perfect and binding. Property matters—be it house, office, shop and so on—will be important in August, November, July, January and March. Yes, there could be law suits. All these are only a part of your life.

Job/Business/Loans/Funds/Investments

Here you are on a good wicket, as we Indians say. There are good chances of earning money, changing a job, if so interested, or launching a new project, if in business. However, if in partnership or collaboration, care and caution should be the guiding principles. You may have to go to court.

Children/Entertainment

Here you will be in your element. From 23 April to 7 May, Mercury will be in your sun sign and it will be Venus from 29 May to 23 June. Both Mercury and Venus will give you joy, happiness, good cheer and great delight. But short are the days of roses and wine. Therefore, enjoy and be happy. Be convivial, that is love good company, be sociable and lively. I am sure you understand.

Trips and Ties

See under the heading Journey and Communication please. Add to it July, September, March and January for good measure.

Publicity, Projects, Performance

January should show the way for the entire year. Therefore, be ready for the window of opportunity which should come your way. Also, as said earlier, till 16 July 2014, publicity, projects and performance are truly highlighted. In other words, the first seven months will be mighty important for it. Push hard and long and you will succeed. Combine enthusiasm and power and you will have both.

Happiness Quota

Strictly speaking, happiness is a personal equation and varies from person to person. But I know that you Taureans like your comforts, your pleasures, and most certainly your food and flowers. Also, I know that you are both artistic and practical and materialistic. A very strange and rare combination. Therefore, taking it all into consideration and knowing very well that Saturn will be opposing your sun sign, my marks for you will be 72 per cent.

Monthly Round-up

January: you will begin on a positive, winning streak, and journey, ceremony and good relationships should be happy events; February: changes on the work and personal front will start and they have to be tackled with tact and skill; March: socializing, friendship, gains, and the fulfilment of a wish; April: expenses, secret deals, looking after the sick and the needy, but you must safeguard your health; May: a progressive, go-ahead month as pointed out in the preceding forecasts for the planets; June: finances, food, family, contracts and comforts; July: meditation, the domestic scene, renovation and decoration, excellent rapport with people and travel and communication will be highlighted; August: home, house, family, immigration, buying/selling/renovation, a continuation of July; September: you are on top of any situation—children, hobbies and creativity are emphasized; October: job, health, pets, projects, colleagues and your relationship with subordinates and servants; November: love/hate, cooperation/competition, collaboration/separation, trips and ties, signing of documents and drafts; December: loans, funds, capital formation, buying/selling, reduced vitality, and the need to take care of your health.

Outer Planets

In Western astrology, Uranus, Neptune and Pluto are the outer planets. They also have their say in the destiny of human beings.

URANUS: Uranus makes things rough and tough for you. Expenses, ill health, possible hospitalization (nothing is certain and final), looking after the poor, the weak and the unfortunate are indicated. Long-distance connections and collaborations fall under the spell and orbit of Uranus.

NEPTUNE: Neptune gives you strange friends, sudden money, gains and losses, exciting company and good cheer. Neptune exhilarates you. Good for you.

PLUTO: Pluto, the powerhouse of the zodiac, certainly helps you in journeys, ceremonies, publicity, pilgrimages, inspiration, intuition and general good luck. In short, Pluto is your bodyguard.

Month by Month

January

The year 2014 starts on a sound footing and there is added zest and power in your endeavours. There is money and honey. By mid-month new emotions are at play. There could be some domestic upheavals, and you may run into stormy weather in your marriage. As the month ends, there is passion. You are in the throes of romance. Emotions are at a peak too and you work with your heart.

If you are in the media or the film industry, a musician, writer, painter or singer, there is worldly success. The month ends in a somewhat eccentric way. You may choose bizarre companions to spend time with. Ganesha blesses you as you look for perfection.

February

There is money to be made and new accomplishments. In this period, you are happy with monotony. You are in your comfort zone and there is success. The mid-month is a period of extravagance. There is new work, love, passion, friends, good living, new accomplishments and a slew of goodies in the bag. By the end of the month there is a lot of movement. There will be new associations. You have the luck of the draw. Ganesha ensures that.

March

You are emotional and introspective. New wounds are opened and you could be in a maudlin mood. You are forced to break out of the confines of your comfort zone of stable emotions. There is a new direction to your life. By the middle of the month you look for new work and moneymaking opportunities. You look for a definite, concrete goal in life and work towards it. As the month ends, the trend continues. You are back to where you started when the year dawned, with your nose to the grindstone. You achieve a lot and set new targets. Ganesha blesses you! You could be signing gilt-edged agreements and moving your business profile to another level.

April

You spend time with domestic concerns. Children will be a source of joy. There could be home renovations and even an addition to the family. You spend a lot on goodies. There could be new love and passion too. Mercury will be in Taurus from 23 April to 7 May. You are brimming with ideas and there will be a flash of genius too. This is a fortnight when you should go all out and make your dreams happen. There is success and happiness. There will be applause and accolades. There is a windfall in store. I may even go as far as to say that you may win the lottery. Ganesha ensures every type of success.

May

There are expenses and new ventures. There is love and passion. The intensity of this period is palpable. You are in line for awards and rewards. The three Ps—power, pelf and privileges, are yours. You could also get carried away in matters of the heart. You may come out with a classic composition if you are a musician or writer. Venus makes its presence felt for over three weeks, from 29 May to 23 June. The simple rule is that when Venus is in your sign you are bestowed with comforts and luxuries, ornaments and money. Ganesha asks you to go for it.

June

You trim all wastage and if you have overindulged, you get on to a strict diet and exercise regimen. There are new relationships and they can blossom, if nurtured. There could be family reunions and alumni meetings. Your life is a whirl. There could be illness in the family and you may be busy with hospital procedures. You are on an emotional roller coaster. Old wounds surface. You put all important projects on the back burner and enter a world of conflicting emotions. Ganesha guides you.

July

You are at the crossroads. There is new love and bonding. By the middle of the month you are back on an even ground. There is work to be done and money to be made. Once again, you are in full flow. There are new ideas, opportunities and openings in your life. You are steadfast and working hard. Bankers, media folk, realty traders, those playing the market have a field day. There are lucrative assignments. Ganesha is happy for you.

August

There is passion and energy in your life. There are expenses and investment opportunities. There is also new love. You also spend on the less fortunate. You are in a philanthropic mode. By the middle of the month there is peace and tranquillity. The month ends with stability. Ganesha is with you.

September

You are stubborn and rigid and believe that you are right all the time. This may alienate you. There will be strong ego clashes and you may feel that you are right all the time. You will rise to great fame and eminence and have power over people. Your skills will be in the open and you will be applauded. By the middle of the month you are filled with compassion. You have an increased empathy for the people in your daily life. You may also become more attracted to mystical philosophies and metaphysics. By the month-end you are filled with idealism and an increased willingness to work for the kind of world you want to see. There are many options and possibilities. Ganesha smiles.

October

You are back at work, slogging away. You look back at the year that was and at all that you have accomplished. You may decide to overhaul your life. You are on the brink of a new cycle of growth and progress. By the middle of the month there are emotional moments as you withdraw into yourself for a deeper understanding of your urges. New vistas open dramatically. There could be profitable travel. The end of the month brings many changes. All structures that have become rigid in your life will now break down. At work you look for stimulation and new opportunities. Ganesha is not worried. This is an incredible period and you will profit from it.

November

You feel invincible as you have learnt your lessons the hard way. You are crowned with success in all your undertakings. There is money and honey. You indulge yourself and go on the overdrive. You live and love lavishly. You throw yourself at work and the party circuit. There are mega projects on the cards and big money to be made. The middle of the month sees you reach out to people and places. You need new inspiration to forge ahead. As the month ends there are stolen moments with a loved one. There are happy times with friends and family. Ganesha wishes you well as always.

December

You look at offbeat openings at work and think out of the box. These are beautiful times and you should make the most of it. You meet with old friends, family and lovers and toast to times gone by. There is a lot on your plate. New work beckons. While there is merriment in the air you will not sacrifice work for anything under the sun. There are good times and you join the party mode. You are propelled with new energy as you enter 2015. There are many plans and you go all out to achieve your goals. This is a great way to end the year and embark on a new one. There are wonderful times to be had. Ganesha is happy for you.

Months at a Glance

January

You will begin on a positive, winning streak; and journey, ceremony, good relationships should be the happy events.

February

Changes on the work and personal fronts will start and they have to be tackled with tact and skill.

March

Socializing and friendship and gains, and the fulfillment of a wish is highlighted.

April

Expenses, secret deals, looking after the sick and the needy are indicated. Also, you must safeguard your health.

May

A progressive, go-ahead month as pointed out in the preceding forecasts for the planets.

June

Finances, food, family, contracts and comforts.

July

Meditation, the domestic scene, renovation and decoration, excellent rapport with people, and travel and communication will be highlighted.

August

Home, house, family, immigration, buying/selling/ renovation. August is a continuation of July.

September

You are on top of any situation. Children, hobbies and creativity are emphasized.

October

Job, health, pets, projects, colleagues and your relationship with subordinates and servants are indicated.

November

Love/hate, cooperation/competition, collaboration/ separation, trips and ties, signing of documents and drafts.

December

Loans, funds, capital formation, buying/selling. Do take care of your health and reduced vitality.

Weekly Review (By the phases of the moon)

1 January: New Moon in Capricorn

The year starts with great ambition and determination. You have many tasks to do and have the stamina and perseverance. The flip side is that you could tire yourself and get gloomy. Try to bring some balance into whatever you do. Taureans are generally lucky and good with money as they understand the practical aspects of life. Unless otherwise indicated in their chart, they end up with a pile of possessions and have a strong materialistic streak. They are also prone to philanthropy and can have a sensitive side to them. They are also hard-working and creative and can be both bankers and writers; they normally rise to great eminence in life. Audrey Hepburn, George Clooney, Andre Agassi, Billy Joel, Al Pacino, Barbara Streisand, Cher, Jay Leno, Pierce Brosnan and several other celebrities in all walks of life are all Taureans. For that matter, even Saddam Hussein! This year too starts on a sound footing and there is added zest and power to your endeavours. Ganesha predicts money and honey. It is a powerful start to a new year. Go for it!

8 January: First Quarter in Aries

The hard work continues. There are new ventures and money to be made. There are also many expenses and you will be busy making purchases, earning well and still trying to balance the budget. A note of caution though, do not burn the candle at both ends, or you could end up with some health problem despite your excellent constitution. As we all know, stress is such a killer in this modern world. There is money coming to you through work and possibly even through inheritance. Without a doubt, Ganesha ensures success and I am happy with it. As you know, I am a great devotee of Ganesha who makes everything happen! But, I repeat, watch your health!

16 January: Full Moon in Cancer

There are new emotions at play. There could be some domestic upheavals and you run into stormy weather in your marriage. There could be problems with the spouse, children, in-laws and friends. Female Taureans will go through an emotional roller coaster. If single, new love will make you toss and turn. Ganesha wishes you well. Of course, I must add here, like I always do, that I do not have your personal chart and so I am only suggesting tendencies. The stars only impel, they do not compel. I do not have the other planetary positions in your individual horoscope and so this is a general reading. But, most certainly, emotions will be at a high pitch. Control your temper and watch your step. Take deep breaths and react only after thinking over an issue thoroughly. Love is many-splendoured but it has its thorns!

24 January: Last Quarter in Scorpio

As the month ends, there is passion. You are in the throes of romance. At least, you find some interest or pursuit, other than a love interest, and go for it big time. You put your heart and soul into it. There is success and you are crowned with applause. Emotions are at a peak too and you work with your heart. If you are in the media or the film industry, a musician, writer, painter or singer, there is worldly success and appreciation for your work. Ganesha is with you all the way and that is all that matters.

30 January: New Moon in Aquarius

The month ends in a somewhat eccentric way. You may choose bizarre companions to spend time with and may go off the beaten path. Routine kills, and you look for offbeat pleasures. You are not led astray but you are looking for unusual pleasures and new ground. You look to reinvent yourself like Sachin Tendulkar. I have been a sportsman in my time and I can see clearly how the god of Indian cricket, the great master, is readjusting his strokes and conserving his energy. Ganesha blesses you as you look for different things in your quest for perfection. You do not want to get off the rails; this is just a time for readjustment.

6 February: First Quarter in Taurus

You are steadfast again with your nose to the grindstone. There is a lot to be done and you do not waste time. There is money to be made and new accomplishments. I am sorry but I have to repeat this, I have known and dealt with many Taureans in my long life. While they can be the most dependable, creative and hard-working people, they also resist change. This can sometimes be their undoing. Any change sends shivers down their spine unless otherwise indicated in the personal horoscope. In this period, you are happy with monotony. You prefer doing the same thing over and over again until the cows come home. Of course, you are in your comfort zone. And there is success. Ganesha ensures that. I am happy too.

14 February: Full Moon in Leo

The full moon is in Leo and this is a period of extravagance. You make purchases. There are many expenses. You entertain a lot; friends will drop in; there could be a family reunion; children will bring joy; and you will run through a period of expansion. There is new work, love, passion, friends, good living, new accomplishments and a string of goodies in the bag. You live larger than life. You live like a king or a queen. You are generally not one to make expensive purchases but you break all rules and may go on a shopping spree. You may purchase land, property, big brands; eat, drink and make merry. Ganesha wishes you well. Enjoy! Look at me. I have always enjoyed my life. Who am I to preach sobriety?

22 February: Last Quarter in Sagittarius

There is a lot of movement. You may travel on work or pleasure. There will be new associations and a lot of fire in your belly. The good and hectic times continue. There could be new romance and unusual thrills. I must add that this is also an expensive period. Nothing in life is free. 'It is a material world,' said Madonna, and I fully agree with her. I should know, having been through the vicissitudes of life in my long and colourful existence on the planet. But you have the luck of the draw in your favour. Ganesha ensures that, and I am happy for you. Finally, good luck is the icing on the cake. Napoleon, the great general, always chose the lucky commanders. Canny man, he had a point there!

1 March: New Moon in Pisces

From the hectic days of the past few weeks, you get into a different mode. You are emotional and introspective. New trends take you by storm. You may remember old hurts. New wounds are opened. You are forced to break out of the confines of your comfort zone of stable emotions. Normally, you don't wear your emotions on your sleeve but this time the floodgates open to offer a catharsis.

This is also important. Life is not always about getting ahead. You have to step back too and reflect on the many furrows of life. No one is perfect. We make errors; you have made them too. You are only human. Come to grips with them and move on. Ganesha wishes you well.

8 March: First Quarter in Gemini

You attempt new things. There is a new direction to your life. People come and go like fairies in a novel. You let go and are in the arms of poesy. Money may slip out of your hands but it doesn't bother you. The year started with a hard slog and you know that life is yet to unwind, and this is what you are doing right now. There is a side to all of us that is in shadow. We could call it the blind spot. We all have it, even the most intelligent and well read. It is difficult to fathom the shadowy side or blind spot but this is a time when you allow the unusual to happen. You may give expression to different urges that you seldom come to grips with in the normal course of life. Go with the flow. Ganesha watches over you.

16 March: Full Moon in Virgo

You are soon back to your practical self. You look for new work and moneymaking opportunities. You look for a definite, concrete goal in life and work towards it. You tighten the purse strings and are back to your usual hard-nosed self. You don't want to waste any more time. Life is fleeting and new openings are falling on your lap. Ganesha blesses you. I join him. You iron out all the creases and once again plunge into the world of work and money.

24 March: Last Quarter in Capricorn

As the month ends, the trend continues. You are back to where you started when the year dawned with your nose to the grindstone. There are investments to be made along with many shrewd and tactful purchases. You love the good life and work hard for it. You look for material and emotional value in whatever you touch. There is no time for love and the niceties of amorous pursuits. It is too distracting in this phase. You are one of the great lovers in the zodiac, there is no doubt about that. But this is not the time for romance. Ganesha is with you all the way and that is important.

30 March: New Moon in Aries

The hard work doesn't let up. In this phase, you achieve a lot and set new targets. Ganesha blesses you! You could be signing gilt-edged agreements and moving your business profile to another level. It is a long way to go! Bankers and media people make hay. The sun is shining like never before and you grab the bull by the horns. I like that! Imagine a Taurean grabbing a bull by the horns! Whatever you embark on now will lead to success. There may be love and lust, and why not? That makes life complete. Life is multidimensional and you experience all facets.

7 April: First Quarter in Cancer

There are quiet moments. You spend time with domestic concerns. The spouse, in-laws, friends, old lovers etc. will demand your time and attention and you are more than willing to share yourself with them. Children will be a source of joy and you will be busy with them. There could be home renovations and even an addition to the family. Ganesha blesses you.

15 April: Full Moon in Libra

You spend a lot on goodies and money flows out of your pockets. I repeat, under all the bluster, Taureans are deeply emotional and sentimental and rarely show the underbelly. You will use this period luxuriating in comfort. There could be new love and passion too. There will be emotional and material pulls. Go with the tide, go where it takes you. Ganesha is with you and finally that is what counts. The flip side is that there will be many opportunities and you will be hard-pressed to make up your mind on what you want. But this is certainly not a situation to be worried about.

22 April: Last Quarter in Aquarius

This is certainly a fruitful period and you have to milk it. To paraphrase the Bard, take the flood that leads to fortune. Mercury will be in Taurus from 23 April to 7 May. Mercury is the winged messenger, the communication expert, the journey specialist. Mercury, the mighty, all-powerful planet is in your sign now. It favours travels, meetings, conferences, interviews, trips, more brain power, contacts, communication, correspondence and contracts. Mercury has a special connection with the circuits of the brain. Chess, crossword and other such games belong to Mercury. Also, short-distance runners and spin bowlers are controlled by Mercury. Mercury, in short, is the ambassador and salesman of the zodiac. Mercury is the symbol of news, views, messages, interviews, contacts, communications, travel and transport. Mercury gives an impetus to all of the above in the sun sign where it is located. You are brimming with ideas and there will be a flash of genius too. This is a fortnight when you should go all out and make your dreams happen. Luck is on your side. Hitch your wagon to the stars and realize your dreams. Aim high. Ganesha is with you.

29 April: New Moon in Taurus

This is a powerful period and you can do wonders. There is success and happiness as Mercury will be in Taurus. Whatever you embark on now leads to glory. There will be applause and accolades. There is a windfall in store. I may even go as far as to say that you may win a lottery, and not a small one at that! There is no stopping you in this phase. Unless otherwise indicated in your personal chart, Ganesha ensures every type of success. The new moon is in your sign and this is also your birth period. The trends are propitious. Go for it!

7 May: First Quarter in Leo

The good times roll on. Money and honey are in store. Those in the media will do exceedingly well. There are expenses and new ventures. You spread yourself thin. There is love and passion. There could be a new love affair and your heart will sing. If married, the bonding will be intense. You could also be playing the field without a care in the world. There are happy domestic events, even travel with the family to some exotic location. Ganesha wishes you well. He is delighted, and so am I.

14 May: Full Moon in Scorpio

The intensity of this period is palpable. You are in line for awards and rewards and your hard work will not go unnoticed. The three Ps—power, pelf and privileges— are yours. You could also get carried away in matters of the heart. It will be a good idea to watch your step. Pride comes before a fall, and nothing is impossible when the going is particularly good. Ganesha is happy for you but cautions against overstepping. Success and its attendant privileges are heady and Taureans have their share of giant egos. Talent and good luck spawn an aura of invincibility. You feel nothing can ever go wrong, and this is where you should be particularly careful. You may trip, and you surely don't want that.

21 May: Last Quarter in Pisces

Emotions take over and you may make commitments without thinking over the pros and cons. You allow your heart to rule. You may jump to conclusions in a weak moment, but I suggest you think before you make the final decision. It is best not to act in haste and repent at leisure. I am not the best example of patience and planning but this is what Ganesha asks me to tell you. You may also come out with a classic composition if you are a musician or writer. Your creative energy soars like the American eagle. This is a maudlin period and you wear your heart on your sleeve, much to the surprise of everybody.

28 May: New Moon in Gemini

The new moon is in Gemini, and Venus makes its presence felt for over three weeks, from 29 May to 23 June. The simple rule is that when Venus is in your own sign you are bestowed with comforts and luxuries, ornaments and money. Ganesha says Venus is the planet of comfort and beauty. It is an important planet and is of great significance. This is a vital phase. I repeat: Venus is the planet for love, romance, sex, beauty and the good life. It is the planet of attraction, wealth, knowledge and prosperity. The compatibility of partners and also the type of life the individual will lead is also judged from the placement of Venus in the horoscope. As a planet, Venus is considered to be beneficial, feminine and gentle. Venus symbolizes the force of attraction in the universe. In human beings, this attractive force manifests as love and beauty. When Venus is well placed in the chart, there is love, art, beauty and all the goodies of life that make life worth living. Venus rules Libra and Taurus, though its role in every sign is important. Like other planets, it also has its transits. In Libra, Venus is aesthetic and cultured. In Taurus it is more earthy, materialistic and sensual. Venus rules the venous system, kidneys, urinary tract, throat, larynx, and is responsible for good looks. In short, Venus in Western astrology stands for comforts, arts, relationships, sex, decorations, luxuries and wealth. Need I say more? Ganesha asks you to go for it like a person possessed. The Venus period comes soon after the Mercury period. You have it all going for you.

5 June: First Quarter in Virgo

The heady period of the last few weeks slowly slips into some discipline, thanks to the influence of Virgo. You trim all wastage and if you have overindulged, you get on to a regimen of strict diet and exercise. You may even settle into a nature-cure clinic and get detoxified. I dare say you need it after the heady period. Ganesha is with you. The rest will follow as it should. Use your free will to your advantage. While destiny exists, do not get too fatalistic. You can tweak your life your way too.

13 June: Full Moon in Sagittarius

There is movement of all kinds. Friends will drop in and you will be reaching out to people and places. Money flows in and out. There are new relationships and they can blossom, if nurtured. There could be family reunions and alumni meetings. You may meet up with school and college buddies and renew old school ties. Your life is a whirl and you are exploring different avenues. Ganesha wishes you well.

19 June: Last Quarter in Pisces

There are maudlin moments. You may meet an old flame and feel that you made a mistake leaving him or her in the lurch. But this is no time for regrets. You have moved on and so has the other person. Time and tide wait for no one. Grapple with the present and I assure you that you will have your hands full. There could be illness in the family and you may be busy with hospital procedures. Children will be a cause of worry. Elders at home may also need special care. You ensure that your loved ones are taken care of and this takes up all your time. This may also be a good time to get a health check-up. If you have put on weight and resorted to unhealthy habits, this is a good period to get back in shape. Ganesha blesses you.

27 June: New Moon in Cancer

You are on an emotional roller coaster. Old wounds surface and you may make a mess of the present with overriding emotions. You put all important projects on the back burner and enter a world of conflicting emotions.

You have been working hard as a form of escapism and you now realize that you have a lot hidden under the carpet. When the situation changes, as it does now, every emotion comes flooding through. It is a period of catharsis. I must insist, though, that astrology only impels and never compels. A lot depends on your personal horoscope. Of course, your favourite astrologer is seldom wrong. But I am not God. I am just another human being interpreting the stars for you. The indications are that it may be necessary to stem the flood. Ask Ganesha for guidance if the situation gets overwhelming.

5 July: First Quarter in Libra

You don't know what to do as there are many possibilities and you don't know what to zero in on. You are at the crossroads. I am not your counsellor; I have also made mistakes but I am just interpreting the stars. If it threatens to rain, use your umbrella. That is the purpose of astrology: to guide you and show you the new inclinations taking centre stage. There is new love and bonding. You want to escape into the comfortable world of amorous pursuits as you don't want to grapple with the world and its challenges. You want to ride fairy-tale clouds far away in the sky. You want to live under a veil. So be it! Ganesha wishes you well.

12 July: Full Moon in Capricorn

Luckily, the full moon is in Capricorn and you are back on an even ground. There is work to be done and money to be made and many challenges of the real world. You cannot escape from it all indefinitely. You have to come to grips with terra firma. Practicality and the Taureans are never separated for long and you see good sense in hard work and get back to the slog. Ganesha is with you all the way, and that is heartening. Money is honey and who knows that better than you?

19 July: Last Quarter in Aries

This is, once again, a period when you are in full flow. There are new ideas, opportunities and openings in your life. There are new businesses and money to be made. It is all happening and you are batting on the front foot like Sachin Tandulkar. Little master Sunil Gavaskar thrashed the famed Windies' pace attack without a helmet. Sehwag reached his double century with a six and Messi scores goals with impunity. This is the mood you are in, and you should be, I dare say. Ganesha watches over you.

26 July: New Moon in Leo

You are steadfast and working hard. Genius is all about perspiration. Inspiration too, but nothing happens without the hard slog. There is no eureka moment without hard work. Believe me when I say this. There are new openings and you move ahead with the speed of a cheetah and the arrogance of a lion in the Savannah. Bankers, media folk, realty traders and those playing the market have a field day. There are lucrative assignments, you cash in on them, the sun is shining on you. Ganesha is confident that you have realized the essence of existence. It is all about now, the present moment. The past is gone and the future is a mystery. Milk the moment. As the Nike advertisement says: Just do it!

4 August: First Quarter in Scorpio

There is no letting up. You zoom like a Formula One driver in pole position. You fly past the curves in life's fast lane. There is passion and energy in your life. There are expenses and investment opportunities too. There is new love as well. The unattached may find a partner and the attached may experience deeper bonding, and maybe a fling or two, I dare say with a wink. Ganesha blesses you.

10 August: Full Moon in Aquarius

Offbeat people and offbeat pursuits take hold of your time. This is a welcome distraction. You also spend on the less fortunate. You are in a philanthropic mode. You are unable to fathom or even handle ugliness and destitution. You may take time off and settle in an ashram or take a vacation from the battlefield of life and work. You want to know what your karma and dharma are. There are many unanswered questions. Ganesha understands your predicament and blesses you. One has to go through the tunnel to see the light.

17 August: Last Quarter in Taurus

There is peace and tranquillity, relatively speaking. You look for answers and find some of them. You are placated. There are domestic chores knocking on your door. The family needs you, and you need them too. You have been away too long. Parents, siblings, cousins and distant relatives want your time. You also need their love and support. No man is an island and you have been on a bare strip of land, divorced from everything for a very long time. There is no need to be depressed or to despair; the cookie crumbles and rebuilds too and the rebuilding process is on. Ganesha watches over you like an eagle. That is what is important.

25 August: New Moon in Virgo

There is some sort of stability in your mind which has been wandering a lot. Remember, we have over 60,000 thoughts a day and the mind is like a monkey on a stick. The best antidote to a restless mind is to keep it busy and occupied all the time. Ask me, I have been writing books for decades! You have to go through the travails of life. The human body, as the yogis say, is made for suffering. There is no escape from the cycle of birth, old age, suffering and death. If you learn your lessons, good for you. If you don't, there will be more trouble ahead. I am putting it as simply as possible so that you, dear readers, understand me loud and clear. I am not looking for brownie points. The shortest distance between two dots is a straight line and I am drawing it for you. That is all. Ganesha is always with you and that is the best part. It is to Ganesha that I go for direction.

2 September: First Quarter in Sagittarius

You are firing on all cylinders. You want to be on pole position all the time but take care that you don't meet the fate of Niki Lauda or Ayrton Senna. Go slow. Taureans are normally slow, deliberate and sure-footed. So this is unusual behaviour but the stars impel you. You are also very stubborn and rigid and believe that you are right all the time. This may alienate you and isolate you. Your peer group may find you hard to handle. There will be strong ego clashes. You are upset at the slightest criticism and feel that your writ should go unchallenged. Ganesha is with you and that is a great help. Learn to bend a little. In the tempest, it is the great oak that falls and not the wiry bamboo. Be like water, ready to choose its path and do not confront opposition all the time. You have to learn to help yourself; a little introspection will help.

9 September: Full Moon in Pisces

This is a sobering influence and you get the chance to examine your life and to sow the seeds for something greater than what you have imagined. This greatness is in the spiritual realm and will manifest in a number of ways as the weeks and months go by. The new urgings will slowly be realized by you; just be patient. You will rise to great fame and eminence and have power over people. Your skills will be in the open and you will be applauded. This is a great time for artistes of all kinds. Ganesha blesses you. Whenever you are in a conundrum, ask him for advice.

16 September: Last Quarter in Gemini

In this period, you are filled with compassion. You have an increased empathy for the people in your everyday life and clearly see and appreciate their angst. You have been working on your inner self and now see vividly the essential unity of yourself and all beings. You help others often by going out of your way, with material and emotional largesse. You may also become more attracted to mystical philosophies and metaphysics. There is possibly a religious or spiritual experience which will have a profound impact on you. Work is also good but it is tinged with mysticism. A guru or godman will make a huge impression on you. Ganesha wishes you well. You have come a full circle.

24 September: New Moon in Libra

Your ego clashes are not threatening now. You are on an even ground in life. You are filled with idealism and an increased willingness to work for the kind of world you want to see. You may join a social movement. You are now more capable of selfless actions and are willing to help, seeking little or nothing in return. You may have conquered your ego for the moment at least. You have been in a rut for long and now you decide on throwing it away and chasing your dream. There are many options and possibilities. Ganesha smiles in appreciation. Change is the only inevitability and without prodding yourself take to a new course of action. There is a long way to go!

1 October: First Quarter in Capricorn

Hard work and a Taurean are never at loggerheads. The bull just loves to work, especially if it means money. So you are back on the work front, slogging away. In this last quarter, you look back at the year that was and at all that you have accomplished in life. You try to evaluate and understand exactly what you have learned. You may decide to overhaul your life entirely. You may even move on in an entirely new direction that will give you more satisfaction. You are looking at new ways in which to handle life. You have searched your soul enough and now want a really fulfilling life. The time is ripe and Ganesha nods in agreement.

8 October: Full Moon in Aries

You are on the brink of a new cycle of growth and progress. But I warn you, do not have exaggerated expectations. Even if there are no sudden windfalls, great wealth or luck, there will be more subtle, but useful effects. This is a period of great learning as you become wiser and more mature and have a broader understanding of the world. While you ask for more from the cosmos, you are also prepared to give more. So the sharing and expectation are equal. There is money and honey, and, most important, there is spiritual growth. Ganesha is happy too.

15 October: Last Quarter in Cancer

There are emotional moments as you withdraw into yourself for a deeper understanding of your urges and inner drives. Ganesha wishes you well. You are in a deeply philanthropic state. Like Mother Teresa, you want to give everything you have. You look at transforming the energies in your life to entirely new directions. New vistas open dramatically. You may also attract powerful events and people into your life and you may have the freedom to do things that you have never done before. There could be profitable travel on the cards or the chance to study something new and different altogether. There is also the distinct possibility of money falling into your lap. Did I hear you chuckle in joy, or was I hearing voices?

23 October: New Moon in Scorpio

The new moon in Scorpio plays a dramatic role in your life now. This can be an upsetting and tense period if you have allowed your life to crystallize into rigid patterns, and you simply resist change. Do not be like a stagnant pond filled with muck that refuses to be cleaned. You desire new experiences but do not do anything that takes you to the law courts. You look for creative change but it is not easy. At the same time, you must desist from destructive measures. It is a tough call and you are at your wits' end. Watch your health, especially for diseases of the reproductive organs. Be discreet in all your undertakings and do not break the law. At one level, this is a very positive phase and you can grow. Take the right course. Either way, Ganesha is with you lest you stumble and fall. Such confusions are necessary in life. It will make you a better person in the long run. After all, life is a marathon race and not a sprint. Even Bolt has to run the marathon of life despite his amazing sprints!

31 October: First Quarter in Aquarius

There are all sorts of changes in store. The change may be sudden and totally unconscious too. The result is a sort of upheaval and this can be upsetting and unpleasant. There may be some accidents and you may trip and fall in the metaphorical sense too. So be on your guard. You will look for freedom from constricting relationships. All structures that have become rigid in your life will now break down and you will experience new freedom. At work too, you look for stimulation and new opportunities. Learn to embrace change in all aspects of your life. You rebel against authority and may just create problems for yourself. Ganesha is not unduly worried. Neither am I. This is an incredible period and you are shown many colours of life. In the end, you will profit from every experience.

6 November: Full Moon in Taurus

The full moon is in Taurus and you are on track once again. You feel invincible as you have learnt your lessons the hard way and feel that no one and no situation can pull you down in any way. Do not get into ego clashes. You are crowned with success in all your undertakings. There is money, honey and applause from the least expected quarters. Your family is proud of you and you are the toast of the locality. You may even win honours from the government for your outstanding achievements. I am thrilled. So is Ganesha.

14 November: Last Quarter in Leo

You indulge and overwork yourself. You live and love lavishly and spend like there is no tomorrow. You plan foreign holidays with a loved one or the family, depending on your personal circumstance. You throw yourself at work and the party circuit. There is love and longing in the air and you may be indiscreet in your amorous pursuits. There are mega projects on the cards and big money to be made. There are also many expenses as you make lavish purchases. Ganesha blesses you.

22 November: New Moon in Sagittarius

This is a time when you reach out to people and places. You need new inspiration to forge ahead with your plans. You continue working hard and use your free will to make dramatic things happen. There is success but even your critics cannot say that you didn't earn it. You made it the hard way and when you look back there is a feeling of quiet satisfaction. Ganesha wishes you abundance.

29 November: First Quarter in Pisces

There are stolen moments with a loved one. There is joy and beauty all around you. There is happiness too but tempered with some disquiet. Sometimes, you think of days gone by in your reflective moments and this brings a tear to the eye. While all this is natural and human, it will be best to live in the moment. Seize the present and leave the past behind lest it sully the flavour of the good times that are to come. There are happy times with friends and family as you fall back into your comfort zone for a breather. Ganesha wishes you well as always.

6 December: Full Moon in Gemini

You are filled with new ideas as the last month of the year unfolds. You look at offbeat openings at work and think out of the box to maximize your returns. These are beautiful times and you should make the most of it before it slips away as always. Ganesha is watching over you and that says a lot. You do a lot of catching up as you meet with old friends, family and lovers and toast to times gone by.

14 December: Last Quarter in Virgo

There is stability now but you are still in a festive mood. There is a lot on your plate. New work beckons. There is money to be made and new peaks to be scaled. You are assimilating new experiences and Ganesha is thrilled, for it will make you a better person. While this has been an exciting year, you also look at changing your wardrobe and reinventing yourself, possibly a new hairdo and a better physique. You look at yoga, meditation, an organic diet and the gym with greater intent. The new year beckons and you are all geared up to project an entirely new vision of yourself to the world at large.

22 December: New Moon in Capricorn

While there is merriment in the air and you are not one to back off from the action, you also know that work will always be the priority in your life. You will not sacrifice work for anything under the sun. It is your first spouse, ultimate passion and greatest love. You are what you are because of your work. It is your identity, your calling card. Without it you feel that you are just another lumpen element guzzling beer and ogling life. For you, that is an assured waste of time, and you know that time is fleeting. There are good times and you join the party mode. But your mind is elsewhere, somewhere far away. Yes, tomorrow is another day but you are planning moves for 2015 and cannot take your foot off the pedal. You are ambitious and want great things for yourself. Like the mother of Puducherry said, you want the highest aspiration to organize your life and this is a tough call! Ganesha blesses you and wishes you great times ahead.

28 December: First Quarter in Aries

You are brimming with new energy as you enter 2015. There are many plans and you go all out to achieve them. There could be family holidays, party times or good old hard work. The choice is yours, says Ganesha. I dare say you will opt for hard work if it makes you laugh all the way to the bank! This is a great way to end the year and embark on a new one. There are expenses and purchases, and wonderful times to be had. There are miles to go!

Key Dates

January

2*–4, 7–13, 20–21, 25–26, 29–31.
Ganesha says, you start with a bang: journeys, ceremonies, publicity and projects. You are truly in the limelight, or at the forefront of affairs, whichever way you care to put it.

February

3*–10, 12–14, 17–18, 21–22, 26–27.
Work at full throttle, and, from it, gain status and power, which is richly deserved. You revel in your success, and the recognition of your worth.

March

2–9, 11*–12, 15–16, 19–21, 24–26, 29–31.
Friends and fulfilment are the two Fs. Therefore, lots of socializing for you and you revel in this now. It makes you feel very good indeed.

April

3–4, 7*–8, 11–17, 20–22, 25–27, 30*.
A mixed bag for you. You will have to take care of major expenses and also cope with the ill health of family members. But you will face difficulties and triumph. Journeys are possible too.

May

1*–9, 13–14, 18–19, 23*–24, 28*–29.
Full power and energy as you play to win, to impress, to dazzle. Naturally so; in your birth month all-round activity, in all spheres.

June

1–2, 5–6, 9–10, 14–15, 19*–28.
Possessions, selling, investing, restoring or improving assets and property or foreign connections, import and export will be the important activities.

July

2*–8, 11*–13, 16*–18, 21*–22, 26–27, 30*–31.
House and home and all therein keep you busy and happy. You enjoy it tremendously. Trips, ties and romance add to the fun.

August

3–4, 7*–9, 22–23, 26–27, 30–31.
All property matters are highlighted, as in June. Lots of ideas and plans come into play as you seek a direction, a new meaning, not just to your life, but also to your actions.

September

4*–5, 9*–10, 14*–15, 18*–19, 21–27.
Many stars for you this month. Creativity, children and joy light your fire. Lots of emotion and excitement, both professionally and personally.

October

1–3, 6*–13, 15–16, 19–21, 24–25, 28–30.
You could compete with Baw Xishun, the world's tallest man, at 2.36 metres. A bittersweet time as you forge new links, and partnerships, even as some existing ones end.

November

1*–8, 12*–13, 16*–17, 20*–21, 25*–26, 30*

Many stars for you once again in this month. Work, health, collaborations, journeys and finances will be the main issues you address. All are important for progress and gain and all keep you busy too.

December

5–6, 9–10, 13–19, 22*–23, 27*–29.
You end the year on a high note. Your mood, your attitude, and your confidence will soar as you have a firm sense of direction, and an equally strong faith in yourself and Ganesha!

Gemini

Vivacity + Versatility + Verve = VICTORY
Ganesha says this is Bejan's formula for Gemini.

YEARLY FORECAST

Till 16 July 2014

Summary and Guidance

Jupiter will be in your second angle. What does it really mean? One illustration is equal to a thousand words. 'A bespoke shirt or trousers is now just a click away, courtesy the cyber tailor,' *The Times of India*, 22 June 2013. The apparel company, says Vidya Natarajan, is more of a technological company. Stiff collar, English shirts, cutaway collars, split yokes, butterfly gussets (triangular or square pieces of fabric inserted into a seam to add breadth and reduce stress) and two-buttoned barrel cuffs. We are talking here about men's clothes. The reason is Jupiter in the second house stands for clothes for man and woman. Other characteristics of the second house include wealth, speech, physical enjoyments, trading in ornaments, pearls and diamonds, buying or selling in general, accumulation of wealth, earning through self-effort, acquisitions from father, inclinations, food, taste, clothes, eloquence, letters, deceitfulness, family members, friends, enemies, servants and close followers. Yes, this is a very exhaustive list and you should be happy about it.

You Geminis are very curious and want to know the reason for everything. Therefore, especially for you, I am explaining that Jupiter is in excellent formation with Neptune, and this formation gives more firepower to all the above predictions. Also Pluto and Neptune are in a great formation.

17 July 2014 to 11 August 2015

Jupiter will be in your third angle of contacts, contracts, communication, correspondence, computers and, above all, consciousness. The signing of cheques, IOUs, promissory notes and instruments of negotiation will be in focus. You will be fully stimulated artistically, because Jupiter will pep you up. The whiz-kids of communication are the Geminis, the Sagittarians and the Aquarians. Now you know the goodies you will get.

A word of caution. Saturn will be in your sixth angle of health, colleagues, pets, food, exercise and animals. Therefore, eat regularly, exercise and do not overstrain. If you do, the batteries of your energy will run dry and you will come apart, so to say. You will be exhausted. You have so many irons in the fire. You cannot afford to be tired or sick or listless. Rest and recreation are absolutely necessary. You have to learn to take it easy from time to time.

Main Trend

I have already explained very clearly that till 16 July 2014 money, clothes, ornaments, buying and selling, trading, speech and food are the main features. After that, from

17 July 2014 the Cs of contacts, communication, contracts, correspondence and, finally, consciousness will be the key to happiness. Physical fitness and hobbies are absolutely necessary. Your relations with your neighbours and relatives should be nice and easy. Geminis are mentally alert and active. Any split in relationships leads to tension and turmoil and psychological problems. Be willing to listen to others. Keep your channels of communication active. Add to your knowledge. Remember, your ideas can be brilliant and therefore don't be afraid to share your thoughts and feelings with others. The more you share, the happier you will be. But please, please do not jump to conclusions. Sometimes, it is best to listen and give others the right of way. Believe me, it helps. Try it and let me know.

I must specially mention that Mars will be in your fifth angle of creativity, children, hobbies, entertainment, tantra, mantra and religion from 1 January to 25 July. It will stimulate you to give your very best. Slight tensions are possible in January, April and July. But that should not come in the way of your creative juices, inspiration, intuition and imagination. You will be both artistic and constructive.

Journey and Communication

As said earlier, journey and communication at all levels is where you really excel and score points, literally. For example, the great tennis player Rafael Nadal is a Gemini. Ravi Shastri, the former cricket all-rounder, in a telephonic conversation told me that he was a Gemini. There you have it. Gossip also comes in communication and here I am joking! Don't we all love to gossip from time to time?

Health

As said earlier, you Geminis live on your nerves. You are alert and agile. Saturn in your sixth angle of health could cause minor problems with breathing, in your private parts, lungs, chest and feet if you are not careful. A word to the wise is enough and you are wise.

Love/Marriage

Love and marriage are to many women the world itself. It is a woman's existence, and rightly so. Venus, the symbol of love and marriage, will be in your sign from 24 June to 18 July. This does not mean that you must fall in love and marry during this period. It only means that it is favourable for affairs of the heart, joy and happiness, romance and attachments, children and sports. Happiness varies from person to person. I have an honest confession. My wife Gooli is a Gemini. I owe a great deal of my success to her. She is my best friend and my soulmate.

Property

Property matters are highlighted till 16 July 2014. The reason is that buying and selling, renovation and decoration, moving house, building and construction often go with monetary transactions. The months for it could well be September, 24 June to 18 July, and 26 October to 4 December.

Job/Business/Loans/Funds/Investments

Funds and investments could make you rich as Jupiter will help you. A job switch is possible. But look before you leap. Make sure of all the facts. Haste is waste. Do business but take only calculated risks because Saturn is favourable only partially, not completely. The months are July, August, September, January, possibly April. As said earlier, funds and investments are favoured partially. I am not God. This is only a sun-based reading. Perhaps July, September and January are best for it.

Children/Entertainment

October, April, June and February favour children and entertainment. From 24 June to 18 July Venus, the planet of entertainment and luxury, will be in your own sign. Also Mercury, planet of communication, will be in your own sign from 8 to 29 May. Finally, Mars will certainly be in your angle of entertainment from 1 January to 25 July. But fiery Mars in the sign of Libra (balance) could cause imbalance and disturbance in the form of great joy or great sorrow. Great turbulence and mighty exhilaration are in store. In short, Mars is both good and bad for you.

Trips and Ties

Trips, ties and communication are the lifeblood of Geminis. Fine months for it are August, October, February and April. Mercury, the winged messenger, will be in your own sign favouring travel and communication and relationships during 8 to 29 May.

Publicity/Projects/Performance

For Geminis publicity and performance are a part of communication, interaction and relationships. Combining all these, the months will be June, July, August, October, February and April. Also, 24 June to 18 July, when Venus will be in your sign, and 8 to 29 May, when Mercury will be in your sign, are good periods. Things should work out for you then.

Happiness Quota

Geminis are at heart children. They are themselves toys who play with toys! Ideas, brilliant ideas and thoughts are their gifts to mankind. But Neptune and Mars are partly good and partly bad for them. My final marks will be 83 per cent.

Monthly Round-up

January: legacy, finances, passion, but low vitality; February: distant places, research, parents and in-laws, education, children, good fortune through meeting the right persons; March: position, prestige, power, parents, home and property rites and rituals for the living and the dead; April: friendship, socializing, gains and glamour, realization of aspirations; May: travel, restlessness despite good fortune, expenses, care of health; June: good going in terms of health, wealth and happiness—thank Ganesha for it; July: finances, family, ties, adornment, home, buying/selling, vehicles; August: contacts, communication, contracts, crash courses, mental brilliance, new projects, courage, determination; September: home, family, treasure, parents and in-laws, work prospects even for the retired—paradoxically, elderly persons will retire shortly; October: journey, ceremony, publicity, children, hobbies, creativity, therefore, a lively and lucky month; November: job, pets, projects, subordinates' health needs care; December: love/hate, partnership/separation, but you do gain and can look forward to the future with great confidence. You deserve it!

Summary

More responsibility, luckily more money, gusts of genuine inspiration, travel and joy, name and fame, comforts and property are indicated. Health precautions will be necessary. This is the kaleidoscope of your life in 2014. Ganesha says happiness, despite tension and turmoil, is your due in life, and therefore, you shall have it.

Outer Planets

URANUS: Uranus will gift you with sudden ups and downs of fortune, eccentric but lovable friends and relationships.

NEPTUNE: Yes, Neptune in your angle of power, prestige and position, pomp and pelf helps you all along. Have faith in yourself and God. If you have faith and trust in God and religion, your work will be much easier. But I do not impel or compel. It is your life, your decision.

PLUTO: Pluto could raise a minor storm in the teacup of loans, funds, wills, inheritance, joint finance, tantra and mantra. I would say go with the flow and make the best of it. Lose a battle but win the war.

Month by Month

January

The year starts on a powerful note, with hard work, direction and ambition. You set your sights on your goals and go for them in earnest. You look beyond yourself now. There is fire in the belly and you push ahead on all fronts. There is purpose in your moves. Media folk do well. There are emotional moments, and domestic concerns raise their head by mid-month. There are inheritances and family investments to take care of. There is love, passion and bonding and you enjoy many special moments with your partner. As the month ends, there are maudlin moments. You look inward and face harsh and deep psychological truths. On the work front, there could be international collaborations and a rise in reputation and prestige. Ganesha is happy for you.

February

You have stability. You roll up your sleeves and get down to the hard slog. You are creatively charged and could win awards if you are a writer, painter or actor. As the month progresses, you live larger than life. You spend recklessly. There is love and passion. There could be power struggles, ego drives and altercations. As the month ends, there is travel and new encounters. You network furiously. You move fast and furious from one happy encounter to another. Ganesha smiles.

March

Your sensitivities are not in tune with your intentions and there could be some sort of struggle for mastery of the self. There is furious activity on social networking sites. You want to share your joys and sorrows with everyone. Those in committed relationships reach ecstatic bonding. As the month progresses, your energy level is high, your ambitions are aroused, but there are roadblocks of all kinds. Family life has emergencies. You suddenly realize that there is a hole in your pocket and whatever you earn gets flushed out. You have to plug your extravagant ways. There are alumni meetings, and long-lost friends and lovers come out of the woodwork. As the month ends, the focus is on all fiscal instruments. There are rewards and accolades at work as you climb many notches. New relationships enter your radar and you project warmth and friendliness. There could be a windfall in the form of an inheritance. Ganesha watches over you.

April

There are many domestic issues that need your attention. This is also an excitingly creative phase for writers. Expenses skyrocket. Your energy level is very high, and you tend to identify your ego with your ideas and opinions. Many doubts, fears and insecurities haunt you as several deep-seated fears in your psyche wrestle out of your subconscious. By mid-month the mood is better but not upbeat. There is low self-image, isolation, loneliness and difficulties in relating to people. You may be in a love triangle and this could cause problems. As the month ends, you plunge into hard work and control your restless mind. You are charged and want to be a person of consequence. Ganesha blesses you.

May

Mercury is in your sign from 8 to 29 May. You zoom ahead. Make the most of this phase. Grab it with both hands. This is a propitious time filled with love, passion, hope, joy, achievement, marriage, engagement, festivities, new vistas, new beginnings, takeovers, makeovers, corporate moves, profitable gambles, money and honey. You are on a bull run. There is very little that can derail you now. You have the Midas touch. There is progress on the material front and now you want to grow as a person. You enjoy life and feel liberated from the routine and the mundane. There is more gusto and freedom in your actions. Ganesha is happy for you.

June

There is a lot of mental activity and you will be communicating furiously with others. There are rewards and awards, plaudits and applause. Family life is pleasant. By mid-month there is a lot of movement at all levels. You will bond with your spouse/lover, children, parents, siblings, in-laws and colleagues. The energies are powerful. Venus is in Gemini from 24 June to 18 July, which is more than a month. This is a great period, and you must make the most of it. This is a powerfully creative phase. Media folk do exceptionally well. Later in the month, there is also a chance to make easy money. There could be problems with the law and a fall in reputation if you are not careful. Ganesha suggests that you steer clear of it all.

July

There are several paths spread out before you and you don't know which one to take. There are expenses, medical emergencies and maybe even a nervous breakdown. There are several emotional challenges and hidden stresses. You look for salvation and could go looking for a guru. There is stability by mid-month. You are ambitious and look for renown. Media folk do well. There is money and honey. Family life is on an even ground. There is success at work, and you also spend time in social work. You help others, reach out to society, and find your true calling. You are in the throes of communicating, and use technology well. You live large and spend like there is no tomorrow. You accomplish a lot. Ganesha watches over you.

August

There is new energy powering you. Along with it is powerful intensity. This is a great time for commercial ventures and all types of negotiations. There is buoyant optimism. There are lucky breaks. There is also personal growth. By the middle of the month there are maudlin moments and you may fall into depression, but this passes quickly. As the month ends, there is stability and you earn big bucks. Your ventures do well. There is money and honey, rewards and awards, applause and accolades. You are in great spirits; you are buoyant, accepting, friendly, agreeable, charming and balanced in your approach towards yourself and others. You may also fall in love with someone from a completely different culture. Ganesha is thrilled for you.

September

People will be a stumbling block and you feel that you are not able to convince anyone. Take precautions, as you could be prone to accidents. On the plus side, this is a good time to embark on new projects. The focus is on finance, commissions, ties, associations, collaborations and other fiscal instruments. As the month progresses, there is emotional intensity. You review the past and make big plans for the future. You are creatively charged. This is a good time for all kinds of mental work, group discussions and negotiations. You organize yourself and are clear-headed. You are at your creative best and are filled with zest and ambition. As the month ends, you are in touch with your feelings. The focus is on relationships, and you spend time with friends and loved ones. Ganesha is happy for you.

October

There is hard work ahead. You want the thrill of life, adrenaline pounding through your veins. But you have to move out of your comfort zone for that. Money slips through your fingers as you splurge on the good life. By mid-month the energies are in your favour. There could be travel and new ventures. You make and spend money. There is love and longing. You are in an upbeat and buoyant mood. You want to tango with love, lust, high stakes and danger. By the end of the month, you look for gods and godmen. You may go on pilgrimages. You could be in the throes of sustained growth accompanied by restlessness and impatience. Your sensitivities are finely tuned. You are filled with grace and gratitude. There are lucky breaks and windfalls. Ganesha is delighted for you.

November

Now you realize that success is a result of sustained effort. You have clear goals for your life and want to achieve them. You spend time in important negotiations and clinch big deals. You conjure up grandiose schemes. You make the necessary changes in your professional life and zoom ahead without full stops. You are in the throes of communication; and those in advertising, marketing, PR and journalism do particularly well. By the middle of the month, you triumph over personal and domestic turbulence with a zeal rarely witnessed. There could be international travel with the family. This is a propitious time for big plans, new collaborations and new contracts. Ganesha is pleased.

December

You look to make fundamental changes in your life, changes that are creative, exciting and alive. There are new ideas, experiences and insights as you evolve into a better person and grow in consciousness. You are on stable ground by mid-month. Hard work and discipline are needed now. If unattached, you could take your relationship to the next level. Those who are married experience powerful bonding. There is ambition powered by sustained work. As the year ends, you are warming up to new challenges. Your growth has been steady and it is visible. Ganesha has carried you through.

Months at a Glance

January

Legacy, finance, passion, but low vitality.

February

Distant places, research, parents and in-laws, education, children, good fortune through meeting the right persons.

March

Position, prestige, power, parents, home and property rites, and rituals for the living and the dead.

April

Friendship, socializing, gains and glamour, realization of aspirations.

May

Travel, restlessness despite good fortune, expenses, health care needs.

June

Good going in terms of health, wealth and happiness— you should thank Ganesha for it.

July

Finance, family ties, adornment, home, buying/selling, vehicles.

August

Contacts, communication, contracts, crash courses, mental brilliance, new projects, courage, determination.

September

Home, family, treasure, parents and in-laws, work prospects even for the retired; paradoxically, elderly persons will retire shortly.

October

Journey, ceremony, publicity, children, hobbies, creativity therefore, a lively and lucky month.

November

Job, pets, projects, subordinates' health care.

December

Love/hate, partnership/separation, but all said, you do gain and can look forward to the future with great confidence. You deserve it!

Weekly Review (By the phases of the moon)

1 January: New Moon in Capricorn

Gemini is an air sign and could be inconsistent, impatient, changeable, creative and restless. A Gemini's world is one of duality. Geminis are curious, talkative, versatile and mentally active. They are born communicators. Every sign has its list of celebrities, and this one is no exception. You share your birth sign with Angelina Jolie, Anna Kournikova, Anne Frank, Ben Johnson, Marilyn Monroe, Johnny Depp, Bob Dylan, Brooke Shields, Che Guevara, Donald Trump, Jackie Stewart, John F. Kennedy, Frank Lampard, Salman Rushdie, Paul McCartney, Steve Waugh, Venus Williams and Gauguin, among others. The year starts on a powerful note, with hard work, direction and ambition. You may be in the habit of starting something and then falling off the wagon. In this phase, you are consistent. You set your sights on your goals and go for them in earnest. Ganesha wishes you well.

8 January: First Quarter in Aries

'Many people know so little what is beyond their short range of experience. They look within themselves and find nothing! Therefore they conclude that there is nothing outside themselves either,' said Helen Keller. You look beyond yourself now. There is fire in the belly and you push ahead on all cylinders. There are expenses and you could lose money in trivial pursuits. The married may see an addition to the family and those who are courting may take the relationship to the next level. There is purpose in your moves. Media folk do well. Love is in the air and you have little time left for the other pursuits of life; it takes you by the scruff of the neck and overwhelms you. Ganesha is with you.

16 January: Full Moon in Cancer

There are emotional moments, and domestic concerns raise their head. Children need attention and there could be medical emergencies at home. You have your hands full. There could also be an unusual degree of selflessness in love. You may just want to help your partner and expect nothing in return. You may relish the martyr role. There are inheritances and family investments to take care of. Business folk may have their hands deep in loans and other fiscal instruments. The start of the year has a full plate on offer. Ganesha wishes you well.

24 January: Last Quarter in Scorpio

There is powerful intensity. You communicate with others hard and fast. You are making many plans to move ahead in life. You hope to act on them later. You are in touch with your feelings and emotions, and your plans are in line with your inner desires. You are overdriving yourself and there are strong ego pulls. There is love, passion and bonding and you enjoy many special moments with your partner. You display your feelings with the flamboyance of a flamingo in heat and attract others like bees to honey; you wear your emotions on your sleeve, and this can work both ways. You are also generous and want to party and have fun times. Ganesha blesses you. You mean no harm but could easily be misunderstood.

30 January: New Moon in Aquarius

These are maudlin times. You look inward and face harsh and deep psychological truths. You are influenced by your surroundings and go within yourself to make the changes that you feel you should. The species that adapts to change survives, said Darwin. You can see quite clearly that you are in a rut. You need to change tack in many areas of your life, not to just compete with a changing world, but to survive. On the work front, there could be international collaborations and a rise in reputation and prestige. You think out of the box and there is applause. Ganesha is happy for you.

6 February: First Quarter in Taurus

You have the stability of Taurus in this phase. You roll up your sleeves and slog hard. There are distractions, and your mind is swept away like flower pots in a tsunami, but you still manage to stay on course. Those in the media do well. You are creatively charged and could win awards if you are a writer, painter or actor. Family life is stable and you spend many cosy moments at home. You are optimistic, you plan and think big. There is money to be made and you can see clearly that a hefty bank account will help your cause. Ganesha blesses you.

14 February: Full Moon in Leo

The full moon is in Leo and you live larger than life. You spend recklessly. If single, you court all but you may somehow return home empty-handed. You may gamble and lose money. There is love and passion, but somehow the deep, spiritual bonding that you expect may be elusive. There could be power struggles, ego drives and altercations. You may have run-ins with the law. You are filled with energy and should use it in the right direction. Learn to optimize your gifts. Ganesha holds your hand.

22 February: Last Quarter in Sagittarius

There is travel and new encounters. You network furiously and are the soul of the party. You are affable and others seek you out. You may move with the family to another country or take up a job away from home. Youngsters do well at examinations and interviews. The energies of this phase make you a good listener and an engaging conversationalist. Domestic issues are placed on the back burner as you move fast and furiously from one happy encounter to another. Ganesha smiles.

1 March: New Moon in Pisces

There are maudlin moments. There is a disconnect between your personal and professional needs. Your sensitivities are not in tune with your intentions and there could be some sort of struggle for mastery over the self. You are overflowing with emotions and are sensitive to others' needs. You may hide in the closet to understand yourself better, as the richness of feeling and emotion that you experience and express may alienate you from your peer group, who can't seem to fathom you. There is furious networking through Twitter and Facebook. You want to share your joys and sorrows with everyone, but is anyone listening? Singles look for partners, and those in committed relationships reach ecstatic bonding. Family life is intense with many outings and fun times. Ganesha is with you.

8 March: First Quarter in Gemini

'Faith is the bird that sings when the dawn is still dark,' said Rabindranath Tagore. You look to creatively transform your world and the world around you. There is a lot of movement and exchange of ideas, power struggles and disagreements. Your energy level is high, your ambitions are aroused, but there are roadblocks of all kinds. Even close family may oppose your plans and you may have to plough a lonely furrow. Family life has emergencies. Children and elders may need medical attention. There could be a sudden bereavement or an illness. Work moves along prescribed lines and there is a lot on your plate. New vistas open. Ganesha journeys with you.

16 March: Full Moon in Virgo

There is more stability. You work hard and count your pennies. You suddenly realize that there is a hole in your pocket and whatever you earn gets flushed out. You have lent money and now you have to chase it. You have to plug your extravagant ways. You sign big deals and run through contracts and the fine print with a magnifying glass. You need a bigger apartment as the family is growing and space is at a premium. 'Loving ourselves works miracles in our lives,' said Louise Hay. Yes, you have to do that. You change your wardrobe and diet, start a new exercise regimen and make way for a new personality. There are alumni meetings, and long-lost friends and lovers come out of the woodwork. There is new love along with the old and that is quite a cauldron of boiling passion, love, hate and disquiet. Singles have a field day and the attached have sombre moments; those who are married may miss the carefree days of courtship. But regrets are out of place now. The energies are good. Use the waxing phase of the moon to your advantage. Ganesha holds your hand.

24 March: Last Quarter in Capricorn

You make headway, albeit slowly. The focus is on all fiscal instruments. There are maudlin moments too, and you may think of your own mortality. If you have had an illness or someone in the family has been diagnosed with a terminal problem, you may be prone to depression. Not that this helps, but I cannot resist quoting Steve Jobs here, 'I think death is the most wonderful invention of life. It purges the system of those models that are obsolete.' Of course, Jobs's take relates more to technology (probably) and is cold comfort for the human condition. There are rewards and accolades at work as you climb many notches. Ganesha blesses you.

30 March: New Moon in Aries

The new moon is in Aries and you are powered by new-found energy. This is a very pleasant phase and you should make full use of it. One part of you wants to take a vacation and just do nothing—to chill, as they say these days; another part of you wants to climb new mountains at work. Use your free will and decide on your course of action. New relationships enter your radar and you project warmth and friendliness. This is contagious. You attract others to you like butterflies to pollen and there could be the seeds of a significant relationship. Fiscal affairs are also in focus. There could be a windfall in the form of an inheritance. Ganesha watches over you.

7 April: First Quarter in Cancer

The home front calls. There are many domestic issues that need your attention. A child may be flying away for higher studies, the spouse and parents may need medical attention and the home may need repairs. You could plunge into panic. This is also an excitingly creative phase for writers. You make hay while the sun sets! I say this deliberately, as many writers and creative folk work late into the night. The single look for true love, but it is elusive. You give your soul in its quest but have nothing to show for it. There are indulgences as you look to escape from the perceived failures of your life. Ganesha is with you; take heart from that.

15 April: Full Moon in Libra

Expenses skyrocket. Apart from the usual domestic requirements, you also spend heavily on things you don't really need. Your energy level is very high, and you tend to identify your ego with your ideas and opinions. Others don't take kindly to this, and there are differences of opinion. You are easily angered and become irritable. This mood spills to the home front too, and there could be domestic upheavals. Many doubts, fears and insecurities continue to haunt you as several deep-seated fears in your psyche wrestle out of your subconscious. You get into a shell and are filled with remorse and self-pity. I must add here that these are mere generalizations, as I don't have your personal details. Astrology never compels. These are mere prods. Use your free will to advantage, says Ganesha. I second that.

22 April: Last Quarter in Aquarius

The mood is better but not upbeat. You have many thoughts in your mind and play with abstractions. You are concerned about your identity. There is low self-image, isolation, loneliness and difficulties in relating to people. Even close family, friends and lovers wonder what you are up to. You find that you are not able to communicate your innermost feelings. It is all a matter of perception. You look at the half-empty glass and feel that you are a failure. This is the right time to make the corrections and zoom ahead. You may be in a love triangle and this could cause problems. Ganesha insists that you look ahead and use your innumerable skills. This phase will also pass, like it always does. No dark cloud remains for long.

29 April: New Moon in Taurus

The new moon is in Taurus and there is a glimmer of stability. You realize that you have to get back on track. You plunge into hard work and control the monkey mind. An Irish proverb says that a good laugh and good sleep are the best cures in the doctor's book. You look for more work, and take time off to be by yourself also. You may take a break in the hills or the beaches to rejuvenate and think your life over. You explore many avenues. You are charged and want to be a person of consequence and not just another human being inhabiting planet earth. You want your own identity and not be known only as somebody's son or daughter. Ganesha blesses you.

7 May: First Quarter in Leo

From 8 to 29 May, Mercury, the mighty, all-powerful planet, is in your sign. It favours travels, meetings, conferences, interviews, trips, more brain power, contacts, communication, correspondence and contracts. Mercury has a special connection with the circuit of the brain. Chess, crossword and other such games belong to Mercury. Also, short-distance runners and spin bowlers are controlled by Mercury. Mercury, in short, is the ambassador and salesman of the zodiac. Mercury is the symbol of news, views, messages, interviews, contacts, communications, travel and transport. Mercury gives an impetus to all of the above in the sun sign where it is located. The first quarter is also in Leo. You zoom ahead.

Make the most of this phase. Grab it with both hands. This is a propitious time filled with love, passion, hope, joy, achievement, marriage, engagement, festivities, new vistas, new beginnings, takeovers, makeovers, corporate moves, profitable gambles, money and honey. As the bard says, take the high tide to fortune. Ganesha is delighted as he wants the very best for you.

14 May: Full Moon in Scorpio

You are on a bull run. There is very little that can derail you now. You have the Midas touch. Take risks and embark on whatever you had earlier dreamt of. You are filled with drive, gusto, ambition, self-belief, perseverance and powerfully healthy ego drives. Ganesha can see that you have turned the corner. There could be international holidays, business expansion, new collaborations, money and honey. And there are miles to go.

21 May: Last Quarter in Pisces

You are in deep thought. There is progress on the material front and now you want to grow as a person. You realize that your troubles have all been a matter of perception, and nothing more. This is a great realization and you begin to count your blessings. You open the throttle and move in a million directions. You need to embrace the world, and technology helps. Travel, money, new friends, relationships, births, marriages, bereavements, engagements, festivities and a lot more will be on your plate. This is also a creatively rewarding phase. Use it well. Your sensitivities are highly tuned. Ganesha is with you all the way.

28 May: New Moon in Gemini

You enjoy life and feel liberated from the routine and the mundane. There is more gusto and freedom in your actions. There are significant encounters with people, and you relish every moment. The new moon is in your sign and you are filled with ideas. There are outings with family and friends, and you are the soul of the party with your wit and repartee. The family will bond like never before and you feel blessed. Ganesha is happy for you.

5 June: First Quarter in Virgo

'Fill the brain with the highest ideals, place them day and night before you, and out of that will come great work,' said Swami Vivekananda. There is a lot of mental activity and you will be communicating furiously with others. There will be paperwork and conferences, and you will impress everyone with your communication skills. There are ego drives but it is in your interest to contain them. There are rewards and awards, plaudits and applause. Family life is pleasant. There are no hiccups to derail you. Ganesha wishes you well, as always.

13 June: Full Moon in Sagittarius

There is a lot of movement at all levels. You are not only ideating furiously but there is also geographical movement. You have many plans for the future based on lessons from the past. You are also the soul of the party with your congenial and affable personality. You are in demand. You throw your ideas at others, seeking feedback. Keep your ears open. Sometimes criticism is valid, and you can change tack if you feel it is in your interest. You will bond with your spouse/lover, children,

parents, siblings, in-laws and colleagues. The singles sow
their seeds without bother. The energies are powerful and
it is a great time to be. Ganesha is happy for you.

19 June: Last Quarter in Pisces

Venus is in Gemini from 24 June to 18 July, which is
more than a month. This is a great period, and you must
make the most of it. Venus is another important planet
and is of great significance. This is an important phase. As
often discussed, Venus is the planet of love, romance, sex,
beauty and the good life. This is the planet of attraction,
wealth, knowledge and prosperity. The compatibility of
partners and also the type of life the individual will lead
are judged from the placement of Venus in the horoscope.
As a planet, Venus is considered to be beneficial, feminine
and gentle. Venus symbolizes the force of attraction in the
universe. In human beings this attractive force manifests
as love and beauty. When Venus is well placed in the
chart, there is love, art, beauty and all the goodies of life
that make it worth living. Venus rules Libra and Taurus,
though its role in every sign is important. Like other
planets, it also has its transits. In Libra, Venus is aesthetic
and cultured. In Taurus, it is more earthy, materialistic
and sensual. Venus rules the venous system, kidneys,
urinary tract, throat, larynx, and is responsible for good
looks. In short, Venus in Western astrology stands for
comforts, arts, wealth, relationships, sex, decorations,
luxuries and wealth. This is a powerfully creative phase.
Media folk do exceptionally well. There are launches,
ceremonies, conferences, publicity meets, PR exercises,
promotions, stocks, shares, mutual funds and so on. You
make money and, for a change, save it. You are able to

make the right investments despite the mounting expenses. Ganesha blesses you. There could be new love too, and the single may take it to the altar.

27 June: New Moon in Cancer

There are emotional moments that threaten to derail you. There could also be deceit. Be careful when lending money or signing new documents. There is also a chance that you look at options to make easy money. There could be problems with the law and a fall in reputation if you are not careful. Remember that it is very difficult to climb the mountain, but very easy to fall from the summit. You may also lose heavily in gambling and other underhand activities. Ganesha suggests that you steer clear of it all. The past also has an uncanny habit of showing up when it is least expected. You could also be prone to indulgences as your shadow side or blind spot seeks to take over. The home front has issues that need solutions. You cope, but it is not easy. Ganesha holds your hand.

5 July: First Quarter in Libra

You are confronted with many options, and that is not a comfortable space to be in. You are filled with ideas and they need approval. There are several paths spread out before you and you don't know which one to take. There are expenses, medical emergencies and maybe even a nervous breakdown. There are several emotional challenges and hidden stresses. You are caught in an ambush like a wounded giraffe in the Serengeti stalked by a pack of lions. You surmount everything and evolve into a better person. You look for salvation and could go in search of a guru. You read the right books and meet with uplifting souls for answers. There is tantra, mantra and yantra. You examine your life, sandpaper the past and give it a fresh coat of paint. You want a new self, a completely different persona, and it is happening. Ganesha holds your hand and journeys with you.

12 July: Full Moon in Capricorn

There is stability after the long haul. Every sign has these moments—ups and downs are a part and parcel of life. Seasons follow one another, and one has to coast through everything. In this phase, your ego drives are back and you are energetic, decisive and belligerent. You want your way at all costs and will not tolerate laggards and passengers in your team. You want to make things happen and have no time or inclination for the sensitivities and weaknesses of others. You are ambitious and look for renown. Media folk do well. There is money and honey. This is a great time for solo players. Family life is on an even keel as you steer a clear path for yourself. Ganesha is with you as you send the right messages to the universe, and it responds with abundance.

19 July: Last Quarter in Aries

'Everyone can be great because everyone can serve,' said Martin Luther King. The energy of Aries pushes you to great heights. There is success at work and you also spend time doing social work. It is a good way to get to know yourself better. You help others, reach out to society, and find your true calling. You are in the throes of communication, and use technology well. Swami Vivekananda called the mind a drunken monkey, and your mind is simply saturated. But you find yourself neck-deep in work, and this could be the beginning of better things. Domestic issues are brushed under the carpet for now. Ganesha blesses you.

26 July: New Moon in Leo

'Be selfish, be generous,' said the Dalai Lama. This is a good phase to formulate your goals and work towards them. You live large and spend like there is no tomorrow. Ego energies are high, and the way out is to cooperate with others, and not run them down for non-performance. You indulge in outdoor activities and may go on treks or take to hobbies like gardening. You may also be investing in real estate. Some of you may even bring home an exotic pet. You accomplish a lot, and manage to use the energies of the new moon well. There is money to be made, and love shows up when least expected. Ganesha watches over you.

4 August: First Quarter in Scorpio

There is new energy powering you. Along with it is powerful intensity. 'I don't know what your destiny will be, but one thing I do know: the only ones among you who will be really happy are those who have sought and found how to serve,' said Nobel laureate Albert Schweitzer. This is a great time for commercial ventures and all types of negotiations. There is buoyant optimism, almost bordering on overconfidence. There are lucky breaks, and you miraculously get your way with authorities and the law. There is also personal growth as you experience the entire gamut of human emotions and emerge the better for it. You may also take time out to help the less privileged. Ganesha journeys with you.

10 August: Full Moon in Aquarius

'Truly it is in the darkness that one finds the light, so when we are in sorrow, then this light is nearest to all to us,' said the mystic Meister Eckhart. There are maudlin moments and you may fall into depression, but this passes quickly. Your mind is sharp like a Swiss army knife and you work at amusing yourself with different kinds of experiences. New vistas open up, and new knowledge and understanding flood through. You are in touch with the world and will be tweeting obsessively. You speak your mind, and impress with your honesty and forthrightness. There are expenses, medical emergencies, past hurts that emerge from the closet and some domestic rumblings. But that is part of the package of life, says Ganesha.

17 August: Last Quarter in Taurus

There is stability and you earn big bucks. Your ventures do well. There is money and honey, rewards and awards, applause and accolades. Ideas flow easily and you are intellectually alive and curious. This is a great time for students and academics. You may chair important meetings, conferences and negotiations, and earn the respect of your peers. There is fruitful and expansive interchange with others. You encourage opposition and learn from it. You also manage to shore up finances and have fun too. You work hard and party harder. Ganesha holds your hand.

25 August: New Moon in Virgo

This is a favourable period for all kinds of activity. You meet with others and may plan a long holiday. You are in great spirits; you are buoyant, accepting, friendly, agreeable, charming and balanced in your approach towards yourself and others. You may also fall in love with someone from a completely different culture as you socialize with a vengeance. Those in settled relationships may have an addition to the family. It is all working out for you and Ganesha is thrilled. You are shrewd, savvy and crack lucrative deals.

2 September: First Quarter in Sagittarius

There is a lot of movement and you speak your mind. You tread on toes and are irritable, emotional and prone to fights and altercations. People will be a stumbling block and you feel that you are not able to convince anyone. You see people as challenges and threats. Take precautions, as you could be prone to accidents. You could hurt yourself and others in the process. On the plus side, this is a good time to embark on new projects. The focus is on finances, commissions, ties, associations, collaborations and other fiscal instruments. You push hard and there are many expenses; money disappears like water on desert sands. There are indulgences and stolen moments with your partner. Ganesha smiles.

9 September: Full Moon in Pisces

There is emotional intensity. You review the past and make big plans for the future. You are also troubled by past actions. Somehow, you are unable to sever yourself from days gone by. Let the past be. It is spilt milk. You coil like a serpent and ruminate endlessly like an ungulate. You simply can't fathom how you did all those stupid things. We all go through this, and hopefully you have learnt from your mistakes, and evolved. You are creatively charged—writers, poets and those in allied fields do well. If your love life is in shambles, you wonder why. The monkey mind possesses you. Your shadow side and blind spots haunt you. 'Show me a sane man and I will cure him,' said Albert Camus. Don't worry. You are in good company—with the rest of humanity, if you please! This mood shall pass. Just hang in there. Ganesha holds your hand. I have been there too, if that is any reassurance.

16 September: Last Quarter in Gemini

'The ability to concentrate and to use your time well is everything if you want to succeed in business—or almost anywhere else for that matter,' said American businessman Lee Iacocca. That is the key—to control the monkey mind and be filled with passion. You have to be driven if you want to be an achiever; nothing in life comes easy or free, barring your inheritance. The moon is in your sign and this is a good time for all kinds of mental work, group discussions and negotiations. You organize yourself and are clear-headed, and have a clear idea of what your ego needs. You are at your creative best and are filled with zest and ambition. But ambition without perseverance is zilch. Ganesha agrees. There are fun times with friends and family. I have said this deliberately. Please remember that I was a professor of English.

24 September: New Moon in Libra

This is a more balanced period. You are in touch with your feelings, and your emotional interactions with others work out well. You are a good listener and are looking for input, criticism and feedback from others, even if it is harsh. You have an open mind. You are filled with interest, sympathy and concern for others and are affable and congenial. Everyone wants to hang out with you. The focus is on relationships and you spend time with friends and loved ones. There are expenses as you shop for pleasure. Children bring joy. Life is on an even keel and Ganesha is happy for you.

1 October: First Quarter in Capricorn

There is hard work ahead. There are emotional issues to wrestle with, but that is the package of life. You are reminded of old wounds and could again lose track. You want more than just routine and the usual everyday exchanges. You want the thrill of life, adrenaline pounding through your veins. But you have to move out of your comfort zone for that. Once again, I repeat, nothing in life comes easy. Money slips through your fingers as you splurge on the good life. People befriend you for your largesse. But you see through it and roll up your sleeves and get down to good, old-fashioned, hard work. Ganesha is pleased.

8 October: Full Moon in Aries

You are propelled by powerful energy. The full moon is in Aries and the energies are in your favour. Make the most of it. There could be travel and new ventures. You make and spend money. There is love and longing. You slog away on the front foot in the final over of the IPL, and it is not fixed! Let me remind you that I was a sportsman in my younger days. You are in an upbeat and buoyant mood. Life is dancing and calling out to you like a koel calling out to the monsoon. You want to tango with love, lust, high stakes and danger. You are like the trapeze artist seeking the thrill of greater heights; you are the lion tamer with your hand in the lion's heart! Ganesha wishes you well as you spread your wings and go for the impossible which a recent commercial says 'is nothing'.

15 October: Last Quarter in Cancer

'On the mountains of truth you can never climb in vain: either you will reach a point higher up today, or you will be training your powers so that you will be climbing higher tomorrow,' said German philosopher Friedrich Nietzche. You search hard for the truth. You look for gods and godmen, go looking for a guru and show renewed interest in tantra, mantra and yantra. You may go on pilgrimages and do havans for yourself and the family. There are festivities at home and possibly an addition to the family. There are quiet and reflective moments. You look for higher meaning and purpose in everything that you do. Ganesha blesses you.

23 October: New Moon in Scorpio

There are powerful influences at play. You could be in the throes of sustained growth accompanied by restlessness and impatience. There may be a job or residence change, and several disturbances to your personal life. I am not at all saying that they are bad. Please note that. With discipline and perseverance you will come up trumps. You will rebel against limitations and evolve and grow as a person. As you surmount the roadblocks, you will see the light at the end of the tunnel. There will be new tacks, new vistas and new windows opening up in your life, leading to a radical transformation. Ganesha journeys with you.

31 October: First Quarter in Aquarius

Your sensitivities are finely tuned. You are particularly perceptive and work towards creating an open, relaxed, secure and sympathetic atmosphere. Others flock to you. There is great bonding and fun times. You are filled with grace and gratitude. You help others, and a philanthropic streak emerges. There are lucky breaks and windfalls. Ganesha is delighted for you as you make rapid progress, both as a human being and as an active member of society. You plough a different furrow and take the road less travelled.

6 November: Full Moon in Taurus

This is a period of stability and hard work. You have been thinking about success for too long. Now you realize that success is a result of sustained effort. 'An ant on the move does more than a dozing ox,' said Chinese philosopher Lao Tzu. You are the ant now. You have clear goals for your life and want to achieve them. Enough of procrastination and dilly-dallying. You spend time in important negotiations and clinch big deals. You prune your expenses and cut your coat according to your cloth. You have to make your inner desires bear fruit, and you are driven. Those in the developing world may look at immigration for a better lifestyle. Youngsters also check into foreign universities. You look for positive change. There is new zeal in you and Ganesha wishes you well.

14 November: Last Quarter in Leo

'A scholar who cherishes the love of comfort is not deemed to be a scholar,' said Lao Tzu. You live and love large. You conjure up grandiose schemes. If you are an architect, you want to build bigger and newer designs. You make the necessary changes in your professional life and zoom ahead without full stops. You are in the throes of communication, and those in advertising, marketing, PR and journalism do particularly well. You see the light at the end of the tunnel. You see the summit of Everest and redouble your efforts. Ganesha holds your hand as you push ever so harder in a bid to be where you visualize yourself to be.

22 November: New Moon in Sagittarius

'When you do things from your soul, you feel a river moving in you, a joy,' said the poet Rumi. You achieve the impossible. You triumph over personal and domestic turbulence with a zeal rarely witnessed. If you have been lonely, isolated and depressed, it is all behind you. There is a force, a power that grips you. You are almost like an evangelist making miracle cures happen. There could be international travel with the family. You make changes in your priorities and move with the winds of change like a feather in the breeze, allowing it to take you where it will. You give yourself to the secure embrace of a higher power. Ganesha is delighted.

29 November: First Quarter in Pisces

There are serious thought processes on the cards. You take on practical issues head-on. This is not a time for games and trivia. You are organized and thorough at work and achieve a lot. You sign on the dotted line with great care. In love, as Osho described it, you transcend the body and enter the realm of superconsciousness. The powerful physicality you feel for your partner has a spiritual glow to it now. This is a propitious time for big plans, new collaborations and new contracts. You feel good about yourself. Isn't that what you always wanted?—asks Ganesha.

6 December: Full Moon in Gemini

The full moon is in your sign and you are ideating with the speed of a cement-churning machine trying to lay a road in Mumbai a day before the monsoon lashes the city. 'It is only when the mind is completely quiet, free of conflict—it is only then that the mind can go very far into the realms that are beyond time, thought and feeling,' said J. Krishnamurti, the famous writer and philosopher. You look to make fundamental changes in your life, changes that are creative, exciting and alive. There are new ideas, experiences and insights as you evolve into a better person and grow in consciousness. There are new relationships, new friends, even a new love. There could also be a new exercise programme and a closer look at alternative therapies. Life is crowning you with glory. Ganesha applauds.

14 December: Last Quarter in Virgo

You are on stable ground. There is hard work and discipline needed now. You feel like enjoying yourself, as the mood is mellow and the peer group is partying away. You could be self-indulgent and squander money. If not yet committed, you could take your relationship to the next level. Those who are married experience powerful bonding. Many positive influences will create a halo around you. Ganesha holds your hand.

22 December: New Moon in Capricorn

The new moon is in Capricorn and there is ambition powered by sustained work. There are, however, powerful forces exerted upon you, and you will have to make radical changes in your life. You junk old patterns of behaviour that are not valid any more and make room for more current and creative changes. As the year ends and the winter chill nestles in your marrow, you are warming up to new challenges. There is work to be done but you are in a fun mood. There could be extended holidays and you defer all life-changing decisions. Right now, you want to tango. Ganesha wishes you well.

28 December: First Quarter in Aries

'He who knows does not speak. He who speaks does not know,' said Lao Tzu. This is the last week of the year and you have been on the roller coaster a few times. Surprisingly, you haven't thrown up yet. Instead, you have evolved into a more mature, sensible, hard-working and determined person. Your growth has been steady and it is visible. Those who haven't met you for a long time are taken aback by the dramatic changes. Ganesha has carried you through, and he will continue to do so. Trust him. You are fired by the energy of Aries now, and you take it with you into the next year.

Key Dates
January

1, 5–6, 9*–15, 18*–19, 22*–24, 27–28.
Ganesha says you start your innings this year dealing with loans, joint finance, insurance, taxes, investment, buying/

selling/house moving, renovation and decoration. Thus, property and money issues dominate.

February

1*–2, 6*–11, 15*–16, 19*–20, 23*–25, 28–29.
Journey, mobility, pilgrimage, rites, religion, tantra and mantra, inspiration and travel are the various possibilities this month. Most of them should happen.

March

1, 4*–10, 13–14, 17–18, 22*–23, 27–28.
Hard work, good rewards. Parents, in-laws and elderly relatives interact very strongly with you. Everything connected with property will come up trumps for you.

April

1*–9, 13*–15, 18*–19, 23*–24, 28–29.
You will walk your way to fame, success, love, riches, power and promotion. The health of parents, in-laws and other people might be a problem.

May

2*–3, 6*–7, 11*–17, 20–22, 25*–27, 30–31.
Both the good and the not-so-good are highlighted; you seek to create harmony. Expenses have to be dealt with too.

June

3*–4, 7*–13, 16*–18, 21*–23, 26*–27, 30*.
You will run the race of life, be it honey, money or good old Indian rice and curry. Gains in terms of jewellery, job, profession and business are highlighted and you work wonders.

July

1, 4–5, 9–10, 14*–16, 19*–25, 28*–29.
July stands for almost all the Fs—finance, family, food (implying entertaining, hospitality), favours and life's different flavours. A month of plenty, and in all the Fs I have mentioned.

August

1*–7, 10*–11, 15*–16, 20*–21, 24–25, 28–29.
News and views, meets and conferences, trips and ties, computers and the Internet all come together. A grand reaching out happens.

September

1–3, 6–8, 11*–17, 20–21, 24*–26, 29*–30.
Home, office, shop, renovation and decoration, that is, property matters. Parents and in-laws, work and business will keep you extremely busy. Try to save time and energy. Watch your heath. Loans and investments are possible.

October

4*–5, 9*–14, 17*–18, 22*–23, 26*–27, 31*.
October helps you be a good parent, cultivate friendship and hobbies, entertain lavishly and be amused. Fun and work both are for you now, says Ganesha. A wider dimension to life rather than merely living.

November

1, 5*–11, 14*–15, 18–19, 22–24, 27–29.
November is for dealing with issues regarding health, finance, loans, pets, servants, bosses, colleagues and job. You will be exhausted with so much to handle, so do take proper rest from time to time.

December

2*–8, 11*–12, 15*–16, 20*–21, 24*–26, 30*–31.
December is for meeting people, marriage, partnerships
of every sort and journeys. Also, for the union or clash of
minds. Both could happen and are equally important.

Cancer

YEARLY FORECAST

Thou art the Symbol of Hope
Thou art the Teacher of Teachers
Thou art the Repository of Knowledge
Thou art the Infinite Source of Wisdom
Thou art the Remover of Obstacles
Thou art the Icon of Creativity
Thou art Lord Ganesha
Thou art the Saviour of Humanity

Imageheads

Till 16 July 2014
Summary and Guidance

The above praise of Ganesha applies to you very specially because Jupiter, the planet of prosperity and spirituality, will be in your complete personality house or first house or first angle. It will give you tremendous enthusiasm and power to set the wheels of any project rolling in the right direction, especially if you worship your own god or deity. And I worship Ganesha. In simple words, you will get what you want. Be happy. Enjoy. My advice is to share your good fortune with others. By doing so, you will double your happiness. Sharing is the secret of happiness, love, laughter and joy. I am sure my darling, sweet and sensitive Cancerians will understand it intuitively and rationally. Let me repeat. Success, achievement, progress, prosperity and happiness are the five pointers for you in 2014.

17 July 2014 to 11 August 2015

From 17 July 2014 to 11 August 2015 Jupiter will be in your second angle. The second angle stands for wealth, speech, physical enjoyments, trading in ornaments, pearls and diamonds, buying or selling in general, accumulation of wealth, earning through self-effort, acquisition from father, truthfulness and falsehood, inclinations, food, taste, clothes, eloquence, humility, steadiness of mind, learning, education, letters, anger, deceitfulness, family members, friends, enemies, servants, close followers, self-control, death. You will admit that this is quite a list.

Cancerians are generous but not extravagant as a rule. Therefore, give your money and a part of yourself to the poor, the weak, the needy, the unfortunate, the ill and the afflicted. Believe me, life is in giving. You will be making deals, purchases, augmenting income, and socializing and clubbing with one and all.

Main Trend

I have already said very clearly that 2014 is the year for all Cancerians because Jupiter, the all-rounder of the zodiac, is in your own sign. Cornucopia is the horn overflowing with flowers, fruit and corn, and is the symbol of plenty. So, now you can easily understand how good the year is for you. Be forceful, be hopeful, be confident but please understand that others are also human beings. Respect them and they will love you. It is so simple. The three great factors will be: (1) travel, contacts, collaborations, foreign affairs, publicity, spirituality; (2) hard work and wonderful rewards; and (3) enthusiasm, self-confidence and hope.

Journey and Communication

As said in the main trend, journey and communication will end in pleasure and profit. From 30 May to 16 June Mercury will be in your own sign and once again from 13 to 31 July, giving you impetus and the imagination to travel and contact others. September, March are the other months for it.

Health

As Jupiter is in your sign, health will improve. The reason is that Jupiter means expansion at all levels. I have to say jokingly that expansion could also mean that you might put on extra weight. My suggestion, for whatever it is worth, is to eat well and wisely but to exercise and cut away the extra fat and flab. Play hard, work hard. Got it?

Love/Marriage

Saturn is in your fifth angle of love and romance. Normally, Saturn acts as a thorn to love and laughter, but Saturn is in good formation with Jupiter till at least 16 July 2015. Therefore, till you are most welcome to woo and coo. Also, Venus, the planet of love, will be in your own sign from 19 July to 11 August 2015. A time to win hearts, to serenade, to exchange glances and hearts. Love, believe me, is the elixir of life. No love, no life. January and July are also good times for romance and laughter.

Property

In property matters you do well and there is a chance of inheritance. But here I must make it very clear that your personal horoscope will really decide the buying and selling, renovating and decorating of home and house. Wait. I have a flash of inspiration. Your sign stands for home and house; therefore, property affairs, buying and selling, renovation and decoration are quite probable. Look at your bank balance please and then go for it, that is my advice. Why this caution and boldness? Because I too am a Cancerians!

Job/Business/Loans/Funds/Investments

Yes, in job and profession, you make a killing. In other words, you will be very successful. Money, a new job, or as we say, window of opportunity for work and advancement will come to you. Be bold, take the initiative and make the best of the numerous chances which come your way. Remember life is sweet, but this sweetness is short. Make the most of it. A job switch, a change in profession or business or additional income by different ways is foretold. Ganesha says, go for it.

Children/Entertainment

Cancers are soft and sentimental and therefore children, laughter, good food, music, comforts of life, films, art come to them naturally. It is time to warm the cockles of your heart, time to love and be wanted. Yes, you will be vibrating with energy and creativity. This sentence should encourage you and stimulate you. Be sure that you will be needed, loved, appreciated, praised. Do not hold back. Be confident. Take life on the upswing.

Trips and Ties

In the very beginning, I had made it absolutely clear that this is a year for contacts, trips, communication, foreign affairs. My only suggestion is, please do not hesitate. Put your best foot forward. In the parlance of cricket, go forward and smash a mighty six.

Publicity/Projects/Performance

Ganesha chuckles and says here you are in your element. Publicity and projection of image will come to you naturally, gracefully, wondrously. You will excel in projecting your image or that of the company or firm you represent. Try something new or different. Those in research, food, drinks, creative enterprises, farming, gardening, mining, fishing, swimming, shipping, medicine, health, do exceptionally well. You might shatter all known records.

Happiness Quota

I must also inform you that Mars will be in your fourth angle till 25 July. This could cause disturbances, sudden changes, upheavals, separations. I mean there is a possibility of it. The finality depends upon your own personal horoscope and the will of God. Therefore, I am not giving you 100 out of 100 but 89 per cent.

Monthly Round-up

January: off and away to a magnificent start, despite pressures and pulls, says Ganesha; February: windfalls, joint finance, legacy, passion; March: right contacts, success, travel, publicity; April: tremendous drive, like Ganguly the crickter, also a Cancer with ambition honed perfectly; May: good news, pressures, delays but all turns out well in the end, and so socialize; June: expenses, losses, ESP and psychic powers, glimpses of Ganesha/God/Allah/ the supreme power, pilgrimages, rites and duties; July: success, happiness, fun and games, family, victory; August: finances, family, the luck of the draw, buying/selling/ investing; September: fanning out to people and places, contracts and contacts, communication channels buzz; October: home, house, in-laws, renovation/decoration in office/shop/home; November: despite changes, you do enjoy yourself and are creative; children give joy; December: work, health, loans, pets and projects.

Summary

In 2014 confidence, conviction, courage, communication will lead you to victory, money, fame, fortune, popularity, smashing success. Ganesha blesses you. Health safeguards are essential.

Outer Planets

URANUS: Uranus will be in your tenth angle of power, pelf, position. Very surprisingly, the best part is that you will have maximum power between 17 July 2014 and 11 August 2015. That means 2014 and 2015 both will turn out to be mighty fortunate.

NEPTUNE: Neptune will be in your ninth angle of publicity, fame, spirituality, intuition, imagination, inspiration. In short, Neptune will mean spirituality +

creativity. You can easily understand that Neptune is your greatest friend.

PLUTO: Pluto, the power planet, will give you great joy and sharp pain. The reason is Pluto is in your seventh angle of partnerships, attachments, ties, collaborations and marriage. Pluto stands for power-plus. Pluto is like a double-edged sword, but it will help you to be bold and take on challenges.

Month by Month

January

You start the year on a good wicket, batting on the front foot. There is hard work ahead, and you have big plans for the future. There is money coming in, and you have a nest egg, but you will have to keep tabs on your health. There is fire in your belly. You sign new deals. There is new love too, and sparks fly. Your emotions are rich, eloquent, flamboyant, powerful and beautiful. There are new vistas beckoning. Get a grip on your inner demons. The end of the month sees a new intensity in your life. There is love, passion and deep bonding. Work is in a bull phase and you make progress. On the personal front, there could be a change in residence. You may also change jobs. Ganesha watches over you.

February

This is a good phase. There could be rewards and awards, applause and accolades. The single could find new love, and those in stable relationships experience powerful bonding. You also mow down the opposition with a mix of charm, seduction and high-handedness. This is an intense period and your vital energies are high. Travel and furious networking are indicated by month-end. You may join a movement for societal change. You expand your horizons, open new vistas and bask in the warmth of popularity. Ganesha is with you all the way.

March

Your emotional life is in a twirl. You may have to make radical changes in your life and leave areas that are not working well. You will have to drop behaviour patterns that are obstacles to your growth. Domestic life will have its quota of problems. There could be altercations, arguments, fights, issues with the law and general mayhem. This is also a period of selfless giving. There is philanthropic intent. By the middle of the month, you will show steadfastness in your dealings. Use the energy of this period well. The hard slog continues. There is money to be made and you can see it clearly. You sign new deals and make rapid expansion on the work front. The end of the month brings fire in your belly, also love, passion and powerful bonding. The health of a parent could be a cause for concern. Ganesha is with you.

April

There will be new discoveries and you may meet exciting people from a totally different cultural milieu. You are open to winds of change. There are expenses, travel, meetings, old and new associations that are strengthened and an entire bag of goodies awaiting you. By mid-month, you make big plans. This could be a tricky yet significant time. There are maudlin moments too. You are in a creative phase and filled with brilliant ideas. You

win the applause of your peer group. The month-end
brings stability and drive. You are assertive without being
abrasive. There is love, passion and bonding. Ganesha
watches over you.

May

There are expenses and many affairs of the heart. You live
large like there is no tomorrow. This is relationship time.
There could be disappointments and unrealistic ideals.
Children could be a source of anxiety. Elders may have
to cope with medical emergencies. The month-end brings
Mercury in your sign from 30 May to 16 June. This is
a great period in which you should optimize. If you use
the energies well for the next fortnight, you could move
into another realm of success and prosperity altogether.
Ganesha urges you on.

June

You roll up your sleeves and get to work in earnest. There
are new contacts, contracts and profitable associations.
There could be travel and negotiations of all kinds. By
mid-month, your emotions are in a twirl. It could be
a tough phase for adolescents and young adults. Your
emotional and psychological demands find an outlet in
social work. There are awards, plaudits and kudos. Your
family rallies around you, offering strength and security.
Ganesha too watches over you.

July

Seize the moment; it belongs to you. This is a time for
making big plans and executing them too. It is the season
for awards and rewards. You continue on the bull run.
There is rapid expansion, money and fame. Venus is

in Cancer from 19 July to 11 August. The good trend continues. Life works in your favour as Venus makes its presence felt for close to a month. The grand times continue without abating. There is intensity, purpose and direction in all that you do. You have the Midas touch. You conquer new frontiers. Ganesha is delighted.

August

There is new love. There are also many new expenses and big investments. There could be conflicts, altercations, arguments and disagreements, but you are back on solid ground by the middle of the month. You roll up your sleeves and get down to solid work. You want to make big money and sign new deals. You will work long, hard and true. You will be good with work that involves precision. This is a favourable time for all business negotiations and commercial transactions. Ganesha is with you.

September

Your spiritual and humanitarian instincts are stirred. This is a great time for scientists, academics, students and seekers. There is rapid movement at all levels. By mid-month, the mood is cheerful and you feel optimistic. This is a stimulating period for artists. There are awards, applause and accolades. There is also love, passion and bonding. Your affairs are in a whirl. You get possessive, insecure and jealous. Ganesha walks with you.

October

There are ego issues, temper tantrums, altercations, misunderstandings, breakdowns in communication, irritations, provocations and perceived threats to your individuality. You are filled with views and opinions, and want to express them to everyone. You are able to influence others and accomplish a great deal. The mid-month brings in emotional issues that you have to deal with. You take incalculable risks. You look for spiritual deliverance. You look for new meaning. Ganesha holds your hand.

November

You sign new deals, expand your business interests, travel overseas, form new businesses and personal bonds. You live large and are in full throttle. There are new associations, contacts, contracts, love and lust. There are awards and rewards, accolades and applause. As the month ends, you are on a high. You network furiously and meet with people from all over the world. You are in the fast lane, partying hard. This is a fruitful period. Ganesha blesses you.

December

You are filled with emotions and let your heart rule over your head. There are domestic issues to handle. Your health is under the scanner. A stable phase brings in rich dividends by the middle of the month. You are on the fast track to success. New destinations, horizons and vistas beckon. You enjoy helping out and working with people and animals. You spend time with friends and loved ones. Ganesha holds your hand.

Months at a Glance

January

Off and away to a magnificent start, despite pressures and pulls, says Ganesha.

February

Windfalls, joint finance, legacy, passion.

March

Right contacts, success, travel, publicity.

April

Tremendous drive, like Ganguly the cricketer (also Cancer).

May

Good news, pressures and delays, but all turns out well in the end; and so socialize.

June

Expenses, losses, ESP and psychic powers, glimpses of Ganesha/God/Allah/the supreme power, pilgrimages, rites and duties.

July

Success, happiness, fun and games, family, victory.

August

Finances, family, the luck of the draw, buying/selling/investing.

September

Fanning out to people and places, contracts and contacts, communication channels buzz.

October

Home, house, in-laws, renovation/decoration in office/shop/home.

November

Despite changes, you enjoy yourself and are creative; children give joy.

December

Work, health, loans, pets and projects.

Weekly Review (By the phases of the moon)

1 January: New Moon in Capricorn

Cancerians can be timid, dull, shy and withdrawn, and most brilliant. They are fundamentally conservative and home-loving. On the surface they can appear formidable, uncompromising, tenacious, purposeful, energetic, shrewd, intuitive and wise, and deep inside they can be sympathetic, kind, imaginative, romantic, idealistic and sensitive. Some celebrity Cancerians include Meryl Streep, Jack Dempsey, George Orwell, Mike Tyson, Princess Diana, Hermann Hesse, the Dalai Lama XIV, Sylvester Stallone, Tom Cruise, Pierre Cardin, Ringo Starr, Tom Hanks, Arthur Ashe, Leon Spinks, Harrison Ford, Ernest Hemingway, Gerald Ford, Bill Cosby and Ingmar Bergman, among others. India has had three highly successful cricket captains in Sunil Gavaskar, Saurav Ganguly and the current skipper, M.S. Dhoni. You start the year on a good wicket batting on the front foot off the first ball like Chris Gayle. There is hard work ahead and you have big plans for the future. There is money coming in and you have a nest egg, but you will have to keep tabs on your health. There are emotional and physical indulgences and, I dare say, discipline is not your strong point. There will be happy times with the family. Children bring joy. Use the energies of the new moon and forge your plans. Ganesha is with you and that is all that matters.

8 January: First Quarter in Aries

You sign new deals, there is money coming in, and there's progress at work. There is new love too, and sparks fly. You could meet someone at work and the chemistry will be electric. Along with this are several domestic responsibilities. Elders need attention, children may be leaving the nest and there may be emotional moments. There could also be an addition to the family. As you can see, there is a lot on your plate. It is like an Indian thali with many dishes. Choose what you want; don't choke on it. Ganesha holds your hand and leads you forward. Your emotions are rich, eloquent, flamboyant, powerful and beautiful. But you don't have to wear them on your sleeve; you will be misunderstood. Discretion is the better part of valour. There could be temper tantrums and ego drives, which may get the better of you.

16 January: Full Moon in Cancer

Your emotions are in a whirl. Inner demons surface, and hold you in a vice-like grip. You are filled with remorse, anger, bitterness, hate, jealousy and possessiveness. You want to take revenge for perceived hurt. Lovers may feel betrayed and want to get back at the one who, they feel, has harmed them. 'An eye for an eye makes the whole world blind,' said Mahatma Gandhi. I agree. Lie low and the phase will pass like storm clouds do. Look at the positives and learn from the past. No one can inflict pain unless you have allowed them to. Move on, open new windows and check out different frontiers. There are new vistas beckoning. Get a grip on your inner demons and you will have conquered yourself. There are domestic issues brewing, and you will have to attend to them before they turn into a tsunami. Life is dynamic. Grab the moment by the collar. Ganesha blesses you.

24 January: Last Quarter in Scorpio

There is a new intensity in your life. You are turning the corner. Your emotions are powerful and you can use them well. Remember, nuclear power has many peaceful uses! 'Don't be trapped by dogma—which is living with the results of other people's thinking. Don't let the noise of others' opinions drown out your own inner voice. And most importantly, have the courage to follow your heart and intuition,' said Steve Jobs in an address to Stanford University. Take life by the collar and plough your own furrow. There is love, passion and deep bonding. Work is in a bull phase and you make progress. New vistas beckon. Family life has its pulls and pressures, but that goes with the territory. Ganesha is happy for you.

30 January: New Moon in Aquarius

There are emotional moments, which threaten to derail you. Your monkey mind is also playing tricks. 'A human being is a part of the *whole* called by us, the Universe. But he experiences himself, his thoughts, and his feelings as something separate from the rest; an optical delusion of his consciousness. Our task must be to free ourselves from this prison by widening our circle of compassion to embrace all living creatures and the whole of nature in its beauty,' said Albert Einstein. I go with him. There is good in all of us. Learn to see that. On the personal front, there could be a change in residence. You may also change jobs. Of course, these are not compulsions. Astrology only impels. I could be wrong. I am not God. But use these proddings as signposts. There could also be medical emergencies. Elders will need attention. Ganesha watches over you.

6 February: First Quarter in Taurus

There is stolidity in your affairs. You roll up your sleeves and get to work in earnest. This is a good phase. Make the most of it. There could be rewards, awards, applause and accolades, as you court success. You see money settling in your bank account and that spurs you. Finally, isn't it money that makes the world go around? You need to prepare a nest egg and there are domestic responsibilities. You can see the uses of money clearly and you get down to the task of making more of it without an argument. The single could find new love and those in stable relationships experience powerful bonding. Ganesha is happy for you.

14 February: Full Moon in Leo

You have fire in your belly as you scorch the tarmac like a Formula One driver. You mow down the opposition with a mix of charm, seduction and high-handedness. You could be arrogant and defiant and yet have your way. It is a skill, I dare say, and you have it. This is an intense period and your vital energies are high. You are filled with confidence and self-belief. You are formidable. There is money and honey. You enjoy a swelling bank account. There are insecurities nestling in your subconscious, and money provides some sort of comfort and solace. It is something you feel you can fall back upon when the chips are down, when relationships don't work and when your cries for bonding are not heard. You make the right investments despite mounting expenses. You may redecorate the home or take the family on a holiday. Your life is rich with anecdotes, adventures and passion. Ganesha is thrilled.

22 February: Last Quarter in Sagittarius

There is travel and furious networking. You use all the tools at your disposal and are on all the social networking sites. You may join a movement for societal change. You are gripped with idealism. You join groups and make your opinion known. You are open-minded and flexible, and this helps. You accommodate others and are a valuable team player. You are vocal and honest in your opinions, and this may hurt others, but you cut no corners and don't hold back your punches. You expand your horizons, open new vistas and bask in the warmth of popularity. You are the toast of the peer group. You are acknowledged, and this certainly helps. Ego drives are strong and your self-belief is at a peak. Ganesha is with you all the way.

1 March: New Moon in Pisces

The new moon is in Pisces and there are powerful subconscious forces working on you. Your emotional life is in a twirl. You may have to make radical changes in your life and eject areas that are not working well. You will have to drop behaviour patterns that are impeding your growth. Make positive creative changes in your life. You may have to adopt better time management skills.

Remember that you have the same number of hours per day that Leonardo da Vinci, Thomas Jefferson, Albert Einstein and others had. You can never buy yesterday for all the gold in the world. Time flies and waits for no man. There will be new assignments and expansion at work. Domestic life will have its quota of problems, with elders and children eating into your time. Ganesha helps you along the way.

8 March: First Quarter in Gemini

Your monkey mind is racing away like a lost hot-air balloon. It is in a mess, and drags you down with its weight. There could be altercations, arguments, fights, issues with the law and general mayhem. You will be prone to temper tantrums and ego issues. You feel that you know it all and will not accept a contrary opinion. This is also a period of selfless giving. There is philanthropic intent. We are a sum of many parts, and different parts of you emerge, causing more than necessary confusion. Even close friends can't fathom you in this mood. You are loving and belligerent at the same time. You are like lichen in the sea swept away by the force of a tide. Ganesha watches over you.

16 March: Full Moon in Virgo

There is some steadfastness in your dealings now. Work moves along predictable lines. You travel and make new contacts. You roll up your sleeves and slog away and this is the best way to quell a disturbed mind; it is an old-fashioned method that works. Use the energy of this period well and success will breed more success. Life has its share of snares, snafus and surprises, but you manage to sidestep them. Ganesha blesses you. Family life is also on an even keel.

24 March: Last Quarter in Capricorn

The hardwork continues. There is money to be made and you can see it clearly. It is a material world and you don't have to be a Madonna to realize it. Don't we all know that? You sign new deals and rapidly expand on the work front. There are festivities at home too. There could be an engagement, a marriage or even an addition to the family. Friends drop by and there are happy moments. Ganesha smiles.

30 March: New Moon in Aries

The new moon is in Aries and the power is all yours. You surge ahead and mow down the opposition. There is also love, passion and powerful bonding. You may take your relationship to the next level if you are going steady. Your ambitions are stirred and there are rewards and awards, applause and accolades. The health of a parent could be a cause of concern and there could be a medical emergency. Despite all of that, you are on a high-growth trajectory. Ganesha is with you all the way.

7 April: First Quarter in Cancer

'People don't notice whether it is winter or summer when they are happy,' said Anton Chekov. And you shouldn't either, as the subcontinent heats up. You carry your joy and sorrow within you. There will be new discoveries and you may meet exciting people from a totally different cultural milieu. You share a lot and learn a lot. There could be new relationships and they could be platonic but inspiring. You are open to winds of change, and that helps. New vistas open and you grow as a person. There are expenses, travel, meetings, old and new associations that are strengthened and an entire bag of goodies await you, including, I may add, some domestic problems. But that is par for the course. Ganesha holds your hand.

15 April: Full Moon in Libra

'I can resist everything but temptation,' said Oscar Wilde. You make big plans now. You have thought through the details for months and this is the culmination of endless rumination. You now want to activate your ideas. You will have to avoid grandiose and impractical plans. This can be a good time for job-hopping or signing new deals. You are careful with contracts and agreements. You could also be arrogant and self-righteous and will lose your cool with those who think nothing of your plans. This could be a tricky yet significant time. Parents, siblings, old and new lovers, friends from long ago, and all sorts of people come together now like the confluence of rivers. There are expenses and partying. Ganesha blesses you.

22 April: Last Quarter in Aquarius

You are in planning mode. There are maudlin moments too. You look at the larger picture and where you fit in it. You may need to change many aspects of yourself, and you do just that. You are in a creative phase and filled with brilliant ideas. You win the applause of your peer group. You may take time off and work with the less privileged. You feel that this way you will be able to understand yourself better. You now have a new grip on yourself and understand your motivations better. You may also spend time in speculation, gambling and betting. There are indulgences too. Ganesha journeys with you.

29 April: New Moon in Taurus

There is stability and drive. You roll up your sleeves and slog away. The new moon is in Taurus and the influences are powerful. You are assertive without being abrasive or pugnacious. You are direct, to the point, and yet congenial and charming. This way, you manage to have your way. You seem to have found yourself and this helps in your interactions. There is love, passion and bonding. Ganesha watches over you.

7 May: First Quarter in Leo

'There are three gates to self-destructive hell: lust, anger and greed,' says the Bhagavadgita. You have powerful ego drives. Crazed lust can also overtake you. There are expenses and many affairs of the heart. You live large like there is no tomorrow. You grab hold of the moment and shake it like a wet dog trying to dry out. You work to break out of the rut. There are blockades, and you may have to muscle your way through them. There are physical and psychological challenges. But Ganesha holds your hand and you sail through it all. At the same time, there is intense bonding, hard work and loads of money. I suggest you bask in your glory. The fruit ripens only when it is beckoned by existence, not before that. If it has now, good going!

14 May: Full Moon in Scorpio

This is relationship time. You hang on to anyone who offers you a shoulder. There could be disappointments and unrealistic ideals. You may feel betrayed. It is all a matter of perception. You feel you are the giver and the unselfish one who sacrifices everything for the other. There are beautiful moments too, but you may tend to gloss over the problems. There is powerful intensity in all your dealings. You are scorching the tarmac like Niki Lauda, the great motor car racer who returned to the track after over seven somersaults and a near-death experience. You show the world that under the soft and sweet exterior, you are as solid as steel. Ganesha blesses you as you evolve into a better person.

21 May: Last Quarter in Pisces

There are solitary moments now. You are looking at a change of residence. Youngsters living in their parents' home may want to move out and find wings. Children could be a source of anxiety. Elders may have to cope with medical emergencies. There are group activities too, but you have many pressing issues to solve. You try to fit into the group dynamic and also manage to keep your integrity. You guard your personal space. The subcontinent is sizzling and so are your thoughts. They are on fire like a kebab on coals. Domestic issues eat into your time. Ganesha watches over you.

28 May: New Moon in Gemini

Mercury is in your sign from 30 May to 16 June. Mercury, the mighty, all-powerful planet, is in your sign now. It favours travels, meetings, conferences, interviews, trips, more brain power, contacts, communication, correspondence and contracts. Mercury has a special connection with the circuits of the brain. Chess, crossword and other such games belong to Mercury. Also, short-distance runners and spin bowlers are controlled by Mercury. Mercury, in short, is the ambassador and salesman of the zodiac. Mercury is the symbol of news, views, messages, interviews, contacts, communications, travel and transport. Mercury gives an impetus to all of the above in the sun sign where it is located. You fly high and meet with your aspirations. This is a great period which you should make optimum use of. Life is calling and you have to be prepared for the dance. If you use the energies well for the next fortnight, you could move into another realm of success and prosperity altogether. Ganesha urges you on.

5 June: First Quarter in Virgo

This is a stable period and you work your heart out. You seem somewhat settled and know your mind. You roll up your sleeves and get to work in right earnest. You work on a satisfactory resolution of long-pending domestic issues. The employed could get pay hikes and promotions, and the self-employed will be on an expansion spree. There are new contacts, contracts and profitable associations. Those in social work win kudos. Ganesha is happy for you. So am I.

13 June: Full Moon in Sagittarius

There could be travel and negotiations of all kinds as you meet people from different cultures and climes. This is a genuine learning experience. You meet with others and ideate. Your soul is on fire. You want to reach out and, in turn, want to be reached too. You are not on an accomplishment drive in this phase; you know that you need to spread your wings and soak in knowledge. There is enhanced confidence and you gain tremendously from this period. Someone from overseas could have a profound impact on you. Ganesha blesses you.

19 June: Last Quarter in Pisces

Your emotions are in a twirl. You feel as though your heart has fallen into a washing machine which has forgotten to stop. You are on a slow burn and a fast churn. You feel isolated, hurt, offended or ignored. You withdraw into a closet with mothballs. You don't want to meet anyone and yet deep down you want to partake of life, love and be loved. You feel let down by a lover or friend. Your image is shattered and your belief in yourself gets a whack on the behind. This may be an overreaction as you could be extra-sensitive in this period. It could be a tough phase for adolescents and young adults coping with jumping hormones and various sensitivities. Domestic issues will be on the forefront. Parents will need special care. Ganesha carries you through the tough times.

27 June: New Moon in Cancer

'True compassion is more than flinging a coin to a beggar; it is not haphazard and superficial. It comes to see that an edifice that produces beggars needs restructuring,' said Martin Luther King Jr, the civil rights leader. Your emotional and psychological demands find an outlet in social work. You may join one of the several anti-corruption movements in India (for those living here) or work in one of the countless hospices. You are filled with the desire to serve. You meet all kinds of people and communicate with intensity and purpose. You are filled with zeal for the causes you believe in and are ready to even court arrest. You are firing on all cylinders. There are awards, plaudits and kudos. The family rallies around you, offering strength and security. Ganesha too watches over you.

5 July: First Quarter in Libra

'Whatever you can do, or dream you can do, begin it. Boldness has genius, power and magic in it,' said Goethe. Seize the moment; it belongs to you. There is no other time but the 'now' in your life. Live like it is the last moment. This is a time for making big plans and executing them too. You look at all aspects of your life, including your inner feelings and desires. You want to chisel your life and fine-tune it. You cut to the chase. You reorganize your home and workspaces both physically and metaphorically. You could even be moving overseas for better prospects. This is action time. You are the lion tamer at the circus. If you don't tame the lions, they will tame you. In this case, time will! You make rapid progress and Ganesha is thrilled.

12 July: Full Moon in Capricorn

Jupiter is the planet of plenty. Jupiter signifies or shows that it is harvest time. It is the season for awards and rewards. Dear readers, I have put it in very simple terms so that you understand it completely and clearly. Jupiter means good luck. Cornucopia is the horn overflowing with flowers, fruit and corn. It shows abundance. Jupiter is also the great teacher, the religious head and bestows position, pelf, prosperity, the three P's. I am saying this now, I have left it till the end, that in 2014 Jupiter will be in Cancer till 16 July. This clearly means that the going has had its share of rewards till now. The ups have been more than the downs. With the full moon in Capricorn, you continue on the bull run. There is rapid expansion, money and fame and, of course, hard work. The thrill will be in earning every penny. Ganesha is happy for you as you court success.

19 July: Last Quarter in Aries

Venus is in Cancer from 19 July to 11 August. The good trend continues. Life works in your favour as Venus makes its presence felt for close to a month. Venus is another important planet and is of great significance. This is an important phase. As often discussed, Venus is the planet for love, romance, sex, beauty and the good life. This is the planet of attraction, love, wealth, knowledge and prosperity. The compatibility of partners and also the type of life the individual will lead is also judged from the placement of Venus in the horoscope. As a planet, Venus is considered to be beneficial, feminine and gentle. Venus symbolizes the force of attraction in the universe. In human beings this attractive force manifests as love and beauty. When Venus is well placed in the chart, there is love, art, beauty and all the goodies of life that make life worth living. Venus rules Libra and Taurus though its role in every sign is important. Like other planets, it also has its transits. In Libra, Venus is aesthetic and cultured. In Taurus it is more earthy, materialistic and sensual. Venus rules the venous system, kidneys, urinary tract, throat, larynx, and is responsible for good looks. In short, Venus in Western astrology stands for comfort, arts, wealth, relationships, sex, decoration, luxuries and wealth. You earn, spend, grow, get nourished, spread your wings, provide succour to all and do well for yourself. 'What more do you want?' asks Ganesha. I want you to be happy and successful, and my prayers are answered.

26 July: New Moon in Leo

You are filled with restless energy and the grand times continue without abating. There could be new property or hugely profitable business deals. There is intensity, purpose and direction in all that you do. You have the Midas touch. You buy all that you fancy and yet you seem to have some money left over. There is love, lust and passion. You may find a new partner if unattached, and those in a steady relationship may take it to the next level. You conquer new frontiers like a killer shark slicing the waters near the shoreline in its quest for baby seals. The force is with you. Ganesha is delighted.

4 August: First Quarter in Scorpio

You are filled with a new intensity. You look for change, a break from routine. You attract new friends and a new facet of your personality emerges, one that you probably never knew existed. There is new love, and if you meet someone now, chances are that this person could play a significant role in your life. It could be an unstructured relationship, and mutually rewarding. There are also many new expenses and big investments as you are in the mood to take risks. Ganesha is happy that you inhale and recharge your soul with the fresh fragrances that rush through the newly opened windows of your life.

10 August: Full Moon in Aquarius

The full moon is in Aquarius and there are maudlin moments. You look at different tacks in your life and could exhibit odd, even bizarre behaviour traits. You will not understand yourself easily and neither will close friends. They will think that you have lost it! 'Show me a sane man and I will cure him,' said Albert Camus. Relationships could be off key and if you try to be dominant or assert your individuality, it could backfire. There could be conflicts, altercations, arguments and disagreements, and the equilibrium of a relationship, a thin line, can be breached. The solution lies in honest communication. Domestic life is also under focus. Children and parents need attention, a pet may need the vet, a sibling may be going through a divorce, and even the problems of friends in your circle may affect you. Shield yourself, says Ganesha. Since you are a natural caregiver, you could be overly sensitive.

17 August: Last Quarter in Taurus

You are back on solid ground. Terra firma beckons. You are like a pilot who has sighted the landing lights after being caught in a hurricane for hours. You roll up your sleeves, thank Ganesha, and get down to solid work. You live in gratitude and want to make up for lost time. You want to make big money and sign new deals like Columbus sighting uncharted territory. There may be a tendency to cut corners and go in for the fast buck. There are several unethical options and I am reminded of Mario Puzo's famous line in *Godfather* – 'Behind every fortune is a crime.' Stick to the straight and narrow, I say. Ganesha seconds the suggestion.

25 August: New Moon in Virgo

You continue on stable ground and hack away. You will work long, hard and true. You will be good with work that needs precision and will not bother much about the larger picture. You know what money means and does to your life and you make no bones about it. You need to prepare a nest egg and there are everyday demands too. So you sit on the drawing board, make big plans and start executing them. This is a favourable time for all business negotiations and commercial transactions. There are profitable new contacts, and legal issues, if any, will be solved in your favour. Of course, these are generalizations and a personal horoscope will provide more details. There are over seven billion people on the planet with their own unique temperaments and personalities. This is the greatest challenge for an astrologer. I do my best and leave the rest to Ganesha.

2 September: First Quarter in Sagittarius

There is a lot of movement now. You network and meet up with new people from all over the world. There are chance encounters and lucky breaks. There could be love too, with an absolute stranger from a completely different cultural context. Your spiritual and humanitarian instincts are also stirred. You look for deep answers to profound questions facing mankind. You are interested in different forms of healing, psychology, astrology, sociology and education. This is a great time for scientists, academics, students and seekers. There are expenses and the real world calls out. But you plunge into the theories of life and its processes with gusto. Ganesha smiles.

9 September: Full Moon in Pisces

There are maudlin moments. You are filled with emotion. You want to change a lot, in you and around you. You may go in for a complete wardrobe overhaul or a new hairdo, or check into a spa or rejuvenation centre and look at alternative therapies with new eyes. There is rapid movement at all levels on several planes. There is money and a lot more honey. I have seen eight decades of life and I have cast lakhs of horoscopes. Sometimes I could be wrong because I am not God. Astrology never compels. I want humanity to be happy and peaceful. That is all. I wish my readers the very best. Your self-worth zooms and you earn plaudits. Ganesha holds your hand.

16 September: Last Quarter in Gemini

The mood is cheerful and you feel optimistic and on top of the world. You tend to go overboard and get indulgent. You are reeking of overconfidence and feel that the world is your oyster. You indulge, shop like it was the last day of planet earth, and get quite wasteful. Watch out for arrogance and ego energies, which could result in conflict situations. You do not have to step on toes to get your point across. Your natural charm and wit will do. This is a stimulating period for artists. There are rewards and awards, applause and accolades. Ganesha blesses you.

24 September: New Moon in Libra

You are torn between options. You cannot make up your mind. There are continued expenses and indulgences. There is also love, passion and bonding. You could love insanely and be in the possession of crazed lust. You could also be moody, irritable, and subject to irrational and compulsive behaviour. If things do not work your way, you snap and exhibit eloquent fireworks. Domestic issues are in sharp focus as hidden and buried tensions surface. Your soul is in ferment. It is on fire, it scorches you. You want to possess your partner and he or she is elusive. This frustrates you. This can be a particularly difficult time for young adults. Your affairs are in a whirl. You get possessive, insecure and jealous, and too constricting. Set yourself free and soar high like the American eagle, says Ganesha.

1 October: First Quarter in Capricorn

There are things to do and your mind is racing away like a greyhound keen on a podium finish at the Macao races. There is a lot of work ahead and you don't know where to start. There are ego issues, temper tantrums, altercations, misunderstandings, breakdowns in communication, irritations, provocations and perceived threats to your individuality. But, despite this, you are on a high-growth trajectory. There are expenses and domestic issues, but work goes on well. Ganesha holds your hand and hauls you over troubled waters.

8 October: Full Moon in Aries

You are zooming away like Mad Max. There is fire in your belly, and a new-found zest propels you like high-octane fuel. You are filled with views and opinions and want to express them to everyone. The news impacts you and you may want to play a part in national affairs. If you aren't already in politics or some related activity, you may be keen on joining some. You feel empowered and are also able to examine yourself with objectivity. You are able to influence others and accomplish a great deal. To paraphrase the Bard, the world is a stage and we have to play our parts. You feel your part is gigantic; you feel you are destiny's chosen child. Life looks hard at you and you look it in the eye. Ganesha watches.

15 October: Last Quarter in Cancer

There are emotional issues that you have to deal with. There could be confusion, anxiety and uncertainty in your affairs. A love affair may cause anxiety. You don't know if the person you are in love with also shares the same feeling. This causes insecurity, depression and anger. You take it out on friends and loved ones, and if you are living with your parents and siblings in a joint family, you will be the cause of a lot of pain. Ganesha guides you through stormy paths. Work is fine, but unless you sort your heart out, it will not be running on full throttle.

23 October: New Moon in Scorpio

You are fuelled with new zeal. You are on the fast track to success as a new self-belief propels you. There is love and passion, and you could even be seized by crazed lust. You are ready to die for a cause or for the person who has pulled your heart strings so dramatically. You are ready to fight for what you believe in, and even die for it. You walk the razor's edge; there is only black and white, there are no compromises, no shades of grey. I paraphrase Somerset Maugham: if you love a woman she is worth everything, if you don't she isn't worth two penny. This is gender specific, but it could run both ways. This is a blitzkrieg. Your heart strings sing, cry, dance and take you to the moon and back, over and over again. The mood is upbeat. You take incalculable risks. I am a Cancerian too. I know what you are up to. Ganesha blesses you.

31 October: First Quarter in Aquarius

You go down memory lane. You think of all the hurt and betrayals. You lock yourself up and cry in the cold confines of solitariness. You feel dejected and let down. You have trusted and reposed faith in people, but they have all pulled the rug from under your feet one way or the other. But the past is the past, and nothing you do now will bring it back. You look for spiritual deliverance, you will look for solace in gurus and godmen, tantra, mantra and yantra. You help out in old-age homes, with the underprivileged and the needy. You look for new meaning. You are torn inside and need a balm. Gaia needs your idealism and nurtures you. Ganesha too holds your hand. Soon you will be on the fast track. These are but the tides of life. They come and go.

6 November: Full Moon in Taurus

You are filled with new zeal and raw energy, like a newly inducted Green Beret. There is nothing you cannot accomplish. In this phase, 'impossible' is truly a word in the dictionary of fools. There is rapid progress in all spheres of activity. You sign new deals, expand your business interests, travel overseas, start new businesses and personal bonds and are on a powerful bull run. You are optimistic and determined to get where you want to. There are also lucky breaks and windfalls helping you in your ascent through life. Ganesha is pleased. Family life is on an even keel.

14 November: Last Quarter in Leo

There are expenses and emergencies. You live large and indulge in comfort shopping, buying several expensive objects. You are in full throttle and preparing to take off like the latest Boeing. You are on a high growth phase and the mood is upbeat. There are new associations, contacts, contracts, love and lust. You bond at every level. There are awards and rewards, accolades and applause. Ganesha is delighted. So am I.

22 November: New Moon in Sagittarius

The bull run continues. As the year ends and the winter chill settles into your bones you are heating up the tarmac. 'It is best and easiest not to discredit others but to prepare oneself to be as good as possible,' said Socrates. Your recent successes have made you confident and you are on a high. You want to achieve more. You realize that the adrenaline charge is obsessive and intoxicating. You are greedy to improve your life, and why not? You excel both in a team and as a solo player. You mind your business and get down to the task of creating wealth. You network furiously and meet with people from all over the world. Sparks fly and love is born. It is a long way to go. Ganesha is happy for you.

29 November: First Quarter in Pisces

'Time rushes towards us with its hospital tray of infinitely varied narcotics, even while it is preparing us for its inevitably fatal operation,' said Tennessee Williams. There is success but your mind wanders. Remember, heaven and earth are here in your mind. No place or person can help you permanently if your mind is not in the right place.

Your fertile mind throws up new ideas. You are in the fast lane, partying hard, sometimes wrong, and yet hoping to live long! Every day has different biorhythms and this is where free will comes in. Handle the smaller details of life and the big picture falls into place. Astrology never compels. I have made charts for decades. Ask me. This is a fruitful period as you grow at several levels. Ganesha blesses you.

6 December: Full Moon in Gemini

'Take the first step in faith. You don't have to take the whole staircase, just take the first step,' said Martin Luther King. Your mind is everywhere, like a yo-yo on a long string. You are filled with emotions and can let your heart rule your head, and this leads to regret. You jump into the deep end of the pool without a life jacket. You are the cat with nine lives. In a bid to come to grips with your core, you look at spirituality, yoga, meditation, new diets and exercise regimens. You go looking for a guru and read the latest books on self-development and personal growth. Your personal life is still in tatters and you wonder why. Singles look hard for partners. They get them easily, but soon there are disruptions. There are domestic issues to handle too. Your health is under the scanner. Children and elders need attention. There is a lot on your plate. Your mind is whirring like the bright wings of a kingfisher with a succulent trout in its belly. Ganesha holds your hand.

14 December: Last Quarter in Virgo

I have been a sportsman in my youth and I know what it takes. I quote Wayne Rooney, the English football player:

'You are trying to put yourself in the moment and trying to prepare yourself to have a memory before the game.' He was referring to visualizing a situation. Do that. Visualize where you want to be and ask the cosmos for abundance. Work hard for it, prepare yourself to accept the bounty of nature, and it will fall into your lap. Dream big and work towards it. Success is yours. Ganesha walks with you. This is a stable phase with rich dividends.

22 December: New Moon in Capricorn

The year is ending and the new moon is in Capricorn. The energies give you balance and stability. Make the most of them. You are on the fast track to success. You have the Midas touch. There are new associations and you work through them cautiously, having been bitten before. You do not want to take chances. The travel bug may bite you, and you feel that you want a trunk containing continents. You set sail. New destinations, horizons and vistas beckon. Life is calling out to you and you are set to tango. Ganesha blesses you

28 December: First Quarter in Aries

'Love is the only reality and it is not a mere sentiment. It is the ultimate truth that lies at the heart of creation,' said Sri Aurobindo. You are filled with love for all creation even in normal times. In this phase, it gets accentuated. You enjoy helping out and working with people and animals. You could be involved in social work, philanthropy, and may even enrol in an NGO. Your inputs are appreciated, and you feel good by giving. You spend time with friends and loved ones, and usher in the new year in a landslide of goodwill. Ganesha holds your hand.

Key Dates

January

1*–7, 10–11, 14*–15, 18*–20, 23*–25, 28–30.
Ganesha says, these three months—January to March form a bridge for you in every possible way, for example: business, marriage, foreign connections, trading, expansion, children.

February

2–3, 6*–7, 20–21, 25–26.
February is important for finance; pending work will be done. Partnership, joint finance, house or office shift/ move, work with the government, multinationals, loans and funds are highlighted.

March

1*–2, 5*–7, 10*–17, 19*–20, 24*–25, 28–30.
This is the launch pad to success, just as the GSLV's success puts the country in the reckoning for a share of the $10 billion global space business.

April

2–3, 6*–12, 15–17, 20*–22, 23–25, 26, 29*–30.
Power, promotion, perks, pelf, position, all the Ps best summarize this month! Nothing more to be said!

May

3–9, 13*–14, 18*–19, 22*–23, 26–27, 30–31.
Socializing, money, property, love, luck, laughter. You have a lot going for you right now, and throughout the month.

June

1*, 4–5, 9–10, 14*–20, 23–24, 27–28.
June will be hot and cold and secret dealings/affairs will be highlighted. The last ten days will be the best, announces Ganesha. June through September will decide your future.

July

1*–3, 6–8, 11*–17, 20*–21, 24*–25, 28–30.
Away to a head start now. Your work will be done, and targets achieved. People will respect you. Success in new projects and mighty romance, says Ganesha.

August

2–3, 7*–13, 17–18, 21*–22, 25*–26, 30*–31.
Honey and money, a turning point, says Ganesha! Your income increases, expenses multiply. Buying and selling will keep you busy. It's also party time, food time, and love and romance time.

September

4*–10, 13–14, 17*–19, 22*–23, 26–28.
Travel, news, computers, exciting news, contacts, contracts, trips, ties, victory. All the Cs, all the Ts!

October

1*–7, 11*–12, 15*–16, 19–20, 24*–25, 29-30.
The focus is on home, house, office, shop, godown. Work to a time schedule. It gets better results in the long run.

November

2*–3, 5–6, 11*–16, 20*–21, 25–26, 29–30.

Romance and dreams, contacts, companions, attachments. A lovely month for marriage, companionships, partnerships, journeys, collaborations, children, sports, arts and crafts, scholarships. A beautifully busy phase.

December

1, 4–5, 8–9, 12*–14, 17*–18, 22*–28, 31.
Important for both work and partnership. December means a job switch, promotion, income from different sources; exceptional hard work but good rewards.

Leo

YEARLY FORECAST

Real success is in great achievements and even greater generosity and kindness. Be a big man and also a great man. Ganesha says there is a double header for Leos. On the one hand, Leos will help people in every possible way. In the words of the Bible, they will help to reach 'where the wicked cease to trouble, and the weary are at rest'. In other words, they will help the poor and the unfortunate. On the other they will strive to motivate, inspire, and work tirelessly for the world. Simply put, it means they will motivate and lead the world to prosperity. When and how?

Till 16 July 2014

Summary and Guidance

Ganesha says Jupiter will be in your twelfth angle of research, studies, inspiration, hospitalization, loneliness and separation, and, very surprisingly, you will be both the doctor and the nurse for one and all. A period of suffering and salvation, expenses and good feeling for everybody. Great knowledge and wisdom accompanied by separation and sorrow. Yes, this is what your Ganesha devotee has to say very humbly about you. He may be right or wrong but he is very honest about it. Also, and this is most important, your energy, your faith and your hopes will be tested and tried in the crucible of fire itself. You will come out brand new and shining clean. I am happy for you.

17 July 2014 to 11 August 2015

As said in the beginning, you will motivate, inspire and work tirelessly for the world in every possible way. The reason is that Jupiter, the planet of plenty and prosperity, will be in your own sign as per Western astrology. Jupiter means hope, love, creativity, power, pelf, prosperity, plenty of goodies and finally spirituality. My God, you have a very tempting and wonderful list!

Listen, Leo, and listen carefully, the strongest shoulders must carry the greatest burden. Now, your year of power has come. I am now eighty-three. I have learnt one very great lesson in life. Power must be used wisely and well. If you do so, power will bless you, so to say, and make you even more powerful. If you misuse power, you will ultimately be thrown to the dogs and the wolves, as we say. I am an Indian. The Americans will say you have a choice. Your Indian astrologer will say you have no choice. Your Indian astrologer says point blank, it is your duty, your karma and your dharma to do the best you can, in every way you can, for as many people as you can. Yes, that is what I say to you softly but firmly.

Leo is personality-plus. Therefore, you must be up close and personal with people and thus influence them. Make the first move. Do not be selfish. Control your pride. Start new work. You will not only impress but guide others.

Here is your big chance. Don't blow it. In the language of cricket, have patience, hit the loose balls and score a much needed century. In female parlance, have the perfect facial and make-up, and use the best lotion and cream in the world for the glow on your skin. I am sure you have now got what I am trying to say. Good!

Main Trend

I have gone out of my way to tell you very clearly that till 16 July 2014 it will be a mixed bag of joy and sorrow: helping yourself and others and also feeling lonely. Again, I have made it amply clear that your real success starts from 17 July 2014. But let me clarify once again that astrology is not perfect. One trend passes into another many times just like the shifting of gears of a car or a motorbike. Strictly speaking, I cannot say that on this date and month the lucky period starts. Also, please remember, this is not a horoscopic, personal reading. This is only a solar reading. Solar reading means a reading based mainly upon the position of the Sun. Sol means the Sun. But this much I do know very definitely. Hard work, goodness and initiative are the three pillars of success.

Journey and Communication

Till 16 July 2014, journeys, communication and pilgrimages will be the essence of your life. Mercury will be in your own sign from 1 to 15 August and that certainly favours it.

Health

I have already said that hospitalization is a possibility but not a certainty. Do not panic. Take care of your back, your spine, your heart and your lungs. Even if you have poor health, Ganesha says you will finally recover. Worry less. Expenses could bore holes in your pocket. Not to worry. Leos will make good money.

Love/Marriage

From 17 July 2014 to 11 August 2015 is the period of romance, fun and the sacred ties of marriage. Just take care of your parents-in-law in terms of both relationship and health. The health of parents, in-laws and other elders may cause grief and sorrow. The reason is Saturn will be in your fourth angle till roughly the end of 2014. This is not to frighten you. It is just to guide you. Please remember that I am not God, I may be wrong and I certainly wish you all the best in life. I am a born optimist. Venus, planet of love, marriage, fun, luxury, money and children will be in your sign from 12 August to 5 September. It speaks of joy and achievement. Again, 17 November to 10 December and 6 March to 5 April should be exciting, if uncertain. Take a chance is what my gut feeling suggests.

Property

Let me explain. The fourth angle in the horoscope stands for both property and parents. There will be an increase in property, possibly with litigation or dispute. But I feel that till 16 July 2014, there are excellent chances of settlement. Afterwards also, provided you are willing to let go, to adapt, to win and to lose some. Property matters, renovation and decoration, anything to do with mining, shops, office, godowns, major shifts, immigration, foreign lands and trips will bring positive results. I go with the flow.

Job/Business/Loans/Funds/Investments

These are highly important. Jupiter enters your sign from 17 July 2014 to 11 August 2015. This is a grand period for work and rewards, achievement and initiative. In simple language, for progress and prosperity. August, October, January and April along with June are the high watermarks. Push but do not pulverize. Remember, others too have a right to life and love.

Children/Entertainment

I do not plan anything. I go with the flow. I predict on the spot at white heat. Like molten lava in a volcano. Therefore, one particular point or aspect slips into another. In other words, connect what I am saying now about love/marriage with what I have stated earlier. Please remember, from 12 August to 5 September Venus in your sign and from 1 to 15 August Mercury in your own sign will favour you.

Trips and Ties

Till 16 July 2014, trips and ties are highlighted. Taking a journey should be fun. Give your best shot in August, September, October, December, February, April and June. I believe I have given you a wide choice.

Publicity/Projects/Performance

Yes, Ganesha says this is where you excel. Your forte. Your real strength. Give your very best from 17 July 2014 to 11 August 2015. If Saturn has a few hurdles for you do not worry. Hurdles are meant to be overcome. If you believe in Lord Hanuman and Saturn you must chant this mantra twenty-one times: Om praam preem proum sa sanaye namah. Please feel free to do your own thing and worship the god you respect. Be free. Be happy.

Happiness Quota

From 17 July 2014 to 11 August 2015 is your good period. Therefore, taking everything into due consideration, I will give 81 per cent.

Monthly Round-up

January: work and projects could tell on your health unless you learn to relax; February: love/hate, attachments/separations, journey/a home away from home, marriage/divorce; March: funds for work/home, trusts, buying/selling/investing/capital formation; April: journey, publicity, exultation, collaborations, a grand reaching out to people and places; May: 'Work is Worship' could well be your motto; for good measure, add duty and beauty; June: love, life, laughter, and the law of chances operate in your favour; so if you feel like it, take a few chances; July: despite expenses and interferences, property matters and family conditions do give some satisfaction; buying/selling/journeying are emphasized; August: go all out for the kill, roaring Leos, and emerge victorious in whatever you do; September: finances and funds will be augmented; October: contacts, contracts, socializing, friendship, good news; November: home, house, family, parents, property, renovation/decoration, buying/selling/leasing/shopping; December: plenty of fun and frolic, children and creativity fulfil you; a great ending to a busy beginning, concludes Ganesha.

Summary

Movement, productivity, creativity, group activities and delays are also paradoxically possible, so do not be in a hurry. More power, heavy expenses and responsibilities and duty, a combination of which, truly speaking, is karma. The bottom line is smashing success for you. There is some danger of accidents and mishaps because of Mars. That's life. Nothing is perfect.

Outer Planets

URANUS: Pilgrimages, charitable causes, dealings with lunatic asylums, holy shrines, tantra and mantra, the arts, specially films, theatre, music and dance are highlighted. Original ideas and research will give you the boost, the extra mileage and the glory you deserve. Uranus will disturb you, will make you struggle hard and long for success and glory but will finally deliver the goods. In modern language you will breast the tape in style and be a winner.

NEPTUNE: Neptune favours loans, funds and relationships at all levels, that is, sexual to spiritual. Avoid drugs and drinks please or enjoy now and pay later. Your choice. Big money will come to you. Investments, funds, trusts are also indicated for you, thanks to Neptune.

PLUTO: Pluto, the planet of pep and push, makes you work extremely hard. Do not buckle or come down under the stress and strain of Pluto. Take periodic rest. Believe me, this is a good suggestion. Follow it. Hard work and recreation should go hand in hand. At least till 2014.

Month by Month

January

The start of the year sees you soaring away. There is fire in the belly. You live larger than life. There is love, lust, passion and bonding. There are ego clashes, altercations and outbursts of anger. There are medical emergencies, and children need attention. There is a lot on your plate. There is hard work and expansion in your affairs. You will have to change your ways to suit the dramatic changes happening all around you. The month-end brings in maudlin moments and periods of depression. You spend time looking for spiritual alternatives. Ganesha urges you on.

February

You sight money and big plans and go for them. Those in committed relationships experience beautiful bonding. You may be looking at expensive purchases and possibly a new home. You live grand and make plans which scintillate. The month-end sees travel. There are parties and fun times and you hog the limelight. You network and make profitable contacts and sign many significant deals. Ganesha watches over you.

March

You are sensitive and filled with emotions. You work with your heart and give freely. You look for soul bonding. You are filled with a zillion thoughts. This could also be a good time for collaborations and new projects as you form new associations. By the middle of the month the domestic front calls out. The month-end sees you make progress.

You make money and win kudos. New vistas open and you are able to pattern your world as you want it. You are firing on all cylinders. You mow down the opposition and get closer to the conscious goals in your life. You are in the throes of regeneration and transformation. Ganesha is with you.

April

You want your writ to rule at home. You realize that unless you change your ideas and beliefs you may be left out of this surge of new thought that is enveloping the world. Your huge ego demands are redundant. There may also be issues with the spouse or partner. There is travel and possibly a new home or even new interiors. You take to the gym and change your wardrobe. There could be domestic issues like serious illness in the family by the month-end. This is a wonderful time for business expansion. Ganesha smiles.

May

There is love and bonding, and new opportunities at work. You are also the soul of the party and win awards and rewards, applause and accolades. There is eating and drinking and bonhomie. There is new intensity in all your dealings. There are new associations too. The indulgences of the past may have taken its toll. Your health could be in the doldrums. The month-end is a great time for group activities and friendships. There are happy moments with peers and family. Ganesha wishes you well.

June

Your ego energies are high and you are able to make your stand clear in no uncertain terms. Use your energies well and you will be able to accomplish a lot. Close associations will be tested and you will have to meet others more than halfway. There is travel and new love. By mid-month your communication skills are enhanced and you succeed in tough business negotiations. You are smart, adroit, charming and cunning. The month-end sees you prone to rash and impulsive actions. Apart from domestic demands, there could be travel, romance, expensive purchases and a host of new activities. Ganesha holds your hand.

July

This is the time when you reflect upon your life and your value system. The main focus of this period is on relationships of all kinds. There are intimate one-to-one encounters. Jupiter will transit the sign Leo from 17 July 2014 to 11 August 2015. I repeat, these placings are only by Western astrology. Jupiter is the planet of plenty. There is expansion on the work front as you profit from the worlds of business and high finance. The energies are powerful; your senses are stimulated and you are fascinated by every new phenomenon. There are high-end purchases as you expand your sphere of influence. Ganesha is with you.

August

Mercury is in your sign from 1 to 15 August. This fortnight sees you embark on new adventures. This is a wonderful period. Whatever you embark on now will lead to success. Venus is in your sign from 12 August to 5 September. Venus is another important planet and is of great significance. This is an important phase too.

New vistas open up almost magically. There could be international travel, love, powerful bonding, many new profitable associations and a general upswing in life. Ganesha is delighted.

September

In this phase you attempt to liberate yourself from unnecessary and inhibiting restrictions. Funds, investments, loans, selling and buying, stocks, shares and realty also occupy your time. In this phase you are intellectually stimulated and interested in new experiences. There are family gatherings, birthday and anniversary parties, alumni meetings and all types of profitable associations. Those in a relationship reach new peaks of attachment. There is fun and entertainment, get-togethers and parties. There are many options courting you as you continue making headway in life. Ganesha smiles.

October

There is powerful energy propelling you. This is a time of confidence and benevolence. You now grow in wisdom and maturity. Mid-month brings in powerful family bonding. There are expenses, expansion, growth, regeneration, rejuvenation, romance, love, passion, rewards and travel. Old loves cross your path and the encounters could be memorable. Ganesha is with you.

November

A new wind is blowing in your face. You become increasingly interested in new spiritual thought or philosophy. The last quarter of the month is in Leo and it goads you to achieve big things. Your ambitions are aroused and you push hard for power and success. You will bulldoze all opposition and may invite conflict. You want to grow at all levels as you look at becoming a person to reckon with in your community. As the year ends, you are flooded with nostalgia. This is not a sign of weakness. It just makes you a more complete person. Ganesha wishes you well.

December

You are filled with new plans for the family and want to tweak all available resources to secure their future. You may need to move to another city, or even another country. This period may have an electric quality to it. There is hard work at the office as also several domestic pressures. Of course, this is party time and you have to allow your natural exuberance, energy and lust for life to take over. There could be new love and some indiscretion thrown in. Ganesha watches over you.

Months at a Glance

January

Work and projects could tell on your health unless you learn to relax.

February

Love/hate, attachments/separations, journey/a home away from home, marriage/divorce.

March

Funds for work/home, trusts, buying/selling/investing/ capital formation.

April

Journey, publicity, exaltation, collaborations, a grand reaching out to people and places.

May

'Work is Worship' could well be your motto. For good measure, add duty and beauty.

June

Love, life, laughter, and the law of chances operates in your favour; so if you feel like it, take a few chances.

July

Despite expenses and interferences, property matters and family conditions do give some satisfaction; buying/selling/journeying are emphasized.

August

Go all out for the kill, roaring Leos, and emerge victorious in whatever you do.

September

Finances and funds will be augmented.

October

Contacts, contracts, socializing, friendship, good news.

November

Home, house, family, parents, property, renovation/decoration, buying/selling/leasing/shopping.

December

Plenty of fun and frolic, children and creativity fulfil you. A great ending to a busy beginning, concludes Ganesha.

Weekly Review (By the phases of the moon)

1 January: New Moon in Capricorn

Leo is a fire sign and can be dogmatic, pompous, intolerant, patronizing, domineering, inflexible, vain, magnanimous, creative, romantic and generous. Leos may just feel that they are the lions of the human jungle. Famous Leos include Garfield Sobers, Pete Sampras, Rod Laver, Aldous Huxley, Alex Haley, George Bernard Shaw, Alfred Hitchcock, Andy Warhol, Sandra Bullock, Usain Bolt, Whitney Houston, Madonna, Arnold Schwarzenegger, Barrack Obama, Robert De Niro and Roman Polanski, among others. The start of the year sees you soaring away. There is stability and hard work. You are ambitious and want to foist your will over others. You want to dominate everybody and everything and in the process create roadblocks to progress. You want life and events to be at your beck and call. This works sometimes, but backfires most of the time. Life may not write the script you want it to write. Ganesha wishes you well as you plough through life. There is hard work ahead and you don't shy away from it.

8 January: First Quarter in Aries

There is fire in the belly. You live larger than life and strut about like an African lion in the rutting season. There is love, lust, passion and bonding. You make waves and make your presence felt in no uncertain terms. Your roar resounds through Serengeti. There are expansion plans and many expenses. There are also domestic demands and you are hard pressed to fulfil them all. There are ego clashes, altercations and outbursts of anger. There is a vacuum in your life, and unless you steer a new course it may just get bigger. Ganesha is with you.

16 January: Full Moon in Cancer

You are on an emotional boil. There are issues at home that you need to handle with urgency. You will be busy firefighting. There are medical emergencies, and children need attention. One of them may be leaving home against your wishes or adopting a lifestyle you don't much care about. There is a lot on your plate as you also realize that your domineering ways don't count any more with people who matter. You want to be the master of the home and that just won't work. Time is valuable and you also realize that you have wasted a lot of it in frivolous pursuits. There could also be money issues as you look at new sources of income. Ganesha holds your hand.

24 January: Last Quarter in Scorpio

The intensity of Scorpio is felt very strongly now. There is hard work and expansion in your affairs. Charles Darwin said that the species that is amenable to change survives, and that is what you have to do now. You will have to change your ways to suit the dramatic changes happening all around you. Life will not run according to your plans and you begin to see that clearly. Your thought processes could be outmoded and your attitudes towards life antiquated. There is love and passion, and you sow your oats without discretion. There are excesses and indulgences accompanied by new realizations. Ganesha is with you as you look for different options when you realize that your writ doesn't hold sway any more.

30 January: New Moon in Aquarius

There are maudlin moments and periods of depression. Those unwilling to change with the times are in a deep rut from which there seems to be no escape. You spend time looking for spiritual alternatives and could be interested in yoga, meditation and alternative health. You are looking at every way to reinvent yourself. You want to stay afloat. You want to continue to be the king of the jungle, to be respected and admired, to be a leader of men and material. You may also indulge in philanthropy and help out with the less fortunate. You need to change the course of your life and are looking at every option to do just that. You may even change your wardrobe or simply get a funky haircut. Youngsters may look at piercings and tattoos. Ganesha urges you on.

6 February: First Quarter in Taurus

There is stability and hard work. You roll up your sleeves and dirty your elbows. You sight money and make big plans and go for them in the way you know best. You may meet an old flame and could stoke the embers of desire. There is love and passion and you may even take it to the next level if you are not already attached. Those in committed relationships experience beautiful bonding. The emphasis in this phase is on realty, construction, insurance, stocks and joint investments. There is also success for those in the media and in showbiz. You may also be looking at expensive purchases and possibly a new home. Ganesha wishes you well.

14 February: Full Moon in Leo

The full moon is in your sign and this is a great period. Make the most of the energies of the moment. You live grand and make plans which scintillate. Nothing holds you back. There is rapid progress as you streak across the night sky like a meteor. There is passion, love, powerful bonding, profitable partnerships and rapid expansion. Your hard work pays off and you see money in the bank which, of course, you promptly spend. You love the good life and make expensive purchases. There are also ego clashes and altercations. You are on the fast track of success without a care in the world. It is often said that pride comes before fall and you will have to watch your step. Do not blemish the harvest with intolerance and anger, says Ganesha. Carry everyone with you. There is love, lust and bonding in this phase.

22 February: Last Quarter in Sagittarius

There is travel, and you may take the family on an exotic holiday. You do not like being alone and so are not a solo traveller. You need others to listen to you and try your best to foist your will on everyone. You are great in leadership roles and like to lead from the front. Those who are employed feel stifled. You need to be the leader of the pack. There are parties and fun times and you hog the limelight. You are generous to a fault and money slips through your fingers like early morning dew. The focus now is on business development. You network and make profitable contacts and sign many significant deals. Ganesha watches over you.

1 March: New Moon in Pisces

You are filled with fears of all kinds. Have you overstepped your limits? Will you be broke? Will your health issues put you in a spot? Is your marriage on the rocks? You escape from it all in alcohol, food, maybe drugs, partying, comfort shopping and every other way you can. You are sensitive, and filled with emotions that bubble like Mount Vesuvius. You work with your heart and give freely. You are generous to a fault and don't care if your resources are drying up. Even if the land is parched, the lion wants to remain the king! You surround yourself with friends, loved ones and well-wishers. You look for soul bonding. You may even get it, says Ganesha.

8 March: First Quarter in Gemini

You are filled with a zillion thoughts. The monkey mind is freaking out, to use a common phrase of the next generation. I may be an old astrologer but as you can see, I am in touch! As I always say, the future belongs to young people. You grapple with emotions, and finally manage to pin them down. You also return to the past and think of the mistakes you have made and the people you have ill-treated. You are filled with remorse but there is no going back. What has happened cannot be undone. Just make sure that you learn from the past. If you manage to do that, you have evolved, says Ganesha. This could also be a good time for collaborations and new projects as you form new associations and links.

16 March: Full Moon in Virgo

There is more stability now and you realize that you have to make up for lost time. There are many issues demanding your attention. The domestic front is calling out. A child may be leaving home and elders may need medical help. There is a lot on your plate. There is a drain on time and finances. But you will have to cope. There could be a change of job, residence, and money flow. But you are able to face everything and conquer the challenges. Ganesha is with you. Please remember that challenges are opportunities for growth. What is important is not what you do when the tide is in your favour but how you manage when the chips are down. That is the real test of character.

24 March: Last Quarter in Capricorn

You make progress and there is equilibrium and balance. You roll up your sleeves and get set for the hard slog. You make money and win kudos. You are the toast of the peer group, and nothing could please you more. You just love the limelight and you crave attention. This goads you further and you are propelled to enter new frontiers of work and play. New vistas open up and you are able to pattern your world as you want it. Success breeds success and you sight the winning spree like Barcelona, Manchester United and Real Madrid in the international soccer leagues. Ganesha is happy as you grow in stature both professionally and as a human being.

30 March: New Moon in Aries

'They are ill discoverers that think there is no land, when they can see nothing but sea,' said Francis Bacon, the philosopher and statesman. You are firing on all cylinders. Nothing can stop you in this mood. You mow down the opposition and make rapid strides. You are getting closer to the conscious goals in your life, and weed out people and attitudes that have outlived their utility. You are in the throes of regeneration and transformation. There is love and passion, and amorous pursuits stir your heart. You may be lost in its arms. No harm in that, says Ganesha. I agree. What is life without love? It is the masala that gives the curry of life its flavour.

7 April: First Quarter in Cancer

The new moon is in Cancer and you are filled with domestic responsibilities. A Leo lights up the room like a large chandelier. You want your writ to rule at home. There could be issues with children. Adolescents will pose many problems and may not listen to you. Apart from the generation gap, your thoughts could also be antiquated. You suddenly realize that unless you change your ideas and beliefs you may be left out of this surge of new thought that is enveloping the world. In fact, you are outdated and outmoded like a Premier Padmini Fiat in a stable of Skodas. Your huge ego demands are redundant. There may also be issues with the spouse or partner. Elders will need attention. Ganesha is with you.

15 April: Full Moon in Libra

You are in an indulgent phase. You do not want to be alone; you just hate it if there is no appreciative audience or a durbar attending on you. 'Music gives a soul to the universe, wings to the mind, flight to the imagination and life to everything,' said Plato. You are looking for just that zing in your life now. You make purchases that clean out your pockets. There is travel and possibly a new home or even new interiors. You take to the gym and change your wardrobe. You try out new jobs and make every attempt to change the tack of your life. You realize your mistakes and get less rigid. Life is a roller coaster at the best of times, and you will have to go with the flow. You do well in creative pursuits. Those who run large organizations sign big deals. You realize that balance, peace and equanimity are essential if you need to stay on course and forge ahead. Ganesha wishes you well.

22 April: Last Quarter in Aquarius

There are maudlin moments. There could be domestic issues like serious illness in the family. You also realize that change is the only way forward and despite the initial reluctance you try hard to work on yourself. You also realize that there is no point in downsizing or browbeating someone else to get your way. 'Charm is a way of getting the answer "yes" without asking a clear question,' said Albert Camus. A change in attitude and behaviour works well in your favour. Ganesha is with you and that is all that matters in the end. The times are changing and the species that adapts survives. It is as simple as that. Gaia has ensured that species that are no longer able to cope with environmental changes simply drop out. Every single day the Amazon forests, the lung of the world, sees new species being born and several dying. There is a lesson here for us.

29 April: New Moon in Taurus

You are in the throes of hard work and stability now. This is a powerfully profitable streak. You sign new deals and make headway in the game of life. Money flows in and it is up to you to see that it doesn't flow out. This is a wonderful time for business expansion. Media barons and those in realty, stocks, pharmaceuticals, armaments, insurance and entertainment find the Midas touch. There is a lot of hard work and team play if you are an employee. But the sight of money is a great temptation and now very little can hold you back. Ganesha watches with glee.

7 May: First Quarter in Leo

There is fire in the belly and you power your way through. There is love and bonding, and new opportunities at work. You are also the soul of the party and win awards and rewards, applause and accolades. There is more than just stability, steadfastness and balance. You surge like a meteor or an Indian rocket in search of Pluto. I say Indian because I am proud of our scientific advancements. You play the field and could sow your oats in every direction. You are like the lion in the rutting season. You make money, sign new deals spiritedly and bat the bouncers of life on the front foot. There is eating and drinking and bonhomie. Enjoy, says Ganesha.

14 May: Full Moon in Scorpio

There is new intensity in all your dealings. There are new associations too, and this is a good time to clarify and explain an issue to someone with whom you are intimately connected. The person could be your spouse or your business partner. You need social intercourse to bounce your thoughts and get feedback to check if you are on the right track. You need the solace of support. In this phase, you will be less domineering and more of a team player. 'Your body is precious. It is our vehicle for awakening. Treat it with care,' said the Buddha. The indulgences of the past may have taken its toll. Your health could be in doldrums and you need medical help or a revamp of your lifestyle. This period is pregnant with possibilities. If you work it right, you will ride high. Ganesha holds your hand. You may go in for a medical check-up or spend time in a health resort.

21 May: Last Quarter in Pisces

There are maudlin and reflective moments when you want to be alone and sort it all out. You feel that you are in a tangle and need to work your way out of the maze. You are quite clear about the path ahead and are mentally alert and sharp. You look for feedback to your ideas but make room for challenges too. You cannot be right all the time. Do not let your point of view blind you to every other opinion. Tweak this phase well and you will come up trumps. There are happy moments too, with love and bonding. This is also a creative phase. The mind has many facets that can either wreak havoc with you or work wonders. If James Hadley Chase had his way he would have called you a puppet on a string. Ganesha watches over you.

28 May: New Moon in Gemini

You play with a zillion thoughts. This is a great time for group activities and friendships. 'Try not to become a man of success, but rather try to become a man of value,' said Albert Einstein. In this phase, you want to add value to yourself. You put your best foot forward and are amiable and affectionate towards all. The affection is reciprocated. There are happy moments with your peer group and family. There is the joy of simple, unadulterated bonding.

You also do well in big business meetings, and your value as a professional and as a human being is appreciated. You are not sitting on a gigantic ego and so do not feel that you are losing ground in discussions. The summer is at its peak, the world is scurrying for cover, and the heat is burrowing a hole in the coldest ice caps. Environmentalists say that it is because of climate change. You couldn't be bothered, lost as you are in the poesy of a faraway world. It is a world of your creation, and you are your world. Ganesha is happy.

5 June: First Quarter in Virgo

'You must be the change you wish to see in the world,' said Mahatma Gandhi. Your ego energies are high and you are able to make your stand clear in no uncertain terms. You are oozing with confidence and could get into unnecessary altercations. The employed could get into a pickle because of this, as 'the boss is always right'. Haven't we heard that before? There are ego clashes and you emerge the victor, like a triumphant lion that has won its territory and its mate. But there is a price to pay, not the least being the loss of goodwill. This is a good time for sportspeople and those in the armed forces. Use your energies well and you will be able to accomplish a lot. There are rewards and awards, accolades and applause. Ganesha urges you to go with the flow.

13 June: Full Moon in Sagittarius

'Life is an adventure in forgiveness,' said Norman Cousins. You need focus now and a lot of patience and tolerance. Close associations will be tested and you will have to meet others is halfway to make peace. There is travel and new love. There is many expenses, maybe a home away from home too. Domestic issues need to be handled. Young mothers will have their hands full with their bundles of joy. There could be marriages, separations, life and death. There is a lot on your plate. Steer clear of controversies, rein in your famed ego and temper and prepare for the unknown. Ganesha will guide you through unfamiliar territory.

19 June: Last Quarter in Pisces

You are in the throes of planning. You want to take the big leap forward. You pay close attention to detail. Your communication skills are enhanced and you succeed in tough business negotiations. You are smart, adroit, charming and cunning. You play your cards well and come up trumps. You have confidence, energy, enthusiasm and determination. You win applause. There is money and honey as new vistas open up and new journeys are undertaken. Just remember that there is never a destination; no journey ends, it just leads to another. Life is filled with new beginnings and it all depends on how you reinvent yourself. Ganesha blesses you.

27 June: New Moon in Cancer

You may be prone to rash and impulsive actions. This will not be in your interest as it will alienate others and create enemies. Ensure that you do not assert yourself at the wrong time and place and with the wrong people. You could get irritable, impatient, argumentative and overtly sensitive. Apart from domestic demands, there could be travel, romance, expensive purchases and a host of new activities. There is fire in your belly and you want to explore all avenues before you surge ahead in the direction you have chosen. Ganesha holds your hand.

5 July: First Quarter in Libra

'I have been and still am a seeker, but I have ceased to question stars and books; I have begun to listen to the teaching my blood whispers to me,' said Hermann Hesse. This is the time when you reflect upon your life and your value system. You begin to examine your relationship with the various pillars that prop your life. There will be change and chopping and cleaning as you junk what you don't need. You look at greater clarity and control of your life. There could be new purchases and new thought processes as you steer away from the beaten path and plough a lonely but profitable furrow. The main focus of this period is on relationships of all kinds. Through them you try to get to know yourself better. Ganesha wishes you well.

12 July: Full Moon in Capricorn

There are intimate one-to-one encounters. You look at yourself and your dealings with a magnifying glass, and tweak what you believe is not working any more. There could be a relook at an existing relationship, even a marriage. If it doesn't seem to work, you may just opt out. You want the best partnership for yourself, one that elevates your soul, and not one to fulfil societal needs. There is hard work too, as you make money and advance in your career. You do well in material terms. Ganesha blesses you as you move heaven and earth to find yourself.

19 July: Last Quarter in Aries

Jupiter will transit the sign Leo from 17 July 2014 to 11 August 2015. I repeat, these placings are only by Western astrology. Jupiter is the planet of plenty. Jupiter signifies or shows that it is harvest time. It is time for awards and rewards. Dear readers, I have put it in very simple terms so that you understand it completely and clearly. Jupiter means good luck. Cornucopia is the horn overflowing with flowers, fruit and corn. It shows abundance. Jupiter is also the great teacher, the religious head, and bestows position, pelf and prosperity, the three Ps. This is a long time and you could use the energies well. There is expansion on the work front as you profit from the worlds of business and high finance. Your personal style statement could also be in the throes of a dramatic makeover as you are working on a new persona. Ganesha is happy for you.

26 July: New Moon in Leo

'The two important days in your life are the day you are born and the day you find out why,' said Mark Twain. The new moon is in your sign and your birth period has just about begun. The energies are powerful; your senses are stimulated today and you are fascinated by every new phenomenon that you encounter. You look for excitement and may get bored with routine. The tempo of life will be brisk, as a zillion thoughts collide. You live large. There are high-end purchases as you expand your sphere of influence. This is a great time for those in the public eye. You can do no wrong and there are awards and rewards. Arrogance, unwanted aggression and ego clashes could get in the way. Anything can happen overnight, says Ganesha.

It takes you weeks to climb Mount Everest and a second to fall from it. A prince can become a pauper in the blink of an eye! Pride comes before fall, so keep rooted.

4 August: First Quarter in Scorpio

Mercury is in your sign from 1 to 15 August. Mercury, the mighty, all-powerful planet, is in your sign now. It favours travels, meetings, conferences, interviews, trips, more brain power, contacts, communication, correspondence and contracts. Mercury has a special connection with the circuits of the brain. Chess, crossword and other such games belong to Mercury. Also, short-distance runners and spin bowlers are controlled by Mercury. Mercury, in short, is the ambassador and salesman of the zodiac. Mercury is the symbol of news, views, messages, interviews, contacts, communications, travel and transport. Mercury gives an impetus to all of the above in the sun sign where it is located. This fortnight sees you embark on new adventures. This is a wonderful period and I suggest you grab the high tide to fame and fortune. Whatever you embark on now will lead to success as a new intensity and purpose consumes you. You will stop at nothing and nothing can stop you. Ganesha smiles.

10 August: Full Moon in Aquarius

Venus is in your sign from 12 August to 5 September. Venus is another important planet and is of great significance. This is an important phase. As often discussed, Venus is the planet for love, romance, sex, beauty and the good life. This is the planet of attraction, love, wealth, knowledge and prosperity. The compatibility of partners and also the type of life the individual will lead is also judged from the placement of Venus in the horoscope. As a planet, Venus is considered to be beneficial, feminine and gentle. Venus symbolizes the force of attraction in the universe. In human beings this attractive force manifests as love and beauty. When Venus is well placed in the chart, there is love, art, beauty and all the goodies of life that make it worth living. Venus rules Libra and Taurus though its role in every sign is important. Like other planets, it also has its transits. In Libra, Venus is aesthetic and cultured. In Taurus it is more earthy, materialistic and sensual. Venus rules the venous system, kidneys, urinary tract, throat, larynx, and is responsible for good looks. In short, Venus in Western astrology stands for comforts, arts, wealth, relationships, sex, decorations, luxuries and wealth. You are in the throes of a lucky period. New vistas open up almost magically, from nowhere. There could be international travel, love, powerful bonding, many new profitable associations and a general upswing in your life. Ganesha is thrilled.

17 August: Last Quarter in Taurus

The going gets better with more stability. There is hard work and success. You are like a road roller in a country lane, defining your path in no uncertain terms. You may embark on a new course of study, go abroad for further qualifications and discover yourself. You have read a lot, but now you need empirical evidence. Until you see what you read, your learning will for ever be incomplete. Youngsters may backpack and elders may take long-awaited holidays. You think big and out of the box. You are brimming with ideas. They seem to spill over from every nook and cranny of your fertile brain. You are imaginative, intuitive and innovative. Success is guaranteed. Ganesha is more than delighted.

25 August: New Moon in Virgo

You make rapid progress. There is stability too, and you are not hot under the collar. If there has been some chronic illness you could see its remission. You may settle into healthy habits and even choose a spa or natural healing centre to detoxify. You want to heal yourself of stresses and chemicals. Those who go under the knife could get favourable results. On the work front, you continue moving ahead with gusto. There are no airs. You just slog, and see the fruits of your labour. This pushes you further, it goads you on to more success. Ganesha blesses you.

2 September: First Quarter in Sagittarius

'Even if I knew that tomorrow the world would go to pieces, I'd still plant my apple tree.' These words by Martin Luther King have great relevance for all time. There may be some stressful moments when you lash out at those who have somehow held you back in the past. As I always say, the past is no more. In this phase, you attempt to liberate yourself from unnecessary and inhibiting restrictions. You junk what you don't need and get on to a new tack in life. There will be more freedom and self-determination in your affairs. You are doing everything to expand and liberate your life. You are looking at the larger picture, at doing big things in life. Funds, investments, loans, selling and buying, stocks, shares and realty also occupy your time. Ganesha blesses you.

9 September: Full Moon in Pisces

'Every great philosophy is a species of involuntary and unconscious autobiography,' said Nietzsche. You realize that it is time to slow down and put the brakes on your mind. You have been moving too fast and could have overlooked small but significant issues. You may have even felt scattered, undisciplined and nervous, as you have spread yourself too thin. In this phase, you are intellectually stimulated, and interested in new kinds of experiences. There is a lot on your plate. The luck of the draw is in your favour. There are family gatherings, birthday and anniversary parties, alumni meetings and all types of profitable and enjoyable associations. The networking will be intense. There could also be international travel. Ganesha blesses you.

16 September: Last Quarter in Gemini

'Clouds came floating into my life, no longer to carry rain or usher storm, but to add colour to my sunset sky,' said Rabindranath Tagore. Your mind is lifted by new ideas and thoughts as you check out every available option under the winter sun. There are strong desires to bond with the opposite sex. Those in a relationship reach new peaks of attachment. Like Osho said, you go through the tunnel of sex to the higher reaches of superconsciousness. There is fun and entertainment, get-togethers and parties. There are new bonds as you meet with people of all colours. This is a gregarious time and your creative instincts are unleashed. You may also have many affairs of the heart. If you are married, you walk barefoot on broken glass. Discretion is the better part of valour. I must add here, like I always do, that these are mere generalizations. I do not have your personal horoscope and so cannot be specific. Ganesha is with you.

24 September: New Moon in Libra

There are many options courting you as you continue making some headway in life. There is hard work as you put everything you have into tasks that fit into a larger plan. Your energies are controlled and you win accolades for your diligence and perseverance. This is a good time to examine the details of your work set-up with a fine-toothed comb. You work patiently towards your objectives and choose your course of action methodically. You are relentless in your efforts and the reward is lasting accomplishments. Interestingly, seniors may find a partner at this late stage and may tie the knot. Love has no age. Ask me! I have seen enough of life's caprices to understand and appreciate the power of love. Ganesha smiles appreciatively.

1 October: First Quarter in Capricorn

You settle down and make a go of it. There is success along with maudlin moments. Children may leave home for higher studies or as a consequence of marriage. There will be happy and sad moments with family members. But it is quality time when you hold hands and thank each other for just being there. You are full of discipline and self-restraint. You check your purse strings and decide that it is best to invest in a nest egg. You are able to use your free will to advantage. Ganesha watches over you and there is nothing to worry about.

8 October: Full Moon in Aries

You are turbocharged. There is a powerful energy propelling you. The full moon is in Aries and there is fire in your belly and in your ventures. The lion is stamping its personality over the entire range and none dare oppose it. Every other species watches in awe as you shake your flowing mane in assertion. This is a time of confidence and benevolence. You know who you are and your life is moving in the direction you have secured for yourself. Your home and work fronts are on strong ground; you are also in the throes of personal advancement and growth. You take on leadership roles in the office and are suitably rewarded. You now grow in wisdom and maturity. Some of you may look at higher studies in law, philosophy and medicine. Youngsters top the class. You are also in touch with your inner feelings and your personality gets more rounded and grounded. There could also be increased religious or spiritual self-awareness. This is also an excellent time for financial affairs. Ganesha is pleased.

15 October: Last Quarter in Cancer

There is powerful bonding. The family gets together. You may decide to take an international holiday together. For the first time, all of you, despite your differences, challenges and situations in life, flock together. There are unexpected breaks and good fortune. There are windfalls and sudden opportunities for personal advancement. If you have been ill for some time, there could be good news from the doctor. Many of you suffering from chronic ailments will check out alternative therapies with enormous success. Life is good, and in a way you have come full circle. You have been there and done that. This is a good time to sharpen your perspective on life and reach a balance. Ganesha is pleased.

23 October: New Moon in Scorpio

There is a powerful intensity cradling you. You may find it hard to keep emotional issues from clouding your interactions with others. There may be powerful and unconscious drives and impulses overpowering you. There could be moments when you slip into old thought patterns but you manage to check yourself at the right time. The work front sees you blazing away. There are expenses, expansion, growth, regeneration, rejuvenation, romance, love, passion, rewards, travel, accolades, desires, bonding, excesses, love and luck. Ganesha blesses you. Your plate is full and the champagne is overflowing.

31 October: First Quarter in Aquarius

Your moods change rapidly like shifting clouds on a windy day. You are like rain in the English countryside, so completely unpredictable. While one aspect of you faces a torrential shower, there is a rainbow on the other side. All this may affect a clear perception of your goals. There is success in your endeavours but there is no point in sullying the euphoria with too much thought. Tame the monkey mind or it will tame you. Everything in life has two sides to it and there is no purpose agonizing over it. The half-empty glass is also half full; it is all a matter of perspective. You may feel that no matter how much you accomplish, there is always something lacking. Old loves cross your path and the encounters could be memorable, to say the least. Life is calling and you want to be a part of the dance. The last tango belongs to Ganesha!

6 November: Full Moon in Taurus

There is stability and hard work as you put your best foot forward and make rapid progress. There are a few tensions along with the potential for great stimulation. It is in your interest to face every situation head-on. Brushing skeletons under the carpet may not be an effective move in the long run. It may just blow in your face later. On the plus side, a new wind is blowing in your face. You become increasingly interested in new spiritual thought or philosophy. You may get involved in the occult, or other esoteric sciences. There is all-round growth. Ganesha is happy with your progress.

14 November: Last Quarter in Leo

The last quarter of the moon is in Leo and it goads you to achieve big things. Your ambitions are aroused and you push hard for power and success. You may get too ambitious and greedy and could resort to unethical means. You will bulldoze all opposition and may invite conflict. There could be issues with the law if you are not careful. You may also get involved in local politics and neighbourhood issues. You may rally people around you demanding social change. You also examine religious, philosophical or metaphysical views very closely. You want to grow at all levels as you look at becoming a person to reckon with in your community. You are also prepared to eject anything that doesn't fit into your new framework. Ganesha blesses you.

22 November: New Moon in Sagittarius

There is a lot of movement. You crave emotional excitement and seek out different people and experiences.

You are impulsive, alive and bubbling with life. You look for change and are ready to take risks. If you feel that you have fallen into a rut, you do everything you can to break free from the comfort zone. The flood waters are rising. You are not one to sink, and you swim through with aplomb. There is travel, and fun times with the family. You spend time in the outdoors, maybe on a farm, or gardening. There could be additions to the family. You may even adopt an exotic pet like an iguana or any other reptile. There are marriages and festivities. There are fun times and you let your hair down. You love being the cynosure of all eyes. Ganesha watches over you.

29 November: First Quarter in Pisces

There are maudlin moments. As the year approaches its end, you are flooded with nostalgia. You are now more tolerant of your own sensitivities. You realize that under all the bravado and the hype there is also pain and hurt. This is not a sign of weakness. It just makes you a more complete person. There is no need to feel sorry for yourself or be prone to self-pity. The truth is that you are now a fuller, more balanced, more mature person who can look into the mirror without flinching. You also realize that you are pushed to higher levels of thought and ideals. You are expressive, creative, attractive, dynamic, austere, fearless, self-confident and analytical. There are many new plans on the anvil; a whole new you is in the making. Ganesha wishes you well.

6 December: Full Moon in Gemini

The year is ending and you are working on a blueprint to plug all loopholes. You are filled with new plans for the family and want to tweak all available resources to secure their future. You may need to move to another city, or even another country. At the very least, you will look at moving to a new and bigger residence to accommodate a growing family more comfortably. This period may have an electric quality to it. Children bring happiness. These are happy times. Make allowances for some medical emergencies as elders will need attention. Ganesha is with you.

14 December: Last Quarter in Virgo

As the winter chill gathers around you, domestic affairs take centre stage. There are sudden expenses and you are pushed to the wall. There is hard work at the office as also several domestic pressures. So you are pushed on all fronts. You can be in a flap but it may be pertinent at this juncture to learn to accept the punches. You have had great times, and we all know so well that good times, like the tough times, never last. Go with the flow and accept what has fallen in your plate. I am not saying these are tough times. All I am saying is that life is beautiful and it is necessary to live in gratitude. This too shall pass. Life has its seasons; one needs the other. Remember, you will be much poorer without the hardships! Ganesha blesses you.

22 December: New Moon in Capricorn

'What a strange illusion it is to suppose that beauty is goodness,' said Leo Tolstoy, the great novelist. Your airs and ego clashes, if any, are immaterial now. You realize that beauty is skin-deep and transitory. If you have won a beauty contest, you feel that the halo is disappearing with time. You look for more substantial answers from life. Of course, this is party time and you have to allow your natural exuberance, energy and lust for life to take over. You are with family and friends, near and dear ones, ushering in another year. Ganesha holds your hand and leads you to new vistas of learning and growth!

28 December: First Quarter in Aries

You are in an explosive mood. You browbeat the opposition into submission. There is fire in your belly. You are the soul of the party. Use this energy well for new projects, if any. Life is calling and you are more than ready for the dance! There could be new love and some indiscretion thrown in. If married or in a stable relationship, you could be holidaying together. But you are beyond caring about the niceties. It is party time and you want to have fun. Ganesha watches over you.

Key Dates

January

1*, 5–6, 9–11, 14*–19, 21–23, 27*– 28.
Ganesha says, work, home, love, journey, the satisfaction of achievement, a possible change of job or a promotion. Stress and strain, though unavoidable, are not good for your health, rest and care are essential. Don't neglect yourself.

February

1*–2, 6*–7, 10*–16, 19*–20, 23*–25, 28*–29.
Marriage, partnerships at all planes, journeys, stopovers, ceremonies and collaborations. Quite a handful! You're at the crossroads, says Ganesha, in several ways.

March

1*, 4–5, 9–14, 17*–18, 22–23, 27*–28.
A very important week around, mid-month. Hard work, loans, funds, investment, joint finance for working full speed ahead are all likely. I'm not saying they're going to happen, but they just could!

April

1 –2, 4*–10, 13*– 15, 18*–20, 23*–24, 28*–29.
Ganesha says, you climb the ladder of success and also achieve real happiness. What is there left to say?

May

3*–8, 11–12, 16*–17, 21*–22, 26*–27, 30*–31.
Tremendous hard work, mighty success. This will be a carryover from April. Friends, supporters will be with you most strongly. Guard your health and make sure you don't fall prey to stress.

June

3*–4, 7*–8, 11*–18, 21*–22, 26*–27, 30.
A month of happy results, fulfilment, the realization of hopes, dreams, and ambitions, predicts Ganesha! You will love and be loved, and that's the greatest news of all!

July

1*, 4–5, 9*–15, 19*–20, 23*–25, 28*–29.
Expenses mount, but from the fourteenth onwards there is much improvement in finances. Health care is essential, learn to be well organized, says Ganesha, in all matters, but especially in looking after yourself.

August

1*–6, 10*–11, 15*–16, 20*–21, 24–25, 28–29.
Life really begins now. You will pick up strength and, energy, and therefore be successful. Love and gains make you happy. New ventures can be launched at this time.

September

1*–8, 11–13, 16–17, 20*–21, 24*–25, 29*–30.
Hard work and good rewards. Foreign lands beckon. Buying/selling/shopping/leasing/funding, investing will be important. Money comes and goes, but you cope well!

October

4*– 5, 9*–10, 13*–11, 22*–23, 26*–27, 31.
The salient features of October will be employment, property, news, views, your inventive genius and ability and the courage to take chances, says Ganesha!

November

1*, 5– 6, 9*–15, 18–19, 22*–24, 27*–29.
November (and December also) run into one somewhat homogeneous unit. House and home, journey and contacts, sum it up for the entire period till the end of the year.

December

2*–4, 7*–12, 15*–16, 20*–21, 24–26, 30–31.
Ganesha says, thrills, spills, mental brilliance, speculation, courtship and wedded bliss. They all last long because you have much to share in every way. In short, happiness and satisfaction, to add to what I said for November.

Virgo

YEARLY FORECAST

> Weapons cannot cleave him (the soul), nor fire burn him;
> water cannot wet him, nor the wind dry him away.
>
> – *Bhagavad Gita*

So powerful is the Jupiter-Saturn-Neptune trio for you, Virgos, that this shloka/ mantra/dictum applies very specially to you.

Till 16 July 2014
Summary and Guidance

Till 16 July 2014, Jupiter in your eleventh angle will make it a truly wonderful 2014 in terms of your personal outlook on life, and on the world at large. High on vitality, confidence, self-knowledge and independence, you will be ready to take on anything that comes your way. One might not be wrong in saying that confidence is your middle name!

Ganesha says money and honey are the twins who will be with you, like your own shadow. As the British say, 'Money is the sinew of love and war.' This love could also lead to a loud and lovely peal of wedding bells. I am sure you know romance and finance make one of the most powerful combinations in the world! Jupiter will also be responsible for marriage, collaborations, ties, journey, publicity, ceremony and excellent PR work at all levels.

17 July 2014 to 11 August 2015

Ganesha says, a certain restlessness caused by anxiety or even nervousness is a distinct possibility. You will have introspective seizures, so to say. You will do a lot of self-evaluation and assessing and judging. Visits to lonely places, hospitals and welfare centres are very probable. Ganesha says you could be into healing, nourishing, helping people, and being helped. Travel would be a good release.

Also, you will be moving house/office, going in for renovation/decoration/installation of gadgets, fashion designing. You will be of great service and use to others, and will be in the news. Expenses, awards, introspection are the other features.

Main Trend

You have it made this year. Jupiter will win the game for you. Friends, money and honey, alliances, group activities, prosperity are destined. Who is wiser than destiny? Later, from 17 July 2014 to 11 August 2015, Jupiter gives you a spiritual and religious expansion of life. Instead of ego problems you will view the world with compassionate detachment. This compassionate detachment is a typical Virgo characteristic. In modern language, you will know that the whole world is on the same page or the same boat. A spiritual teacher, an old friend, study of metaphysics, reiki, different methods of faith healing are the numerous avenues open to you. Those interested in psychiatry will do wonders. In short, honey + money + spirituality = Virgo. My only suggestion is not to be critical, sarcastic or too analytical.

Journey and Communication

In all spiritual, religious and metaphysical matters, journey and communication will be a huge success. But delays and difficulties and even hindrances in the actual journey may (not must) happen because of Saturn in your third angle. Neptune in your seventh angle also indicates unusual meets, journeys, conferences and happenings. Mercury in your own sign from 16 August to 1 September favours journey and communication in a fantastic manner.

Health

Scorpios and Virgos are very health conscious and sometimes even extreme about it. Ganesha asks you to make a conscious effort and say every day to yourself, 'I am healthy and therefore happy.' You may call it auto-suggestion but it helps. Jupiter in your eleventh angle will also sustain your vitality till 16 July 2014. Good health can lead to major achievements in life this year. A little bit of exercise and fresh air cannot hurt anybody.

Love/Marriage

As already said in the beginning, Jupiter in your eleventh angle will also be responsible for marriage, collaborations, ties, journey, publicity, ceremony and excellent PR work at all levels. Venus, the indicator of love, marriage, comfort and beauty, will be in your sign from 6 to 29 September. Other months could well be November, January, March, May, July. But in November tread softly because you will be treading on your own dreams and those of others. This is a slight change from the poem of W.B. Yeats.

Property

Directly or indirectly you do gain through property, be it shop/office/godown/house/warehouse and so on. Uranus in your eighth angle could cause sudden disturbances and scuttle your plans. Be patient. Treat people with care.

Job/Business/Loans/Funds/Investments

As said earlier, being high on vitality, confidence, self-knowledge and independence, you will be ready to take on anything coming your way. One might not be wrong in saying that confidence is your middle name. This is another way of saying that power, promotion and perks will be with you. In simple language, success is certain.

Children/Entertainment

Pluto in your fifth angle gives a big boost to children and entertainment. Your creative juices will run high and strong. Films, the arts, research, tantra, mantra, spirituality and different forms of healing are some of the many routes through which you will travel and prosper.

Trips and Ties

Trips and ties go well with journey and communication but for ties we have to take a look at Venus, the planet of relationships. Venus will be in your own sign from 6 to 29 September, that is your birth month. January, March, May, July are the other months for life, sweet life. Enjoy. Life is sweet but short. Make the most of it.

Publicity, Projects, Performance

Till 16 July 2014, push yourself with all that you have. Jupiter works for you and that means campaigns, long-range planning for projecting yourself or the company or both. You will do a good job of it. Make use of technology and learn to socialize with ease and confidence. That's the trick and the ticket.

Happiness Quota

On this court, you score 86 per cent.

Monthly Round-up

January: open sesame to fame, fortune, children, romance, hobbies, creativity; February: health, work, colleagues, irritations over pets, projects and important trifles; March: collaborations, partnerships at all levels, journey with a stopover, reaching out to people, places; April: joint finances, insurance, loans, public trusts, low vitality, sex and love in a strange mix; May: the luck of the draw, knowledge, evolution, wisdom, ancestors and rites, genuine spirituality, long-distance connections, pilgrimages; June: a high-powered month for work and play, prestige and promotion, parents and in-laws, boss and life partner; July: a golden harvest for the trouble taken and the seeds planted, and that says it all; August: expenses, work, contacts, secret work, affairs of the heart, illumination of the soul, though there could be inflammation in the sole (of your foot); September: wishes granted, rewards, wish-fulfilment is possible. You will feel wonderful and strong, ready to take on anything coming your way; October: finance, food, family—and that does not mean entertainment—amusement, doing the social rounds; November: gains, friends, children, creativity, group activity, joy and delight in life; December: house, home, parents, in-laws, a home away from home, travel, get-togethers and separations.

Summary

The pinnacles of pelf, power, prestige—the three Ps. Beware of pride and prejudice. A wish-fulfilment comes your way. Let me whisper a secret. Be confident, do not criticize, and game, set and match will be yours.

Outer Planets

URANUS: As it is, you and Scorpios often have problems connected with health. Sometimes you can be a hypochondriac. Health for you is half in the mind. The stomach could misbehave in more ways than one.

NEPTUNE: Both love and deception, spirituality and illusion, magic and madness will be your lot because of Neptune. Neptune will be in good position with Pluto and Jupiter and therefore the good will conquer the bad at least till 16 July 2014. Afterwards also, to a lesser extent, joy will fly in your pocket.

PLUTO: Pluto in your third angle helps you in trips and ties, love, romance and marriage. But if you try to overreach yourself your health may not help you. In other words, be bold, adventurous but learn to know your limits. I agree that it is easier said than done.

Month by Month

January

The new moon is in Capricorn and your feet are firmly on the ground. The year starts with a definite game plan. You have concrete goals in mind. You also look at your health seriously and may look at alternative healing with new eyes. There could be illness at home and you may have to care for your spouse and old parents. The month-end fills you with ideas. You may spend time in offbeat yoga, nature camps or in a new type of meditation programme. Your moods see-saw and sometimes you appear cold, impersonal and insensitive. There may be misunderstandings and tough emotional situations. Ganesha holds your hand.

February

This can be a great time for bankers, those dabbling in realty and the markets, even media folk. You are on fire. There is money and honey, love and romance, birth and death, as your entire life coalesces into something new. You balance idealism and euphoria with practicality. You throw parties, buy goodies for the home and invest in a new wardrobe. There may be foreign travel and visits to exotic locales. Your canvas is large and your palette rich in colours. Ganesha blesses you.

March

There are many domestic issues that you have to resolve. There will be maudlin moments and you may feel crushed. The sooner you get out of this mode, the better. Myriad thoughts are coursing through your veins. The energies are high but you are not able to zero in on any one course of action. There is consolidation at work and the home front is stable. You are busy with investments. The mood is thick with thoughts of love by the end of the month. One manifestation of this influence is a pleasant, day-dreaming mood. Work piles up but you look for softer creative options, even some form of social work. Ganesha wishes you well.

April

There are good portents for business and professional life as you attract persons and circumstances that help you grow both as a person and as an entrepreneur. Compared to the fury of several events in your life, this is a happy, emotional, agreeable and soft phase. By the middle of the month there are many opportunities knocking on your door. There could be associations with gurus and godmen as you process new spiritual thoughts. The end of the month sees ego drives, low self-esteem and low body image. There is also work and money. Ganesha is with you.

May

There is expansion and growth in all areas as you get indulgent and live large. There are possibly some indiscreet alliances too. There could be windfalls. Many structures that you have built in your life will be challenged. If you are going through a divorce, the settlement will unbalance you. There are emotional moments. You want to sort out your life. The idiosyncrasies of the world stare you down. There could be jealousy, deceit, controversy and intrigue. Ganesha holds your hand.

June

New vistas beckon. There is some semblance of stability along with the newness. You are networking furiously. There could be overseas travel and new love and happiness. You make headway and clean up the cobwebs.

By the month-end you open your arms and embrace change. There could also be power struggles. Life will soon be beautiful and the new moon augurs well for a leap into the future. Ganesha guides you.

July

There are many subconscious influences at play and your attention may get distorted. There is some confusion about your core needs. There are delusions and illusions. The full moon is in Capricorn by mid-month and you do well. Make the most of this positive influence. There is more stability now. There are grandiose schemes on the anvil. There could even be new love and powerful bonding. You make rapid progress as the month comes to a close. The pace of life accelerates. Ganesha wishes you well.

August

Your confidence is at an all-time high. You may take a family holiday in exotic locales. You look to reinvent yourself and are attracted to spiritualism and mysticism. There is churning and soul-searching. Mercury is in your sign from 16 August to 1 September. This is the time to make hay when the sun shines. Go for it! The hard times seem to be a thing of the past. There is money and honey, rewards of all kinds, applause and awards. Ganesha smiles.

September

Venus is in your sign from September 6 to 29 September. It is also your birth period and you are on a dream run. There is health, happiness, money, love and plaudits. New vistas do open up and you look at metaphysics, astrology, natural healing, the occult, tantra, mantra, godmen, yoga, meditation and related areas. There could also be new love and great bonding. The month-end sees a grand reaching out to people and places. Those in the teaching profession, the arts, media, films, direction, editing, do exceedingly well. There are rewards and awards, honours and plaudits. Ganesha is happy.

October

There will be business expansion. You are riding high and may be subject to serious ego conflicts. There are new collaborations/ventures, research and discoveries. You show great discipline. You examine your life and the structures that you have built into it and make the necessary changes for maximum results. There are emotional moments by the middle of the month. The spouse and elders may need medical attention. The month-end brings passion, love and multiple affairs. It is not a bad phase by any means. It just means that you want to rope in a lot into your life. There could be deceit and betrayal. Ganesha walks with you.

November

You are rushing through life and make big leaps forward. There will be happy moments with friends and family. Home/house/property affairs come into sharp focus. There is money and honey, new love, passion, lust, purchases and expenses, travel, ego and ecstasy, finance and fortune. There is long-distance travel on the cards. Whatever you embark on now will lead to success. Ganesha is pleased.

December

You reach out to people and old friends. Long-lost extended family and others drop by to savour your hospitality. You will be busy with inheritance issues, family matters and old longings. You have emerged as a better person now. The new moon is in Capricorn by mid-month and lucrative work opportunities grab you by the collar. You rush into the new year with money and honey and a broad smile on your face. There is new energy and new healing. By the month-end there is enough on your plate to excite you, keep you occupied and motivated. Ganesha blesses you.

Months at a Glance

January

Open sesame to fame, fortune, children, romance, hobbies, creativity.

February

Health, work, colleagues, irritations over pets, projects and important trifles.

March

Collaborations, partnerships at all levels, journey with a stopover, reaching out to people, places.

April

Joint finances, insurance, loans, public trusts, low vitality, sex and love in a strange mix.

May

The luck of the draw, knowledge, evolution, wisdom, ancestors and rites, genuine spirituality, long-distance connections, pilgrimages.

June

A high-powered month for work and play, prestige and promotion, parents and in-laws, boss and life partner.

July

A golden harvest for the trouble taken and the seeds planted, and that says it all.

August

Expenses, contacts, secret work, affairs of the heart, illumination of the soul, though there could be inflammation in the sole of your foot.

September

Wishes granted, reward, realized, wish-fulfilment is possible. You will feel wonderful and strong, ready to take on anything.

October

Finance, food, family—and that does not mean entertainment—amusement, doing the social rounds.

November

Gains, friends, children, creativity, group activity, joy and delight in life.

December

House, home, parents, in-laws, a home away from home, travel, get-togethers and separations.

Weekly Review (By the phases of the moon)

1 January: New Moon in Capricorn

Every zodiac sign has its list of celebrities and you are no exception. You are in the company of Michael Jackson,

Sophia Loren, Stephen King, Mickey Mouse (created on 19 September 1928 by Walt Disney), Mother Teresa, Ingrid Bergman, Ivan Illich, Agatha Christie, Jesse Owens and so many others. As you can see, I am only naming a few. Every sign has all types of personalities and several shades too. This is no template, but Virgos are generally careful and trustworthy though sometimes too critical. You are normally sensible, practical and logical. You are ruled by Mercury and could be interested in many things. You will make good copy editors because you are good at finding fault; you are overly fastidious and this helps. In relationships, you may be considered a pain in the neck due to your fastidious and critical nature! Of course, I must add here that this is a general reading, so accurate conclusions cannot be drawn unless it is a personal horoscope. Astrology is complicated and the stars only impel. I repeat this all the time so that you do not get carried away and assume a fatalistic attitude. The new moon is in Capricorn and your feet are firmly on the ground. You work hard and well. You can be trusted to deliver. You look at the pros and cons of a situation with a fine-toothed comb and ensure success. The year starts with a definite game plan. You have concrete goals in mind. Ganesha is with you.

8 January: First Quarter in Aries

There is hard work on the cards. You try your hand at different things. Those of you who freelance will make steady progress with many opportunities falling in your lap. You are on the fast track to success. You also think about your health seriously and may rediscover alternative healing. There is money coming in but it also rushes out. So you need to be careful. The family may make many demands on your time and resources. Ganesha blesses you. There may be an addition to the family and some couples and single parents may even choose adoption. Needless to say, you will make a great parent. Children could also leave the nest in search of their own identities. There is a lot churning in your life now.

16 January: Full Moon in Cancer

There are emotional moments and a lot of soul-searching. Some of you are just locked in the past and keep wandering back to a period in your life dead and gone. It is pointless. If you have recovered from a terminal illness, you keep going for check-ups and relive the gory and dismal days. The check-ups are good but there is no point in living in the past. Move on and make the present count for a better tomorrow. There could be illness at home and you may have to care for your spouse and old parents if they live with you. You may meet up with old colleagues and long-lost siblings. If you have embarked on a new assignment, there will be success. You network furiously and pave the way for profit. Ganesha blesses you. That alone is half the battle won!

24 January: Last Quarter in Scorpio

There are intense moments. There could be new love, and young Virgos may disobey the family and elope with someone quite inappropriate. This is not a judgement call, but young love, as we all know, is blind. You will not listen to anyone. There will be a lot of tension in the family. It may be a good idea to hold your horses and seek wiser counsel. I know from my own life that you will do what has to be done. Finally, circumstances and natural inclinations determine our life path. You could overstep your boundaries and also extend yourself financially. Your emotions are at fever pitch and you need to negotiate this phase with care. Ganesha is with you all the way. Children could also pose trouble. As you can see, a lot is happening in your domestic life at the moment.

30 January: New Moon in Aquarius

You are filled with ideas and a new, path-breaking mode of work. There is strong idealism coursing through your veins. You look at gods and godmen and new modes of healing. You may spend time in offbeat yoga, nature camps or in a new type of meditation programme. You want to find yourself in the din and bustle of life. If you have the time and have retired from work, you do not want to waste time idling away. You look for challenges of all kinds to goad you away from lethargy. You look for freedom and want to escape the humdrum of life. But there is no other way. We all have to go through the patchwork of life. Your moods see-saw and sometimes you appear cold, impersonal and insensitive. There is no real connect with the family and you are just doing your duty to them as you feel it has to be done. There could be fears of a money shortage too. There may be misunderstandings and tough emotional situations. Ganesha smiles as he knows that you are being tested for greater challenges. You will emerge stronger.

6 February: First Quarter in Taurus

There is work and money. If you are the type who picks up a job for life, there will be consolidation at work. There will be promotions and security which you crave.

You are generally not one for dramatics in the normal scheme of things. In this phase, you will be doing nothing else but working hard. You will provide for the home and for the future. This can be a great time for bankers, those dabbling in realty and the markets, even media folk. You will be making big money. Of course, this is a general reading and I cannot get into specifics unless I know the personal chart. I am your favourite astrologer but I am not God. There is love and happiness all around and Ganesha is happy.

14 February: Full Moon in Leo

You are firing on all cylinders. It is all happening at once and in a hurry. There is money and honey, love and romance, birth and death, as your entire life coalesces into something new. The transformation is intense. You balance idealism and euphoria with practicality. You earn and spend and live larger than life. You are like the grandest of lions in Serengeti. This is a stolid period; you know what you want and go for it. You are as sure-footed as an alpine goat. Nothing can get at you now as you scale the peaks of success with dexterity. Ganesha is delighted. So am I.

22 February: Last Quarter in Sagittarius

You are generally not one to waste money but in this period you spend like there is no tomorrow. You throw parties, buy goodies for the home and invest in a new wardrobe. There is richness and grandeur in your life and you are unabashed about it. Old friends drop in, there is new love and you play the field. It is said that Virgo is the virgin, but you are anything but that now. You are luxuriating in style. There may be foreign travel and visits to exotic locales. People from overseas may also drop by. You experience life from a broader perspective. Your canvas is large and your palette rich in colours. You break all chains as you move into fifth gear and steer ahead like an Indian rocket. I say Indian rocket because our space programme is doing quite well and we are in the nuclear club. Of course, I must add here that all this is for peaceful purposes! Ganesha blesses you.

1 March: New Moon in Pisces

There is a lot happening in your life at the moment. There are many domestic issues that you need to resolve. Those going through a divorce will be hard-pressed to reach a settlement fast. You do not want to lose well-earned assets, so it may be necessary to hire the best lawyers and counsellors. An out-of-court settlement will be ideal. But all that depends on the personal horoscope. These are just the trends that I am interpreting. But warm and positive energies surround you. Friends help out. You have a close bond with many people and they will not let you down. There will be many maudlin moments and you may feel crushed. The sooner you get out of this mode, the better. There is no use crying over spilt milk. Ganesha nods in agreement.

8 March: First Quarter in Gemini

You are rushing around with new ideas and plans. Myriad thoughts are coursing through your veins. You need to make up your mind and steer a concrete course of action. The energies are high but you are not able to zero in on any one course of action. You are all helter-skelter, searching hard for the right game plan. Remember, the mind is a monkey on a stick. Keep it steadfast or you will lose track of what to do. Ganesha blesses you. He knows that you will come through. Delusions and illusions are all a part of the grand design. No one is exempt from it.

16 March: Full Moon in Virgo

The full moon is in your sign and this is a good period. Take the chances that come your way. There is consolidation at work and the home front is stable. You are busy with investments and count your pennies zealously. You plan assiduously for the future. There will be substantial returns on investments and you are elated. If married, there will be intense bonding with the spouse. If single and fancy-free, new love will catch your eye and hook you. You will struggle with the bait like a giant carp. But amorous pursuit wins in the end and you find that love is indeed a spiritual experience. The sexual route is but a path to superconsciousness. Ganesha walks beside you. I am delighted.

24 March: Last Quarter in Capricorn

As our Indian readers know all too well, this is the financial year-end so a lot of tax planning is done. There are expenses, investments, purchases and many new plans on the anvil. You may buy a new home or a fancy car. Life is dynamic and change is the order of the day. But you plough the furrow even if single-handedly. You refuse to be ejected from your comfort zone. Ganesha knows what you are going through, of course, and blesses you. You are conscious of health needs and keep a tab on annual health check-ups. You listen to the doctor and watch your diet and gym schedules with great care. Like with every other sign, you also have opposites. One type of Virgo breaks all the rules, the other type is just too scared to do anything of that kind. Which type are you?

30 March: New Moon in Aries

You are sizzling like the Indian summer. You make progress and seize every opportunity. The mood is thick with thoughts of love. You are conscious of your loved ones and your feelings for them. You are filled with love and may fall in love with someone new. But this has more to do with ego drives than with any real feeling of love. One manifestation of this influence is a pleasant, day-dreaming mood. Work piles up but you are not alive to the demands of hard work. You look for softer creative options, even some form of social work. You feel warm and friendly towards everyone and look for company that uplifts you. Watch this trend carefully. If you are not with the right people, you could end up feeling terribly lonely. Like Mother Teresa said, and I wholeheartedly agree, loneliness is worse than AIDS. Personal relationships are favoured in this influence and it will be a good idea to hang out with compatible people. Ganesha wishes you well.

7 April: First Quarter in Cancer

There are taut emotions at play but this can also be a useful influence in many ways. There are good portents for business and professional life as you attract persons and circumstances that help you grow both as a person and as an entrepreneur. People in authority are favourably inclined towards you, and your professional life will run smoothly. Everyone realizes that you are primarily interested in working harmoniously with others, and they respond by being agreeable. You may be inclined in this period to involve yourself in artistic matters like design, journal layout, office redecorating, etc. Compared to the fury of several events in your life, this is a happy, emotional, agreeable and soft phase. Ganesha blesses you as you make your way through the labyrinths of life.

15 April: Full Moon in Libra

There is love and passion. There is also money and honey. But there are so many opportunities knocking at your door that you are simply unable to make up your mind one way or the other. This is an interesting phase in your life. If used well, it could be a time for expansion and growth. There could be associations with gurus and godmen as you process new spiritual thoughts. You may dwell on past lives and look for different modes of salvation. New vistas open up dramatically. Love could also pop out of the bottle suddenly like a genie. There are many trends. It all depends on what you do with them and how you steer your life. Astrology only impels, never compels. I have been reading horoscopes for decades and know how capricious it is. Use your free will to your advantage. Life is many-splendoured and there is magic everywhere. It all depends on what you connect to. Ganesha walks the walk and talks the talk with you.

22 April: Last Quarter in Aquarius

There are maudlin moments. You could go into a shell and think of the unhappy days gone by. This could also be a stormy period in your personal relationships.

You and your partner won't see eye to eye about some project that both of you are closely involved in. The clash in perspective may be due to a difference in your backgrounds and conditioning. There will also be ego drives, low self-esteem and low body image. You want to triumph and feel that if your view is not considered it is akin to a blot on your honour. Let me assure you that such thoughts died with the Neanderthal man, and the modern man has to move ahead in the Age of Aquarius, the age of communication and new spirituality. If you don't move on, you will be stuck in a rut. Obviously, under the current influence, any kind of team effort will fail. It may be a better idea to go solo. Ganesha watches over you. Some said the world would end in 2012. If it did, I wouldn't have been writing this and you reading it. But old concepts and thoughts have to die for newness to emerge from the rubble.

29 April: New Moon in Taurus

The new moon is in Taurus and there is a lot of consolidation on the work front. You find stability and put your nose to the grindstone. There is money to be made and to be spent and you are filled with the business of living. Be wary of deceit, though. Ensure that people you deal with represent themselves truthfully. Life is never about having things your way; we have to meet people midway. You may also be tempted to get into some underhand deal and go for a quick buck. All this will boomerang. There will be a price to pay. Others will try to deceive you. It takes two hands to clap so you cannot excuse yourself from the consequences of your actions. It always catches up some time or the other. You may also have to face the unpleasant consequences of past actions. You will look at routes of escape and take refuge in drugs or alcohol. Ganesha is with you. I am too. This is a mixed bag. Always think hard and opt for the right path. Like Mahatma Gandhi always said, there is no substitute for truth.

7 May: First Quarter in Leo

There is fire in your belly. There is money and work, fame and fortune. There is expansion and growth in all areas as you get indulgent and live life large. There are possibly some indiscreet alliances as you look for freedom in its truest sense. There could be sudden windfalls or unexpected gains. There is growth of a very profound kind. You mature overnight and feel blessed. You count your blessings and suddenly realize that you are in a very lucky space and live in gratitude. Ganesha is happy for you. Such realizations are a gold mine and if it emerges from your soul, you have arrived in more ways than one!

14 May: Full Moon in Scorpio

There will be many changes and challenges in your growth trajectory. Many structures that you have built in your life will be challenged by circumstances. There could be many life changes in the offing. Change is never easy or happy, and you will have to make several adjustments. If you are going through a divorce, the settlement will unbalance you. You will feel a strong sense of uneasiness, because the unexpected looms large now. There will be hidden and apparent tensions as your world order changes. You may just completely break off a close relationship. All this will take a toll on your health. Ganesha asks you to take care.

21 May: Last Quarter in Pisces

There are emotional moments and you take a back seat. You want to sort out your life. Of course, I repeat, the specifics depend on your personal chart and I am only making a general reading. You find the time to network and look for suitable diversions. There is deep bonding with friends who bail you out of tight situations. Ganesha is with you. You are filled with new realizations. New aspects of your life are revealed to you and you have close encounters with all kinds of people. Your life is intense and in a whirl.

28 May: New Moon in Gemini

Your mind wanders in many directions like a puppy that has lost its leash. The idiosyncrasies of the world stare you down. There could be jealousy, deceit, controversy and intrigue. Ganesha believes that you should stand your ground if you feel you are right and are being falsely victimized. There could be new job openings and you look for new associations and new vistas. Family life is tenuous. You feel alone, lonely and lost as the children may have flown the coop. Retired people could feel depressed if they are not gainfully employed. Research has suggested that most retired people die within a short span of leaving their jobs. So the idea is to keep using your brain and body lest they atrophy. You wrestle with self-created confusions and even your peer group will find you hard to fathom.

5 June: First Quarter in Virgo

You are back to stability and new ground. There is new energy and you settle down on terra firma. You busy yourself with family matters. There are siblings, children, spouse and parents demanding your attention. Ganesha helps you seek answers. New vistas beckon, windows and doors open, there is fresh air and you take deep breaths. There is some semblance of stability along with the newness. There is freshness all around. The mist has cleared and the early morning dew is just magnificent. The radiance of the cosmic dance takes your breath away. You take lungfuls of invigorating air and are born anew. There is a new dawn; for fleeting moments that seem like eternity you believe the dawn is everlasting. It is a long way to go!

13 June: Full Moon in Sagittarius

Along with some balance and equilibrium, there are many changes in your life now. You are networking furiously and meeting all and sundry in a bid to expand your circle and your consciousness. There are many expenses. There could also be overseas travel and purchases that you simply cannot avoid. There is new love and happiness. You live large, without a care in the world. You have emerged from tough times and are battle-scarred and hardened; you can now wear your epaulettes with pride. You don't want to become a stagnant cesspool as you seek out new interests and friends. You don't want to be driftwood either. You want to be a person to reckon with. Ganesha is with you all the way. Life is all about instilling fresh blood, and you are going about doing it with earnestness.

19 June: Last Quarter in Pisces

You make headway and clean up the cobwebs. There is a lot to be done. It may also be a good idea to get into a fitness programme or to detoxify at a nature cure clinic. At the very least, you may need to go for a medical examination. All the tension of the past few weeks can result in a psychosomatic illness. We are all connected in some way or the other and you could be better off by getting in touch with the root of the problem and releasing the accruing tension. You don't have to complain and be pessimistic. Do not imagine ghosts, ghouls and demons where none exists. You could be moody and pessimistic but these are all the machinations of the mind. Take to yoga, meditation and positive affirmation and shed it all. Look at positivity, bask in the sunlight. Make room for more of the right ingredients so that you may roar again like a finely tuned Honda engine. Ganesha wishes you well.

27 June: New Moon in Cancer

The subcontinent is boiling over in the scorching summer with all the attendant problems of lack of power and water. Your emotions are also taking a huge toll on you, even in the shade! You look for answers about a new reality. Open your arms and embrace change. The more you resist, the more difficult it will be. While there is money and honey, my favourite phrase, there could also be power struggles. Ganesha holds your hand while you walk over burning coal. Life will soon be beautiful and the new moon augurs well for change and a leap into the future. Embark on new projects during the waxing phase of the moon and you will come up trumps.

5 July: First Quarter in Libra

Your mind is in a whirl. Fancies and illusions take over. They become more important than reality. You will daydream a lot which is quite harmless, but since there won't be much clarity this is not a good time to make decisions or to embark upon a course of action that requires clear thinking. There are many subconscious influences at play and your attention may get distorted. Do not resort to alcohol or drugs as you feel like leaving the real world and escaping into some faraway land. There is some confusion about your core needs and you may have to re-evaluate your priorities. There are delusions and illusions, so take time off before you rush to conclusions. Take some time before you form a concrete course of action. Ganesha blesses you.

12 July: Full Moon in Capricorn

The full moon is in Capricorn and you do well. Make the most of this positive influence. There is money and honey and many idealistic dreams. There is reflection and many plans are made for the future. Ganesha blesses you. There is more stability now and your feet are firmly on the ground as you go about the task of living in a practical way. You are not one who can be swayed from practical concerns for too long. You say 'enough is enough' to yourself, and dust the cobwebs from your life and march on like a true soldier.

19 July: Last Quarter in Aries

Last year, around this time, it was an exciting period when it all went your way thanks to the influence of Venus. You probably had the best of both worlds. It may not be as luxurious now but the accent is most definitely on positivity and forging ahead. There are grandiose schemes on the anvil. There could even be new love and powerful bonding which can snare you and shake you off your feet.

Ganesha is with you. There is domestic harmony, children do well, and health is good. You are poised for more joy, maybe even greatness. Success will crown you and you will drown in applause.

26 July: New Moon in Leo

The new moon is in Leo and you are making rapid progress. There is a lot of networking and the pace of life accelerates. You live large and spend like crazy, to use next-generation lingo. You acquire many new gadgets and make some high-quality purchases. Ganesha wishes you well as you scorch the runway with speed, dexterity and elan. It is as if life is preparing for you a golden harvest. Wonderful is all I can say! Remember, projects started in the waxing phase of the moon are generally successful.

4 August: First Quarter in Scorpio

There is new intensity in all your dealings. Your confidence is at an all-time high. You may take a family holiday and move to exotic locales. You also look to reinvent yourself and may take up a new course of study. You are attracted to spiritualism and mysticism. You meet with alternative healers and godmen and look for new ideas. You want to change your life at the root, at the very core. Ganesha blesses you. I am happy too. There is churning and soul-searching.

10 August: Full Moon in Aquarius

There could be needless disputes, irritability and rash action. You may have a problem getting along with others. If you are in a team, you will have to make compromises. You may feel a bit let down and discouraged by the attitudes of others. You react defensively to people and may get too hasty and overcritical. You could also be accident-prone now so take the necessary precautions when you drive. These are the indicators. This is a general reading and the stars, I repeat, never compel. Ganesha walks with you all the way.

17 August: Last Quarter in Taurus

Mercury is in your sign from 16 August to 1 September. Mercury, the mighty, all-powerful planet, is in your sign now. It favours travel, meetings, conferences, interviews, trips, more brain power, contacts, communication, correspondence, contracts. Mercury has a special connection with the circuits of the brain. Chess, crossword and other such games belong to Mercury. Also, short-distance runners and spin bowlers are controlled by Mercury. Mercury, in short, is the ambassador and salesman of the zodiac. Mercury is the symbol of news, views, messages, interviews, contacts, communications, travel and transport. Mercury gives an impetus to all of the above in the sun sign where it is located. 'There is a tide in the affairs of man, when taken at the flood it leads to fortune,' said Shakespeare. This is the time to make hay when the sun shines. Go for it! The tide is in your favour now; set sail with a song on your lips. Ganesha blesses you. As your favourite astrologer, I am happy.

25 August: New Moon in Virgo

The new moon is in your sign and the good times continue to roll. The influence of Mercury also continues. The hard times seem to be a thing of the past. 'To have great poets, there must be great audiences,' said Walt Whitman.

Likewise, to make a great prediction, I need the right audience. Of course, accurate predictions depend on personal details. I also feel happy when I predict happy times. Now that a great period is in store for you, I am sure you are hanging on to every word. There is money and honey, rewards of all kinds, applause and awards. Make the most of this period. Ganesha smiles. The family is delighted and friends toast to your health and success.

2 September: First Quarter in Sagittarius

It is a double whammy. Venus is in your sign from 6 to 29 September. Venus is another important planet and is of great significance. This is an important phase. As you know, Venus is the planet of love, romance, sex, beauty and the good life. This is the planet of attraction, love, wealth, knowledge and prosperity. The compatibility of partners and also the type of life the individual will lead are also judged from the placement of Venus in the horoscope. As a planet, Venus is considered to be beneficial, feminine and gentle. Venus symbolizes the force of attraction in the universe. In human beings this attractive force manifests as love and beauty. When Venus is well placed in the chart, there is love, art, beauty and all the goodies of life that make life worth living. Venus rules Libra and Taurus, though its role in every sign is important. Like other planets, it also has its transits. In Libra, Venus is aesthetic and cultured. In Taurus, it is more earthy, materialistic and sensual. Venus rules the venous system, kidneys, urinary tract, throat, larynx, and is responsible for good looks. In short, Venus in Western astrology stands for comforts, arts, relationships, sex, decorations, luxuries and wealth. It is also your birth period and you are on a dream run. There is health, happiness, money, love and plaudits. What more do you need? Ganesha is thrilled. So am I. Of course, this is not a personal horoscope and these are generalizations. But the indications are there. There are no compulsions, only gentle prods. I hope what I say here materializes in your life. Finally, your favourite astrologer wants humanity to be happy, content and fulfilled.

9 September: Full Moon in Pisces

While the going is good, there could also be some sensitivities and insecurities. New vistas do open up and you look at metaphysics, astrology, natural healing, the occult, tantra, mantra, godmen, yoga, meditation and related areas. There are many opportunities as you will be striking out in several directions. There could also be new love and great bonding if you are already attached. Ganesha blesses you. There is domestic peace and times of deep reflection. You are filled with gratitude as it is all going your way. Sometimes you wonder what the grand plan is, how it is all working out. All life is a miracle. 'All life is yoga,' said Sri Aurobindo. You can feel it in your bones now.

16 September: Last Quarter in Gemini

There is a grand reaching out to people and places. You are networking furiously and are in great demand. Social networking is the new buzzword and you don't have to be a kid or generation-next to exploit the many advances in science and technology. The world is shrinking by the day, thanks to the new gizmos and gadgets. Your real gifts are knowledge, skills and wisdom. This is the time when it all comes in handy and you flower; the stars are also propitious. Generally, it is best to take risks and venture into uncharted waters when the stars augur well, like they are doing now. Those in the teaching profession, the arts, media, films, direction and editing do exceedingly well. There are rewards and awards, honours and plaudits. Ganesha is delighted. Money also flows in. Investments pay off. Health is good. If you want more, I am sorry, but then that is sheer greed!

24 September: New Moon in Libra

Your life flows smoothly. Of course, nothing in life can ever be silky smooth but you show great strength and stamina and deal with all that is thrown at you. You are in demand. People will listen to you and you could be addressing large audiences. You emerge as a leader in your community. Ganesha is happy. So am I. There are expenses too as you will be making luxurious purchases and spending like there is no tomorrow. But in the phase you are in, why worry about tomorrow?

1 October: First Quarter in Capricorn

You are rooted to the ground. You are very practical and there is no room for idle fancies. There is money to be made and new job offers. There will be business expansion. Those who are employed are in line for promotion. Life has many shades, it is many-splendoured and miraculous. Ganesha knows it all and will guide you. Whatever will be, will be! There will be frenetic communication between you and others. You are riding high and may be subject to serious ego conflicts. Be careful of that and avoid turbulence in encounters with people. You may have to compromise a bit and let others have a say even if you are not in complete agreement with them. Discretion is the better part of valour and sometimes even great generals have retreated to win the battle. Read about Rommel, the great general, the Desert Fox, and you will know. You are impulsive and may get carried away with your own importance. Others have opinions too. Allow dissenting voices to be heard.

8 October: Full Moon in Aries

You are shooting ahead like a meteor in the night sky. There are new collaborations/ventures, research and new discoveries. Ganesha eggs you on. Of course, there are work pressures and a lot on your plate. And why not? How is being idle a virtue? You show great discipline and are able to channel all your energies towards your goal. You examine your life and the structures that you have built into it. You make the necessary changes for maximum results. You are thorough and meticulous in your approach towards work and life. There will be lasting results. You are able to focus, concentrate and attend to detail. You can't go wrong, and you know it.

15 October: Last Quarter in Cancer

You spend time in domestic chores. Children need attention. Youngsters may be leaving home for higher education and the nest will be empty. There are emotional moments. The spouse and elders may need medical attention. There is a lot on your plate, like an Indian thali. You are stable and reliable and cope well with all that is thrown at you. You do not make unrealistic demands and recognize that your loved ones are human. You are objective in all your dealings and the import of your words resonate. Any relationship now will be characterized by sobriety and stability. You may not be unduly demonstrative and could be more practical than romantic, but there is a steadiness of feelings. Others can see it. Ganesha blesses you.

23 October: New Moon in Scorpio

You are in an intense phase. There are powerful emotions at play. There are passion, love and multiple affairs. There are many emotional moments too, which take you off the rails. It is not a bad phase by any means. It just means that you want to rope in a lot into your life and so will be multitasking furiously. There could be great lust too, I dare say, and youngsters may be taking undue risks. But life is a game of roulette. Don't we all know that? Ganesha wishes you well.

31 October: First Quarter in Aquarius

You could spend some dark moments. Communication with others may break down. There is confusion and it is not the right time to make important decisions. There could be deceit and betrayal. Take extra precautions when you deal with others. Misunderstandings in this period could lead to unpleasant situations. Ganesha walks with you. That could be a great help. There could be issues of low self-esteem and a lack of confidence in your abilities. Ride the waves. This shall also pass. Good times, like bad times, never last. Ask Muhammad Ali, three-time world heavyweight champion. Ask Nelson Mandela, who came out of jail to lead a country. For that matter, just ask me.

You have to ride life like an expert surfer. That is the only way. Just bob with the tide, ride the waves.

6 November: Full Moon in Taurus

This is a practical and fruitful phase. You are rushing through life and making big leaps forward. You could also be swayed by the period and its success and make rash decisions. In business deals, take extra precautions. Do not get greedy. Check the fine print. Read agreements and documents carefully and possibly enlist the services of a professional. Ganesha warns against deceit. You may feel like making more money. Avoid schemes that are dishonest. On the flip side, there will be happy moments with friends and family. Home/house/property affairs come into sharp focus. You are in the driver's seat. Wear your seat belt and drive carefully!

14 November: Last Quarter in Leo

There is money and honey, new love, passion, lust, purchases and expenses, travel and some tribulations, ego and ecstasy, finance and fortune. There is tremendous growth in business and you look at earning money from several sources. You are planning for the future. You grab every opportunity that comes your way. The stars are smiling at you. Smile back. Ganesha is happy, so am I. You have the luck of the draw. Go for it. If you watch your step, nothing will go wrong. Like Nadia Comaneci, you will pirouette on a dainty toe with precision.

22 November: New Moon in Sagittarius

There is long-distance travel on the cards. Youngsters seeking admission in foreign universities will get good news. You are free, frank and fearless and will be sharp in your comments too. This can be a time for real growth and expanded opportunities. Ask yourself honestly what you want from life and how far you will go for what you want. You have to know precisely where you are and what your real needs are. This is a good time to go the distance. Of course, you must also know when to stop. Make the most of the waxing phase of the moon. Whatever you embark on now will lead to success. Ganesha is pleased with the developments. Nothing else matters.

29 November: First Quarter in Pisces

The workings of your mind take you by storm. You could become obsessed by delusions. Take the beaten path now as it is tried and tested. This can be a period for real growth and opportunities. There could be ego inflation and excessive pride. Be careful not to act in an overbearing manner or you will lose out in the popularity sweepstakes. There could be brushes with the law, even court cases, as you could well get on the wrong side of people without much reason. Every trifle seems to outrage your honour and dignity. Keep an even keel, use your free will, and remain calm. There could be travel. Ganesha is with you as the winter cold shrivels the skin and cuts into the bones. A more accurate reading will depend on your personal horoscope. Until then, this is all that I can say.

6 December: Full Moon in Gemini

Your mind is moving fast in different directions. Your discipline and self-restraint are tested. You tend to overextend yourself and believe that nothing can go wrong. There is luck on your side but why push it? You

squander resources without a care and live in delusions
of grandeur and plenty. There are maudlin moments and
fun times too. You may seek out gurus and godmen, lucky
charms, tantras and mantras. You are in the mood to help
others. Ganesha is with you as you ford the last weeks of
the year with care.

14 December: Last Quarter in Virgo

There is stability and hard work. You are back to being
the sniffer dog that smells big bucks even if it is highly
camouflaged. You reach out to people and old friends.
Long-lost extended family and others drop by to savour
your hospitality. The year has passed in a jiffy and problem
areas have been sorted out to your satisfaction. Ganesha is
happy for you. You will be busy with inheritance issues,
family matters and old longings. You have emerged as a
better person now as life has taught you many lessons. I
am glad that you have come up trumps.

22 December: New Moon in Capricorn

While the whole world is partying, you could be working
hard. Yes, you have sniffed out gold and the methods
to mint it, and you are ready to postpone the partying.
The new moon is in Capricorn and lucrative work
opportunities grab you by the collar. Ganesha is delighted.
I am happy too. You rush into the new year with money
and honey and a broad smile on your face. Your emotions
are bubbling over and you are in touch with them. You
have a philanthropic bent of mind and want to establish
empathetic relationships with others. You are healed
of past wounds as you have managed to confront the
unconscious areas of your psyche. There is new energy

and new healing. You emerge from it all like the sphinx. No Trojan horse can catch you off guard.

28 December: First Quarter in Aries

You are pushing ahead, fast and furious. There is a lot to be done. There could be marriages, engagements, even divorces and childbirth. There is enough on your plate to excite you, keep you occupied and motivated. Sometimes you may find it difficult to understand others and they may also wonder what is going on in your head. But despite being a bundle of contradictions, which we all are, you are filled with an innate stability and drive. You know where your bread is buttered and you go for it. You are in touch with reality. Ganesha blesses you.

Key Dates

January

2*–4, 7–13, 20–21, 25–26, 29–31.
Ganesha says, you will have the ambition and the luck to carry through any venture you take up. Your creativity will conquer everything. Even domestic problems will be solved. Home life will improve.

February

3*–10, 12–14, 17–18, 21–22, 26–27.
Work is important, and your desire to reach out to others, as well as express yourself fully, will be realized. If you are interested in pets, new projects, change of staff/job, this is the right time for it. Health precautions are a must.

March

2–9, 11*–12, 15–16, 19–21, 24–26, 29–31.

Both kisses and kicks, partnerships and separations, in short, both the good and the bad have to be dealt with now.

April

3–4, 7*–8, 11–17, 20–22, 25*–27, 30*.
April is a collage of loans, funds, romance, joint finance, journey, children and property. The pace will be hectic. So safeguard your health, and also avoid overdoing things.

May

1*–9, 13–14, 18–19, 23*–24, 28*–29.
Most important for decisions, pilgrimage, collaborations, finance and investment, foreign connections. Import-export, tours and trading will come into play in a recurrence of the theme of reaching out.

June

1–2, 5*–6, 9*–10, 14–15, 19*–28.
A turning point, bringing power, fulfilment, gains. Also, disturbances in the home, taking care of the health of elders, a time to be brave and forward looking. You'll have to deal with many things simultaneously.

July

2*–8, 11*–13, 16*–18, 21*–22, 26–27, 30*–31.
You start with delivering a wallop and knocking out the opposition. Gains and success are certain for you, says Ganesha!

August

3–4, 7–9, 12*–19, 22–23, 26–27, 30–31.

A topsy-turvy month. Income, expenses, work, medical care, journeys, buying and selling are some of the features. Finances are therefore important.

September

4*–5, 9*–10, 14*–15, 18*–19, 21–27.
Power gains, promotion, children, hobbies, confidence and victory, says Ganesha! A powerful, fulfilling birth month, bringing both achievements and satisfaction.

October

1*–3, 6*–13, 15–16, 19–21, 24–25, 28–30.
New deals, bargain hunting, wheeling and dealing, furniture, commissions, trading, festivals, food and celebrations. After 14 October, trips, ties, trading are the important Ts.

November

1*–8, 12*–13, 16*–17, 20*–21, 25*–26, 30*.
November is truly action time. Your home, your work and inner development all come together. You make personal and spiritual gains now, which also reflect on family life.

December

1*, 5–6, 9–10, 13–19, 22*–23, 27*–29.
Home, shop, office (therefore, property too), immigration, decoration, children, carnival, celebrations, ceremonies, Vaastu and house warmings are the salient features of the period between December 2014 and March 2015.

Libra

YEARLY FORECAST

Renowned poet Adil Jussawalla writes, 'Your universe was built to dance on a pin.' Later on he says:

> Learn balance with nothing to stand on.
> Though you've lost heart, lost ground,
> Go rootless, homeless, but balance.

Till 16 July 2014

Summary and Guidance

Ganesha says my devotee Bejan has unleashed the tiger, poet Adil Jussawalla, on you because Libra is essentially about balance. Note this well, Amitabh Bachchan and Ranbir Kapoor are Libras. I may go back to more than thirty years to cite others like Premnath, Raj Kapoor and certainly Krishna Kapoor, his wife. There are two distinct aspects to 2014. a) You will be in top form, at your brilliant best, pole-vaulting to power, pelf, popularity. The reason is Jupiter will be in your tenth angle of fame, fortune, fate. Who is wiser than destiny? b) The other feature is that Mars, the planet of war, energy, ambition, accidents, sudden decisions, will be in your sign from 1 January to 25 July. I know very well that you like balance and poise and calm. But the energy of Mars is restless and wild and very powerful. Mars is not happy in Libra therefore, and I hope I am wrong. Along with great power will come upheavals, separations, sorrow and sudden violence. I repeat. I am not God. I hope I go wrong; but as a Ganesha devotee, I must give you both sides of the coin. In simple language, extremes will be your lot in 2014.

17 July 2014 to 11 August 2015

Here we are on a totally different wicket as the cricket commentators like to say, and I am writing this today, 23 June 2013, the day of the final cricket match between England and India in the Champions Trophy. What a coincidence! Jupiter in your eleventh angle promises gains and gaiety, laughter and love, companionship and concord, and certainly favours group activities, meets, conferences, ties, interaction with crowds, huge chunks of humanity, as I love to call it. Be affable, be sociable, put on that mighty winning electric Libra smile and slay the world. Believe me, I know you are good at it. Go for the sweet kill! Ha ha! I am quoting writer and historian Belloc: 'In this world there is nothing worth the winning, except the love and laughter of friends.' This saying is meant very specially for you, Librans. In the end, let me tell you very politely but rather firmly, please do not hesitate to speak your mind. You may do it in Libra fashion, namely sweet, soothing and soft, but do it you must. You have to share your rare insights with one and all, even though it might mean a hurt or two, a scratch or two. Yes, dear Librans, it will be well worth your while. This Ganesha devotee and former professor of English is eighty-three. I am not a Libran, but my rising sign is Libra. Therefore, I do know how difficult it is for Librans to ram it down anybody's throat. Be diplomatic if you like, but be sure that the message gets home.

Main Trend

I have often said that Libra = beauty + utility. In 2014, it will be mighty apt. Art and commercialism will blend into a seamless whole. In other words, they will marry. Great for you. But wait, there is also a flip side to the coin. Do take care of your health and try not to overreach yourself financially. Have beautiful objects, wear wonderful clothes, live in style, be trendy and fashionable, speak with kings and queens, have a bit of fun on the side if you are interested (don't blame me for the consequences!), but try to keep your position, dignity and balance. It is here that you may have problems because of the behaviour of others. You all know it is difficult to control our own behaviour and almost impossible to manage those of others. That is the root of the problem. Sharp Librans should have no difficulty in getting this into their head.

Journey and Communication

Mars in your sign till 25 July makes you restless, impulsive and raring to go. Journeys, maybe with a stopover, are predicted in December, February, April and June. Also from 2 to 28 September, Mercury, the planet of journey and communication, will be in your own sign according to Western astrology. Go for it, then. December is also journey time. I am sure I have given you quite a few openings.

Health

Neptune, the planet of both illusion and inspiration, is in your sign of health. Maybe, even you will not know the real cause and problem of your health, your mood swings, your sudden ups and downs. During September and March through May, you should be careful about your health. But worrying will not help. I suggest that you keep your cool. The rest will follow. Back, throat, spine and feet could be the culprits.

Love/Marriage

Libra is all about love and relationships. Single bliss, loneliness, is not for you, at least not for most of you (there may always be exceptions). Venus is in your sign from 13 September to 23 October and readies you for a bout of romance and wedlock. At eighty-three, I know that marriage is a serious but funny business. As I have said, 'In love and in cricket, even the great Daruwalla can lose his wicket.' The other months are December, June and February. April will be something of a halfway house between joy and disturbances. It is your choice.

Property

Saturn in your second angle favours property, provided you do not overreach yourself and read the small print in the contract. Yes, there is a chance of deception. January, July and, to some extent, September seem to be your best bet.

Job/Business/Loans/Funds/Investments

As said at the very beginning, you will be at your brilliant best, pole-vaulting to power. Now you know it is excellent. The months for it are July, December, January and February. April could be a mixed blessing, both good and bad.

Children/Entertainment

Librans are fun and can have fun like Leos and Sagittarians. Mars in your own sign definitely propels you towards children and entertainment, fun and side shows. The months for it should be October, June, December. In July, you combine work and pleasure. Good for you.

Trips and Ties

Trips and ties go well with journey and communication, as said earlier. For ties, very specially, October, February, April, June, December should be outstanding. As a rule, February and June are lucky for the Librans. I have actually asked many Libras about it. I have said what I have known.

Publicity/Projects/Performance

Aries, Cancer, Libra and Capricorn are the four cardinal signs of the zodiac. These four signs specialize in publicity, projects and performance. Please do not misunderstand me—this is only a reading based on the solar signs. Any person from any other sign can be great and achieve all that he or she desires. All the twelve signs have a right to greatness and glory. I have just mentioned what I have seen and known with my limited knowledge. I could be wrong. The months for power, name and fame will be January, July, June, February and December. Please read what I have said at the very beginning of the annual forecast. It will boost your confidence.

Happiness Quota

Thanks to Jupiter and Neptune, you will be happy most of the time. But Mars and, to a certain extent, Uranus, the planet of rebellion and revolution, will rattle you, shake you up a little. My advice is to keep your cool, pray to God; and if you believe in astrology, I am suggesting the mantra of Venus, which is your main planet. The mantra for Venus is, 'Om dhram dhreem dhroom sa sukraya namah'. Venus suggests Devi. But I always say that you are free to do whatever you like and believe in. All roads lead to the supreme power. This is my simple, sincere message. I give you 82 per cent.

Monthly Round-up

Take January: for house, home, family; February: romance, children, creativity; March: work and health improvement measures; April: marriage, relationships, contacts, trips, ties and opposition; May: loans, funds, health, taxes, accidents, legal matters; June: publicity, publishing, fame, religious rites, matters to do with parents and in-laws; July: parents, in-laws, work, rewards, family, the effort you put in; August: contacts and group activities, gains and joy; September: expenses, health, but also God's grace and success in ventures and fine connections, collaborations; October: confidence, success, charm; November: finances, family, food, fortune—the four Fs; December: communication and contacts at all levels.

Summary

'Excelo' in Latin superbly sums up 2014 for you. It means to surpass, to be the very best, to be eminent, to be all that you ever wanted to be! Ganesha agrees.

Outer Planets

URANUS: Uranus, I am afraid, will cause disputes, legal action, disturbances and perhaps separation if your personal horoscope indicates it. This is a reading based only on your zodiac sign. My advice is to take it easy. Be balanced. 'Be calm of mind, all passions spent.'

NEPTUNE: Neptune gives you intuition, inspiration, bright ideas and great success. Matters related to pets, servants and colleagues will be of extreme importance. Mood swings are possible. At times, you may not know what happens to you health-wise. Consult a good doctor, therapist or an ayurvedic expert/healer. Yes, there is a chance of misplacing important documents and deeds and even theft and robbery. A chance, please remember, is not a certainty. It is only a possibility. Don't get worked up over it. Easy does it.

PLUTO: Pluto helps you in house, home, office, parents, in-laws and all property matters. But the health of elders is certainly suspect. Medical care for them and also for you; frequent check-ups are a must. Do not neglect it please.

Month by Month

January

You begin the year sorting out several issues in your domestic and professional spheres. There could be make-or-break situations. It will be a good idea to take care of your health. The work arena is steaming hot. Avoid altercations, temper tantrums, scuffles or confrontations of any kind. By mid-month, the domestic scene will be top priority. There are medical emergencies. You are at a crossroads. The month-end sees escapist indulgences. You tend to go overboard. Ganesha helps you.

February

There could be new job openings and several options to make big money. You realize that the tide is changing and feel happy. There are many expenses and some travel too. There are many fears lurking in your subconscious. It may be a good time to check out new vistas in spirituality. By the month-end, you network and meet new people. There are tricky family situations. Remove dead wood and make way for the new. Ganesha is with you.

March

You look at yoga and meditation, yantra, tantra and mantra. You are looking to reinvent yourself. Your mind is on a razor's edge. There is conflicting interests. You have mood swings. There is wealth and diversity in your emotions. By mid-month, there is travel and new collaborative efforts. There is success in all your ventures. If you are in showbiz, there are awards and rewards, accolades and applause. You are moving ahead with great speed and burning the tarmac. The new moon is in Aries and this is a propitious time to sign new deals. There is love and passion. Ganesha wishes you well.

April

There are emotional storms. Children need attention, there are illnesses in the family, love life goes kaput, and you are at your wits' end. By mid-month, there is love and bonding, good health and many indulgences. There is overseas travel and accolades. You want a new course in life. You look for deeper meaning, something more profound that you can hold on to. You help the less fortunate and take to spiritual reading. As the month ends, there is a semblance of stability and direction. You are energized, excited and enthused. There is money and honey, hard work and success, love and lust, bonding and break-ups, hope and despair. Ganesha watches over you.

May

Your energies are running high. This is a powerful period and you are filled with ideas and expansion plans. There are expenses, love, lust, passion, purchases, increased prestige, status, triumphs, awards, rewards, accolades and applause. There is expansion, expense, ambition, stamina and determination in your endeavours. By the month-end, you are able to relax and enjoy yourself with friends and loved ones. You embark on new collaborations, higher education, research and new discoveries. There are a zillion thoughts flitting through your mind. Ganesha blesses you.

June

You could get excessively jealous and possessive and all interactions are likely to be intense. Expenses skyrocket and you keep dilly-dallying on important decisions. There is fire in your belly and you are zooming away on jet fuel. This is also a time of confidence and benevolence. By the month-end, you could take up yoga and meditation and there could be increased religious or spiritual self-awareness. Ganesha is with you.

July

A lot of time and money is likely to be spent in decorating and making your personal space, both at work and home, more attractive. You become indulgent and there could be parties and fun times. By mid-month, there is balance in your affairs. There is success at work and you win awards. There is powerful energy and you are filled with passion. There could be travel and new contracts. The end of the month end sees you live and love larger than life. There is money and honey, rewards and awards, and appreciation and accolades. Ganesha is happy for you.

August

There could also be problems in communicating with others. There could be misunderstandings. There is love and bonding and many challenges on the home front. Your relationships are in a tizzy, thanks to mutual mistrust. There are arguments and altercations. This is a time for introspection. By mid-month, there is stability in your affairs. Your individuality stands out. Family life is smooth and children bring joy. This period could signal the birth pangs of a powerful growth cycle. Ganesha is with you.

September

Mercury makes its presence felt from 2 to 28 September. This is a great period. Take risks, expand your business and personal interests and strike hard when the iron is hot. This is your time in the sun. Your emotions are at a peak and your sensitivities are at a high. There is travel, romance, rewarding work, love and bonding. You are in a powerfully creative phase and artists, writers, actors and others in the media have a field day. You win kudos and are the toast of your industry. This is a great time for creative folk. While there are rewards on the material plane, you also check out spiritual options. You want to grow at every level. Ganesha is delighted.

October

Venus is in Libra from 30 September to 23 October, which is another propitious period. The latter half of the year is filled with good tidings. Make the most of this period. You have the Midas touch. There is love, longing, bonding, passion, new ventures, quality purchases and a home away from home. There is exotic travel, and a new love that is significant enters your life. There is money and honey and most importantly, you have the maturity and balance to use it well. By mid-month, you spend time with family and friends renewing old ties. I see achievement and progress, passion and infidelity. Ganesha watches over you.

November

This could be a great time for parliamentarians and policymakers debating issues. You are able to defend your position successfully. You emerge as a person to reckon with and are in line for prestigious awards. There is love, passion, lust, expenses, romance and good times. You make quality investments which will stand you in good stead in the days to come. By mid-month, there is love in the air and a new person enters your life. There are fun times with get-togethers and parties. There is travel, new associations, gaiety, joy and festivities. Ganesha is thrilled.

December

You are bubbling with creative energy and can come up with masterpieces, thanks to all the contradictions, fears and insecurities playing havoc with your core. This is a powerfully creative phase. By mid-month, you are able to accomplish all kinds of tasks. Your energy is high, your health is good and you perform at your peak. You assert yourself and mow down the opposition. You are graceful and charming. You show a resolve of steel. End of the month brings in love and bonding. There are family issues to settle, property matters to look into. You have great plans for the future. Ganesha blesses you.

Months at a Glance

January

House, home, family.

February

Romance, children, creativity.

March

Work and health improvement measures.

April

Marriage, relationships, contacts, trips, ties and opposition.

May

Loans, funds, health, taxes, accidents, legal matters.

June

Publicity, publishing, fame, religious rites, matters to do with parents and in-laws.

July

Parents, in-laws, work, rewards, family.

August

Contacts and group activities, gains and joy.

September

Expenses, health and God's grace and success in ventures and fine connections, collaborations.

October

Confidence, success, charm.

November

Finances, family, food, fortune—the four Fs.

December

Communication and contacts at all levels.

Weekly Review (By the phases of the moon)

1 January: New Moon in Capricorn

Mars has been in your sign from 8 December last year. Mars is the commander-in-chief of the army, the warrior. Courage, ferocity, power and strength go with Mars. In short, Mars becomes a very positive influence if you can control your feelings and temper. Mars is a fighter. Mars will be in Libra from 1 January to 25 July. This is an unusually long time for Mars to be in one sign. Note it well. Your Ganesha devotee feels that Libra is the sign of balance and Mars is intense, extreme and very forceful. What will be the result? The result will be that the balance will be upset. What does it mean in practical terms? Trouble, disturbances and even upheavals in relationships—be it marriage, partnership, friendship or social relationships. Luckily, the horoscope has other planets too, and they too play a part in your relationships and your destiny. Therefore, do not be afraid. Astrology is only a part of life. Do your best. Take life as it comes. My advice is to live and let live. The choice is yours. You begin the year sorting out several issues in your domestic and professional spheres. There are many pressing emotional issues. There could be make-or-break situations. You may feel distraught. It will be a good idea to take care of your health. You are working now with game-changing situations. Ganesha wishes you luck.

8 January: First Quarter in Aries

There is fire in your belly and a lot on your plate. The work arena is steaming hot with many pulls and counter-pulls. You are charged up. There is fire and brimstone in all your dealings, which could work in your favour. There are dark clouds hovering, and your inherent love for peace gets waylaid. Avoid altercations, temper flare-ups, scuffles or confrontations of any kind. There are ego issues riding high and it will be good to take time off and let off some steam. Ganesha is with you and that helps.

16 January: Full Moon in Cancer

The domestic scene has top priority now. There are problems at home. Children, maybe even grandchildren, need your attention. There are medical emergencies. There could be issues with the spouse or partner. The unattached may go through a rough patch with the person they are courting. There are unnecessary expenses too, and bouts of depression, and you feel the whole world has conspired against you. There are many challenges, and, like Edmund Hillary, you look to scale the many Everests of your life. For that matter, you could be even the lesser-known Sherpa Nawang Gombu, who has scaled Everest innumerable times, or even like Bachendri Pal, the famous Indian female mountaineer. Ganesha blesses you.

24 January: Last Quarter in Scorpio

There is powerful intensity pushing you ahead. Your love life is in a quandary. You are at a crossroads. There are many options, but they are all life-changing and it is difficult to decide. Those in the media and in showbiz do exceedingly well. There are parties, get-togethers and happy times too, including a new love on the horizon. You may just decide to sow your oats without worrying about the consequences. I have often stated this and I repeat, Librans are ruled by Venus and love the good life. The bubbly flows like the Ganga or a Himalayan spring. Ganesha is with you.

30 January: New Moon in Aquarius

The question of finance crops up. If there is a divorce or marital disagreement, you stand to lose a lot. Learn to go with the flow. There is nothing you can do about the situation. Go with the punches. Muhammad Ali was battered by Joe Frazier for the world heavyweight title but he finally won the bout. You will scrape through, but there could be bruises. Relationships of all kinds could be tricky. I have done thousands of charts and I know that Librans hate being alone. As a result, they end up spending time with people they shouldn't be with. There could also be escapist indulgences. You tend to go overboard and regret it all later. Some of you may need psychiatric help. Ask Ganesha for guidance.

6 February: First Quarter in Taurus

There is more stability now and you come to grips with the situation. You look at work with more meaning and get down to the hard slog. There could be new job openings and several options to make big money. You realize that the tide is changing and feel happy. Use free will to your advantage. There are many expenses and some travel too, and you indulge in comfort shopping. You also look at a home away from home. Ganesha blesses you.

14 February: Full Moon in Leo

Ego issues run high. You may lose your temper over trifles and might spend like there is no tomorrow. You may even be looking at unscrupulous options. You will have to decide how much is enough and where to draw the line. There are many fears lurking in your subconscious. The fear of losing your good looks and being alone and left to fend for yourself is the deepest insecurity that plagues you. Just remember that the body disintegrates with time. Learn to handle the demons nestling like unwanted guests in your soul. It may be a good time to check out new vistas in spirituality. If you don't change tack, life may force you to. Ganesha walks the tightrope with you.

22 February: Last Quarter in Sagittarius

This is a period when you network and meet new people in a rush. There are many new experiences. There could also be tricky family situations. You suddenly realize that even those you shower your love on are not reliable when it comes to the crunch. Or have you been expecting too much? No one can trifle with your life if you don't allow them to. Many problems you face are your own creation. Ganesha wishes the very best for you as always. Learn to take life by the horns and not get locked into dead-end situations all the time. Remove dead wood and make way for the new.

1 March: New Moon in Pisces

Your emotions are at fever pitch. You are bubbling over. You may spend time at ashrams, go on a pilgrimage and seek out gods and godmen for salvation. Ganesha is with you. 'If your eyes are blinded with your worries, you cannot see the beauty of the sunset,' said J. Krishnamurti. You take the cue and want to rid your mind of emotional debris which is like shrapnel nestling in your soul. You look towards yoga and meditation, yantra, tantra and mantra. You are looking to reinvent yourself. It is a step in the right direction.

8 March: First Quarter in Gemini

Your mind is on a razor's edge. There are conflicting interests playing havoc with your core. You are overtly sensitive and get hurt easily by stray remarks. Then you allow them to play in your mind like a broken record. You seek for love to escape it all. You look at all the social networking sites in the hope of finding someone who will understand you and provide support. You have mood swings and the depth of your emotions is unfathomable even to near and dear ones. There is wealth and diversity in your emotions. Those involved in the acting profession blaze a distinct trail. There is applause but it may not bring happiness. Ganesha smiles.

16 March: Full Moon in Virgo

I may add a bit about Librans here. Libra is considered to be one of the most desirable signs on the zodiac. Libras look for peace and harmony and are conflict resolvers. They seek beauty, luxury, and drama. Libra is a cardinal air sign and can be indecisive, flirtatious, self-indulgent, dependent and fickle. Libras are charming hosts and are the diplomats of the zodiac. In this phase, there is travel and new collaborative efforts. You have a problem deciding exactly what to do and this could be your undoing. There are many options and you keep changing your mind. Ask Ganesha to sort out your priorities. You are in the thick of experimentation, and make new discoveries along the way.

24 March: Last Quarter in Capricorn

There is power and stability. You are on firm ground. There is success in all your ventures. If you are in showbiz—and a lot of Librans are, considering their desire for the limelight, their good looks and penchant for drama—there are awards and rewards, accolades and applause. There is money and honey, my favourite phrase. You work hard and are ambitious and determined to make it all happen in your life. Ganesha promises success. There are happy domestic moments and money flows into your pockets. Ensure there is no hole in them!

30 March: New Moon in Aries

Libras are drawn to showbiz. Amitabh Bachchan, Rekha and a host of other legends from this zodiac sign have scorched the Indian screen. You also share your birth sign with Michael Douglas, Catherine Zeta-Jones, Kim Kardashian, Doris Lessing, Serena Williams, Martina Navratilova, John Lennon, Manmohan Singh, Mohandas Gandhi, Oscar Wilde, Groucho Marx, Alfred Nobel, Bruce Springsteen and several other celebrities. You could be self-obsessed and think that you are the maker's gift to the planet. You live with delusions of grandeur. At this point, you are moving ahead with great speed and burning the tarmac. The new moon is in Aries and this is a propitious time to sign new deals. Make the most of the waxing phase of the moon. Those in the media and in showbiz do exceedingly well. There is love and passion, including amorous passion. There are ego issues, and many expenses too, as you go on a spending spree. Ganesha is not worried.

7 April: First Quarter in Cancer

'You give but little when you give of your possessions. It is when you give of yourself that you truly give,' said Kahlil Gibran. There are emotional storms as you whiz past the dark tunnels of life. Children need attention, there are illnesses in the family, love life goes kaput, and you are at your wits' end. There are temper flare-ups as emotions run high and you look at life solely in abstractions. Don't make hasty decisions. Ganesha wants you to take a deep breath and slow down a bit. Do not retaliate impulsively.

15 April: Full Moon in Libra

The full moon is in your sign and you want to have fun. There is love and bonding, good health and many indulgences. You are emotional, picky, choosy and sensitive. You want to love everyone, and lose them all in the process. Commitment becomes an issue and the grass on the other side is always greener. There are expenses, many purchases and grand times. I must add here, like I always do, that I am not God. These are mere indications, inclinations, prods and nudges. I try my best, but my words are not writ in stone. Use your free will and steer your course. This is a good time to embark on a new project. There is overseas travel and accolades. Harvest the moment, says Ganesha.

22 April: Last Quarter in Aquarius

You are pushed to the wall and stare at multiple opportunities. You need to reinvent yourself and take a serious look at prayer, meditation, chants, pilgrimages, godmen, gods, yantra, tantra, mantra and salvation. You want a new course in life. You look for deeper meaning, something more profound that you can hold on to, that can permeate your core. The search is intense. You help the less fortunate and take to spiritual reading. You look for a balm for your tormented soul. Ganesha is with you.

29 April: New Moon in Taurus

There is a semblance of stability and direction. You have searched hard and found some answers. You are energized, excited and enthused. There is money and honey and you set a cracking pace in your dealings. There is hard work and success, love and lust, bonding and break-ups, and hope and despair. Ganesha watches over you as you climb one mountain after another and make your world a little better. In the end, all your efforts pay off.

7 May: First Quarter in Leo

'Courage is grace under pressure,' said Ernest Hemingway. Your energies are running high and there is a lot of pressure too. It depends on what you do with both situations. Will you show courage or will you just crack up? This is a powerful period and you are filled with ideas and expansion plans. There are expenses, love, lust, passion, purchases, increased prestige, status, triumphs, awards, rewards, accolades and applause. Your ego could get you into a spot of bother. There could also be medical emergencies and trysts with the law. Ganesha is with you, though, and that is a big help. Be discreet and wise with your choices.

14 May: Full Moon in Scorpio

'Be like a flower and turn your face to the sun,' said Kahlil Gibran. You will have to do just that now as a new intensity takes over your life. This phase is as hot as it gets and I am not talking about the weather. There is expansion, expense, ambition, stamina and determination in all your endeavours. There will also be altercations at work, mood swings and temper tantrums. Librans who are older and fall in the senior citizens category will have to take health precautions. Children will give joy and there will be family gatherings, festivities and a lot of bonding. Ganesha wishes you well.

21 May: Last Quarter in Pisces

The flow is easy now and you are able to relax and enjoy yourself with friends and loved ones. You will spend time in groups and express your affection. Your need is to feel wanted, and so you seek out like-minded people for fun times. You are confident and make a favourable impression on everybody. You could even be the life of the party. You strive for greater balance and embark on new collaborations, higher education, research and new discoveries. You have been imprisoned in routine, and now you want to free-fall into experimentation. Ganesha is with you. Those in creative fields do well.

28 May: New Moon in Gemini

There are issues with others built on misplaced ego drives. There are arguments and altercations and you get into a rage and a sulk. But in the process you also get to know yourself. If you are able to take the cue and prevent repetitive behaviour, all this will have helped. There could be loss of some sort. People may leave you in the lurch or an old love may disappear. There could be depression and some of you may need psychiatric help. There are a zillion thoughts flowing through your mind and you have no idea what to do or where to start. Ganesha blesses you.

5 June: First Quarter in Virgo

Personal relationships are in focus now. There will be emotional confrontations with your partner, spouse or loved ones. You are frothing with emotions and might be difficult to handle. If you have hidden your emotions over the years, they may come to a boil now. You desperately need the security of feeling loved and wanted and you also go out of your way to reciprocate feelings. You could also get excessively jealous and possessive, and all interactions, regardless of gender, are likely to be intense. You look hard for new directions, new vistas, new doors and windows to open and save you, but you have been in a comfort zone for so long that it is almost impossible to change tack. Expenses skyrocket and you keep dilly-dallying on important decisions. Ganesha watches over you.

13 June: Full Moon in Sagittarius

There is fire in your belly and you are zooming away on jet fuel. This is a positive influence and you are filled with benevolence towards others. You contemplate the loftier aspects of life and skip everyday murmurings. You are emotionally stable and are filled with optimism and positive energy. There could be ego issues to handle, though, as you get a bit self-righteous and arrogant. You are gifted by nature and so feel superior to others. This expresses itself in your actions and words. You will not tolerate dullards and ignoramuses, and tell them off in no uncertain terms. There is also fun and bonhomie, associations, meetings and collaborations. I can say for certain that astrology is not a definitive science, so these are mere indications. Astrology never compels. Just leave it to Ganesha.

19 June: Last Quarter in Pisces

Emotions run high and their is a lot on your plate. But this is also a time of confidence and benevolence. You are secure in yourself and believe that you will succeed, no matter what the obstacles. You are checking out new vistas and there are many curves in the direction your life is taking. Career and home life are good and there are opportunities for spiritual advancement. There are rewards and awards and you are appreciated. This means a lot to you as, subconsciously, you are looking for appreciation. Some may even think of returning to their country if they have been working overseas. Ganesha is with you. That is a given.

27 June: New Moon in Cancer

You grow in wisdom and maturity. You have been through it all and it has been a learning experience. Students do well. Many of you will be deciding on higher studies in foreign universities. Senior citizens may also take up various study courses, not only to keep themselves occupied, but also to learn more. You also find the time to get in touch with your inner feelings. There could be a confrontation with your inner self. You look back at old hurts and how the past has affected the present. There is a lot of sifting and prioritizing. You could take up yoga and meditation and there could be increased religious or spiritual self-awareness. There are many domestic compulsions too, and even additions to the family. Ganesha blesses you.

5 July: First Quarter in Libra

The first quarter is in your sign and this is a good time for creative activity. You love beauty and all the goodies money can buy. You want luxuries, not just comforts. You might spend a lot of time and money on decorating and making your personal space, both at work and home, more attractive. You are filled with love and could well be in the throes of amorous pursuits. You are congenial too, and others enjoy your company. You are indulgent and there could be parties and fun times when you go overboard. Youngsters most certainly will. Ganesha watches over you.

12 July: Full Moon in Capricorn

This is a period when there is more balance in your affairs. You work with caution and are deliberate in your words and actions. You try your best not to focus on the negatives of people and concentrate on their positive traits instead. There is success at work and you win awards. You are capable of detailed planning and of running things over with a fine-toothed comb, leaving nothing to chance. Success is yours for the asking. There are meetings with old and new acquaintances and you spread cheer and bonhomie. Ganesha is pleased. The maudlin moments are few and far apart.

19 July: Last Quarter in Aries

There is a lot of energy and you are filled with passion. If you don't have one already, you look hard for a partner. There is good cheer all around, but if there is unexpressed or repressed sexuality in your relationship, the fuse may just blow up. You may also be in the mood to sow your oats and not be very discriminating in your affections. On the work front, you continue to make progress. There could be travel and new contracts. With some hard work, discipline and perseverance, your success can touch new heights. You realize that some new facet of you emerges every single day. You are a work in progress, forever moving in a new direction. Ganesha watches over you with paternal concern.

26 July: New Moon in Leo

You live and love larger than life. You make fancy purchases and could move into a bigger home or have an exotic holiday. You are feeling happy, balanced and optimistic. There is great success in all kinds of contractual negotiations, conferences and discussions. Since you court success so easily, there are ego issues and aggressive behaviour. Slow down a bit and accommodate everyone if you want to be a team player. Solo artists are, anyway, an island unto themselves. There is money and honey, rewards and awards, and appreciation and accolades. Librans love the good life. No harm in that, says Ganesha. You live once. So why not live it up?

4 August: First Quarter in Scorpio

There is intensity in all your dealings. You are not able to focus though you work hard. Somehow, you find it hard to be disciplined. Editors, and those in the business of looking for errors or sharpening or polishing what is with them, may have to take another look at their work after a few weeks to avoid mistakes which can creep in. There could also be problems in communicating with others. There could be misunderstandings. There is love and bonding and many challenges on the home front. But do not worry, says Ganesha. No problem can run you over. Of course, you continue to be seized by passion in a vice-like grip!

10 August: Full Moon in Aquarius

'I am not upset that you lied to me. I am upset that from now on I can't believe you,' said Frederich Nietzsche. Your relationships are in a tizzy thanks to mutual mistrust. There are arguments and altercations. Young couples may even be on the verge of breaking up. Those in long-term relationships also need to look inwards. There is a lot of cementing to do on the cracks. Family life runs into trouble and there could be court cases and expensive settlements. You may have been playing the field and it is found out. Your life is shrouded by a deep fog right now. This is a time for introspection and not for depression and maudlin thoughts. Get deep into the inner recesses of your life and ferret out the dark secrets. Use this period to get to know your real self, possibly your shadow side or blind spot. Ganesha watches over you.

17 August: Last Quarter in Taurus

There is stability and headway in your affairs. This is an interesting period. You plough a lovely furrow and also manage to be a good team player. Your individuality stands out, but in a complementary way. You still manage to blend in easily with the team. You approach your goals methodically and are diligent in your approach. You are rewarded with success. Family life is smooth and children bring joy. You are busy preparing a foundation for the future, and slog away. You feel insecure without a nest egg and go all out to make one. Ganesha blesses you.

25 August: New Moon in Virgo

Osho said, 'It is one of the fundamental laws of life that compassion cannot be defeated by hostility. Compassion simply changes the hostile person. Just start looking into people's eyes with grace.' While there is stability and you surge ahead, it will also be a good idea to let go of old hurts that weigh you down. You cannot do anything about the past. At best, you can learn from it and avoid repeating errors. Make new ones, maybe. But moping about the past never helped anyone. Also, no one has the perfect cards. We have to make do with what has fallen into our plate. No person is truly happy. Something or the other is always lacking. That is what makes life so exciting. Even identical twins have different personalities and temperaments. This period could signal the birth pangs of a powerful growth cycle. When Ganesha is with you, why worry?

2 September: First Quarter in Sagittarius

Mercury makes its presence felt from 2 to 28 September. Mercury, the mighty, all-powerful planet, is in your sign now. It favours travels, meetings, conferences, interviews, navel, trips, more brain power, news, views, contacts, communication, correspondence and contracts. Mercury has a special connection with the circuits of the brain. Chess, crossword and other such games belong to Mercury. Also, short-distance runners and spin bowlers are controlled by Mercury. Mercury, in short, is the ambassador and salesman of the zodiac and gives an impetus to all the things it symbolizes in the sun sign where it is located. You are in a lucky phase for close to four weeks. Make the most of it. 'There is a tide in the affairs of man, when taken at the flood it leads to fortune,' said the Bard. Ensure that you do just that. Take risks, expand your business and personal interests, and strike hard when the iron is hot. This is your time in the sun. There is growth and success. Ganesha is thrilled.

9 September: Full Moon in Pisces

'This turning towards what you deeply love, saves you,' said Rumi. Those in love may well take it to the next level. Your emotions are at a peak and your sensitivities are at a high. Trifles may get you worked up. There is travel, romance, rewarding work, love and bonding. You are in a powerfully creative phase and artists, writers, actors and others in the media have a field day. You win kudos, and are the toast of your industry. Ganesha smiles. You manage to take unimaginable risks but manage to carry them off without careening off the tarmac. You can do no wrong in the phase you are in.

16 September: Last Quarter in Gemini

This is a great time for creative folk. You display the awesome hitting ability of Chris Gayle, the magical moods of Maradona, the pace of Usain Bolt, the dancing feet of Nureyev, the vision of Stephen Hawking, the genius of Bill Gates, the passion of Rasputin, the stamina of Yifter the Shifter, the erudition of Rabindranath Tagore and the dazzle of Marilyn Monroe. Mercury propels you to great heights. There are no full stops as you plug away. New windows open and there is magic and miracles. You shine like the North Star on a dark night. Ganesha chuckles in delight.

24 September: New Moon in Libra

The new moon is in your sign and this is a propitious period. Use the energies in this waxing phase well. While there are rewards on the material plane, you also check out spiritual options. You want to grow at every level and iron out the deficiencies in your personality. You look at holistic change. There is love, passion, bonding, longing and its attendant complications, but you can't have it all, can you? Ganesha says no.

1 October: First Quarter in Capricorn

Venus is in Libra from 30 September to 23 October, which is another propitious period. Venus is another important planet and is of great significance. This is an important phase. As often discussed, Venus is the planet for love, romance, sex, beauty and the good life. This is the planet of attraction, love, wealth, knowledge and prosperity. The compatibility of partners and also the type of life the individual will lead are also judged from the placement of Venus in the horoscope. As a planet, Venus is considered to be beneficial, feminine and gentle. Venus symbolizes the force of attraction in the universe. In human beings, this attractive force manifests as love and beauty. When Venus is well placed in the chart, you get love, art, beauty and all the goodies of life that make life worth living. Venus rules Libra and Taurus though its role in every sign is important. Like other planets, it also has its transits. In Libra, Venus is aesthetic and cultured. In Taurus, it is more earthy, materialistic and sensual. Venus rules the venous system, kidneys, urinary tract, throat and larynx, and is responsible for good looks. In short, Venus in Western astrology stands for comforts, arts, wealth, relationships, sex, decorations, luxuries and wealth. The latter half of the year is filled with good tidings. Make the most of this period. You have the Midas touch. There is love, longing, bonding, passion, new ventures, quality purchases and a home away from home. There is exotic travel, and a new love enters your life that is significant. This is also your birth period and I suggest that you use the energies well. The omens are good for success. Ganesha is happy.

8 October: Full Moon in Aries

The good times continue unabated. You do well at work and the domestic scene is much more settled when compared to the early months of the year. You have changed a lot as a person, and there are new realizations as you become more attracted to, and involved with, mystical philosophies and metaphysics. There is money and honey and, most importantly, you have the maturity and balance to use your riches well. You are in full throttle and live life to the fullest. You may go sky-diving, bungee-jumping and check out other adventure sports. You want to do it all in a rush. Go for it, says Ganesha.

15 October: Last Quarter in Cancer

You spend time with family and friends renewing old ties. There are alumni meetings and parties where you let your hair down. There are happy days and new energy, and you are able to put your energy to full use. You are networking across the globe and your enthusiasm for life oozes like a river in spate. There is clarity and single-mindedness of purpose. You move hard and fast like a rocket seeking the moon. Ganesha is happy for you.

23 October: New Moon in Scorpio

The intensity continues. A lot of time is spent with the family. 'I believe a leaf of grass is no less than the journey-work of the stars,' said Walt Whitman, the poet. The small things matter. Get them right and the larger picture will become perfect. That is what you do now. There are domestic issues that have piled up and you need to address them as soon as possible before they get out of control. There are maudlin moments and there is a tinge of sadness when you think of what you may have lost in the past. It is dead wood and nothing can be done, says Ganesha. I agree. Ask me, I have seen a lot of life. Move on. That is the only way.

31 October: First Quarter in Aquarius

'Our chief want in life is somebody who shall make us do what we can,' said Ralph Waldo Emerson, the writer. You travel down memory lane and remember all those who impacted you one way or the other. Thoughts crowd you. Remember, the mind is a restless monkey. It has to be tamed. We have over forty thousand thoughts assailing us every day, wreaking havoc. Control your monkey mind or become its slave. You have to make many important decisions which could be game-changing. There is achievement and progress, but at some cost. There is passion and infidelity. Watch where you sow your oats, says Ganesha.

6 November: Full Moon in Taurus

There are stable energies working in your favour. You present your case with enthusiasm, energy and vigour, and are able to floor the opposition. This could be a great time for parliamentarians and policymakers debating issues. You are able to defend your position successfully. You are not spoiling for a fight but just taking a stand for something you believe in. Many opportunities fall into your lap and you are able to make the most of them, thanks to confidence in your ideas and beliefs. You emerge as a person to reckon with and are in line for prestigious awards. Ganesha blesses you as you consolidate your position as a person of knowledge, skill, power and authority.

14 November: Last Quarter in Leo

The good times continue. You make money and honey. There is love, passion, lust, expenses, romance and good times. You are in a congenial and expansive mood and have a great time with peers, friends, neighbours, relatives and business associates. You are in communication mode and ooze out energy. There is fire in the belly as you court success. This is a time for consolidation despite the big spending and purchases. You make quality investments which will stand you in good stead in the days to come. Ganesha is pleased.

22 November: New Moon in Sagittarius

There is a free flow of thoughts. Writers and creative people mint the moment. You network furiously and your presentations get you applause. There is love in the air and a new person enters your life. Youngsters are in the throes of passion. There are ego drives too, and temper tantrums. But you are able to swing things your way. Watch your weight. There could be health concerns too, as you oscillate from one sweet tooth to another. You are in an indulgent mood and cannot make up your mind about the course of action to take. Ganesha is with you.

29 November: First Quarter in Pisces

You yearn for love and romance. Powerful forces are pushing you. Those in a committed relationship reach heights of ecstasy. There are fun times too, with get-togethers and parties. This elevates your mood and so this is a great time for artistic activities. 'That sorrow which is the harbinger of joy is preferable to the joy which is followed by sorrow,' said Saadi, the poet. You have been through the grind, and have came through it, a better and stronger person. As the winter chill sets in, there is travel, new associations, gaiety, joy and festivities. You are the soul of the party. Ganesha is thrilled.

6 December: Full Moon in Gemini

Your mind is plagued by thoughts that create havoc in you. To others, you appear as an independent, self-reliant person who is willing to serve the larger cause. But deep inside nestle insecurities and you realize that you need material backing as well as moral support from others. You realize that you could be as fragile as bone china. There is outer confidence, which helps as a mask. Others see clarity, deliberation and decisiveness in you, little realizing that you are like a duck in water, calm at the surface and struggling hard beneath the waterline. But you are bubbling with creative energy and can come up with masterpieces, thanks to all the contradictions, fears and insecurities playing havoc with your core. This is a powerfully creative phase. Ganesha watches over you.

14 December: Last Quarter in Virgo

There is more stability as you hit terra firma. It is a soft landing. You are now able to accomplish all kinds of tasks. Your energy is high, your health is good and you are at peak performance, like a well-oiled machine. You may give extreme adventure sport a closer look. There could be travel and fun times. You are assertive and are able to put your foot down when needed. This aggression helps you. As your favourite astrologer, I always wish you well. Like I always say, I could be wrong sometimes, just sometimes. The final call is left to the Almighty, whatever name you give Him. Ganesha walks with you.

22 December: New Moon in Capricorn

There is deliberation and caution in whatever you do. You are thorough, professional and attract success. You have broken free like the Brahmaputra in spate. You assert yourself and mow down the opposition. You are graceful and charming and are also able to state your case in no uncertain terms. You show a resolve of steel and no one can walk over you. You are not seething; you are just being strong. Away from work is fun time; you manage to work hard and party harder. You want to be surrounded by love, beauty and happy thoughts, and escape into the arms of romance. Ganesha smiles.

28 December: First Quarter in Aries

The year is ending well for you. There is love and bonding, and you ensure that you spend time with loved ones. There are family issues to settle, property matters to look into, and several other problems that raise their ugly heads. Children and grandchildren, if any, take up your time. You want to be with everyone everywhere, but that is physically impossible. You manage to resolve everything, and handle everything thrown your way comfortably. Ganesha is thrilled. You move into the new year with great plans and hopes for the future. You have taken hard decisions and you come up trumps.

Key Dates

January

1, 5–6, 9*–15, 18*- 19, 22*–24, 27–28*.
Ganesha says that it's a fine time for property matters, parents, in-laws, buying/selling, land, building and construction. You get domestic happiness as well as progress.

February

1*- 2, 6*–11, 15*–16, 19*–20, 23*–25, 28*–29.
Romance, marriage, children, speculation, entertainment, new projects, religious ceremonies, functions, the spheres of the arts and sports are all energized. All full-plate, and you relish it hugely.

March

1, 4*–10, 13*–14, 17–18, 22*–23, 27*–28.
Romance and finance, work and play, make March memorable. But you must learn to take care of your health and that of your dear ones. Financially, March to May is for loans and funds.

April

1*–9, (an important week) travel, neighbours, 13*–15, 18*–19, 23*–24, 28*–29.
Ganesha says that marriage and personal, professional and platonic partnerships, journeys, legal cases—all come together now. Different kinds of excitement await you.

May

2*–3, 6*–7, 11*–17, 20–22, 25*–27, 30–31.
Loans and funds, joint finance, insurance, inheritance,

investment vis-à-vis finances. Also, moving house or office. Once again, take care of yourself.

June

3*–4, 7*–13, 16*–18, 21*–23, 26*–27, 30*.

There are stars on half the dates simply because June will be most important—lucky for meeting people, contacting them, finishing pending work, starting new projects, realizing your dreams and aspirations. It is a month for breakthroughs.

July

1, 4 -5, 9–10, 14*–16, 19*–25, 28*–29.

Socializing, tremendous pressure of work, but home conditions will improve and make you happy. From 20 July, you have more energy, more vitality, and that reflects on all your activities. Look after your parents.

August

1*–7, 10*–11, 15*–16, 20*–21, 24–25, 28–29.

Friends will help you; your enthusiasm will be seductive and welcome. You will socialize and have a ball.

September

1–3, 6–8, 11*–17, 20–21, 24*–26, 29*–30.

Expenses, taking care of the sick and the weak, medical check-ups, journeys and spirituality are the highlights. A slight slowdown before your birth phase.

October

4*–5, 9*–14, 17*–18, 22*–23, 26*–27, 31*.

Ganesha says that you have both pleasure and profit. Once again, the home will have your attention. Progress at work too, so that the picture is rounded off, in your birth month.

November

1, 5*–11, 14*–15, 18–19, 22–24, 27–29.
Socializing and work come together now. Buying/selling, investing, wining and dining keep you busy, indeed! It's finances and fun, to sum up!

December

2*–8, 11*–12, 15*–16, 20*–21, 24*–26, 30*–31.
December will be specially important for trips and ties, communication and computers, contact and contracts. Reaching out to people, places and the new year, says Ganesha.

Scorpio

YEARLY FORECAST

Magic, mystery, life-death-regeneration, heaven and hell, serpent and eagle: yes that's what Scorpio is all about.

Till 16 July 2014
Summary and Guidance

Ganesha says you Scorpios are both spiritual and sexual. That is your real power. Use it wisely and well. You will have a chance to be among the great leaders of the world and help humanity. Jupiter will be in your ninth angle of spirituality, religion, past karma, journeys, pilgrimages, research, world view, inspiration, intuition, prophetic dreams. You will know the difference between reality and maya and you will live in both worlds. That is very great praise and well deserved. Remember, dear Scorpios, you will have the ability and the capacity to change your life and those of others.

Yes, I understand that you are a human being. You are proud, rigid, determined, obstinate and not easy to live with. You are a difficult person to be with. But that is the way you are made. Try to be more tolerant, more pleasing, more gentle and less assertive and cunning. Throw out revenge from your heart as you would throw out or sweep out dust and dirt from your own house. Sadness and darkness will also come to you because Saturn will be in your sign till roughly the end of 2014. If you believe in Hanuman you may chant the mantra 'Hum hanumate ramdootaye namah' twenty-one times. You are completely free to follow your own religion and do what you like. I keep an open mind. All I want is your happiness. My son Nastur is a Scorpio.

17 July 2014 to 11 August 2015

Peak performance, says Ganesha, will be the result of Jupiter in your tenth angle. Power, pelf, perks, prestige, promotion await you with open arms. The only thing that can bring you down is your own pride and I am sorry to say that most Scorpios, but not all, are proud. To be dignified is fine and necessary. To be proud is to prepare for a fall. I am eighty-three. I have seen the world. Nothing remains forever, dear readers. Nothing. Just act your part honestly, intelligently and sincerely.

Pious deeds, lotteries, windfall, leadership, eminence, apex of career/profession/fame/name are distinct possibilities. Your income could come from more than one source.

Let me pay you a mighty compliment! Prophets of doom, dismay and death and the end of the world go wrong because they do not know or do not care to acknowledge one great quality of human beings. That quality, simply put, is resourcefulness. This is the great lever or advantage we humans have over all others. At least, I believe it. To me not power, not consciousness but compassion is the greatest thing in the world. The Dalai Lama XIV has spoken about it. I bow my head to the Dalai Lama. Great humanity is true spirituality.

Main Trend

As said in the beginning, your two main characteristics are the serpent and the eagle. You are capable of great goodness and mighty evil. It is not your fault. It is the way you are made. Also, I admit that I may be right or wrong in my astrological analysis. Scorpio is one of the signs of the master or adept. On the other hand, Scorpio is also the sign of strategy and conspiracy. The two major examples are General Rommel of Germany and General Montgomery of the Allies. Cheiro, one of the world's greatest astrologers, was a Scorpio. I am sure you get the message loud and clear.

Journey and Communication

Jupiter in your ninth angle till 16 July 2014 certainly propels you forward in the direction of journey and communication. Be it home, office, shop or even a foreign land, you will communicate in style and élan. Therefore, success is your due and you will have it. February and perhaps April could be risky for it.

Health

Saturn in your first house does indicate a slight problem, maybe psychological or anxieties or even phobias. Scorpios are prone to it as per my observation. But thanks to a boisterous and powerful Jupiter, you are in no danger of losing your mind! Perhaps a little bit of caution in February, April through June, August and October should do the trick for you. In other words, worry but do not scurry. Eat Indian curry and be happy. Take it easy.

Love/Marriage

Here you are strong and stylish and suave (smooth). Neptune helps you in romance and ambience (ambience is necessary for romance!). Venus in your sign from 24 October to 16 November will help you to win a fair lady or a handsome man. The other months should be March, May (half and half), July and certainly September. Go for it then.

Property

The four fixed signs, Leo, Scorpio, Aquarius and Taurus, are great in property. Be it housing, shop, office and so on. Do not take undue risks and try to settle all disputes with a wide smile. It will pay to be amiable and good to people. If you can do so, property will come to you.

Job/Business/Loans/Funds/Investments

From 17 July 2014 to 11 August 2015, profession, business and career are highlighted. As I have said in the beginning, power, pelf, perks, prestige, promotion await you with open arms. I have always believed that power should be used wisely and well. The words 'wisely' and 'well' are very significant.

Children/Entertainment

Children and entertainment go naturally with love and marriage because both are many times a part of each other. Children will be brilliant, your creativity will be at white heat, hobbies and pastime and leisure pursuits give not only satisfaction but great delight. That's what life is all about.

Trips and Ties

Trips and ties fall under journey and communication but ties indicate relationships and therefore ties come under Venus. From 24 August to 16 November, Venus is in Scorpio and from 9 to 27 November Mercury, the indicator of travel and journeys, is in Scorpio, showing you the way the wind blows. January, July and September are also happy times for trips and ties.

Publicity, Projects, Performance

Publicity, projects and performance have a direct relationship with job, business, loans, funds and investments. If I combine both of these, practically the whole year is favourable. That's a very big plus point, a bonus, a huge leverage for you. Be bold but not a bully. That is my suggestion.

Happiness Quota

Saturn in your sign and Libra in your twelfth angle of loss, separation, expenses, hospitals, lonely spots, welfare centres, robbery, theft till 25 July could come in the way of your progress. But from 26 July to 13 September Mars will be in Scorpio and so you will recover lost ground. Taking all of it into active consideration, you get 81 per cent.

Monthly Round-up

Ganesha sums it up. The merry-go-round of the months reveals as follows. January: the three Cs: contacts, communication, computers; February: home, house, parents, in-laws, property, retirement for the elderly, foundations for new projects; March: entertainment, love, engagement, hobbies, sports, games of chance—in a word, creativity; April: health, employment, pets, subordinates, colleagues, debts and funds; May: marriage, legal issues, friends and enemies, trips and ties, collaborations, competition—it is a mixed bag; June: money, passion, joint finance, buying/selling/shopping, taxes, real estate, insurance, focusing on health, strain and drain (on the purse and perhaps on you physically); July: fame, publicity, spirituality, fulfilment, journey, education, future plans, relations; August: tough decisions, health of elders, parents, in-laws, work pressure issues of prestige and status are possible; September: friendship, the social whirl, romance, material gains, hopes, desires, ambition—happy days are here again; October: expenses, losses, contacts, love, secret deals, journeys, spirituality—October will be a paradox, a big contradiction; November: confidence, power, gains, happiness, right timing, the realization of wishes; December: finances, food, family, taxes, buying/selling/shopping, property, functions and meets. You will be a crowd-puller! That's great.

Summary

'Siegheil!' Hail, Victory! You will shout in typical German fashion, and remember Germany is a Scorpio country! Power, pelf, progress, publicity, the pinnacle of success will be yours! Ganesha also wants you to guard against ill health, unwise investments, relationship with partners. But the balance is very much in your favour. So go for it!

Outer Planets

URANUS: Uranus is the culprit, the danger in your health sector. It means sudden ups and downs, sudden mood changes and illness which may not have a complete explanation. It is commonly believed that Scorpios are hypochondriac, that is, neurotic and overanxious. But it is most certainly not true of all Scorpios.

NEPTUNE: Neptune helps to ignite your imagination and inspiration in all creative pursuits, say hobbies, films, music, dance, sculpture, painting and so on. Artists and scientists in research, specially if the research is connected to the sea and the ocean, will work wonders. Expect a discovery in a miraculous way between 17 July 2014 and 11 August 2015.

PLUTO: Pluto in your angle of journey, trips and ties certainly helps you to forge ahead. The Internet, the mobile, the iPod, iTouch were meant just for you. Push the envelope as the Americans say.

Month by Month

January

There is hard work. You slog like one possessed. Success cannot elude you. There is applause and rewards, money and honey, flattery and finance. There are new associations. You are reaching out to new frontiers of experience and being enriched by it. The month-end sees love, lust, hate, possessiveness, jealousy, oneupmanship, fights, strife, altercations, innuendos, many dark shades of the moon. Ganesha is with you.

February

There is money and honey as you make headway at work. This is a great time for those in finance, insurance, realty and banking sectors. There are new projects and new love. Your hands are full with work expansion and domestic chores. As the month ends, there is travel. You are networking furiously and meeting new people from all over the world. Ganesha is pleased.

March

This may be the period for the start of a new and significant relationship. You examine your life and decide to chop and churn. You need to get trimmer and so you get rid of all the driftwood. By mid-month you are scorching the tarmac like a Formula One driver. There is triumph over adversity. You are intellectually alive. There could be travel, conferences, applause and accolades. You are busy with loans, funds, joint finances, leasing and buying/selling. Trust in Ganesha.

April

There is new love and several domestic issues that you have to deal with. There could be illness in the family and you will be pushed to the wall. There are many opportunities staring at you and you are in a quandary. What should you do? Which direction should you take? You may have to take a close look at your health. But, despite this, you make considerable headway in life. This is a time for big bucks. There could be a windfall. You could receive an inheritance or even win a lottery. Ganesha is pleased.

May

You may rebel against restrictions and old patterns of behaviour. There is love, passion, raw lust, buying, selling, investments and stocks. You live large and wild. As the month ends you are busy with the three Cs—contacts, communication, correspondence. You spend time at home, with the spouse and kids, or with aged parents. Youngsters will rebel and have intense disagreements with their parents. The home will be on fire with arguments and counter-arguments. Ganesha watches over you.

June

There are inflated expectations, excessive and impractical idealism and a few disappointments. You are in a lucky phase but do not push your luck. New people and events enter your life as it pulsates like a volcano. You look for danger and excitement. You look for new ways to live, new spirituality, new religion, new ideology, new friends, a whole new 'you'. By the month-end you want to help people and share your good fortune. You are deeply emotional and may make wrong choices. Ganesha is with you.

July

This could be a good time to sign lucrative business deals. You may alienate others by being self-righteous or arrogant. The pace is frenetic and you are inundated by events. There is rapid work expansion. This is also a good time to explore your spiritual and inner needs. Mars is in your sign from 26 July to 13 September, quite a long period. Mars is like the volcano of vitality inside you. You could be unduly aggressive during this period.

There is love and passion, work and money, applause and accolades, friends and foes, gains and loss. Ganesha walks with you.

August

New frontiers open up at work and you are crowned with success. You go after everything that you want in the material world without caring about who or what is in your path. This is an extremely productive and growth-oriented period. There is friendship and love, messages, journeys, bonding, spirituality, tantra and mantra. By the month-end you spend beautiful moments with loved ones. There is a family outing and you build on existing relationships. You share joys on a higher consciousness. Ganesha blesses you.

September

There is entertainment, romance and sheer joie de vivre. In the phase you are in, you just zoom ahead without breaks or headlights! There are maudlin moments but they help refine you, humanize you. By mid-month you break free from all restrictions and obligations of the past. You look for ultimate freedom. Mercury makes its presence felt from 29 September to 9 October. You are on a roll. There is money, honey, love, success, applause, accolades, rewards, awards. You have the Midas touch. Take the high tide to fortune. Ganesha is happy.

October

While there is new meaning and direction in your life, there is also hard work and money. Your affairs run smoothly without much effort. Your plate is full. You learn to live in gratitude and thank existence for all its favours. Venus is in your sign from 24 October to 16 November. This is quite a long time and you are in luck. This is an important phase. There are luxury purchases, in all probability a new home. It is a time for the big Ps—position, pelf, perks and privileges. It is also time for awards, accolades and applause. This is also your birth period and the energies are multiplied. Ganesha blesses you.

November

Guard against arrogance, possessiveness, emotional flare-ups and dominance. These are your natural personality traits depending, of course, on the type of Scorpio you are. You are fast and furious. There is success. There are ego drives and you brook no opposition. Your appreciation of beauty, your interest in art, music or poetry is heightened. Mutual funds, shares, stocks, capital-raising and all other money matters come to the fore. There could be foreign travel, meetings, conferences, interviews, trips, more brain power, contacts, communication, correspondence, contracts, networking, matchmaking and every other conceivable human association. Success crowns you. Ganesha is delighted.

December

There is indulgence, pleasure, joy and satisfaction. You buy luxuries and go on a shopping spree. You are happy, content, cheerful and gregarious. You radiate warmth and emotion. You are amorous. The month-end brings in irritants at work and in relationships. There are domestic issues that need handling. You are fiery and have the resilience and stamina to work through it. Ganesha holds your hand.

Months at a Glance

January

The three Cs: contacts, communication, computers.

February

Home, house, parents, in-laws, property, retirement for the elderly, foundations for new projects.

March

Entertainment, love, engagement, hobbies, sports, games of chance; in a word, creativity.

April

Health, employment, pets, subordinates, colleagues, debts and funds.

May

Marriage, legal issues, friends and enemies, trips and ties, collaborations, competition; it is a mixed bag.

June

Money, passion, joint finance, buying/selling/shopping, taxes, real estate, insurance, focusing on health, and strain and drain (on the purse and perhaps on you physically).

July

Leapfrog to fame, publicity, spirituality, fulfilment, journey, education, future plans, relations.

August

Tough decisions, health of elders, parents, in-laws, work pressures absolutely tremendous, issues of prestige and status are possible.

September

Friendship, the social whirl, romance, material gains, hopes, desires, ambition; happy days are here again.

October

Expenses, losses, contacts, love, secret deals, journeys, spirituality. Therefore, October will be a paradox, a big contradiction.

November

Confidence, power, gains, happiness, right timing, the realization of wishes.

December

Finances, food, family, taxes, buying/selling/shopping, property, functions and meets. You will be a crowd-puller! That's great.

Weekly Review (By the phases of the moon)

1 January: New Moon in Capricorn

There have been many changes last year and this year sees you consolidate them. Those who have changed jobs will flourish and grow from strength to strength. There is hard work. Nothing in life comes free. There are some expenses too and many changes in your personal and professional life. But you brook no opposition and slog like one possessed. Success cannot elude you. There may be domestic issues to handle like the health of old parents, siblings, spouse or children. But you are able to take on the challenges head-on without batting an eyelid. This is a good time to sally forth and make miracles happen. Ganesha is pleased.

8 January: First Quarter in Aries

There is great movement as you fly high. There is applause and rewards, money and honey, flattery and finance. There is also travel on official work. There are new associations. You make investments and see that your bank account is swelling by the day. Nothing makes you happier than this. Along with all this, there is love, passion, fun and bonding with old friends. You are reaching out to new frontiers of experience and being enriched by it all. Ganesha blesses you and wishes you well.

16 January: Full Moon in Cancer

I must mention here that, like with all other signs, you are also in exalted company. You share your birth sign with Leonardo Dicaprio, Julia Roberts, Bill Gates, Martin Luther King, Wayne Rooney, Pablo Picasso, Hillary Clinton, Sylvia Plath, Ezra Pound, Charles Bronson, Marie Curie, Albert Camus, Indira Gandhi, Robert Kennedy, Voltaire, Leon Trotsky, and Diego Maradona, to name a few. Scorpions are achievers. They are also very intuitive and can be sensitive and emotional. There are normally different types of Scorpio personalities which we won't go into now as it will take a lot of space and is also out of the ambit of this reading. But it depends on the type of Scorpio you are and, of course, like I always insist, this is a general reading and is not individual-specific. In this phase, there are many emotions that are tearing into you. You are a water sign and so with the moon in Cancer, you will have to be steadfast and not succumb to the pulls and pressures of your heart. You spend time hosting friends and family and look to make a nest egg. There is love and intimacy, sensitivity and solace. Ganesha blesses you.

24 January: Last Quarter in Scorpio

'We're here for a reason. I believe a bit of the reason is to throw little torches out to lead people through the dark,' said Whoopi Goldberg. Your heart-strings are tugged and you help others. You are a kind soul and though you are hell-bent on worldly success, you also know that it is all too ephemeral. You make money for the security it provides. Beyond that, you have nothing to do with it. There is power and intensity in this period. You make your mark in the world but in moments of deep reflection you wonder if the hype, applause and accolades are really worth it. Ganesha knows that you are in a thoughtful phase. From this will emerge a new you like the lotus emerging from the muck. We all need different facets of our personality to emerge so that we understand ourselves better.

30 January: New Moon in Aquarius

Your moods are changing in a hurry. You seem trapped by them. There is love, lust, hate, possessiveness, jealousy, oneupmanship, fights, strife, altercations, innuendos, many dark shades of the moon. You are in turmoil. If self-employed, there could be trouble with the authorities. You may be spreading yourself too thin, obliging everyone and getting nothing done. Ego drives are also strong and you test your will against others. Do not take a confrontationist attitude. Everyone has a right to his or her voice. Ganesha is with you and that is a big help. Take a step back and wait for better times.

6 February: First Quarter in Taurus

There is a lot of stability now. There is money and honey, my favourite phrase. You are making headway at work and wearing down the opposition. This is a great time for those in finance, insurance, realty and banking sectors. It is also a good time for sportspeople. Scorpions have a lot going for them and in the game of life they manage to court success with ease. But, as we all know, you also have your blind spots. You could be your worst enemy. But in this phase you manage to cover a lot of ground as you go on a consolidation spree. You may even buy new property and make expensive purchases. It is a long way to go, says Ganesha.

14 February: Full Moon in Leo

You are on fire and there are massive ego drives. You earn and spend and yet save a lot. So the accountant in you is happy. There are new projects and new love. Your hands are full with work expansion and domestic chores. Children bring joy. Those of you who are ritualistic may go on a pilgrimage. This is a frenetic, action-packed time. In the mood you are in, you take every chance, work till the cows come home and yet survive to tell the tale! Ganesha is happy for you. So am I.

22 February: Last Quarter in Sagittarius

As the month ends, there is travel. You are networking furiously and meeting new people from all over the world. Social networking has changed the paradigm of life today. There are profitable associations and fun times with people you grew up with. You are at alumni association meetings and bonding with the old school tie. 'Happy days are here again,' said a beverage jingle long ago. It is very apt in your life now. You are hardworking and ethical. You have created your present. You deserve it. Ganesha is pleased. Enjoy!

1 March: New Moon in Pisces

You are in the midst of an extremely pleasant time. You give and receive affection. This may be the period for the start of a new and significant relationship. You smooth ruffled feathers and enjoy being with others and having a good time. You take a few days off and want to be self-indulgent. You indulge, eat, drink and make merry. You have slogged hard and believe that it is your duty to pamper yourself. Why not? You have a devil-may-care attitude. Ganesha smiles. I also like the mood you are in. Spread the cheer. Laugh and the world laughs with you, cry and you cry alone.

8 March: First Quarter in Gemini

You are like a beehive, buzzing away. Your mind is in a tizzy. You turn your attention to your career. You also examine your life and decide to chop and churn. You need to get trimmer and so you get rid of all the driftwood. You work with the future in mind. You go over your work routine with a comb and clear all the cobwebs. You want to clear it all, get rid of the crap, and make way for a new 'you'. Like I always say, these are mere generalizations. Astrology impels and never compels. Use free will to your advantage. Never be fatalistic. Ganesha is happy that you are taking positive steps.

16 March: Full Moon in Virgo

You are scorching the tarmac like a Formula One driver. You have cleaned up the litter and are trim and aerodynamic. You are running on the highest-grade turbo fuel. There is triumph over adversity. You make your presence felt in no uncertain terms. There is success and it can go to your head. Do not let ego drives take you by the scruff of the neck. It is a good idea to be flexible in your dealings. Ganesha is with you. What more can I say?

24 March: Last Quarter in Capricorn

In this period, you communicate well with others. You are intellectually alive. You step back and accommodate other voices. You want to broaden your vision and all interactions are fruitful and expansive. There could be travel, conferences, applause and accolades. There is optimism and a new perspective. You are like a pond with fresh water. There is equilibrium in your affairs and you find balance, which is most appealing. Ganesha smiles. Your famed discipline is back and you are where you belong—on the treadmill of life, slogging away happily to greater glory. You court success like a peacock courting a peahen in the mating season.

30 March: New Moon in Aries

There is energy and movement. You achieve a lot. You meet up with colleagues, friends and acquaintances and 'chill', to quote the generation next. You are decisive, impatient and possibly even belligerent. You want action and want to get things done in the fastest and best possible way. Try not to alienate others in the mood you are in. It always helps being a team player if you are working in an organization. Solo players working on their own have no such problem. In teams, there will be opposition, objection and obstacles to your style of functioning and you could be brought back to earth. You are busy with loans, funds, joint finances, leasing and buying/selling. There is money to be made and to be spent as you make stolid investments. Trust in Ganesha and sally forth.

7 April: First Quarter in Cancer

As the sun rises to scorch the subcontinent, you are set to scorch the tarmac of life. There is fire in your belly and whatever you lay your finger on now comes alive. You have the Midas touch. There is new love and you have several domestic issues to deal with. There could be illness in the family and you will be pushed to the wall. There will be medical emergencies; even trifles like a pet falling sick could derail your routine. You like being the boss and there could be promotion at work. Ganesha blesses you. You also look at yantra, tantra and mantra to better your life at a holistic level.

15 April: Full Moon in Libra

There are many opportunities staring at you and you are in a quandary. What should you do? Which direction should you take? It is all happening now and falling in your lap. There are maudlin moments too and you indulge in comfort eating and shopping. But work continues well and you are in store for rewards and awards. You may go in for a new car and other gizmos. Ganesha wishes you well. You are the toast of your peer group and just love all the attention.

22 April: Last Quarter in Aquarius

You may have to take a close look at your health now. You could fall sick and may need expert medical opinion. All the accumulated stress has taken its toll. I hope I am wrong as this is a generalization. But, in any case, it is better to be forewarned. It may be a good idea to check into a nature care clinic and detoxify if you are so inclined. You may also go down memory lane and long for times past. But, despite it all, you make considerable headway in life. Ganesha is with you. You want life on your terms all the time and love dominating a situation. Remember, you have to give in too. You cannot have it your way all the time.

29 April: New Moon in Taurus

You are steadfast in your goals. You sign new deals and are the toast of the organization. This is a time for big bucks in your life. There could be a windfall. You could receive an inheritance or even a lottery. You are filled with gratitude and use the unexpected largesse to help the less fortunate. Ganesha is pleased. Whatever you throw into the world comes back to you. Hindus call it the law of karma. But I believe it holds true for everyone. Life is dancing and you are dancing with it. You are in free flow allowing existence a free rein. You are freed from controls and move like water.

7 May: First Quarter in Leo

There are new influences in your life and they could either be quite disruptive or quite liberating. You may rebel against restrictions and old patterns of behaviour. You may act in haste, compulsively and blindly. You don't care for anyone's opinion now and all of a sudden get rid of all the benchmarks that have outlined your life. You live large. You spend like there is no tomorrow. Yes, there is money in the kitty and, yes, it is your money to do with as you please. If anyone suggests otherwise, you are not in any mood to listen. There is love, passion, raw lust, buying, selling, investments and stocks. It is all happening in your life now. Discretion be damned. You are in no mood to compromise. If you are burnt, you will handle the pain! Ganesha watches over you.

14 May: Full Moon in Scorpio

The full moon is in your sign. You live large and wild. There is more money and even more romance. Scorpions are considered the most passionate lovers of all. You will stop at nothing in this period. There are no full stops, no punctuation marks. This is a hectic, power-packed and fruitful period. You go with guns blazing like in a shootout. You put Clint Eastwood to shame as you fire away and 'make your day'. Ganesha smiles. Your holster is smoking fire.

21 May: Last Quarter in Pisces

You are busy with the three Cs—contacts, communication, correspondence. There are maudlin moments too. The softer side of your personality comes through. You spend time at home, with the spouse and kids, or with aged parents. You take them out on a holiday. The vacation does you good. You are rejuvenated. You may take up a new hobby like playing a new musical instrument, or bonsai, or even get a new pet. Ganesha watches over you. This phase is interesting, to say the least. You somehow show the world that you have a soft underbelly, and there are good reasons why you don't wear your emotions on your sleeve!

28 May: New Moon in Gemini

You have many thoughts plaguing you. You break away from routine without any apparent thought for others or of the consequences of your actions. Youngsters will rebel and have intense disagreements with their parents. The home will be on fire with arguments and counter-arguments. You are in no mood to listen or relent. You want freedom to express yourself the way you want to. Ganesha is happy despite this. You are asserting yourself. This behaviour is affirmative and calls for great mental and emotional strength. It is vital to stand for your rights. It is a tough world. There is also a generation gap. A lot has changed in recent times, and maturity and understanding are called for on both sides, particularly from elders.

5 June: First Quarter in Virgo

This is not a sober period. There are inflated expectations, excessive and impractical idealism and a few disappointments. You have to ensure that your feet are on the ground and not to fly off the handle. There are ego drives that could result in your undoing. You feel that you are invincible and nothing can upset the applecart. You are in a lucky phase but do not push your luck and take foolish risks. This is not the time to play with money and indulge in shady deals with unscrupulous people. This is not a good idea even at the best of times. In this phase, this is a patently bad idea. You are overconfident and think you can jump off the plane without a chute. These are general indications. Your personal chart may be different. But the bottom line is that you should not overextend yourself financially. New people and events enter your life as it pulsates like a volcano. Sort the grain from the chaff. Ganesha is with you and that is important.

13 June: Full Moon in Sagittarius

You are in an experimental mood. You may elope with a new love or may decide to scale the Alps. You may go rafting in the Ganga. There are many possibilities as you look for something different to do. You look for danger and excitement. Youngsters will experiment with recreational drugs, alcohol and partners. You want to do different things. Nothing is in the closet any more. There is alternative sexuality in the open. I am not suggesting that you are prone to it. All I am saying is that in this mood you will experiment with life and with yourself. You look for new ways to live, new spirituality, new religion, new ideology, new friends, a whole new self. Nothing wrong with that, I may add. It is your life and you are entitled to your experiments. Each of us has many personalities and they emerge depending on the circumstances. Ganesha blesses you.

19 June: Last Quarter in Pisces

In this phase you are idealistic. The limitations of the real world may seem very difficult to bear and you want to break free. You want new roles. This can be disruptive if you are in a family situation with domestic chores to attend to. You network with extreme religious, spiritual or mystical sects. You do not want to harm anyone but you want to know yourself better in the larger scheme of things. Do not get carried away. Keep your feet on the ground. There is tantra, mantra, yantra, hypnotism, mysticism and adventure. You want it all, but don't get lost in its maze. Your mind is like a wandering mendicant. Tether it. Ganesha watches over you.

27 June: New Moon in Cancer

You are in a generous mood. There is great compassion for others. You want to help people and share your good fortune. There is money in the kitty but ensure that it is well spent and those you help are benefiting from your largesse. You could be preyed on by hangers-on who will think nothing of taking advantage of your generosity. Scorpios are energetic and hardworking as a rule. But you are deeply emotional and may make wrong choices. Use the mind and not the heart. Ganesha is with you. That is a consolation.

5 July: First Quarter in Libra

You make big plans. This is the time when many ideas come to fruition. But ensure that your ambitions have a semblance of reality. There is no point at all in grandiose and impractical ideas. This could be a good time to sign lucrative business deals. Of course, I insist, read the fine print with a magnifying glass. There is no room for sloppy planning. You may alienate others by being self-righteous or arrogant. It will be a good idea to temper the mood with kindness, tolerance and generosity. The pace is frenetic and you are inundated by events. Family life is pleasant. Friends and lovers express solidarity. Ganesha is happy.

12 July: Full Moon in Capricorn

There is rapid work expansion. You do not allow the mind any more fancies and get down to the hard slog. You are ambitious and money has a special charm. You have seen its power. Do not get unscrupulous and get into easy underhand deals. 'Behind every fortune is a crime,' said Mario Puzo in *Godfather*. He is not wrong. The law will finally catch hold of you. This is just a gentle prod from Ganesha. Mahatma Gandhi emphasized that honesty is the best policy. So stick to ethics and make your bucks.

Finally, the best things in life are free, even in the material world! Ganesha watches over you. Without his blessings, nothing is possible. Ask me. I have been his follower for more decades than I can remember. You have no time for the family now. Love and longing are distant emotions.

19 July: Last Quarter in Aries

The trend is positive. Many projects that you had embarked on years ago culminate now as you look for furious expansion. There is hard work and success. There is material growth; this is a given. This is a good time to explore your spiritual and inner needs. Materialism will satisfy ego drives and provide some comforts. After that is met your spiritual needs have to be satiated. The great saints have always asked their followers to visit them after their basic needs have been met. So this could be a good time to embark on a spiritual process. Ganesha wishes you well. Your spiritual drives power you and there are new, profound realizations.

26 July: New Moon in Leo

This is an interesting phase. Mars is in your sign from 26 July to 13 September which is quite a long period. Mars is like the volcano of vitality inside you and influences endurance, persistence and discipline. Mars was named after the Roman god of war, and is also known as 'the bright and burning one'. Red is the colour of Mars and it stimulates the dynamic, potent and fertile drives that power our lives. Mars rules physical energy and action and governs energy, strength, courage, life force and expansion. Well-placed Mars endows powerful energy and an indomitable will to succeed. Mars propels us like an ignited rocket. It is an important energy since it determines how we pursue what we want to achieve in life. In short, Mars represents energy, force, violence, aggression, sports, combat, wars, battles, accidents, operations. You could be unduly aggressive in this period and want everything your way. There is love and passion, work and money, applause and accolades, friends and foes, gains and loss. Sportspersons win laurels. Ganesha walks with you.

4 August: First Quarter in Scorpio

The pace is frenetic. You move fast and furious getting things done. You brook no opposition and are moving around like a roadroller mowing things down in a slum improvement scheme. New frontiers open up at work and you are crowned with success. You can tame the largest lion in Serengeti in the mood you are in. There is luck on your side. And there is Ganesha. What more do you need as you embrace it all and come up trumps in the battle of life. Just a word of caution: watch out for accidents. Don't take hasty steps and hurt yourself.

10 August: Full Moon in Aquarius

You now go after everything that you want in the material world without caring about who or what is in your path. You hoard and accumulate, but it could well be an empty exercise. You could be arrogant and feel that you are right all the time. You should look for mutual growth. There is enough place even on the Everest for a team! But whatever said and done, this is an extremely productive and growth-oriented period with substantial meaning too. Along with the hard work are maudlin moments too.

But you are human and a bundle of emotions. Ganesha blesses you.

17 August: Last Quarter in Taurus

There is success in all that you undertake. This is a period of reconciliation and consolidation. There is friendship and love, messages, journeys, bonding, spirituality, tantra and mantra. You have achieved a lot. Now you look for more, something beyond mere material accomplishment. You are adamant in your pursuit. Of course, one eye still remains on the bank account. Money is a great intoxicant. It is difficult to let go. It is also like a double-edged sword. Do not allow it to control you. As long as you control it, all is fine. Of course, a paucity of money can be disastrous and I am not advocating it in the least. There are expenses as you make investments and fancy purchases. Ganesha blesses you.

25 August: New Moon in Virgo

Life is good. That is saying a lot in these strife-ridden times. You have a smile on your lips and a song in your heart. You spend beautiful moments with loved ones. There is a family outing and you build on existing relationships. Children bring joy and the spouse is just perfect! Imagine having a perfect spouse! But yes, that is the mood you are in. It is all about love and bonding. You share joys on a higher consciousness. You have gone beyond the body into the ethereal reaches of the superconsciousness. There are no squabbles, fights, altercations, disputes, disagreements. Instead, there is bliss and harmony and it is all-pervasive. Is this for real? Ganesha blesses you. Need I say more?

2 September: First Quarter in Sagittarius

There is frenetic movement. You are filled with energy and are excited and enthused by life. You network furiously and meet new people from all over the world. There is entertainment, romance and sheer joie de vivre. Your body language is a winner's. You are also shrewd and cunning in a good way and roll with the waves. Charles Darwin said that the species that survives is not the strongest or the swiftest but the species that adapts to change. You are doing just that and have finally befriended your fears. Now nothing daunts you. Like Shah Jahan you cock a snoop at your critics and go about building the Taj Mahal! The epic monument took twelve years to build and almost drained the treasury in addition to the enormous human cost. In the phase you are in, you just zoom ahead without breaks or headlights!

9 September: Full Moon in Pisces

There are soft moments. You know your road map well and there is peace and security in the knowledge. You have come to terms with all your inner demons. Now there is no stopping you. There are maudlin moments but they help refine you, humanize you, and not demonize you. You forgive those who have hurt you and ask for forgiveness too. You know that you could have unwittingly harmed others and you want a clean slate to start afresh. You want to forget the bitterness and move ahead to new frontiers and vistas of knowledge and greater learning. Ganesha is delighted. You have reached a state of sadhana, a higher consciousness. You may have found Buddhahood. Of course, these are generalizations but the indications are there. Without a personal chart, I cannot say more.

16 September: Last Quarter in Gemini

You break free from all restrictions and obligations of the past. You rebel against all chains and external limitations. You move out of your inner circle and make social intercourse with those who are radically different from your inner circle. If married, there could be a break-up or, at the very least, serious problems with your partner. The institution of marriage may just get too stifling. You look for ultimate freedom, a final liberation of the soul, if something like that indeed exists. There is also love, bonding and many graceful and momentous occasions with friends and family. Ganesha watches over you with a hawk-eye.

24 September: New Moon in Libra

Great times are in store for you. Mercury makes its presence felt from 29 September to 9 October. Mercury, the mighty, all-powerful planet, is in your sign now. It favours travel, meetings, conferences, interviews, trips, more brain power, contacts, communication, correspondence and contracts. Mercury has a special connection with the circuits of the brain. Chess, crossword and other such games belong to Mercury. Also, short-distance runners and spin bowlers are controlled by Mercury. Mercury, in short, is the ambassador and salesman of the zodiac. Mercury is the symbol of news, views, messages, interviews, contacts, communications, travel and transport. Mercury gives an impetus to all of the above in the sun sign where it is located. Along with the new moon in Libra, you are on a roll. There is money, honey, love, success, applause, accolade, reward, award, the works. You have the Midas touch and cannot go wrong. You are in for a windfall. In cricketing terms, you are batting on the front foot on the last day of a Test match on a spinning track and pockmarking the stands with huge heaves over the fence. To paraphrase the Bard, take the high tide to fortune. Ganesha is happy.

1 October: First Quarter in Capricorn

It is a gold rush. Nothing can stop you now. Unless I know your specific astrological details, I cannot make accurate predictions. But this is the general trend. You realize the good fortune that has smiled on you. In this period you are liberated from illusion. You seek out gods and godmen and finally realize that all paths, though apparently different, lead to the same thing. You realize that all the structures for interpreting the world have the same limitations and rigidity, and a belief in a superior theology or way of life could be way off the mark. Study them all and come to your own conclusions according to your needs and aspirations. All ideologies are different and appeal to different people. But, away from all this, you are making headway at work. While there is new meaning and direction in your life, there is also hard work and money. You are practical and know which side of your bread is buttered. Ganesha is happy.

8 October: Full Moon in Aries

There is progress on all fronts. There is balance and equilibrium in your life. Your affairs run smoothly without too much effort. You are in your comfort zone. Your life is working out well on your terms. Your consciousness is raised and there is elevation in your personal and professional life. You are less frenzied and look at life with some calm and detachment. Ganesha is pleased. You could travel for experience or get in touch with your real self with specialized study. This is also a good time to expand your business. There are expenses too, but you are fine with the tenor of life. Your plate is full.

15 October: Last Quarter in Cancer

You spend time with the family. You realize that you have received unconditional love from many and have taken it for granted or been unable to reciprocate it for a variety of reasons. You have often been critical and now you realize that you were wrong. Such realizations are powerful. They are cathartic and take you to new heights as a human being. You learn to live in gratitude and thank existence for all its favours and making your life so wonderful. Of course, you love control and power and are happiest in the driver's seat. But you temper such desires with compassion. You have the ambition of Alexander, the ruthlessness of Genghis Khan and the wisdom of Buddha. Ganesha smiles.

23 October: New Moon in Scorpio

Venus is in your sign from 24 October to 16 November. This is quite a long time and you are in luck. Venus is another important planet and is of great significance. This is an important phase. As often discussed, Venus is the planet for love, romance, sex, beauty and the good life. This is the planet of attraction, love, wealth, knowledge and prosperity. The compatibility of partners and the type of life the individual will lead is also judged from the placement of Venus in the horoscope. As a planet, Venus is considered to be beneficial, feminine and gentle.

Venus symbolizes the force of attraction in the universe. In human beings this attractive force manifests as love and beauty. When Venus is well placed in the chart, there is love, art, beauty and all the goodies of life that make it worth living. Venus rules Libra and Taurus, though its role in every sign is important. Like other planets, it also has its transits. In Libra, Venus is aesthetic and cultured. In Taurus it is more earthy, materialistic and sensual. Venus rules the venous system, kidneys, urinary tract, throat, larynx, and is responsible for good looks. In short, Venus in Western astrology stands for comforts, arts, wealth, relationships, sex, decorations, luxuries and wealth. The good times keep rolling. There are luxury purchases, in all probability a new home. It is a time for the big P's—position, pelf, perks and privileges. It is also time for awards, accolades and applause. Ganesha smiles.

31 October: First Quarter in Aquarius

You spend time with the less fortunate. You may make donations to an old people's home or to a street charity. You want to give. You look at hospices, hospitals, shelters, even the street to choose the recipient of your largesse. This is a fantastic period. This is also your birth period and the energies are multiplied. Scorpios are indomitable. Nothing can beat them. Most of our beauty queens have been Scorpios. They are fiercely ambitious and once they set their sights on something, they do not give up easily. They want to be counted in the world. But in this phase you remember those who have helped you along the way and help them out in the manner you feel best. It is payback time. You have a heart of gold. Without intending to, you are playing into the law of attraction. You are giving abundance and the cosmos will repay you with it. Guru Nanak said, 'What you give is yours, what you keep is not yours.' Ganesha blesses you.

6 November: Full Moon in Taurus

You are back to the hard slog. There is partying and fun times too, but there is hard work on the cards. Guard against arrogance, possessiveness, emotional flare-ups and dominance. These are your natural personality traits, depending, of course, on the type of Scorpio you are. You sign important documents. Those in insurance, realty, banking and the media strike pay dirt. It is written in the *Dhammapada*, 'A ship which is not well prepared, in the ocean, goes to destruction together with its goods and merchants.' You are the well-prepared ship having gone through all the tribulations of the mind and soul and have come out stronger. You know where you are headed and how to get there. You join the dots in a straight line. You are fast and furious. There is success. You have the right formula. Ganesha is pleased. I am delighted.

14 November: Last Quarter in Leo

You are zooming ahead of the opposition. You are an asset to the organization with your hard work, ethics, amiability and reliability. There are ego drives and you brook no opposition. Your appreciation of beauty, your interest in art, music or poetry are heightened now. You are also filled with love and want to share it with that special person. There are expenses and purchases and many investments. Mutual funds, shares, stocks, capital-raising and all other money matters come to the fore. You live large. There is wining and dining and great moments with friends and family. The winter chill is not hardening your zest for life. You relish your success as it has been hard-earned. You have earned every penny, every accolade. You are the toast of your peers. Ganesha smiles.

22 November: New Moon in Sagittarius

You are on the move. At the risk of repetition, there could be foreign travel, meetings, conferences, interviews, trips, more brain power, contacts, communication, correspondence, contracts, networking, matchmaking and every other conceivable human association. You climb the Everest many times like Nawang Gombu, the great Sherpa. Nothing daunts you. There is fire in your belly. You are free, frank and fearless like a morning tabloid. Ganesha is happy. He has watched your every step, all your life, possibly without you even being aware of it.

29 November: First Quarter in Pisces

There is continued success. The wheel has been set in motion. There are accolades and money. You address large gatherings, chair prestigious committees. There could be awards and rewards. You want to expand your activities. You resent anything that narrows your freedom. You make serious plans to forge ahead with enlightened self-interest. You also understand your limitations and work within them for success. You are at the right place at the right time and your sense of timing is perfect. Success crowns all your endeavours. Ganesha is delighted, to say the least.

6 December: Full Moon in Gemini

There are emotional moments. You are working too hard and, as they say these days, it is time to chill. Your favourite astrologer may be an old man but he knows the lingo of the younger generation! You need to take a break. There are things to do for the family. There will be family gatherings and a new love in your life. Make time for all this. All work and no play makes for a dull person. Ganesha agrees with me. Take time off and be with nature. You have slogged long and hard. There is more to life than just work.

14 December: Last Quarter in Virgo

There is indulgence, pleasure, joy and satisfaction. You buy luxuries and go on a pleasant shopping spree. You eat and drink till you can't move. But your common sense and logic do not allow you to go to extremes. Surely life is not just the hard slog. You can't go on working forever. This is the last month of the year and you are in an indulgent frame of mind, and why not? I did this last year too and I must add it here again at this very juncture. Please remember that life has unhappy events too. No one is immune to the caprices of life. Please remember that these are mere generalizations and an accurate prediction will depend on the individual horoscope. Also, astrology impels and doesn't compel. There are many factors influencing one's life, including one's circumstances, the family, the country, and one's free will. I am your favourite astrologer and am known for my accuracy but I am also human, and to err is human! I wish my readers well and pray to Ganesha for their well-being. Humanity is at a turning point. I see a new consciousness taking over and every single one of us is responsible as it is a collective consciousness.

22 December: New Moon in Capricorn

It is party time and you are the soul of the party. You are happy, content, cheerful and gregarious. You radiate warmth and emotion. You are amorous. People want to be around you. This is a great time for beautifying and renovating your home. You are entertaining, shopping, and enjoying the good life. There are house parties, probably a house-warming celebration for a new home. What a year it has been!

28 December: First Quarter in Aries

You can be quite a control freak. If things don't work to your advantage, it just freaks you out, to use a term of generation Next. But life is not according to you, and the sooner you realize that the better. You could be raving and ranting and losing your cool and this won't help. There are irritants at work and in relationships. There are domestic issues that need handling. You are fiery and lose brownie points in your associations. You have the resilience and stamina to work through it. Ganesha holds your hand as you steer through troubled times. But you are not one to suffer for long. You steady the boat soon and move on. Great times are in store.

Key Dates
January
1*–7, 10–11, 14*–15, 18*–20, 23*–25, 28–30.

Ganesha says the tremendous efforts made in December 2013 will start to pay now. You will have the power needed to be successful as well as happy. A month of progress as well as travel. It is action time, definitely.

February

2–3, 6*–7, 20–21, 25–26.

The key is that November to February are definitely interconnected, and you should push hard for what you desire in these three months. February is also for anything to do with house, home, shop and property in general, including buying/selling.

March

1*–2, 5*–7, 10*–17, 19*–20, 24*–25, 28–30.

March is the time for exploring and developing new ideas, having new experiences, loving and being loved, earning and spending.

April

2–3, 6*–12, 15–17, 20*–22, 23–25, 26, 29*–30.

Love and passion, sex and salvation, finance, job as well as employees and servants, earned income and loans are the highlights now. Quite a list!

May

3–9, 13*–14, 18*–19, 22*–23, 26–27, 30–31.

Be sure of what you want, because you will be meeting a lot of people in May. It is all a question of meeting the right people at the right place and right time. Journeys, collaborations are probable. Take care of your health; be positive.

June

1*, 4–5, 9–10, 14*–20, 23–24, 27–28.
Finance, inheritance, gifts, opposition, lawsuits, and after 21 June, journey and ceremony too, says Ganesha!

July

1*–3, 6–8, 11*–17, 20*–21, 24*–25, 28–30.
You start with a bang—a journey, ceremony, publicity and projects. You're in the public eye and very visible in your success.

August

2–3, 7*–13, 17–18, 21*–22, 25*–26, 30*–31.
Thanks to the quick and fine start in July, you succeed in your enterprises in August. It will be very hard work, but it's well worth it. Rewards and great satisfactions accrue to you.

September

4*–10, 13–14, 17*–19, 22*–23, 26–28.
Take the help of friends, well-wishers, your boss/superiors and loved ones, and you will find joy and fulfilment. It is a time to work in groups, and in the social circle.

October

1*–7, 11*–12, 15*–16, 19–20, 24*–25, 29–30.
A mixed bag for you. Ganesha says, take care of expenses and ill-health of family members and yourself. But you will face difficulties and triumphs. Journeys are possible too.

November

2*–3, 5–6, 11*–16, 20*–21, 25–26, 29–30.
This is a month for both finance and romance, work and joy. Go all out for what you want. You will be popular and loved, and the birth of a child is possible. The world comes to your door.

December

1, 4–5, 8–9, 12*–14, 17*–18, 22*–28, 31.
Possessions, selling, investing, restoring of foreign connections, import and export will be important. There is luck and joy for you, and hope, as you look ahead.

Sagittarius

YEARLY FORECAST

Listen to the melodious music of the divine poet/The earth,
the sea, the sky, the stars are/all woven together by the/
soft strains of the divine music.

– *Sama Veda*, 446

Till 16 July 2014
Summary and Guidance

Ganesha says Jupiter will be in your eighth angle of tantra
and mantra, health foods and exercise, spiritual prayers
and shrines and hymns and words of power, in short, light
and elevation of the spirit itself. Glimpses of God, and
remember your sign represents the archer, the horse and
the fire. This triple combination makes you restless and
research-oriented. My God, what a formidable force! The
other aspect of Jupiter in your eighth angle is to do with
windfalls, inheritance, joint finance, loans, funds, public
trusts and mighty welfare schemes and projects, perhaps
undreamed in the history of the world. I know this is a
lot of praise. I know we all like flattery. I know that even
lions purr when petted. But this is the prophecy I predict
in the name of Ganesha. I may go wrong. But my son,

Nastur, says, 'Daddy, do not be negative, have faith in yourself.' Who is like my readers? My son or I?

17 July 2014 to 11 August 2015

Jupiter will be in your ninth angle where it favours the music of the plants, herbs, space, black holes and so on. Your sign, Sagittarius, strictly speaking, shows the last frontier in research. I am emphasising this in different ways, so that you get the message loud and clear that 2014 is for research, discovery and expanding the boundaries of your heart, mind, body and spirit. Astrology is all about timing. And the timing for you to evolve, to develop, to grow will be just right in 2014 and 2015. Let me be as precise as possible. The period from 2 August 2014 to 27 August 2015 could well be one of tremendous expansion, research, growth, maturity, capability, with more potential power, journey and pilgrimage than you will experience in your entire life.

Now that you know how exciting and powerful the period is, you should get ready to take your best shot by letting your arrows of desire fly from your bow of burnished gold.

Main Trend

For you particularly, I have been very exhaustive in the beginning. I can only add that by piety and good deeds you could well be the chosen one of the Lord. Who am I to say more?

Journey and Communication

Sagittarius along with Gemini and perhaps Aquarius are the three main signs of journey and communication.

This will be specifically true from 17 July 2014 to 11 August 2015. But even before that the possibility is there. Mercury, the communication expert, the journey specialist, will be in your sign from 28 November to 16 December. Make the most of it. Travel and communication are also highlighted from 8 to 29 May, 17 June to 12 July, 1 to 15 August and from 21 January to 19 February. Have your fill of it and be happy.

Health

Saturn in your twelfth angle can be troublesome in the form of monetary and/or psychological problems. Expenses and losses could be sudden and great. But please remember that this is only a reading based on the solar sign and not a horoscope reading. I am not God. Who is wiser than destiny? If you believe in Hanuman, the controller of Saturn, chant this mantra twenty-one times: Shree Ram Jai Ram Jai Jai Ram. Charity to orphans, the disabled and other disadvantaged people will make you happy and rich. What a wonderful combination. Go right ahead, you are Sagittarius. Spread generosity and kindness as only you can. Why? Because you and you alone are the real child of Jupiter, the generous one.

Love/Marriage

Sagittarians are known to break hearts, including their own, not once but a thousand times over. I do not blame them. Astrologically, they are made that way. This year also favours sex and salvation, an unusual but possible combination. Venus will be in your sign from 17 November to 10 December. The period from 24 June to

18 July, 29 May to 23 June, 12 August to 5 September are almost tailor-made for love and marriage. They say love and marriage are like horse and carriage. You are free to agree or disagree.

Property

The mighty signs of property are Capricorn, Sagittarius, Cancer and Aquarius. Property matters are Emphasized. Loans, funds and investments are probable. But let me warn you that it could be something of a risk because Saturn is in your twelfth angle. Normally, Sagittarians take risks. The months for it are March, July, September and January. Renovation and decoration, house, home, office and so on come under property.

Job/Business/Loans/Funds/Investments

If you really ask me for all these matters, from 12 August 2015 to 10 September 2016 Jupiter will be the most auspicious. Therefore, I want you to prepare for it. Sagittarians are far-sighted. They are equipped for it. The year 2014 is more or less a great preparation for it, with some fine results thrown in for good measure. In simple words, it can start in 2014.

Children/Entertainment

The period from 17 July 2014 to 11 August 2015 is particularly favourable for children, entertainment, the arts, research, fun and fanfare, publicity and salesmanship, teaching and writing, and you may please read the entire paragraph during 17 July 2014 to 11 August 2015. All of it applies.

Trips and Ties

For trips, please read journey and communication. For ties, 24 June to 18 July and 17 November to 10 December. Thanks to Venus, the ties may not be tensionfree. Everything in life is not given on a silver plate.

Publicity, Projects, Performance

Yes, this is where you excel and leave all others far, far behind. Sagittarius and Gemini are the mighty signs of publicity, projects and performance. This will be particularly true from 17 July 2014 to 11 August 2015. I repeat, please read the big paragraph for 17 July 2014 to 11 August 2015. That is why I have given it in detail. It should satisfy you.

Happiness Quota

Sagittarians always rebound from extremely difficult and critical situations. They are like the bouncing ball used in Wimbledon tennis. Yes, I love tennis. The big booming service which goes with tennis also goes partially with you Sagittarians? Got it? I give you 81 per cent. A word about Mars. Mars, the warrior planet, will be in your eleventh angle of group activity, children, entertainment, hobbies and creativity from 1 January to 25 July and in your own sign from 14 September to 25 October. Combat and competition are possible. You are good at these. Give your best. Be sporting. Win or lose, be free and frank and fearless. That is what you Sagittarians are all about.

Monthly Round-up

January: money, honey, riches, beautification, augmentation of income, good food, jewellery; February:

research, contacts, communication, correspondence, brothers, sisters and other relatives; March: home, house, property, renovation, decoration, alteration; April: love, romance, children, relationships, hobbies, sports; May: health, pets, servants, job, hygiene, colleagues; June: love, marriage, divorce, journey, reaching out to people, also separations and lawsuits; July: joint finances, funds, loans, legacy, family issues and problems; August: sweet-and-sour relationships, publicity, conferences and meets, inspirational and intuitive moves and manoeuvres; September: prestige, status, power struggle, perks, new ventures and means of communication; October: Socializing, group activities, marriage, love affair, happiness, laughter, the goodies of life; November: secret activities, health expenses, visits to hospitals, welfare centres, medical check-ups; December: fulfilment, happiness, money, marriage, confidence.

Summary

Pressures and opposition bring out the best in you. Also, Jupiter helps you in money, journey, publicity, ceremony and discovery.

Outer Planets

URANUS: Uranus in your fifth angle of pleasure and creativity, love and romance makes for a great see-saw. In simple words, it means pleasure and pain. Believe me, you will have your full share of both. Everything might happen suddenly. Be ready. Be alert. Life is sweet but short.

NEPTUNE: Neptune in your angle representing property, parents, home, house, office, shop, godown certainly gives you a window of opportunity in these directions. It is my humble suggestion that you trust your own judgement. The months for property could well be March, July, September and January. May could be a mixed bag.

PLUTO: Pluto in your second angle favours family, food and finance. Here also I see many ups and downs but as a rule Sagittarians are lucky and so you will win. But please remember I do not have your complete horoscope. I cannot give you a guarantee.

Month by Month

January

You start the year with ferocity. There is energy and intensity and you are able to execute the plans you have made for yourself. A lot of issues were piling up last year and now you go about sorting it all. There is both inner and outer growth. You are torn by several compulsions and pulled in different directions. There will be fissures in relationships and you may feel lonely and alone. You look at philosophy and religion, meet with gods and godmen. New windows open. The month-end sees powerful intensity in all your dealings. Several aspects of your life will be tested. There are many demands on the home front. Ganesha watches over you.

February

You roll up your sleeves and get down to the task of building your home. There is luck, even a windfall. You are filled with powerful energies now. There is happiness and you feel inspired. You throw light and impress and influence everyone you meet. The month-end sees happy travels. Work is on track and there is stability at home. Ganesha looks after you.

March

There is a flurry of activity. Travel, new associations and many unusual encounters. You feel energetic and vigorous. Business people excel at negotiations. There could be profitable travel, new experiences and encounters. By mid-month there will be unspoken differences, reservations or sensitivities that emerge in your communications with others. As the month ends you are powered by new energy. Relationships come into focus. There is success at work and there is new love. Ganesha wishes you well.

April

You do well at lectures, teaching, group discussions, interviews and negotiations of all kinds. At work there are rewards and applause. There is progress and substantial headway in all your dealings. This is a great time for those in creative fields. You get on to social networking sites and make contact with the world. There is progress on all fronts. By the end of the month you are more stable. You are steadfast and persevering. The employed are in line for promotions. The luck of the draw is with you. There could be a windfall. Ganesha blesses you.

May

You realize that it is high time for you to clean up your act and to get to know your real self. It is time you shimmer like gold and come into your own. There are expenses, travel and new associations. You may migrate with the family or due to a job. You look for new vistas. As the month ends your emotions are on fast forward. You are plagued by thoughts. You need an identity. You are looking for a purpose, a definition, a direction. You want your life to be unique and at the same time you want to be emotionally and spiritually fulfilled. All this calls for change. Ganesha wishes you well.

June

There are important domestic and job concerns that confront you. You are focused, and are able to concentrate and work with great clarity. This is a propitious time to surge ahead. There are fun times and you participate in social get-togethers, picnics and outings. The end of the month sees medical emergencies. Those in business look for expansion and the employed get pay hikes and promotions. There are realty deals, blue chip stocks and investments of all kinds. There are emotional moments too but you handle them with maturity. Children bring joy and there could be an addition to the family. Ganesha is overjoyed.

July

There are new projects and collaborations. Those in any type of social activity do exceedingly well. Use this phase for making decisions, planning, negotiating and concluding deals. You fire on all cylinders and are focused. You have set your sights high and will not stop at anything to achieve your goals. Youngsters do well in examinations and interviews. You are filled with optimism, drive, enthusiasm and guts. There could be exotic travel and new love. There are expansions and growth. By the month-end there are major expenses, renovations, redevelopment of property, setting up of new manufacturing units if you are in business, and some medical emergencies. Ganesha is with you.

August

You look for answers to profound questions about life. You seek out gurus and godmen, the latest esoteric thought, and more meaning in life. There are maudlin moments. This is a mixed period, indeed even a nixed period. There could be joy and sorrow, life and death. There is more stability by mid-month and you will be back on track. You straighten out relationships that are not working. There will be financial gains with legacies, inheritance, loans, stocks, realty, manufacturing, pharmaceuticals, retail and related sectors. This is a period of hope, promise and new beginnings. Ganesha is with you.

September

You fly high with new speed and energy. Your emotions are stable though you emit fire in all your dealings. There is love, bonding and fun. You reach out to others and new people enter your life. You attend alumni meetings and spend quality time with family and friends. From 14 September to 25 October, Mars will be in your sign. Mars is like the volcano of vitality inside you and influences endurance, persistence and discipline. Mars is in your sign for over a month and you could be in a combative mood. Watch out for accidents, altercations, disagreements and the law. Life is a roller coaster now. Ganesha watches over you.

October

You try your best to be stable and follow the beaten path. You want to be accepted and do not want to rebel. Your energies are high and you are filled with confidence. This is a good time for business expansion. You meet with worldly success as you sign important documents and detail new plans for expansion. There could also be favourable out-of-court settlements. By mid-month you are highly emotional. There are marriages, engagements and many festive occasions calling out for you. There will be money, love, joy, travel, friends, parties and fun of all kinds. By the month-end there could be a shifting of residence. As the winter chill enters your bones, you are filled with new plans. Trust in Ganesha.

November

This is a great time for both creative and business folk. Your vision is grand and you stop at nothing to achieve your goals. Venus will be in your sign from 17 November to 10 December, which is quite a long period. Venus is another important planet and is of great significance. This is an important phase. Your business deals may have clicked and there is a lot of money to spend. You let your hair down and party. This is also your birth period and the energies of the new moon are intense. There are rewards and awards, applause and accolades. Mercury will be in your sign from 28 November to 16 December. There is rapid growth in all spheres of your life. There are new ventures and collaborations. There is money and honey. Ganesha is delighted.

December

You have a clear idea of the larger picture and are able to handle your ego well, without becoming overbearing. The past is forgotten as you open new windows and see a new dawn. This is an extremely favourable influence for close relationships and encounters of all kinds. There is love and bonding. You want to make waves, make things happen. You demand to be yourself and are filled with powerful assertive energies. You party for ever. This is your time in the sun. Ganesha is delighted.

Months at a Glance

January

Money, honey, riches, beautification, augmentation of income, good food, jewellery.

February

Research, contacts, communication, correspondence, brothers, sisters, other relatives.

March

Home, house, property, renovation, decoration, alteration.

April

Love, romance, children, relationships, hobbies, sports.

May

Health, pets, servants, job, hygiene, colleagues.

June

Love, marriage, divorce, journey, reaching out to people, also separations and lawsuits.

July

Joint finances, funds, loans, legacy, family issues and problems.

August

Sweet-and-sour relationships, publicity, conferences and meets, inspirational and intuitive moves and manoeuvres.

September

Prestige, status, power struggle, perks, new ventures and means of communication.

October

Socializing, group activities, marriage, love affair, happiness, laughter, the goodies of life.

November

Secret activities, health expenses, visits to hospitals, welfare centres, medical check-ups.

December

Fulfilment, happiness, money, marriage, confidence.

Weekly Review (By the phases of the moon)

1 January: New Moon in Capricorn

As with all the other signs, you are in good company. You share your sun sign with André Gide, Monica Seles, Britney Spears, Madame Tussaud, Charles de Gaulle, Joseph Stalin, Nostradamus, Woody Allen, Walt Disney, Gianni Versace, Aleksandr Solzhenitsyn, Kim Basinger and others. Sagittarius is a fire sign and can be tactless, outspoken, frank, quarrelsome, versatile and enthusiastic. Sagittarians love their space and need freedom even in friendships and more intimate relationships. Of course, I must add here that this is a generalization but holds true for a majority of Sagittarians. You start the year with ferocity. There is energy and intensity and you are able to execute the plans you have made for yourself. A lot of issues were piling up last year and now you go about sorting them out. There will be maudlin moments, no one can get away from it, there will be bouts of depression too, but you will be focused on getting your way. You will sort out your finances, your love life and relationships. Junk what you don't need, and move on to new vistas without a pause. There is both inner and outer growth as you work on profound, unresolved issues that may have strangulated your potential. You spend time with parents, children and the spouse. Ganesha is happy.

8 January: First Quarter in Aries

You are pushed by powerful energies. You are brash and outspoken and don't hold your tongue. There are ego issues and you want your way all the time. There are expenses. You know that money is important but you also don't want to spend your life chasing currency notes. You believe money is a means to an end and nothing more than that. You are practical and idealistic and spread yourself thin in too many directions. There are domestic responsibilities you cannot get away from. You are torn by several compulsions and pulled in different directions. You will have to weigh the pros and cons and decide the chosen path for yourself. You could also get obstinate and refuse to see another point of view. There will be fissures in relationships and you may feel lonely and alone. But it is all your creation; you can't blame anyone. Ganesha watches over you.

16 January: Full Moon in Cancer

There are many emotional issues burdening you. Children need attention and there are medical emergencies and several property and tax matters that push you to the wall. You look at philosophy and religion, meet with gods and godmen, do poojas and havans, yantra, tantra and mantra, abstractions, and have new insights. New windows open, many old ones shut. But you are a fish out of water, and you find yourself floundering. The journey is long and, I dare say, you could be making it longer and more complicated for yourself. Ganesha walks with you.

24 January: Last Quarter in Scorpio

There is powerful intensity in all your dealings. You push hard, overextend yourself, gamble, take risks, and move about like a zombie in a zillion directions. There are illusions and delusions, snares and snafus, purchases and expenses, settlements and break-ups, loneliness and pairing, confusion and clarity, selection and indiscrimination, hope and despair. I could be wrong, but these are the indications. Ganesha will see you through as you evolve into a better person.

30 January: New Moon in Aquarius

You spend time helping the less fortunate and visit hospices for destitute people, old-age homes, and may even sponsor free dispensaries. Several aspects of your life will be tested. There are crises you have to deal with and a lot of time will go in firefighting. You are not one to mope but in this period you take setbacks to heart. Health issues surface. There are many demands on the home front. Children need your attention and there are issues to sort out with your spouse or partner. Those living abroad may change jobs, some may even return home. Ganesha watches over you and that indeed is a great blessing. You will emerge stronger. Ganesha will ensure that!

6 February: First Quarter in Taurus

'The enlightened man is the greatest stranger in the world; he does not seem to belong to anybody. No organization confines him, no community, no society, no nation. An awakened person is the master of his own destiny. She/he holds the light of her/his own hard-won truth,' said Osho. You want to be just that, and strive hard to find your true inner nature without compromises. You have the stabilizing influence of Taurus, and get down to business. You roll your sleeves and get down to the task of building your home. Nation building can wait! Charity begins at home and you sort out the business front too. There is luck, even a windfall. Deals swing your way with ease. If you have been trying to broker a deal for a long time, it may happen now without much effort. Ganesha is pleased.

14 February: Full Moon in Leo

'Life finds its purpose and fulfilment in the expansion of happiness,' said Maharishi Mahesh Yogi. 'The very purpose of life is to seek happiness,' said the Dalai Lama. I second it. It is my core belief. I also try to spread good cheer. I have lived long enough and seen the caprices of life. I have also done thousands, possibly lakhs, of charts and seen the ebb and flow of life from close quarters. Man is a bundle of contradictions and every move is a mystery. There is free will too, along with a lot of factors outside our control. You are filled with powerful energies now and are almost unrecognisable from the person you were a few weeks ago. There is happiness and you feel inspired. It is as though you have been struck by lightning, a bolt from the blue. You celebrate love, spread it around, are invigorated by it, and become a candle in the dark. You throw light and impress and influence everyone you meet. Ganesha is pleased.

22 February: Last Quarter in Sagittarius

The last quarter is in your sign and there could be happy travels in store. You love exploring new places, looking for new adventures and offbeat trails. You may plan an exotic holiday with family, friends or even alone. There is new energy propelling you, and all the earlier negativity is replaced by a powerful zest for life. You are like a seed that has just sprouted and seeks the life-giving force of the sun. Work is on track and there is stability at home. Ganesha had promised you that it would all work out well. You look for a welcome break and want to seize the moment. It is a long way to go!

1 March: New Moon in Pisces

'One who condones evil is just as guilty as the one who perpetrates it,' said Rev. Martin Luther King Jr. the great civil rights leader. Taking a cue from his words, you set out righting all the wrongs in your neighbourhood. If you live in the subcontinent, every aspect of life is ridden with anarchy and inequity. All this jars you and you feel you have to do something about it. There are emotional moments as you have to convince family members who warn you of the dangers of activism. You join existing committees and start new ones if none exist. There is a flurry of activity. You meet with law-enforcing agencies, elected representatives, NGOs, citizen's groups and everyone interested in social change. There is travel, new associations and many unusual encounters. Ganesha is an ally. So am I. In the mood you are in, you believe you are carrying the world on your shoulders like Charles Atlas. You believe you are more than a match for Arnold Schwarzenegger. Good luck!

8 March: First Quarter in Gemini

You feel energetic and vigorous. Your health is good and you seek the outdoors and exhilarating physical activity. You are dashing and raring to go. Use this energy well. If you are a sportsperson or in the defence forces or even an extreme adventure enthusiast, this is the time to scale new peaks. You feel alive and bubble with zest like a cola advertisement. Those in sedentary jobs also do well. Business people excel at negotiations and achieve desired results. You are filled with confidence and make a positive impression on others. There could be profitable travel, new experiences and encounters. You could be intellectually restless and keen on ploughing your own furrow, making your own identity. You want to stand out, be different from the flock. Ganesha is pleased.

16 March: Full Moon in Virgo

While life is steady, there will be unspoken differences, reservations or sensitivities that emerge in your communications with others. There could be arguments and altercations. You are full of yourself and with some reason too. You do not tolerate fools gladly. Ignoramuses pile their views on you. They also crowd you out physically. You resent all this and retaliate. Some empathy will help but you do not have the patience or the inclination as you feel your private space is being intruded upon by people who have nothing better to do. You are a maze of pulls and pressures and yet make progress as you have set your magnetic needle and are aggressive in your desire for goals. There are domestic demands on you. Children may fly away and there could be emotional moments. There could also be illness and medical emergencies. Ganesha is with you.

24 March: Last Quarter in Capricorn

Your attention and energies will be focused on work. You plan for the future and meet with others to come up a new direction. This is also a good time to be with yourself, to understand the new winds blowing in your direction. You have many long-term plans and this is a good phase to go over them. There are also strong ego needs. You do not want to fall flat on your face and so you go through the details. You are hoping for success in all your dealings and the homework has to be thorough. You are like the lone ranger now, sorting it out all in your head before making the final push. You don't share details with others and keep it all close to your chest. Ganesha holds your hand.

30 March: New Moon in Aries

You are powered by new energy. Relationships come into focus. There are hidden tensions and you have to face them head-on. You will get to know yourself better through your relationships. There will be a lot of sifting too, as you get rid of those people who mean nothing to you. But you also realize that you do not want to be alone and need a close relationship with a lover, a friend or someone with whom you can share your innermost secrets. There is success at work and new love. There are many expenses too. You are driven, and want it all to happen now. Your impatience doesn't allow you to wait. You are like a jaguar, ready to pounce on anything. Ganesha wishes you well.

7 April: First Quarter in Cancer

There are emotional moments but this is also a favourable time for all kinds of mental work. You communicate furiously and state your case with force. You do well at lectures, teaching, group discussions, interviews and negotiations of all kinds. At work there are rewards and applause. You are clear in your head and spell out your needs and priorities clearly without beating around the bush. You are well organized and are ready to accommodate others. There is progress and you make substantial headway in all your dealings. Expenses skyrocket. There are tears both of joy and sorrow, it's a mixed bag. Ganesha blesses you.

15 April: Full Moon in Libra

There are powerful physical energies at play. Your sexual desires may peak and you want a roll in the hay with that special person. If you suppress your desires, you could become irritable and feisty. You may have to initiate love. Youngsters will be swept by this wave, and the power of infatuation will be as potent as nuclear fission. This is also a great time for those in creative fields. There is enormous energy oozing from every pore and this could be a good time to sublimate it in all creative endeavours. There are expensive purchases, and many opportunities showing up at your door. Ganesha wishes you well. Of course, you dilly-dally for eternity as you do not know which road to take as all the opportunities look alluring.

22 April: Last Quarter in Aquarius

You are in communication mode. Your thoughts are clear and precise. You may take up a new course of study or chill with friends at the movies or an art gallery or museum. As you can see, I am deeply influenced by generation next and use their lingo as often as I can. The future belongs to youth, and I feel they should be encouraged in every possible way. You may be in search of a godman and looking for instant nirvana. You are curious to know more about everything you can lay your hands on. There is clarity and you are objective in all your dealings. You get on to social networking sites and make contact with the world. There is progress on all fronts and Ganesha is pleased.

29 April: New Moon in Taurus

The new moon is in Taurus and you are more stable. The bull lends some balance to the archer! You are steadfast and persevering and slogging away at work. The employed are in line for promotions. Those on their own moonlight and find new ways to make big bucks. You feel happy and are at peace and in harmony with others. You enjoy the good feeling. There is work to be done but not much is accomplished now as you want to enjoy the moment. You are filled with enthusiasm and optimism and send the right signals to the cosmos. The luck of the draw is with you. There could be a windfall. You have planned well and there is bound to be success. It is not just luck, but the result of prolonged planning and good execution. Ganesha blesses you.

7 May: First Quarter in Leo

Leo Tolstoy, the well-known novelist and philosopher, said, 'Truth, like gold, is to be obtained not by its growth, but by washing away from it all that is not gold.' You do just that in the phase you are in. You realize that it is high time that you cleaned up your act and got to know your real self. It is time you shimmer like gold and come into your own. You are in touch with the real world now. You have come to grips with terra firma. You are worth much more than what is commonly acknowledged. You are worth your weight in gold and it is high time you shed all the modesty. I believe it will happen now and you will shine like a jar of glow worms in pitch darkness. Ganesha watches over your every move. You cannot go wrong.

14 May: Full Moon in Scorpio

You live in the world of dark desires. Carl Jung, the great psychoanalyst said, 'The world today hangs by a thin thread, and the thread is the psyche of man.' You have to come to terms with the dark secrets permeating your soul. There is love staring at you but your hands are tied. You crave for love, and when you get it you don't know what to do. You feel lonely, and when that space is occupied you feel crowded. There are expenses, travel and new associations. You may migrate with the family or due to a job. You look for new vistas, for the rush of a warm breeze on your neck. The subcontinent is sweltering, and so is the intensity in your life. But luck and Ganesha are on your side.

21 May: Last Quarter in Pisces

You are in an emotional whirl. Your emotions are on fast forward. This is one of the most emotionally trying influences associated with domestic or professional problems, depression and various types of difficulties in personal relationships. There will be break-ups and you wonder what happened. But you could well be the cause of it all. You realize that you may have been neglecting your emotional and psychological needs and consequently feel alone and disconnected. You feel no one understands you. Ganesha watches over you.

28 May: New Moon in Gemini

You are plagued by thoughts. You need an identity. Suddenly, you feel that you have no identity of your own. You are looking for a purpose, a definition, a direction. Till now, you have been like algae floating in the water without a specific goal. You want your life to be unique and at the same time you want to be emotionally and spiritually fulfilled. All this calls for change. You will need to overhaul your life and change the sails. You have built walls and alienated others. You want to do too many things, but life is fleeting and there is little time to waste. These are indicators but I could be wrong as I do not have your specific details. Ganesha blesses you.

5 June: First Quarter in Virgo

There is an element of practicality that steps in. You look at work and funds at your disposal. There are important domestic and job concerns that confront you. You want to solve all the puzzles on your plate and move forward. You are focused, and are able to concentrate and work with great clarity. You have a sharp eye for detail and the little pieces that make up the whole. You are thoughtful, deliberate and hard-working as you comb through every minor detail with a magnifying glass. Those who are employed are applauded. I belong to the old school and believe that success comes only through perseverance. Hasn't it been repeatedly said that genius is 99 per cent perspiration and only 1 per cent inspiration? Ask me, your favourite astrologer, writing book after book, well into his eighties. Ask Ganesha too.

13 June: Full Moon in Sagittarius

The full moon is in your sign and this is a propitious time to surge ahead. There are fun times and you participate in social get-togethers, picnics and outings. You spend time in genial company and enjoy yourself. This is a light-hearted influence and you can happily sort out various issues bothering you without fear or guilt. There are happy moments with the family as you may attend a concert, or an art exhibition or go to the beach or on a trek into the woods. You have cordial relations with friends, neighbours, relatives and peers. There is happiness all around and you bask in it. You are also a good listener, and that is an integral part of being a good conversationalist. Ganesha approves.

19 June: Last Quarter in Pisces

I have often spoken about the shadowy side of one's personality. Call it the blind spot. Even the most intelligent and the educated cannot escape silly errors of judgement. It is an inclination we are born with. You are no exception as you find your love affairs floundering repeatedly. You make a habit of picking up the wrong partner and investing your emotions in that person. When it doesn't work out you feel doomed and are left to pick up the pieces. Then you call it destiny. I am also fallible and so do not want to be judgemental. This is just a statement of fact. I am also a published poet and I guess it is these shadowy sides that make for great poetry. Ask Ganesha for guidance. You may be in that situation now, in a sort of pickle.

27 June: New Moon in Cancer

There is a lot on the domestic front calling out to you. There are medical emergencies, children need attention, and the spouse or partner needs your time. Those in business look for expansion and the employed get pay hikes and promotions. Make the most of this period. There is frenetic activity and you are like a tsunami. There are realty deals, blue chip stocks and investments of all kinds. There are emotional moments too but you handle them with maturity. Unless otherwise indicated in your personal chart, Jupiter will always be an ally. Children bring joy and there could be an addition to the family, even adoption, if I may add, and many festivities. Ganesha is overjoyed.

5 July: First Quarter in Libra

You are in communication mode. There is a lot going on in your head and you want to spill it out. You also await the right response and are all ears. There are new projects and collaborations. Those in any type of social activity do exceedingly well. You have big ideas and plans and like Michael Jordan, the great basketball player, you want to get better and better and keep raising the bar. He always said that he was only as good as his last game and his best would be the next game! In the process, he kept pushing the frontiers of excellence. Use this phase for making decisions, planning, negotiating and concluding deals. A long way to go! Ganesha is with you.

12 July: Full Moon in Capricorn

Here is a good period for hard, sustained work. You are on fire. You have set your sights high and will not stop at anything to achieve your goals. People help out and luck favours you. Napoleon wanted lucky generals to lead his men into battle. I agree too that luck is more important then anything else. It is how the cards are drawn in your favour, and very little can be done about it. Youngsters do well in examinations and interviews. There could be new job openings and those who are doing well simply excel. Ganesha is pleased.

19 July: Last Quarter in Aries

You are raring to go. You are filled with optimism, drive, enthusiasm and guts. You feel you can achieve the impossible. You may also get carried away and overextend yourself. The pace is frenetic and you often go overboard. Obviously, you are not in any mood to accommodate others. So there could be resistance to your ideas and opinions but you stand your ground. You are not cowed by it. On the contrary, you are encouraged to stick to your guns. There could be exotic travel and new love. Youngsters will enjoy many dalliances. I suspect that senior citizens who are so inclined will also make the most of this phase. There is expansion and growth as you scorch the tarmac on all fronts. Ganesha blesses you.

26 July: New Moon in Leo

The movement continues. There is no let-up. It could be difficult for loved ones and friends to keep pace with you. You are infatuated by travel and are forever seeking someplace exotic. But it remains elusive. There are major expenses, renovations, redevelopment of property, setting up of new manufacturing units if you are in business, and some medical emergencies. Siblings will need care and children may cause anxiety. The single find new love and have a quick roll in the hay. There may be nothing more to it than that. There is progress on the external plane. Ganesha is with you.

4 August: First Quarter in Scorpio

A new intensity takes you over. You look for answers to profound questions of life. You seek out gurus and godmen, tantra, mantra and yantra, pilgrimages, havans, the latest esoteric thought, and more meaning to life. There are new associations; a stranger of the same sex and from an entirely different culture may establish a huge presence in your life now. It need not be sexual in nature. Earlier, a different culture meant a foreign country. It won't be long, I feel, before we start interacting with aliens from other planets on a more routine level. I am an astrologer who has seen over eighty summers but I know and see how technology is changing the world. I am open to new events. Although I am scientific and empirical in my research, I also know that magic exists. We miss a lot with our eyes; the magic exists on a more subtle plane. It won't be long before technology rules us, despite it all. But the magic will remain, insists Ganesha.

10 August: Full Moon in Aquarius

There are maudlin moments. You feel depressed and lonely for no apparent reason. You may fall sick and a persistent skin ailment could recur. The body and mind are connected and it may be due to all the imagined stress you carry like a heavy load. There could be indulgences like alcoholism and drugs. You look at all escape hatches as you want to avoid taking life head-on. This is a mixed period, indeed even a nixed period. There could be joy and sorrow, life and death. Life is a mixture of it all and none of us can escape its vagaries. You don't care too much about money as long as your needs are met. Yet, sometimes, even this can become difficult. Trust in Ganesha. He will lead you across troubled waters.

17 August: Last Quarter in Taurus

There is more stability now and you are back on track. You work hard and make money. There is nowhere to go, you can't play hide-and-seek with life. You have to grapple with whatever is thrown on your plate. There is no arguing with it. You decide to do just that. You are through with the debates and the questioning and the futile search for El Dorado. The answers lie within, not in geographical spaces. Change your mind and change your life. You straighten out relationships that are not working. There will be financial gains with legacies, inheritance, loans, stocks, realty, manufacturing, pharmaceuticals, retail and related sectors. Ganesha watches over you.

25 August: New Moon in Virgo

'Understand the present moment and you have understood the whole phenomenon of eternity,' said Osho. I urge you to live in the present. Your mind wanders and you think of past hurts, relationships that have broken down, and things that didn't work and you can do nothing about them. There no is point in crying over spilt milk. You understand this well too, and work at being in one place with stoicism. You look at rooting yourself. You want to belong and yet you want to be free. You long for love and enter it with open arms. Sooner rather than later you realize that you want to exit from it as you love your freedom more than anything else. This cycle is getting repetitive. This is a period of hope, promise and new beginnings. Ganesha is with you.

2 September: First Quarter in Sagittarius

The first quarter is in your own sign and this is a good time to make the impossible happen. You fly high with new speed and energy. You are in the pole position like Vettel. Just make sure that you don't crash out like Niki Lauda. Your emotions are stable though you emit fire in all your dealings. You have no time for fools and laggards. You display impatience and tell others where to get off. There is travel and you soar like a giant balloon across the beautiful English meadows. Ganesha ensures that you find your way. Why worry?

9 September: Full Moon in Pisces

There is love, bonding and fun. You reach out to others and new people enter your life. You attend alumni meetings and spend quality time with family and friends.

Elders at home may need attention. There could be new job offers for the employed, and rapid business expansion for those on their own. Freelancers will also flourish. You are in a sensitive phase and emotions could boil over. Express it in writing, music, screenplay, dance and in other creative ways. It may help to be persistent as you are quick to lose interest once you start something. Ganesha watches over you.

16 September: Last Quarter in Gemini

From 14 September to 25 October, Mars will be in your sign. Mars is like the volcano of vitality inside you and influences endurance, persistence and discipline. Mars is named after the Roman god of war, and is also known as 'the bright and burning one'. Red is the colour of Mars; it stimulates the dynamic, potent and fertile drives that power our lives. Mars rules physical energy and action and governs energy, strength, courage, life force and expansion. Well-placed Mars endows us with a powerful energy and an indomitable will to succeed. Mars propels us like an ignited rocket. It is an important energy since it determines how we pursue what we want to achieve in life. In short, Mars represents energy, force, violence, aggression, sports, combat, wars, battles, accidents and operations. Mars is in your sign for over a month and you could be in a combative mood. Watch out for accidents, altercations, disagreements and the law. You cannot have your way all the time and you will have to acknowledge that. Retreat sometimes, like the great generals. You could be on edge, rushing through rash decisions. There could be break-ups and marital discord. Life is a roller coaster. Control your temper, your words and your actions.

Sometimes, it is not necessary to be outspoken. Ganesha watches over you.

24 September: New Moon in Libra

The focus is on relationships of all kinds. You will have your hands full with your children, parents, spouse, partner, in-laws, friends, near and dear ones. It may not be too comfortable and you will have to go with the flow. There is an ebb and flow to life and the seasons change all the time. Even the cells of the body change every moment, and our biorhythms vary from day to day. There is cosmic time that is overpowering and you will have to understand that. There is no point breaking your head against the wall. You make trips to shrines and holy places seeking deliverance from the trials of life. I add here, like I always do, that a lot depends on the individual horoscope. These are, at best, generalizations. Use your free will to your advantage. Ganesha watches over you.

1 October: First Quarter in Capricorn

You are in the throes of change. There is more stability too, thanks to the influence of Capricorn. You try your best to be stable and follow the beaten path. You want to be accepted and do not want to rebel. You try your best to belong to the world of normal human beings. I cannot help but quote Edgar Allan Poe here. He said, 'I became insane, with long periods of horrible sanity.' That may well happen to you too. Control and discipline are fine, but in moderation. Allow what is to happen to happen. The straight and narrow may not suit you. Fly with the wind, flow with the water. Along with this are domestic pressures and maudlin moments. You take time off to be with yourself. Ganesha is with you though.

8 October: Full Moon in Aries

Your energies are high and you are buoyed and filled with confidence. This is a good time for business expansion and you have the foresight and insight to make the right decisions. Your decisions now are usually spot on. You may also indulge in a bout of gambling. Luck is on your side, but don't go overboard. You meet with worldly success as you sign important documents and detail new plans for expansion. There could also be favourable out-of-court settlements. There are expenses and a lot of pruning and chopping in your life. Ganesha looks after you.

15 October: Last Quarter in Cancer

You are highly emotional now and feel that you have to express your feelings. This is an explosive period and not great for rationale and reason. You are also able to empathise with others and are a good listener. So others fill you in with their problems and issues. A lot of time is spent with your family and its concerns. There is romance too, and if you already have a partner there is intense bonding. There are marriages, engagements and many festive occasions calling out for you. Leave it to Ganesha and he will show the way.

23 October: New Moon in Scorpio

This is a good time for all types of communication. The employed could have altercations and misunderstandings with their boss. There could also be some marital discord. Nip it in the bud. There could also be pressing medical issues and you may need to consult a specialist. This is a period when going solo may not be the answer. It will be in your interest to work out collaborative enterprises.

You are moving ahead and life is flamboyant. There is money, love, joy, travel, friends, parties and fun of all kinds. Enjoy, says Ganesha. The aroma of hard-earned success is enchanting.

31 October: First Quarter in Aquarius

There are many emotions at play here. Ensure that you do not lose your objectivity in discussions or lose your sense of perspective. Regardless of your gender, women will play a prominent role in your life now. There could be shifting of residence and this may faze you. Objects, persons and places that are familiar to you, from whom you have got emotional sustenance or reassurance, will now be replaced by unfamiliar things. All this can be disturbing and disorienting and you will have to learn to adapt. Finally, as Darwin said, the species that adapts survives. As the winter chill enters your bones, you are filled with new plans. You are moving in many directions but energies are low and there could be fatigue and even illness. Trust in Ganesha and all will be well.

6 November: Full Moon in Taurus

There is substantial progress at work. You think and plan big and manage to execute it all. You are inclined to make big plans and set long-range goals. You are able to see the larger picture and plan accordingly. This is a great time for both creative and business folk. You are able to think in ideal and abstract terms and also have the foresight and planning to hit the jackpot in commercial transactions. Your vision is grand and you stop at nothing to achieve your goals. You roughshod others and could be arrogant and self-righteous. You are forging ahead and may even twist the law to achieve your goals. You have an alibi for all your actions and believe that the end justifies the means. Ganesha watches with some concern.

14 November: Last Quarter in Leo

Venus will be in your sign from 17 November to 10 December, which is quite a long period. Venus is another important planet and is of great significance. This is an important phase. As often discussed, Venus is the planet for love, romance, sex, beauty and the good life. This is the planet of attraction, love, wealth, knowledge and prosperity. The compatibility of partners and the type of life the individual will lead are also judged from the placement of Venus in the horoscope. As a planet, Venus is considered to be beneficial, feminine and gentle. Venus symbolizes the force of attraction in the universe. In human beings this attractive force manifests as love and beauty. When Venus is well placed in the chart, there is love, art, and beauty. Venus rules Libra and Taurus, though its role in every sign is important. Like other planets, it also has its transits. In Libra, Venus is aesthetic and cultured. In Taurus it is more earthy, materialistic and sensual. Venus rules the venous system, kidneys, urinary tract, throat and larynx, and is responsible for good looks. In short, Venus in Western astrology stands for comforts, arts, wealth, relationships, sex, decorations, luxuries and wealth. Your business deals may have clicked and there is a lot of money to spend. You splurge on life's goodies. You let your hair down and party. There is money and honey. Your investments are doing well. Ganesha is pleased.

22 November: New Moon in Sagittarius

The good times continue to roll. This is also your birth period and the energies of the new moon are intense. There are rewards and awards, applause and accolades. You are the cream of your peers and the industry you represent. Media folk do exceptionally well. Chronic illnesses are in remission and relationships are happy. Your bonhomie is contagious. People flock around you and there is magic wherever you go. You flourish and Ganesha is happy.

29 November: First Quarter in Pisces

Uncork the bubbly. Mercury will be in your sign from 28 November to 16 December. Mercury, the mighty, all-powerful planet is in your sign now. It favours travels, meetings, conferences, interviews, trips, more brain power, contacts, communication, correspondence and contracts. Mercury has a special connection with the circuits of the brain. Chess, crossword puzzles and other such games belong to Mercury. Also, short-distance runners and spin bowlers are controlled by Mercury. Mercury, in short, is the ambassador and salesman of the zodiac. Mercury is the symbol of news, views, messages, interviews, contacts, communications, travel and transport. Mercury gives impetus to all of the above in the sun sign where it is located. The year is ending on a fantastic and fascinating note. There is rapid growth in all spheres of your life. There are new ventures and collaborations. There is money and honey. Most importantly, you are happy. If I may stretch it a bit, you are deliriously happy. Ecstasy envelopes you. There is lust and love, bonding and meaning; work is good, family life is stable, health is on an even ground and there is money in the bank and in your pocket. Ganesha is delighted. If you want more, it is pure greed, he says.

6 December: Full Moon in Gemini

You are in success mode. You have the Midas touch. This is a favourable time for all kinds of mental work. You excel in communicating with others and are able to state your case forcefully. You are good at group discussions and negotiations. Youngsters do exceedingly well. You have a clear idea of the larger picture, and are able to handle your ego well, without becoming overbearing. You breast the tape with the speed of Asafa Powell leaving the opposition far behind. Let me remind you that I was a 100-metre champion in my youth. So I know my athletics well. You are riding the wave like an expert surfer, scoring goals from acute angles like Lionel Messi, designing the future like the late Steve Jobs, pulverising bowling like Chris Gayle, and still retaining the calm of Buddha. I quote Søren Kierkegaard, the Danish philosopher, 'Life can only be understood backwards, but it must be lived forwards.' That is what you do now. The past is forgotten as you open new windows and see a new dawn. Ganesha is delighted. Carpe diem! Seize the moment.

14 December: Last Quarter in Virgo

You continue batting on the front foot even on a damp Kotla wicket on the last day of the match! This is an extremely favourable influence for close relationships and encounters of all kinds. There is love and bonding. Courting couples take the relationship to the next level.

Work is also good. There is money and honey as you sign on the dotted line and ink profitable collaborations. You meet new people and any association that begins now will be rewarding. You party and spend time with loved ones. You want to be with others; this is not the time to be alone as you are filled with gratitude and want to share all the goodies that existence has dropped in your lap. Ganesha smiles. He always wants the best for you.

22 December: New Moon in Capricorn

One year is ending and another is beckoning. You wonder how fast time flies! So much has happened and so much remains to be done. While you may not be particularly keen on empire building, you want to make waves, make things happen. You demand to be yourself and are filled with powerful assertive energies. This is not the time for self-denial or discipline. You are looking to express your energies in as eloquent a fashion as possible. Those in the armed forces and in the field of sports, in particular, do exceptionally well. You are assertive in love too, and if you have set your sights on someone, you make a go for it with a no-holds-barred Greco-Roman style, if I may add in jest! Your desires are powerful and the moment is all that you have in your hands. You party for ever. This is your time in the sun, says Ganesha happily.

28 December: First Quarter in Aries

You could be on cloud nine if there is a new love in your life. There is powerful intensity, passion and deep bonding. You are enriched by the other person's presence in your life and you give it all. It is a love that captivates you, ensnares you and leaves you delightfully breathless;

every touch is electric. You feel that you have finally found your soulmate. Ganesha is delighted. So am I. We all know the power of love. Family life is good. You are often torn between wanting to be free and wanting to belong to someone. In this phase, belonging has a better fragrance as you clasp hard onto the whiffs of romantic pleasure.

Key Dates

January

1*, 5–6, 9–11, 14*–19, 21–23, 27*–29.
Ganesha says January stands for finance, family and food, favours and life's flavours. A month of plenty, in all the Fs, and otherwise too.

February

1*–2, 6*–7, 10*–16, 19*–20, 23*–25, 28*–29.
News and views, meets and conferences, trips and ties, computers and the Internet, all come together. The Cs are all therefore important, since communication is the main thrust now.

March

1*, 4–5, 9–14, 17*–18, 22–23, 27*–28.
Home and journeys, money, rentals, loans, health, servants, court cases, all these keep you on your toes. Lots to do, indeed.

April

1–2, 4*–10, 13*–15, 18*–20, 23*–24, 28*–29.
This month helps you to be a good parent, cultivate friendship and happiness, entertain lavishly and be

amused. Fun and work combine to make April very special. Good luck.

May

3*–8, 11–12, 16*–17, 21*–22, 26*–27, 30*–31.

May, June, July are interconnected regarding home, house, shop, property, health, money, servants, hard work, colleagues and more work, says Ganesha!

June

4–7, 10*–11, 15*–16, 19–20*, 23–27 (important).

June is for meeting people, marriage, partnerships of every sort, journeys both short and long. Also, the union or clash of minds. Ties and a major outreach sum it up.

July

1*, 4–5, 9*–15, 19*–20, 23*–25, 28*–29.

You open the account with loans, joint finance, insurance, taxes, legacy. A shift/transfer/house move is also indicated, says Ganesha; but money matters are the dominant note.

August

1*–6, 10*–11, 15*–16, 20*–21, 24–25, 28–29.

Journey, mobility, pilgrimage, rites, religion, tantra and mantra, inspiration and travel are the possibilities for this month. Once again, a very busy time.

September

1*–2, 3–6, 11–14, 18–19, 23–24 (fine), 28–29.

You will be working and slogging hard like a trooper/soldier, and also enjoying the fruits of victory, like a commander. Good news and views make for great intellectual stimulation.

October

4*–5, 9*–10, 13*–18, 22*–23, 26–27, 31.
You will walk your way to fame, success, love, riches, power, promotion. The health of parents, in-laws might be a problem, but you're able to cope.

November

1*, 5–6, 9*–15, 18–19, 22*–24, 27*–29.
The balance sheet of life will be mixed, that is, profit and loss, income and expense, joy and sorrow, in this phase. Take care of health issues, both yours and those of elders.

December

2*–4, 7*–12, 15*–26, 20*–21, 24–26, 30–31.
Ganesha says you will run the race of life, be it honey, money or Indian rice and curry. Jewellery and valuables, job, profession and business are the themes that are energised, and you work wonders in terms of acquisitions and gains.

Capricorn

YEARLY FORECAST

Poets say, 'Short are the days of wine and roses.'

> – Speaking Tree, *Times of India,* 30 June 2013

Knowledge, experience and observation are the tripod of astrology. I am now eighty-three (born11 July 1931). By mundane Western astrology, Capricorn is the main sign of our beloved India. Mundane means earthly; and by mundane astrology I mean astrology of countries rather than of persons.

Till 16 July 2014

Summary and Guidance

Jupiter in your 7th angle gifts you 'partnerships, attachments, trips, ties, collaborations with yourself and nature and society and God is what it is all about. Hurry! There is no time to waste. The Buddha welcomes you with a smile.' Add to it marriage, romance, foreign collaborations, journeys with a stopover, perhaps court cases, and Supernatural powers and Energies helping you all the way. This completes the picture. There is only one snag. The Bible says, 'Do unto others what you expect others to do to you.' That's it.

17 July 2014 to 11 August 2015

Jupiter will be in your eighth angle of loans, funds, taxes, insurance, investment, buying/selling/shopping, inheritance, religious rites, tantra and mantra, seances, using the planchette for producing automatic writing, even necromancy, the art and ritual of raising the dead.

You must learn to be discreet, to conserve your energies, and not to overindulge in food, drinks and sex. Everything in excess has a repercussion. But I do understand at the same time that you like extremes, and I am not your moral custodian. Essentially, a favourable money period for sure!

Main Trend

Please read the very big paragraphs at the beginning. In short, honey till 16 July 2014. After that, money. In money we also include joint finance. Surprisingly enough, tantra and mantra also come in this bracket. Prayers and great charity will be the directions for not only success and achievement but genuine happiness. Capricorns specially should always remember that achievement and success may not always be real happiness and joy. Joy comes from within and has to be shared.

Journey and Communication

Mercury, the spearhead of journey and communication, will be in your own sign from 17 to 31 December. Again March, May, July (certainly), September (surely) and perhaps November also favour it.

Health

Take care of acidity, legs, knees, feet and private parts of the body. Mars will be in your tenth angle of extreme hard work and rich rewards from 1 January to 25 July. This could really tell upon your health. April, June, August and to some extent, December are red signals for you. Please remember this is a reading based only on your sun sign. I am not a god.

Love/Marriage

Till 16 July 2014 love and marriage are strongly accentuated. Strictly speaking, we have begun the forecast with love. Read it. Venus stands for love and marriage. Venus will be in your own sign from 11 to 31 December. Romance and finance will lead to great ambience (atmosphere, mood, setting). July, May and September will make your heart sing and dance. Remember the saying, 'If there is a green bough in your heart, the singing birds will surely come.' As a rule, Capricorns are not great at love and romance. But I will be happy if you prove me wrong. Human beings are capable of everything. That is my motto, for sure.

Property

Yes, Capricorns are not only good but great in property matters. Avoid disputes and legal matters please because of the warrior planet Mars. That is the only danger. Rather than fight, be adjusting and cooperative. That is easier and better. Renovation, decoration, alteration, buying and selling, renting and leasing, shifting and foreign lands all come under the label of property.

Job/Business/Loans/Funds/Investments

Mars in your tenth angle till 25 July makes you work like a donkey and enjoy like a king! Your managerial skills, common sense, practicality, patience, perseverance will lead to victory. March, July, September and 26 October to 4 December will be mighty rewarding.

Children/Entertainment

Children and entertainment are closely related to love and marriage because emotions and the heart and inspiration and imagination are involved. Add to it hobbies, all the arts, specially music, research in science and technology, and you know what a wide horizon you have to work on.

Trips and Ties

Read journey and communications please. Ties come very much under Venus. May, July, September, 11 to 31 December should be ideal for ties. In ties we include all partnerships and attachments, including evidently marriage and collaborations and extramarital affairs.

Publicity, Projects, Performance

Capricorns are one of the mighty masters of publicity and performance. Like the goat they climb to the very top of the hill. Nothing can stop them. They have the determination and the patience to do so. The months for it will be January, October, June and November.

Happiness Quota

I allot 82 per cent to you.

Monthly Round-up

January: power, pelf, perks, promotion, prosperity; February: finances and family; March: contacts and joy; April: property, parents, renovation/decoration, in-laws; May: joy, creativity, children, hobbies, you make news and win others over; June: work, funds, employment, health and medical check-up, servants, subordinates; July: marriage, ties, love, collaborations, romance, meeting and reaching out to people and places; August: health, funds, vitality, tantra and mantra, change of locale, moving; September: journey, publicity, ceremony, collaborations, functions, rites and religion; October: stepping up on efficiencty, work, status, prestige, taking care of parents, elders; November: help, socializing, friendship, fraternity, camaraderie; December: expenses, losses, spirituality, helping others, charity, long-distance connections.

Summary

Romance and finance fuse happily for you. Health safeguards will be essential. Plenty of movement physically, mentally, emotionally, spiritually, points out Ganesha and His is the last word.

Outer Planets

URANUS: Uranus is the hurdle. In all domestic and property affairs a little care and caution are most certainly advisable. After 17 July 2014 and up to 11 August 2015, loans, funds and investments are very surprisingly possible. Life is not a straight line. Life is a circle. Therefore astrology is also a circle. There are ups and downs.

NEPTUNE: Neptune in your third angle helps you in contacts, contracts, communication, correspondence. In short, you will be able to fan out to people and places. Use this prediction to your advantage, says Ganesha.

PLUTO: Pluto is in your own sign and that gives you the ability to overcome all obstacles and clear your way. Pluto gives you the firepower to win. I am sure you Capricorns understand firepower and the will to win very clearly.

Month by Month

January

You are zooming ahead. Nothing can stop you as you power away and mow down the opposition with scant respect. There are new deals, and more money and authority. While you make rapid career progress, there will also be several luxury purchases. There are new investments, exotic travel, love and passion, festivities and celebrations. What a way to start the year! There is also love and deep bonding. Ganesha is with you.

February

There is balance and stability and hard work. The results are stupendous. There is money and honey, rewards and awards, accolades and applause. You smell money, and the fragrance is heady. The best part is that you are not just fantasizing. You are making it all happen. Your energy level is high. There is travel and networking. You take on new responsibilities at work and the applause is deafening. Ganesha is delighted.

March

You know all there is in the material world and now want to taste the ethereal and the esoteric. There may be pilgrimages. There are new activities and new encounters. There is growth at all levels. You work hard to take advantage of every opportunity for growth and expansion. There are also happy times and a roll in the hay. You may be sidetracked from work by the pleasures of the flesh. There could be overindulgence. Ambition goads you. You take risks and live dangerously. Ganesha holds your hand.

April

There are emotional moments. The past catches up with you. You could be irritable, foul-mouthed and bad-tempered. You look inwards and examine your life. You grow and evolve as a person. This is also the time for love. You may work on subjective concerns that bother you and help with the poor and downtrodden. There are maudlin moments too and you look at a complete personal revamp. This is an excellent time for making plans for the future. Ganesha blesses you.

May

This is a powerful phase. You slog away. You may buy a holiday home. There is love and bonding, journeys, festivities, even an addition to the family. This is the time for love and laughter, companionship and shared joy. There are emotional moments tearing you down. You have many affairs of the heart. You are also pulled by the 'drunken monkey', as Swami Vivekananda called the human mind. There are sentimental moments as you play out a fantasy world. Ganesha holds your hand.

June

You have evolved as a person and you realize in moments of reflection that although you have made errors you have managed to pull through. Your energy levels are high and you look at the future with hope and belief. There are expenses and medical emergencies. You may also tread on someone's toes due to strong ego drives. You look for spiritual balms and go in search of gurus and godmen. There are happy moments with the family. There is love, passion, partnerships and collaborations. You consolidate your situation and move on. Ganesha helps you.

July

There are opportunities galore falling squarely on your lap. It is a crisis of abundance. You are spoilt for choice. You are cheerful and gregarious and feel like socializing. You radiate warmth and emotion. There is new love. This is a period of quiet optimism and positive thinking. Money flows through your fingers despite new contracts, partnerships and collaborations. Family life is stable. Your energies are high. You are filled with ambition. But there are discordant moods, and your heart and mind are at loggerheads. There is new love and indulgences. You invest and gamble recklessly. You are filled with love and longing. You want to be with others, particularly with that special person. There could be international travel. Ganesha is happy for you.

August

There are profound changes which derail your life. On the plus side, you may be throwing out junk, and that could be a great psychological burden off you. There is a purging, a catharsis of sorts. You are normally strong, independent and a leader, but in this phase you need the moral support of others and the fellowship of kindred souls. You also look at philanthropy. You may take to writing poetry, screenplays or a book. There could be a few brushes with the law and with colleagues. There are hidden tensions which erupt suddenly. The work front consumes all your energy. You have been working too hard and need to get out and smell the roses and feel the grass grow under your feet. You look for spiritual answers. Ganesha holds your hand.

September

You may look at a new home or even accessories for your wardrobe. This is an excellent time for mental work as you obsess about details and the fine print. You are in a critical mood and are acutely attentive to detail. You are grappling with issues, including, possibly, the hint of your partner straying. This is a time for reflection. You look inwards and try to fathom the rumblings of your soul. You look for spiritual guidance. You are meeting a lot of people and there will be an interesting mishmash of cultures. New vistas open dramatically. You are feeling happy, confident, optimistic and healthy. You are generous, understanding and tolerant and are a hit with the peer group. Ganesha smiles.

October

The first Quarter is in Capricorn and you are filled with energy and optimism. You are open to new winds and make rapid progress. There is zeal, vigour and power in all your dealings. Your communication skills are excellent and you go about forming new friendships and associations. You are creatively charged and look for innovation and invention. You plough your furrow, hack your way through the thicket of life, take the road less travelled and work smart. There is fire in your belly and you blaze. You are a winner all the way. Mars enters your sign from 26 October to 4 December. Mars becomes a very positive influence if you can control your feelings and your temper. Your emotions are stimulated, your passions are aroused. You want new vistas to open in your life and take you away on the wings of poesy. Ganesha approves.

November

There could be foreign travel. Youngsters do well at examinations and interviews. You are filled with new ideas and perspectives. The energies are powerful. There are expenses but fun times too. You are the soul of the party, wining, dining and shaking a leg. There is love and passion. You speak your mind and don't pull your punches. You look for change, for unadulterated happiness and joy. As another year begins pulling down the shutter, you are filled with big plans. Loved ones drop in after long. Ganesha is with you.

December

Venus is in Capricorn from 11 to 31 December. What an appropriate time for Venus to make its presence felt, when the world is charged with year-end festivity! Venus is the planet for love, romance, sex, beauty and the good life. This is the planet of attraction, love, wealth, knowledge and prosperity. This is a double whammy. Along with Venus comes Mercury which will be in Capricorn from 17 to 31 December. This is a fantastic period and a super way to crown the year. It cannot get better. You have the Midas touch. There are festivities and big career breaks. You dazzle like a million chandeliers. You cast your spell everywhere. The year ends in a blaze of glory. The tide is in your favour. Take it at the flood and court fortune (I confess to having twisted the Bard a bit). Ganesha is delighted for you.

Months at a Glance

January

Power, pelf, perks, promotion, prosperity.

February

Finances and family.

March

Contacts and joy.

April

Property, parents, renovation/decoration, parents, in-laws.

May

Joy, creativity, children, hobbies, you make news and win others over.

June

Work, funds, employment, health and medical check-up, servants, subordinates.

July

Marriage, ties, love, collaborations, romance, meeting and reaching out to people and places.

August

Health, funds, vitality, tantra and mantra, change of locale, moving.

September

Journey, publicity, ceremony, collaborations, functions, rites and religion.

October

Stepping up on efficiency, work, status, prestige, taking care of parents, elders.

November

Help, socializing, friendship, fraternity, camaraderie.

December

Expenses, losses, spirituality, helping others, charity, long-distance connections.

Weekly Review (By the phases of the moon)

1 January: New Moon in Capricorn

Capricorns revel in challenges. They are ambitious, sometimes ruthless, pragmatic and persevering. If anyone can turn a shortcoming into a blessing, it is they. Capricorns are generally successful. Like mountain goats, they climb slippery slopes and ensure that no pursuer can reach them. Ruled by Saturn, they look for reputation, money and power, and, more often than not, get it. Famous Capricorns include Nicolas Cage, Denzel Washington, Tiger Woods, Anthony Hopkins, Mel Gibson, Elvis Presley, Richard Nixon, Rod Stewart, Martin Luther King Jr, Muhammad Ali, Kevin Costner, Mao Zedong, Louis Pasteur, Rudyard Kipling and Swami Vivekananda, among others. The year starts well. The new moon is in your sign and nothing can stop you as you power away and mow down the opposition with scant respect. There are new deals, more money and more authority. You work hard and get where you want to. Ganesha is with you.

8 January: First Quarter in Aries

The turbocharged run continues with the power of Aries. There is great success in store. While you make rapid career progress, there will also be several luxury purchases. There are new investments, exotic travel, love and passion, festivities and celebrations. It is also your birth period and the energies are powerful. Make the most of them, says Ganesha. Life is calling out to you and you take the dance to new heights of excellence without missing a step. Ganesha applauds.

16 January: Full Moon in Cancer

There are quieter moments of reflection and solitude. You have been moving ahead at a scorching pace and now you take a back seat and spend time with the family. You have provided for them materially and there are emotional and spiritual demands to be met. The children need a break and so does the spouse. You will also be caring for aged parents and in-laws. There is a lot on your plate but you are fully aware that the family has to be indulged too. What is the point of position and pelf if the family is unhappy? Ganesha agrees.

24 January: Last Quarter in Scorpio

There is new intensity in whatever you do now. There is luck on your side and windfalls galore. What a way to start the year! These are indicators, mere prods. The stars never compel, they only impel. Use these prods well, along with free will. There is love and passion and deep bonding. The unattached may enter wedlock and those who are single may be sowing their seed as though Nostradamus had predicted the end of the world by sunrise tomorrow. There are indulgences, ego drives, excesses and some emotional turbulence. But Ganesha sees you through.

30 January: New Moon in Aquarius

The mood is mellow and softer. Your heart strings are pulled. You spend quality time at home and with friends. There are alumni association meetings, and relatives whom you may have forgotten drop by. You listen to music, go on long drives and look to recharge your batteries before your return to the arena like a gladiator keen on devouring the lions. You need the warm embrace of the family and it is there. You feel secure in its folds. Now, nothing can hold you back. Ganesha is also with you. But please don't think you are invincible. Life can change in a moment!

6 February: First Quarter in Taurus

The earth is calling out to you. There is balance and stability. You roll up your sleeves and soil your hands as you slog away. The results are stupendous. There is money and honey, rewards and awards, accolades and applause. Those in realty, construction, stocks and the media do exceptionally well. Your plate is overflowing with goodies. This is a bull run and you simply go from strength to strength. You smell money, and the fragrance is heady. You want more and more of it. You see the cheques coming in and dig your heels in harder. Money has a certain power, and you smell the ink on new greenbacks and chuckle with pleasure. Ganesha watches over you.

14 February: Full Moon in Leo

You live large with grandiose schemes. The best part is that you are not just fantasizing. You are making it happen. You are not one to idle your time in ruinous fantasies. You can be ruthless too. If something doesn't work, you just junk it and move on. There can be a lot of hurt in the process but that doesn't deter you. You can slice life clean even with a blunt kitchen knife! You are not too bothered about social change but in this phase you may look at a creative transformation of the world around you. Your energy level is high, you are aggressive, and there are huge ego clashes. But you don't back off in the face of enemy fire. Ganesha watches over you.

22 February: Last Quarter in Sagittarius

There is travel and networking. You meet with different people, and a person of the same sex from an entirely different culture will have a significant impact on you. You look to maintain your individuality within the relationship. This is not really a compromise, but sometimes you need to retreat to come up trumps later; it is a strategic move. You take on new responsibilities at work. You are blazing the track and careening like crazy, with sparks bellowing from the tarmac. The applause is deafening. The other aspects of your life will have to wait as you swallow mile after mile in less time than it takes to wink. Ganesha watches from the sidelines.

1 March: New Moon in Pisces

'The soul's first adventure is the fight between two ideas: the wish to return to earth in a human form, and the desire to feel the freedom of having no form,' said Paramahansa Yogananda. You know all that there is in the material world and now want to taste the ethereal and the esoteric. You look for gods and godmen and go in search of a guru. Tantra, mantra and yantra fascinate you. There may be pilgrimages. Relationships may jar, and it is necessary to work in a spirit of compromise to smoothen the folds. You are moving ahead fast and furious. There are powerful and stimulating influences at play. Ganesha blesses you.

8 March: First Quarter in Gemini

You are moving fast and your mind is in a whirl. There are new activities and new encounters. There is a lot of excitement and growth at all levels. You look to break away from routine and inject freshness into your life. You are getting jaded and need to reinvent. Routine can be a killer and it seems to be getting to you now. This can be a time of personal growth and self-discovery. Use the energies well, suggests Ganesha. Attachments, ties and bonds will be of paramount importance; you relive the past in a frenzy of recollections. The monkey mind tries to dominate you but you are well armed psychologically and stave it off.

16 March: Full Moon in Virgo

There is stability and hard work. You are back on terra firma. You work hard to take advantage of every opportunity for growth and expansion. You have the stamina and the will to persevere. You work quietly behind the scenes. There is no show of flamboyance, but your mind is fixed on the target like a pistol shooter at the Olympics. You don't flinch; all that you see is the bull's eye. You create your luck and the windfalls accrue. You build a strong foundation for success. Family life is stable. You don't have much time for them, but there are no complaints. Ganesha is pleased.

24 March: Last Quarter in Capricorn

There is continued hard work. There are also happy times and a roll in the hay. You may be side tracked from work by the pleasures of the flesh. There could be overindulgence. In the midst of it all, your creative energies are stimulated, and those in the media and allied fields receive kudos. There is money, love, expenses, buying, selling, engagements, marriages, bereavements and festivities. There are contradictions, but isn't life a bundle of contradictions? We are churning all the time as a minuscule part of the cosmos. Walk with Ganesha. He knows it all.

30 March: New Moon in Aries

The new moon is in Aries and you are powered by turbo fuel. You are like a new Boeing that is showing off, not just in the hangar or on the runway, but also in the air. You are also able to get material and moral backing from others. You have confidence, clarity and decisiveness. You plan and execute; it is as simple as that. If there are roadblocks you find a way around them like water. If needed, you also adopt the rapier to hack your way through the undergrowth of dissent with the clinical precision of a recruit in the special forces. You are obsessed with money, fame and glamour, and stop at nothing to get what you want. Ambition goads you. You take risks and live dangerously. Ganesha holds your hand, lest you fall off.

7 April: First Quarter in Cancer

There are emotional moments. The past catches up with you and recollections make you look oh, so foolish! Wipe your slate clean and move on, says Ganesha. It is the only way. 'Everything that is happening at this moment is the result of the choices you have made in the past,' says Deepak Chopra. But you do not have to be burdened by the past. In this phase you are irritable, foul-mouthed and bad-tempered, and overreact to the slightest criticism. You withdraw and clam up. This is a good time to get to know yourself. You look inwards at your motivations, and examine your life. There is spiritual growth. Life is not just about making money, and you realize that. You grow and evolve as a person. This holds you in good stead in times to come.

15 April: Full Moon in Libra

This is the time for love. Amorous pursuits gather you in its warm, sometimes lustful embrace. You are smitten. Your heart races. If you go for a cardiac function test, the machine will be flummoxed. You will do anything for the person you want; you tattoo the name on your body and spend your free hours dreaming of your beloved. Love oozes out of every pore and you just cannot contain yourself. If you don't get the object of your desire—your muse and your inspiration to live, you are damned, doomed and wasted. You know it, and are prepared for the descent into hell if it were to happen. 'Love knows no riches or poverty. It is beyond both,' said the poet Kabir. Nothing could be more true for you now. You want to junk orthodoxy and conservatism. You are willing to experiment and take risks. If there is opposition to your plans, you may just elope, migrate or do anything as long as you can just hold the person in your arms and dream big together. This is an interesting time for young adults. The coin can fall on either side. Of course, these are mere indicators. I cannot be accurate unless I have your personal details. But I have also been in love—more than once—and let me tell you, the feeling is 'deadly heady'. Ganesha nods solemnly.

22 April: Last Quarter in Aquarius

You spend time at home and busy yourself with domestic chores. You prefer being in familiar surroundings. Your territory, or turf, is reassuring. You may spend several hours by yourself and work on subjective concerns that bother you. You may also help with the poor and downtrodden. This is not your style normally, but you are looking for profundity in your evolution. The material world is neatly sewn up, and now you need to grow at all levels. Ganesha eggs you on. There are maudlin moments, and some dark clouds hover over you. But that is par for the course. The seasons change, and good times and bad times come and go.

29 April: New Moon in Taurus

You look at a complete personal revamp. There is a change in wardrobe, diet, attitude and perspective. You may check out the gym, yoga, meditation, natural therapies and new systems of thought. 'If we are creating ourselves all the time, then it is never too late to begin creating the bodies we want instead of the ones we mistakenly assume we are stuck with,' says Deepak Chopra. You believe that you can overhaul your life, and you go about doing just that, with sincerity and purpose. This is an excellent time for making plans for the future. You are filled with positive energy and see clearly all the possibilities inherent in a situation. As the subcontinent swelters, your thoughts are heating up. The energies are powerful with the new moon in Taurus. Ganesha blesses you.

7 May: First Quarter in Leo

'Pray as though nothing else will work, and work as if no prayer will help,' goes a German proverb. This is a powerful phase. Your affairs are in order, but you leave no stone unturned and slog away. There are expenses, but it is not wasteful expenditure. You busy yourself with fiscal instruments and may buy a holiday home or start building a nest egg. There is love and bonding, apart from journeys, festivities, even an addition to the family, and this time I am including a pet! Ganesha is with you and that is all that matters.

14 May: Full Moon in Scorpio

The subcontinent is sizzling. In some parts of the developing world there is no electricity, so a lack of air conditioning cannot be blamed! As I say often, circumstances play a major role in shaping our lives. Astrology only impels. 'What dreadful hot weather we have! It keeps me in a continual state of inelegance,' said Jane Austen. You are sizzling with intensity, in keeping with the shooting thermometer. Everything that you embark on is nothing less than grand. This is the time for love and laughter, companionship and shared joy. There are powerful ego drives. The singles look for partners and the married bond. Ganesha wishes you well.

21 May: Last Quarter in Pisces

There are emotional moments tearing you down. You have many affairs of the heart. Watch out for any action that goes against the law. You could be cheated out of hard-earned money or conned into doing something that you regret. Friends and loved ones drop by and you have fun times. Family life goes through rough patches. Children, the spouse, parents and in-laws may simply not see eye to eye with you. Ganesha watches over you.

28 May: New Moon in Gemini

You are pulled by the 'drunken monkey', as Swami Vivekananda called the human mind. Your mind is scattered like feathers that have spilled out of a pillow. You are in the midst of a million thoughts and desperately want to be alone. I quote Henry David Thoreau. He preferred solitude and said, 'I find it wholesome to be alone for the greater part of the time.' Yes, there is power, knowledge and learning in silence and aloneness; you want so badly to be in that space now. There are sentimental moments as you play out a fantasy world. Life is dancing, and maybe taking you for a ride. You want to stand still and hold the railing hard till your knuckles turn white, for all that you are worth. Ganesha holds your hand.

5 June: First Quarter in Virgo

The influence of Virgo steadies you somewhat. 'All that we are is the result of what we have thought,' said the

Buddha. You have evolved as a person and you realize in moments of reflection that although you have made errors you have managed to pull through. Like Muhammad Ali in the epic battle with Joe Frazier for the world heavyweight title, you have come out triumphant despite being somewhat battered. Your energy levels are high and you look at the future with hope and belief. The family is well settled, and that's a blessing. Ganesha is with you.

13 June: Full Moon in Sagittarius

Your life isn't as parched as the earth on the subcontinent calling out desperately for rain. I am reminded of Rabindranath Tagore's poem on the monsoon: 'Come pleasant beauty, bring your pleasant companionship and quench the thirst and heat.' There is travel and furious networking. There are expenses and medical emergencies. You may also tread on others' toes due to strong ego drives and say what you please without worrying about the sensitivities of others. Words can cause great harm, but you are not bothered. There are alumni meetings, and friends and loved ones drop by. You are wanted by everybody and that is not a bad place to be. Ganesha blesses you.

19 June: Last Quarter in Pisces

These are maudlin times. There is luck, and work goes your way, but you are not satisfied. You want more but you cannot place your finger on exactly what you want. Your core emotions are not fully met. There is a vacuum in your life and you try out various options at work and play, but the emptiness just doesn't seem to go away. You look for spiritual balms and go looking for gurus and godmen. There are happy moments with the family, and youngsters will be wild and wanton. But that is the nature of youth and there is no point in censuring them. We have all been through that. Ganesha journeys with you.

27 June: New Moon in Cancer

The new moon is in Cancer and your emotions are raw, like a mango yet to ripen. You want seclusion, time to reflect and understand what life is all about. 'Your worst enemy cannot harm you as much as your unguarded thoughts,' said the Buddha. There is love, passion, partnerships and collaborations. You are unsure if a new association, however profitable, is what you really want. You want to dust it away and start anew. Those with families feel stifled. The householder's life is one of responsibility, and you wonder if you did the right thing by getting into it. But now it is too late for regrets. Consolidate your situation and move on. Ganesha helps you.

5 July: First Quarter in Libra

You are torn by choice. There are opportunities galore falling squarely on your lap and you don't know what to do. It is a crisis of abundance. You are spoilt for choice. It is like having to pick one spinner from the team when there are at least three on the squad with world-class credentials. You are cheerful and gregarious and feel like socializing. You radiate warmth and emotion. There is new love. You spend time at home, beautifying it. There are many moments of sensitivity and sentimentality as you work through illusions and delusions, fact and fantasy. There are indulgences too. But all this is a churning of life, says Ganesha. Nothing to worry about.

12 July: Full Moon in Capricorn

The full moon is in your sign, and this is a period of quiet optimism and positive thinking. This is a good time to make long-range plans and to get your act together. There could be profitable travel. Those who have been ill recover completely. Money flows through your fingers despite new contracts, partnerships and collaborations. Family life is stable, and that is saying a lot. You realize that you need a secure home to sally forth into the world and make powerful strides, and so you indulge the family and there are no complaints. Ganesha blesses you.

19 July: Last Quarter in Aries

You scorch the tarmac. Your energies are high. You are filled with ambition and want to make it all happen. But there are discordant moods, and your heart and mind are at loggerheads. You earn and spend in the same breath. There is new love and indulgences. You invest and gamble recklessly, but it may just work in your favour. Ganesha watches over you.

26 July: New Moon in Leo

You live large. Work is going great and you make rapid progress. You are filled with love and longing. You want to be with others, particularly with that special person. You want to express your love in no uncertain terms. There could be international travel. Those in the media and in the sectors of finance and investment do exceedingly well. There are indulgences, but your health is not affected. Friends and loved ones drop by, you are in party mode, and life is smiling. There could be an addition to the family, and those fond of pets may bring home something exotic, like a rare iguana or a green snake! Ganesha is happy for you.

4 August: First Quarter in Scorpio

There is powerful intensity at work. There are profound changes which derail your life. On the plus side, you may be getting rid of junk, and that could be a great psychological burden off you. Friends and colleagues help out and you are able to get a fresh peek into your life. Old wounds may reopen, which is a good sign. There is a purging, a catharsis of sorts. As you recognize your problems and deal with them, you evolve and heal. Please remember that you are the sum total of all past influences. Work is good and family, life has its fissures, which will heal gradually. Ganesha walks the walk with you.

10 August: Full Moon in Aquarius

You are in a pleasant mood and enjoy being with people. They also enjoy your company. You are normally strong, independent and a leader, but in this phase you need the moral support of others and the fellowship of kindred souls. It could be loosely termed a weak moment. You also look at philanthropy and help out the less fortunate. You may take to writing poetry, screenplays or a book. This is a creative period and you are well rewarded for it. Ganesha watches over you.

17 August: Last Quarter in Taurus

You are slogging away with stamina and determination. There could be a few brushes with the law and with colleagues. There are hidden tensions which erupt suddenly, catching you off guard. There could be crises at the workplace and you need to fight with fire. Little issues that you have taken for granted blow up in your face. But you chip away like a sculptor working on a giant statue. 'You may never know what results come of your action, but if you do nothing there will be no result,' said Mohandas Gandhi. You are not one to give up in the face of adversity and you take it as another challenge. The family is well provided for and you are not worried for them. The work front consumes all your energy. Ganesha blesses you.

25 August: New Moon in Virgo

Your affairs are in order but you need to work on your identity, which you feel is lost. It could be an abstraction and you could be lonely and depressed. You have been working too hard and need to get out and smell the roses and feel the grass grow under your feet. You probably haven't taken a holiday for a long time and need to 'chill'. You see the situation clearly and are able to make the necessary changes. There could be travel, tantra, mantra, yantra and new positive associations which reaffirm your belief in yourself. You look for spiritual answers. Ganesha holds your hand.

2 September: First Quarter in Sagittarius

There are expenses as you shop with a vengeance, buying almost everything under the sun. You may look at a new home or even accessories to your wardrobe. 'Every increased possession loads us with new weariness,' said John Ruskin, the social reformer. How true! You buy it all and wonder if you could have used the money better. This is an excellent time for mental work as you obsess about details and the fine print. You are in a critical mood and are acutely attentive to detail. You are outspoken and may step on someone's toes, leading to altercations. Control your ego drives. You are grappling with various issues, including, possibly, the hint of your partner straying. Hold on to relationships that add value to life and junk those that don't. This is a good period for self-realization. Ganesha is with you.

9 September: Full Moon in Pisces

This is a time for reflection. You look inwards and try to fathom the rumblings of your soul. Your career is going fine and you are well thought of in society, but you need to know what is happening inside you. The externals look good but you are curious to discover your real self, which is very different from the image you present to the world. You look for spiritual guidance and want to map out a strategy for the days to come. You deal with the past to avoid repeating mistakes. I must add here, as I do every year, that every week (valid for every sign) there are new influences and a lot depends on the exertion of your free will. Astrology does not compel, it only impels. You may also meet a new partner, someone as different from you as can be, and there could be fireworks in more ways than one. Ganesha journeys with you.

16 September: Last Quarter in Gemini

You are meeting a lot of people and there will be an interesting mishmash of cultures. New vistas open dramatically and you just love the aroma from this cauldron of global fragrances. There will be powerful ego drives as you surge in confidence. But you have learnt your lessons and avoid altercations and misunderstandings.

There will be dramatic changes in your life and you will be tossed around like driftwood in the Arabian Sea. The universe may be sending you signals to change tack altogether. You may marry, take up a new job, and move overseas. You work through success, failure, love, heartbreak, passion and a variety of other emotions as you charge away on a speed board without brakes. Ganesha holds your hand and steadies you.

24 September: New Moon in Libra

There is love, lust and bonding with the new moon in Libra. You indulge, attend parties, dance away till the cows come home, and let your hair down. You are feeling happy, confident, optimistic, healthy, and willing to learn from anybody who knows a trick or two that you don't. You are generous, understanding and tolerant and are a hit with the peer group. Your communication skills are perfect and you attract everyone to you in droves. Teachers, analysts, counsellors, health care professionals, lawyers and others dealing with people, do very well. Your life has beauty and balance but you may find it difficult to make fast decisions as you are presented innumerable choices on a platter. Ganesha smiles.

1 October: First Quarter in Capricorn

'A healthy attitude is contagious, but don't wait to catch it from others. Be a carrier,' said Tom Stoppard. The first quarter is in Capricorn and you are filled with energy and optimism. You are all eyes and ears, and as keen as a baby elephant to learn from the world around you. You are open to new winds and you embark on an expansion drive. You make rapid progress and grow from strength to strength. The focus is on realty, deeds, bonds, insurance, construction, media and other fiscal instruments. Defence personnel and professional athletes do well. Family life has few hiccups. Ganesha is happy for you.

8 October: Full Moon in Aries

There is zeal, vigour and power in all your dealings. You zoom ahead like a meteor in the night sky. 'The single biggest problem in communication is the illusion that it has taken place,' said George Bernard Shaw. Your communication skills are excellent and you go about forming new friendships and associations with abandon. You are in a state of balance with your personal needs and the needs of others; you are able to give and receive equally. You are creatively charged and look for innovation and invention, and different ways of doing things. You are the master of the original move. Ganesha smiles.

15 October: Last Quarter in Cancer

I am a published poet and cannot help but quote Rabindranath Tagore: 'Where roads are made I lose my way. In the wide water, in the blue sky there is no line of a track. The pathway is hidden by the birds' wings, by the star-fires, by the flowers of the wayfaring seasons. And I ask my heart if its blood carries the wisdom of the unseen way.' You plough your furrow, hack your way through the thicket of life, take the road less travelled and work smart. There is fire in your belly and you blaze through the stratosphere like the latest supersonic marvel. You are a winner all the way. Ganesha is delighted as you climb every mountain in sight and look for more. Achievement spurs you on.

23 October: New Moon in Scorpio

Mars is in your sign from 26 October to 4 December. Mars is the commander-in-chief of the army. Mars is the warrior. Courage, ferocity, power and strength go with Mars. In short, Mars becomes a very positive influence if you can control your feelings and your temper. Mars is a fighter. Your emotions are stimulated, your passions are aroused, and you are fierce and aggressive like a Maori warrior on his first hunt. The focus is on the four Fs—finance, friendship, fun and fraternity. You think and execute out of the box and make waves in uncharted territories. Ganesha smiles.

31 October: First Quarter in Aquarius

As the Greek philosopher Heraclitus put it, 'There is nothing permanent except change.' We may not notice it but we are changing all the time; every macro moment our cells change, and our body changes completely every few years. You look for something entirely different to do. You change your sartorial look, go in for a new hairdo, maybe get some tattoos, change your diet, hit the gym, possibly take to yoga and meditation, and pick up new hobbies and interests. You want new vistas to open in your life and take you far away on the wings of poesy. Ganesha approves. Routine can kill and you are getting suffocated by it.

6 November: Full Moon in Taurus

You take off on a new tack but there is stability and balance in your dealings. There could be foreign travel, and some of you may even be returning home for good after being expatriates for decades working in different parts of the world. Youngsters do well at examinations and interviews. You meet with people from different cultures and benefit greatly from the exchange. You are filled with new ideas and perspectives. This is also a great time for fashion designers, hair dressers, diplomats and those in international trade. You may split from your partner without much acrimony. You will either decide to remain by yourself for a while or slip into another relationship easily. You flow like the Brahmaputra. Ganesha watches over you.

14 November: Last Quarter in Leo

The energies are powerful. There are many expenses and fun times. The year is ending and the winter cold is disquieting. But you are the soul of the party, wining, dining and shaking a leg. There is love and passion, and if you don't partake what falls on your lap in a heap it will only be free will at play. You look for a second home and make the necessary arrangements. Singles have a field day. Ganesha blesses you.

22 November: New Moon in Sagittarius

Travel and powerful ego drives are highlighted. You speak your mind and don't pull your punches, unlike a politician canvassing for votes. You look for change all the time, for unadulterated happiness and joy. Life is mundane for most of us, it's probably the same for all of humanity. It is the human condition. The sun rises and sets in a pattern. Likewise, we have an order to our lives. You seek to change all that, but it is not to be. Acceptance is the key here. You realize that you have to work within certain set parameters of cosmic and man-made time. The peace that you long for is within you. You cannot find it anywhere else, however hard you may try. Ask me. I have seen life in all its varied moods. Ganesha agrees. Go within, he says.

29 November: First Quarter in Pisces

I quote Thich Nhat Hanh. 'Feelings come and go like clouds in a windy sky. Conscious breathing is my anchor.' Yes, that is the key. Your restless mind is looking for more from life. But what else is there? There is work, money, relationships, health, fun times and sad times. What else can you extract from existence? If you have had a semblance of joy most of your life, I suggest you live in gratitude. As another year begins pulling down the shutter, you are filled with big plans. Loved ones drop in after a long while. Time is fleeting and you want to optimise it. Planet earth is a fraction of the cosmos, and we are as large and as important as the smallest grain of sand. Nothing more, possibly less. Accept that and you will not be perturbed. Ganesha is with you.

6 December: Full Moon in Gemini

Venus is in Capricorn from 11 to 31 December. This is fun time, and what an appropriate time for Venus to make its presence felt, when the world is charged with year-end festivity! Venus is another important planet and is of great significance. This is an important phase. As often discussed, Venus is the planet for love, romance, sex, beauty and the good life. This is the planet of attraction, love, wealth, knowledge and prosperity. The compatibility of partners and also the type of life the individual will lead is also judged from the placement of

Venus in the horoscope. As a planet, Venus is considered to be beneficial, feminine and gentle. Venus symbolizes the force of attraction in the universe. In human beings this attractive force manifests as love and beauty. When Venus is well placed in the chart, there is love, art, beauty and all the goodies of life that make life worth living. Venus rules Libra and Taurus, though its role in every sign is important. Like other planets, it also has its transits. In Libra, Venus is aesthetic and cultured. In Taurus it is more earthy, materialistic and sensual. Venus rules the venous system, kidneys, urinary tract, throat, larynx, and is responsible for good looks. In short, Venus in Western astrology stands for comforts, arts, wealth, relationships, sex, decorations, luxuries and wealth. You play the field and have fun times. Your plate is full with inheritance, wills, travel, negotiations, collaborations, settlements, associations, love, hate, despair, agony and triumph. Your hunches point the right way, your intuition works well, and you finally bow down to the majesty of the universe. You seem to have learned your lessons. Ganesha is delighted.

14 December: Last Quarter in Virgo

This is a double whammy. When it rains, it pours. Along with Venus comes Mercury, which will be in Capricorn from 17 to 31 December. This is a fantastic period and a super way to crown the year. It cannot get better. I can be wrong, as I do not have your personal horoscope, but I shall stick my neck out. Mercury, the mighty, all-powerful planet, is in your sign now. It favours travels, meetings, conferences, interviews, trips, more brain power, contacts, communication, correspondence and contracts. Mercury has a special connection with the circuits of the brain. Chess, crossword and other such games belong to Mercury. Also, short-distance runners and spin bowlers are controlled by Mercury. Mercury, in short, is the ambassador and salesman of the zodiac. Mercury is the symbol of news, views, messages, interviews, contacts, communications, travel and transport. Mercury gives an impetus to all of the above in the sun sign where it is located. You have the Midas touch, and several options fall squarely on your plate. You are spoilt for choice. There are festivities and big career breaks. You are rushed to be everywhere at the same time. Ganesha smiles.

22 December: New Moon in Capricorn

You dazzle like a million chandeliers. You cast your spell everywhere. This is also your birth period and the energies have added power, thanks to the beneficial placement of Venus and Mercury. The year ends in a blaze of glory. You could run for the presidency! You charm your way through and are in the arms of windfalls galore. You can't put a foot wrong. Even blindfolded, you step on a lucky break. There are fortuitous associations and somehow you are at the right place at the right time. Ganesha is happy for you. So am I.

28 December: First Quarter in Aries

In the words of Ralph Waldo Emerson, 'Do not go where the path may lead, go instead where there is no path and leave a trail.' That is exactly what you do. You coast along effortlessly. You are like Kapil Dev, also a Capricorn, when he lifted the World Cup. The odds favour you. Take risks. The tide is in your favour. Take it at the flood and

court fortune (I confess to having twisted the Bard a bit).
Ganesha agrees wholeheartedly.

Key Dates

January

2*–4, 7–13, 20–21, 25–26, 29–31.
Ganesha says, January will bring you the horn of plenty
along with several new beginnings. Both power and
pelf will be yours. You will be amused, entertained,
delighted.

February

3*–10, 12–14, 17–18, 21–22, 26–27.
Insurance, heavy expenses, gifts, taxes, but wining and
dining, buying and selling, lots of fun and frolic make this
month a happy one on the whole, says Ganesha.

March

2–9, 11*–12, 15–16, 19–21, 24–26, 29–31.
Ganesha has you reaching out to people and places. Your
work will be done and your dreams realized. Friends and
well-wishers make you happy and proud.

April

3–4, 7*–8, 11–17, 20–22, 25*–27, 30*.
Home, house, renovation, decoration, good news,
domestic happiness, joy, harmony and merrymaking for
you from Ganesha.

May

1*–9, 13–14, 18–19, 23*–24, 28*–29.
A time for revelry, ceremony, functions, children,
romance, hobbies, socializing, making and spending

money. Both give you happiness, adds Ganesha, since that is what money is for.

June

1–2, 5*–6, 9*–10, 14–15, 19*–28.
You will get your just and due awards and rewards, promotions and inspirations, Ganesha assures you. Health will improve. Funds and loans will be available. Servants, employees and colleagues will love and respect you.

July

2*–8, 11–13, 16*–18, 21*–22, 26–27, 30*–31.
It's people time, for sure! Marriage, companionship, travel, trade, foreign affairs, meetings give you publicity and fame. The going is good indeed.

August

3–4, 7–9, 12*–19, 22–23, 26–27, 30–31.
Gains by several names come to you! Inheritance, joint finance, loans, investments, windfalls, litigation, buying and selling, a second marriage, if that's the way the wind blows, says Ganesha.

September

4*–5, 9*–10, 14*–15, 18*–19, 21–27.
Pilgrimage, ceremonies, name and fame, publicity, foreign connections, all spell out success and victory for you.

October

1–3, 6*–13, 15–16, 19–21, 24–25, 28–30.
You will be working hard for success. Changes in your work scenario/environment are possible. You will be recognized, appreciated, rewarded, says Ganesha.

November

1*–8, 12*–13, 16*–17, 20*–21, 25*–26, 30*.
You will be at your best. Love, money, attention and praise are all there and should make you happy. You look back at a good and productive year, says Ganesha.

December

1*, 5–6, 9–10, 13–19, 22*–23, 27*–29.
Secret work, meets, conferences and travel. Expenses and visits to hospitals and distant places. Take care of your health. Be positive, advises Ganesha. You have much to be grateful for!

Aquarius

YEARLY FORECAST

Work is not a curse, it is the prerogative of intelligence, the only means to manhood, and the measure of civilization. Savages do not work.

– C. Coolidge

This is specially true till 16 July 2014:

a) 'Wedlock, padlock, lip-lock,
Marriage is a crazy tick-tock.'

– Bejan Daruwalla

b) Crazy but fun, and at times crazy but kindly cruel, like the surgeon's knife, is marriage. In all fairness, marriage at times can be: 'Two minds with but a single thought, two hearts that beat as one,' quoting Maria Lovell.

This is specially true from 17 July 2014 to 11 August 2015: Aquarians are crazy but fun. True.

Ganesha says we have tackled you Aquarians in a slightly different way. In the beginning, we have given you something special and extra because our Bejan is very spontaneous and as he says, he goes with the flow. In other words, he does what comes naturally. The reason is very simple. Bejan feels what is natural is right and proper.

Till 16 July 2014

Summary and Guidance

Jupiter, the great benefic, will be in your sixth angle focusing on health and relationships with colleagues, subordinates, servants and relatives, and here you are advised by Ganesha to stay cool. Financial muddles are possible, but you will pull through because of Jupiter's blessings, which I will expand on later. Still, do remember that loans and funds, buying/selling, borrowing and lending will have their sharp edges and difficulties. Danger of theft, pilferage, misplacing of documents, valuables and money. Take care. Pets, dependents and relatives could pose problems, maybe because of circumstances beyond their immediate control, says Ganesha. You will have to work systematically and give your best because of stiff competition. Eat intelligently, serve others but take enough rest. Cultivate moderation in all that you do. That's best. Earlier, I had said that you will pull through because of Jupiter's blessings. Ganesha talks about it. For all the hoopla being made of figure consciousness, you don't have to be wafer-thin and look like the dried twig of a tree. A little weight causes no big harm usually, though, I admit, your doctor knows best. In short, you will work hard, do your duty and have your promotion and perks.

17 July 2014 to 11 August 2015

Jupiter steps into your seventh angle from 17 July 2014 to 11 August 2015. Let me illustrate the happenings by an example. *Hip-Hip-Hurrah*, a painting by P.S.Koyer (1888), showing glasses held high in an enthusiastic, lively and welcoming toast best explains 2014 for you. Rejoice. Your hour and year of deliverance are at hand, children of Saturn and Uranus. Ganesha says it's time to lighten up, let your hair down, relax, enjoy, be of good cheer, carouse, make merry, also marry, have a ball, spin, leap, dance, give yourself up to joyous abandon. You need it, and do deserve it.

Collaborations, foreign connections, ties and journeys, publicity and advertisement, TV and computers, all electronic items, jets, and space, galaxies and astronomy, astrophysics, dynamics of spirituality and all the modern therapies—namely, reiki, yoga, crystal healing, necromancy—come under the ample ambit of Jupiter in your seventh angle. In short, it is a wide spectrum you will cover.

Main Trend

We have spoken at length and very clearly about three things: a) hard work and rewards; b) marriage, collaboration and ties; c) research, space, contacts, astronomy, aeroplanes and most certainly, technology, humanity and the arts. Read the opening paragraphs please.

Journey and Communication

This is specially true from 17 July 2014 to 11 August 2015. From 12 January to 17 April, Mercury, the messenger, moves in your sign and Pisces, and that is the real time for it. August, December and October also propel you towards it.

Health

Health certainly improves, thanks to Jupiter in your sixth angle, till 16 July 2014. Colleagues, subordinates and your boss will favour you and psychologically it will be mind over matter and therefore better health. But be careful in November, May and August.

Love/Marriage

Remember the poem about wedlock and padlock in the very beginning. Also, please read the complete forecast from 17 July 2014 to 11 August 2015 which is already given. In other words, marriage is on the cards, as we say. In short, all connections and relationships, including marriage and love, are strongly highlighted for you.

Property

The fixed signs Aquarius, Leo, Scorpio and Taurus are, as a rule, really good in property matters. This year, because of Saturn, you might have to face confrontation and conflict and perhaps legal disputes. Even then funds and loans and investments will be available. Around July and May expect developments. Property includes renovation and decoration of house or a move or shift of office.

Job/Business/Loans/Funds/Investments

This is the Aquarian age or the New Age. Therefore, your brilliance and intelligence could very well outshine and outsmart all the other signs of the zodiac. But more importantly, your individual horoscope has to be seen. What I am saying only applies generally and that also only to some extent. This year Saturn in your job/business/

loans/funds/investments might (not must) cause conflict and clashes with superiors. But thanks to Jupiter and Neptune you can overcome it and get a promotion or a position. Very frankly, those in service do better than those in business. I may be right or wrong. The months for these are July, September, November, December and March.

Children/Entertainment

Children and entertainment depend upon both Venus and Mercury in your individual case. The reason is that every sign and every human being are different. From 6 March to 2 May, 24 June to 18 July, 30 September to 23 October, 17 November to 10 December should be inspiring and exhilarating. My choice are the months of June and December. Take your pick.

Trips and Ties

By modern astrology your main planet is Uranus. By ancient astrology it is Saturn. Taking both into active consideration, April, June, October and December should give you a window of opportunity for it. Be creative. Be bold. Be imaginative. Move it!

Publicity, Projects, Performance

Everything will go well and under control provided you are not erratic and push too hard for achievement and success. Give a little margin for error in judgement. Tolerate other people, even though you think they are fools and you are wise. In other words, be a diplomat and win the game. Happily enough, Jupiter works wonders for you.

Happiness Quota

I give you 79 per cent. I admit that you Aquarians are so complicated that it is difficult to decipher and judge you with precision. Let your heart be in tune with your brilliant mind. That's the secret.

Monthly Round-up

January: expenses, secret deals, negotiations, trips, ties; February: success, projects, ventures, funds, children, creativity, good luck; March: money, family promises, promotion, perks; April: contacts, communication, contracts, research, import-export; May: home, house, renovation, buying/selling, ill health, retirement; June: fine all-round performance, you strike it lucky, and win applause; July: loans, funds, joint finance, domestic matters, job, health; August: love, hate, marriage, divorce, contradictory influences; September: loans and funds, health and pets, religion, spirituality, rites for the living and the dead; October: freedom, intuition, inspiration, publicity, long-distance connections; November: work, parents, status, rivalry, prestige, tremendous pressure; December: friendship, wish-fulfilment, material gains, socializing, group activities, happiness and health. You end on a positive, winning, winsome note.

Summary

Cooing and wooing, marriage, collaborations, work and rewards, mind-blowing experiences, creativity at white heat, journeys and trips and immigration, children, hobbies, entertainment, communication expertise at all levels—well, that's as exciting an adventure as you can hope to have, winks Ganesha.

Outer Planets

URANUS: Uranus, your planet by modern astrology, will be in your third angle of contacts, communication, advertisements, publicity, knowledge, information, education, aerospace, technology, inventions, and therefore, you will be at your best. Yes, there will be opposition and conflicts. But that is real life. Astrology deals with real life as well as the future.

NEPTUNE: Neptune in your second angle gives you money, good food and family happiness. In simple terms, eat well, earn well, speak well, sing well and be well.

PLUTO: Pluto in your twelfth angle could cause expenses, ill health, thefts, robbery, losses. Paradoxically enough, it is Pluto that leads you to selfless service, caring and welfare of others, great spirituality and even glimpses of God. Life is a kaleidoscope.

Month by Month

January

If the last year had its lows, they get straightened out now. Those in the arts or in the teaching profession find many windows opening. Family life is happy and children bring joy. There will be reunions and alumni meetings. Mercury is in Aquarius from 12 January to the month's end. This is a great time to strike it rich. You are filled with energy, and several opportunities open up in your life. Make the most of this period. You have the stamina and determination to make your life count. There is growth, both material and spiritual. There is love, passion and spectacular success. You open your purse strings and help the less fortunate. Ganesha is delighted.

February

There is palpable power and direction in your dealings. You are filled with innovative and out-of-the-box ideas, and those in the media dazzle with their creative genius. There is love, lust, power, ego, anger and a lot of emotions on your plate. There is confidence and enhanced prestige as you make the rounds of life with guts, glory and gumption. By the month-end you check out new vistas to see what exactly suits your growth trajectory. You also explore loans and funds and other fiscal instruments. Ganesha walks with you as you embark on this period of self-discovery.

March

The new moon is in Pisces and Venus is in your sign from 6 March for almost a month. Wow! This is an important phase. This is a propitious period and you live and love in grand style. There is great success for media folk, writers, singers, painters and those creatively inclined. There are new assignments and collaborations that excite you. There is profitable travel and you could be invited to speak at international conferences or chair prestigious groups. You are ambitious and want to make a mark in the world. You are crowned with success. Ganesha is pleased.

April

There are stolen moments with your loved one. This is a sensitive period and you are inflammable. You may take to religion and spirituality and may seek out a new guru or godman. You are filled with empathy and your heartstrings are easily tugged. You are in a process of regeneration. You have magical powers of attraction and are the cynosure of all eyes. This is the time to prepare a nest egg. Ganesha is with you.

May

You could be impulsive and jump into the fray without much thought. By mid-month there is a new intensity as there is psychological and emotional equilibrium. Money slips through your fingers. You look for intense and powerful experiences to understand the inner workings of the world and your life in particular. You look within yourself. At work, you are able to express yourself forcefully. Live in abundance and the universe will take care of you. Ganesha blesses you.

June

Your mind is like a forest fire. There is rage and you cannot fathom it. There is transformation, expansion and spiritual awakening. You look at fantasies and wish to escape the boredom of the mundane world bearing down on you. You want to live as a work of art. There could be travel, new spiritual paths, gods and godmen. By the month-end there are many domestic preoccupations. There are also separations, inheritance, wills, court cases, joys and sorrows of various kinds. Ganesha watches over you.

July

There could be international travel and you meet with all types of people. There is great exchange of energy and you will profit from it. You are finding yourself, and it is not through work but from life experience. You junk the flab, get rid of all the accessories you don't need and trim your mind, home, emotions and surroundings. The health of elders will need attention and there could be an addition to the family. You will also be working through wills and inheritance issues. By the end of the month you dazzle with the brilliance of your genius. Ganesha is pleased.

August

This is indeed a significant period. There are new ventures, a hectic social whirl, indulgences, reinforcements and rebellion. You are looking at new frontiers and vistas. There will be windfalls, exploration and growth. There are marriages in the family, possible ill health of spouse and parents, business expansion and much more. Ganesha is with you.

September

You make positive changes in your life to enrich it. You are attracted to new ideas that are challenging and positive. You have a new approach and perspective to life. By mid-month you crave for freedom. As the month ends it is party time. There could be an inheritance coming your way. There are new friendships and associations. Ganesha blesses you.

October

A lot is on your plate: buying, selling, love, passion, money, expenses, purchases, the good life, travel and everything else that makes life worthwhile. At work, there are rewards and awards. There is money, honey, new projects/assignments, investments, stocks, realty, buying, selling, financial and legal issues. Your relationships are beautiful. Bonding reaches a new peak. By the month-end there is fire in your belly and also a raw, pulsating energy. There are new discoveries and realizations. Ganesha is with you.

November

You contemplate the loftier aspects of life. There is an aura of optimism and positive affirmation. You live large and play with grand schemes. There is great intellectual precision and strategy in whatever you embark on. There is rapid growth as you reach out to frontiers of change. As the month ends there are maudlin moments but there is balance and equilibrium. Ganesha walks with you.

December

Mars is in your sign from 5 to 31 December. Mars is like the volcano of vitality inside you and influences endurance, persistence and discipline. You are filled with dynamism and energy and move about with a rare frenzy. Those in the media and in academia dazzle. You reinvent yourself. It is party time and everyone wants you. Your plate is full and overflowing with goodies and contradictions. There is also time spent with the family and deep bonding. Ganesha is with you.

Months at a Glance

January

Expenses, secret deals, negotiations, trips, ties.

February

Success, projects, ventures, funds, children, creativity, good luck.

March

Money, family promises, promotion, perks.

April

Contacts, communication, contracts, research, import-export.

May

Home, house, renovation, buying/selling, ill health, retirement.

June

Fine all-round performance, you strike it lucky, and win applause.

July

Loans, funds, joint finance, domestic matters, job, health.

August

Love, hate, marriage, divorce, contradictory influences.

September

Loans and funds, health and pets, religion, spirituality, rites for the living and the dead.

October

Freedom, intuition, inspiration, publicity, long-distance connections.

November

Work, parents, status, rivalry, prestige, tremendous pressure.

December

Friendship, wish-fulfilment, material gains, socializing, group activities, happiness and health. You end on a positive, winning note.

Weekly Review (By the phases of the moon)

1 January: New Moon in Capricorn

The year starts well for you. You have new assignments and added responsibilities. If the last year had its lows, they get straightened out now. Those in the arts or in the teaching profession find many windows opening in their lives. Family life is happy and children bring joy. There will be reunions and alumni meetings. Children may leave for further studies in foreign universities. There are marriages, engagements and additions to the family. As they say, Lakshmi enters your home. These are happy days. Enjoy, says Ganesha.

8 January: First Quarter in Aries

Mercury is in Aquarius from 12 January to the month's end. This is a great time to strike it rich. You are filled with energy, and several opportunities open up in your life. Make the most of this period. Mercury, the mighty, all-powerful planet is in your sign now. It favours travels, meetings, conferences, interviews, trips, more brain power, contacts, communication, correspondence and contracts. Mercury has a special connection with the circuits of the brain. Chess, crossword puzzles and other such games belong to Mercury. Also, short-distance runners and spin bowlers are controlled by Mercury. Mercury, in short, is the ambassador and salesman of the zodiac. Mercury is the symbol of news, views, messages, interviews, contacts, communications, travel and transport. Mercury gives an impetus to all of the above in the sun sign where it is located. There could be travel, and friends from overseas will visit. You have the stamina and determination to make your life count. You will also be networking furiously. Technology has made the world a tiny place and you make full use of all the gadgets at your disposal.

16 January: Full Moon in Cancer

There are family issues hogging your attention now. There could be a marriage in the family. Single senior citizens on the lookout for love may find their partners. The going is good. The tide is in your favour and you are making the most of the period, hitting six sixes in an over like Yuvraj Singh. You are batting on the front foot and that is what matters in life. Children may leave home for higher studies and family gatherings take up your time. There is both material and spiritual growth. There is also time for reflection and consolidation. Ganesha is happy.

24 January: Last Quarter in Scorpio

There is great intensity in your life now. You are zooming ahead like a race car. You are energized, excited and enthused by life. There is love, passion and spectacular success. There could be new love and many affairs of the heart. You are spreading yourself too thin but you are not a rolling stone. You are learning a lot and making the most of the situation. You are reaping the whirlwind. Your life now is like an apple orchard in harvest. Ganesha is delighted for you and wishes you well.

30 January: New Moon in Aquarius

The new moon is in your sign. Go for it. Make the best of the waxing moon. The good times continue. The impact of Mercury gets over now but if you have made the most of this period, it will stand you in good stead. The idea is to optimize the good periods and lie low when the going gets tough. Ganesha is happy that you are on the right course. There are maudlin moments too, but they are necessary. You open your purse strings and help the less fortunate. Your heart beats for the impoverished.

6 February: First Quarter in Taurus

There is consolidation and hard work. You normally don't care too much about hoarding money but this is a period of accumulation. You do not allow your moods to overtake you and there is palpable power and direction in your dealings. Ganesha is happy for you. You have wild ideas and, if given free rein, a wild lifestyle too. Of course, all this depends on circumstances and your personal chart. These are mere generalizations, but they hold true most of the time as you know. You are filled with innovative and out-of-the-box ideas and those in the media dazzle with their creative genius. You are on a roll. In your soft and oblique way, you get past the opposition.

14 February: Full Moon in Leo

You live and love deeply. Your life is king- or queen-size. There is money to be earned and to be spent. There is love, lust, power, ego, anger and a lot of emotions on your plate. You are capable of deep bonding and tangible affirmation. You could lose your cool at times and it will be wise not to vent your anger. Count to ten before you retort and take deep breaths like they say in all the yoga books. Ganesha wishes you well and that is important. There is confidence and enhanced prestige as you make the rounds of life with guts, glory and gumption. There is money and honey. Life is smiling at you. This is your birth period and the energies unleashed work in your favour.

22 February: Last Quarter in Sagittarius

You are meeting new people and being besieged by new ideas and ways to live. You want to change the routine. It chafes. You check out new vistas to see what exactly suits your growth trajectory. You also explore loans and funds and other fiscal instruments. There are lots of expenses too. The family may take a lot of your time and money. You attend weddings, receptions, house-warming ceremonies, gatherings of all kinds, and you are the toast of the moment. Ganesha walks with you as you embark on this period of self-discovery. You could be misunderstood as your behaviour is often erratic and non-conformist. Watch out for deceit and being waylaid by people you trust. Ensure that you sign documents after reading the fine print with a magnifying glass or get legal help.

1 March: New Moon in Pisces

The new moon is in Pisces and Venus is in your sign from 6 March for almost a month. Wow! Venus is another important planet and is of great significance. This is an important phase. As often discussed, Venus is the planet for love, romance, sex, beauty and the good life. This is the planet of attraction, love, wealth, knowledge and prosperity. The compatibility of partners and the type of life the individual will lead is also judged from the placement of Venus in the horoscope. As a planet, Venus is considered to be beneficial, feminine and gentle. Venus symbolizes the force of attraction in the universe. In human beings this attractive force manifests as love and beauty. When Venus is well placed in the chart, there is love, art, beauty and all the goodies of life that make life worth living. Venus rules Libra and Taurus, though its role in every sign is important. Like other planets, it also has its transits. In Libra, Venus is aesthetic and cultured. In Taurus, it is more earthy, materialistic and sensual. Venus rules the venous system, kidneys, urinary tract, throat and larynx, and is responsible for good looks. In short, Venus in Western astrology stands for comforts, arts, wealth, relationships, sex, decorations, luxuries and wealth. This is a propitious period and you live and love in grand style. There is great success for media folk, writers, singers, painters and those creatively inclined. You could also be in the throes of multiple affairs of the heart. There is love and longing and you disperse your affections like confetti. Ganesha smiles.

8 March: First Quarter in Gemini

Your mind is in several places at the same time. Yes, the mind is a monkey on a stick and you have to tame it. You are filled with desires and inclinations and don't know where to begin. You want to make money and yet you want to gift it away. You want to strike it rich and then also feel that it is all an illusion and you don't want to be a part of that game. There are many emotions at play. There is love and romance, fun times and deep bonding with your partner or spouse, better rapport with colleagues, peers and family. But, despite it all, you are restless and looking for more. Elders may face medical emergencies and youngsters will excel at academics. Ganesha is with you all the way.

16 March: Full Moon in Virgo

There is stability and you keep your nose to the grindstone. There are new assignments and collaborations that excite you. There is profitable travel and you could be invited to speak at international conferences or chair prestigious groups. You love being with people and sharing yourself with them. Professors, counsellors and salespeople do well. You also decide to take care of your health. If you indulge in drinking, smoking and other such habits, you decide to put a stop to it and change the course of your life, moving towards greater health, harmony, peace and contentment. You often go off the rails and feel that it is time to get organized and work within the parameters of a concrete structure. Sure, routine kills, but some sort of routine is vital for performance. Ganesha wishes you well.

24 March: Last Quarter in Capricorn

There are domestic chores to attend to. There are also many expenses. There could be family holidays, renovation, redevelopment of property and other distractions. You are ambitious and want to make a mark in the world. You want to streamline your life and eject the junk from it. There are many dark areas and unless you de-clutter and remove the cobwebs, there will be little progress. Ganesha is pleased. The opportunities are knocking at your door but it requires wisdom to choose the right path. Like it is said, genius has lapses proportionate to its triumphs, while mediocrity is always at its best. You do fabulously well at times and then go through lows. You realize this and work on yourself. It is never too late.

30 March: New Moon in Aries

This is a great period to push forward. You are filled with zeal and make headway in all that you do. You are crowned with success. Like with other signs, you share your birth period with scores of celebrated people like Federico Fellini, Christian Dior, Jack Nicklaus, Humphrey Bogart, W.S. Maugham, Virginia Woolf, Wolfgang Mozart, Lewis Carroll, Anton Chekov, Ramakrishna, Charles Darwin, Abraham Lincoln, Mark Spitz, Boris Pasternak, Jules Verne, James Dean, Ronald Reagan, Norman Mailer, Sir Francis Bacon, James Joyce, Anna Pavlova and Yoko Ono. You are an inventive genius, a type of maverick who doesn't fit in. But in this frenetic and frantic period, you strike gold. Your ideas mint money. Ganesha is pleased. You are charged and face the idiosyncrasies of life frontally. There is success and the price you pay is not much.

7 April: First Quarter in Cancer

I must point out here that like those of other signs, Aquarians can have different personalities. Their ruling planet is Uranus. They can be shy, sensitive, gentle and patient, and also quite the opposite—exuberant, lively and exhibitionist. They normally are far ahead of the times and don't belong to the everyday mundane world. They are humane, sometimes ethereal, intuitive, imaginative and idealistic. This is the Age of Aquarius and a time for spiritual regeneration. In this phase, there are stolen moments with your loved one. You spend time at home, with the family, kids, friends and loved ones. There could be family holidays too, as you bask in a happy time under the glorious sun. Ganesha wishes you well.

15 April: Full Moon in Libra

Many emotions surface, asking for attention. You are in a bind. There are also many work opportunities staring you in the face and you have to choose one course of action. Your relationships get more intense and if you have been courting someone you will express your love forcefully. There could also be increased sexual desire. This is a sensitive period and you are inflammable. You are apt to make errors. So go slow and don't rush into situations without understanding them well. You may take to religion and spirituality and may seek out a new guru or godman. You are looking for answers. There is too much on your plate now and your mind is in a whirl. Ganesha is with you though.

22 April: Last Quarter in Aquarius

You have an infallible feeling for the fine, unnoticed sensitivities of others. You are filled with empathy and your heartstrings are easily tugged in this phase. You are also filled with grand visions to change the world. You are able to create an open, sympathetic atmosphere with your peer group. You are not in battle mode and make for congenial company. You are not keen on confronting others and are willing to accommodate even the most outlandish thoughts. This works well for you as the gesture is reciprocated. This is also an excellent time for a new relationship to begin. You are in a process of regeneration. There are new vistas opening up and a new you being created. Ganesha wishes you well.

29 April: New Moon in Taurus

You are more steadfast now in all your dealings. You have magical powers of attraction and are the cynosure of all eyes. While you are drawn to tantra, mantra and deeper questions on life, you are also practical enough to know which side your bread is buttered. There is hard work and money to be made. You understand the value of a large bank balance and are propelled in that direction. You do not allow moods and emotions to affect you now. This is the time to prepare a nest egg. Ganesha is with you.

7 May: First Quarter in Leo

You live larger than life and have a strong desire to experience every aspect of existence with all your faculties. Your beliefs are emotional and passionate and you seek out relationships that arouse your emotions and your intellect. There is love, deep bonding and strong sexual desires. You could be impulsive and jump into the fray without much thought. Do not reach conclusions in a hurry. Never judge a book by the cover or for that matter even a 'brook' by its water. You will have to take careful steps and check the waters lest they be filled with piranhas or alligators. But, despite the contraindications, there is progress. Those dealing with large groups of people are in the limelight. Ganesha is happy for you.

14 May: Full Moon in Scorpio

There is a new intensity and also psychological and emotional equilibrium. Different aspects of your personality are in tune with each other. You face everyday life with relative ease. Relations with friends will be cordial. You may be in a reflective mood to figure out your personal and emotional life, to tame the demons that normally strangulate you. Money comes and goes. It slips through your fingers like morning dew. You think of the past and wonder if you could have changed anything. You think of your parents and several dear friends who have been a part of your life. You shed an unseen tear. You wish you hadn't made so many errors. But then life is all about making mistakes and learning from them. The past is dead and gone. Let it be. Ganesha blesses you.

21 May: Last Quarter in Pisces

You look for intense and powerful experiences to understand the inner workings of the world and your life in particular. You look within yourself. You want to understand your purpose, your motivation and the changes you need to make for your life to run more smoothly. There are transformative energies in your life now and this is the right time to incorporate changes. At work, you are able to express yourself forcefully and make a considerable impression. Life now is relentless and restless. You are evolving fast as you make deep inroads into all areas of life. If there is a new love on the horizon, you are hoping it will materialize in something concrete. But before that you must understand if you really need the person or if it is just your inner inadequacy showing up. You are ready for the next step if the other person even suggests it. Ganesha is with you as always.

28 May: New Moon in Gemini

As the subcontinent burns in the summer heat, your mind is at several places all at once. You meet many people from disparate backgrounds and may trust blindly. Be careful of deceit. You will not be able to have things your way. You may also be tempted to get into several get-rich-quick schemes and could land in trouble. The past is also catching up with you and you could be looking for escape routes. But you have to face it all head-on. There is no other way. Or they will emerge later in some other form. Ask Ganesha for help. There is also no point in penny-pinching. Live in abundance and the universe will take care of you. Even if you are not honest with others, the least you can do is to be honest with yourself.

5 June: First Quarter in Virgo

Your mind is like a forest fire. There is rage and you cannot fathom it. You have no idea of what has given birth to this angst. It could be the inequality in society and the rampant corruption all around and the fact that you are unable to do anything about it. You wonder how long you will continue ignoring the inequity all around. You want to achieve a lot and do grand things and leave your mark behind but you feel defeated. There is transformation, expansion and spiritual awakening. You are waking up to new realizations. You also feel alone in this cosmic vastness. You know that everyone is unique but you suddenly feel that you have no one to share your thoughts. You even distance yourself from family and friends and begin to feel sad for no apparent reason. Keep a low profile till you snap out of this phase. In this mood you could be combustible and flare up easily. Maybe, take a break and be by yourself for a while till the energies change. Do not go out of your way to provoke those in power. Ganesha asks you to chill.

13 June: Full Moon in Sagittarius

You don't want to be an island and so reach out to people. You want to belong to the tribe. You are a social animal, after all. The process of change can be slow and deliberate but when it happens, it does so in a flash. There is reality and there is illusion. Learn to see the difference. You look at fantasies and wish to escape the boredom of the mundane world bearing down heavily on you. You wish you had a magic wand and could disappear. All human beings are a bundle of contradictions. Various facets of our personality emerge in different circumstances. There are weak moments and we commit follies for which sometimes we are punished severely. You want to live as a work of art. You are looking for a major explosion of consciousness. But the real world with its taxes, ill health, old age and death beckons. Where can you go, where can you run in this human form, where can you even hide? You plead with Ganesha for deliverance.

19 June: Last Quarter in Pisces

You are in a contemplative mood. Your shadow side and blind spots emerge at such moments. There is energy but you need to direct it well and in the right direction. You are highly inflammable. There are altercations and you burst a blood vessel at the slightest provocation. You look for a change of scene. There could be travel, new spiritual paths, gods and godmen. The present is boring and you need a change. You go on a pilgrimage, look at new religious, philosophical or metaphysical views. You may take up a new course of study and may change tack altogether. The fences are closing in and you need infinite space. You are like an African lion cooped in a Mumbai studio apartment. I admit these are generalizations and I could be wrong as I am not God. A more accurate reading will require personal details. Ganesha is with you and that is all that matters. He will escort you through the tunnel.

27 June: New Moon in Cancer

There are many domestic preoccupations. The family needs attention. A child or sibling is to be married off and your inputs are needed. Elderly parents also need solace. Friends beckon you and there is no escaping the demands of the everyday world. There are all kinds of social contact and you benefit from the fellowship. There is new love and bonding. There are also separations, inheritance, wills, court cases, joys and sorrows of various kinds. There are many new directions calling for you and your plate is rich and overflowing. Ganesha watches over you with paternal love.

5 July: First Quarter in Libra

You are in a whirl like a dervish in a trance. You expand your contacts and meet with the larger world head-on. There could be international travel and you meet with all types of people. There is great energy exchange and you will profit from it all. The idea is to keep an open mind and not be a stagnant pool. Everyone is unique and different and if the differences cannot be celebrated, at least they should not be ridiculed. All human beings are in different layers or levels of consciousness. There are new realizations and you are benevolent and well disposed to friends. Ganesha wishes you well as always. You are finding yourself, and it is not through work but from life experience.

12 July: Full Moon in Capricorn

'Art is the elimination of the unnecessary,' said Pablo Picasso. And this is what you do now. You junk the flab, get rid of all the accessories you don't need and trim your mind, home, emotions and surroundings. Feng shui insists on decluttering and you have taken the cue well. You need to get back to work and straighten the labyrinths of your mind. Work will anchor you. You are practical and set goals and go for them. You think, deliberate, ponder and then act. There is no haste and you don't fly off the handle. You work towards making a foundation for the future. Ganesha is happy for you.

19 July: Last Quarter in Aries

There is frenetic movement on all fronts. You bulldoze your way through life. You fight with turbulence like a hang-glider lost in a tempest. But you pull through. Nothing can get you down now. The health of elders will need attention and there could be an addition to the family. You may even consider adoption. I cannot be more specific as I do not have the personal details. You will also be working through wills and inheritance issues. There is money coming in and you are delighted. There is expansion at work. A lot is on your plate. Start chewing, says Ganesha.

26 July: New Moon in Leo

There is money and honey. Many new opportunities beckon and you have to make the most of what falls in your lap. You dazzle with the brilliance of your genius. Those in the media make themselves heard. There are awards and rewards, applause and accolades. Ganesha is pleased. You party and spend. But deep within is a restlessness, an inner craving for more. You cannot put your finger on it and wonder if you need a shrink! Use the energy of the new moon to move ahead. Time heals all wounds and so allow it to be the balm. Let go of the past and enjoy the moment that has so gratuitously thrust you into the full glare of the limelight. Enjoy your moment in the sun.

4 August: First Quarter in Scorpio

There is new intensity as also a winner's attitude that has nestled in your bones. 'If we have no peace, it is because we have forgotten that we belong to each other,' said Mother Teresa. You realize that you belong to the larger family of man and what you do resonates throughout the universe. Finally, you want peace. You are reminded of Homer's *Odyssey*. After his wild adventures, all Odysseus wants is to come home and bounce his grandson on his knee. You feel that you have wandered enough even if it is just metaphorically and you want to rest, reflect, recollect and rejuvenate. This is indeed a significant period. There are new ventures, a hectic social whirl, indulgences, reinforcements and rebellion. You are looking at new frontiers and vistas. You are also looking for peace. There is a lot of juggling to do and Ganesha wishes you well.

You will have to sort out your priorities before stepping into the next level.

10 August: Full Moon in Aquarius

The full moon is in your sign. Use the energies well to get ahead in life. There will be windfalls, lucky breaks and large doses of good fortune. You feel empowered. The shadow side emerges too. There are confusions galore. You waver between exile and return, between wandering and home. The inner life is as important as the outer, said the great psychoanalyst, Carl Jung, and if the inner life is unexplored it could show up in different ways. You ideate and want to take on new experiences. You realize that an inner transformation will also transform the outer world. If you stay static in unexamined ideas and rigidity, you will stink like a stagnant pool. As a species, if we don't willingly go beyond our constructs, the universe will likely catapult us there. It is akin to Darwin's theory of the evolution of the species. Life is a process of discovery and if you shy away from it, you will be the loser. Ganesha blesses you as you find yourself and wriggle out of the maze like a caterpillar that finally turns into a dazzling butterfly.

17 August: Last Quarter in Taurus

You settle down and that is a good feeling. The hard slog keeps you occupied. The mind is a restless monkey and it has to be tethered. Your focus shifts to work and money. This phase sees you more settled. You are busy with seminars, conferences and meetings. You enjoy social intercourse and the meeting of minds. There is exploration and growth. Youngsters excel in examinations and interviews. You allow new vistas of understanding to visit you. You are ready for the hard slog. Ganesha is happy.

25 August: New Moon in Virgo

You continue with zeal and determination. There is a lot on your plate. There are domestic expenses. There are marriages in the family, possible ill health of spouse and parents, business expansion and much more. You are careful with money and wise with your words and action. This is a period of self-control. Ganesha is pleased. You step back, evaluate your potential, and then surge ahead. There is planning and deliberation in your moves. You are like a battle-hardy general marshalling his resources. You cannot go wrong.

2 September: First Quarter in Sagittarius

There is a lot of movement now and you are progressing as well as reaching out to people and places. There could be new love, flirtations and a few disruptions at work. You make positive changes in your life to enrich it with greater knowledge and experience. You are not disruptive but you want more and are fed up with routine. You do not want limitations and you are impatient when things don't happen as fast as you want them to. You are outspoken to a fault and assertive enough to make the necessary changes. You feel that you are the master of your destiny and you want to be in the driver's seat. There is nothing wrong with that, says Ganesha. But the changes are subtly taking place anyway, without much fanfare. You will see that in the near future.

9 September: Full Moon in Pisces

You may take a break from routine. You may go for a long overdue vacation. There are expenses and many demands on you but you are adamant that you need a holiday. This influence can be mentally very exciting. You are attracted to new ideas that are challenging and positive and ensure progress. You are open to any gust of wind that reinforces your affirmation that life is in your hands and can be moulded by you irrespective of the challenges. You solve problems that could normally faze you. You have a new approach and perspective to life. There is joy and hope. Ganesha is pleased.

16 September: Last Quarter in Gemini

There are many thoughts tearing into you. You are like a wild flower in the desert, tended by no one in particular, but flourishing under the desert sun, in the wind and rain. You are pollinated by the cosmos and are enriched. You crave for freedom, the vastness of infinity and for what lies beyond the horizon. There is love but you cannot hold on to it. In your core, you know that it is fleeting and silly and only fills a void. When that void is filled, as it will be in due course, the love will serve no purpose. You know all that and break free from all shackles. There are tears and misunderstandings. But you have a distant drummer goading you on. Ganesha is with you. He alone understands what you are going through.

24 September: New Moon in Libra

It is party time. There is money coming in and some expenses too. There could be an inheritance coming your way that will change your life. There are new friendships and associations but nothing sticks. You do not want commitment. You cannot give it and you cannot accept the pain of parting either. Ganesha blesses you. The limelight beckons. You enjoy it all but remain unruffled. Life is dancing and singing and you are a part of the choir. Sometimes, in the recesses of your aloneness, you worry about money and earthly desires. Then you somehow realize that existence has given you much more than you deserve. So why worry at all?

1 October: First Quarter in Capricorn

There are new dimensions now. A lot is on your plate: buying, selling, love, passion, money, expenses, purchases, the good life, travel and everything else that makes life worthwhile. There may be a meeting with a former partner and there could be emotional moments. There may be a child involved and the meeting and subsequent parting will hurt. It has been many years now and old wounds surface. You may also be attracted to social reforms at a community level as you feel that old solutions are not adequate and there is need for change. At work, there are rewards and awards and you also take a chance at speculation. There is extra money to play with. There are many influences at play now and the results are quite unpredictable. But the changes that happen will be favourable and life will be pregnant with possibilities. Ganesha smiles.

8 October: Full Moon in Aries

This is a lucky time. Go ahead and do what you really feel like doing, of course within the ambit of propriety. There is money, honey, new projects/assignments, investments, stocks, realty, buying, selling, financial and legal issues. Ganesha watches over you. This is a good period for work that calls for disciplined thinking. Your critical faculties are on fire. No one can take you for a ride. You look at both sides of the coin and comb through every document. The practical streak in you gets highlighted and you stand firm in your views. You take legal counsel if required.

15 October: Last Quarter in Cancer

This is a good period and you experience pleasant times. You reach out to others and give and receive affections. Your relationships are beautiful in this phase. Bonding reaches a new peak. You go out of your way to be pleasant and charming and smooth over ruffled feelings wherever you go. Others enjoy your company because you are agreeable and fun. You are in an indulgent frame of mind and want to have a good time. You feel that you have worked enough and now just want to hang loose. There are expenses as you buy things that catch your fancy even if you don't need them. In this phase, self-discipline is the last thing on your mind. All new associations are profitable and you feel content and happy with your world. I must state here, like I always do, that these are mere generalizations. A more accurate reading will depend on personal details. These are indicators; you can use your free will to alter them. Astrology never compels; it just impels like a gentle prod. Ganesha watches over you.

23 October: New Moon in Scorpio

There is fire in your belly and a raw, pulsating energy. You are filled with intensity, energy and passion. You could be indiscreet in the display of your affections. The dark forces may also motivate you and you have to be on guard. Smoking, drinking, gambling, gluttony, indulgences of all kinds, loans, funds, capital, mutual funds, mortgages, rewards, even punishment, land on your plate. There is a lot happening and several opposing influences are at play too. You look at ways to expand your consciousness. There will be renewed interest in tantra, yantra, mantra, yoga, meditation and new ways of living. You may be excited by alternative healing and alternative lifestyles. You want to look more closely at same-sex relationships. If you are a scientist, this is a great time for new discoveries as you are pushed in that direction. You are not after money or honey. It is not your propellant right now, actually it never has been. You want new ideas and a new consciousness. I am happy for you and so is Ganesha.

31 October: First Quarter in Aquarius

You coast along uncharted waters. There are new discoveries and realizations. You now see clearly that you have been so wrong in the past in judging others. It is not that you are unsure or are on slippery ground. It is just that you are moulding yourself into becoming a better person. Current events, social inequity and other such upheavals in your world sadden you. Avoid prolonged depression. Ganesha is with you as you sally forth in the quest for truth. You are also filled with hope and optimism for the future. This is a propitious time for those in the teaching profession. You get applause for your skills as a communicator. You have a long way to go!

6 November: Full Moon in Taurus

You feel good with yourself and spend time helping the weaker sections of society. You feel benevolent and generous towards all. You spend time in libraries poring over tomes on self-improvement. This is a very positive influence. You contemplate the loftier aspects of life and skip the irritating details. There is an aura of optimism and positive affirmation that has taken over your life. You may also feel self-righteous and arrogant and the epitome or fountain of all the wisdom in the world. This attitude may not win you brownie points and your peers may find you insufferable. But all that is part of the rocky terrain of life. Ganesha wishes you well.

14 November: Last Quarter in Leo

You live large and play with grand schemes. Despite that, you are cautious and deliberate in your moves. There is great intellectual precision and strategy in whatever you embark on now. There is detailed planning and you behave like Napoleon in one of his wondrous campaigns. There is money and honey as you sign big deals with flair. There is love, passion and many affairs of the heart. You have a maudlin side to you which the opposite sex finds enchanting. You are a charmer. Even your tears have takers. Those in insurance, realty, stocks and banking do exceptionally well. There is rapid growth as you reach out to frontiers of change. Ganesha is pleased.

22 November: New Moon in Sagittarius

You are moving for the kill like a cheetah in Serengeti that has sighted its quarry. There is rebellion against antiquated ideas and old patterns of behaviour that have curtailed your natural inclinations. You could break away from home and family and plough your own furrow. There could be domestic upheavals as you compulsively, without forethought or consideration, mark your territory. You just break away like a lone wolf seeking its destiny under the sun without its pack. Your needs and priorities are most important now. The generation gap gets exacerbated in families, and youngsters could just elope or break away from the fetters. There are disruptions as you make changes in your life that allow for greater self-expression. You want to fly with the wind like a kite that has cut loose. Ganesha watches over every move as you enter uncharted territory.

29 November: First Quarter in Pisces

There are maudlin moments but there is balance and equilibrium in life. Your life is humming along with direction and intent like a migratory bird. You work on the personal and business fronts and tie up loose ends. Your life is reaching a critical point and you want to be ready for it. The countdown to the rocket launch has begun! You may opt for a live-in arrangement with an unusual partner from a completely different culture and ethos. You may be making a mistake or even a series of mistakes, but you don't know it now. Neither do I. You are plunging into the unknown. It is like a bungee jump and you are not even sure of the straps. Your approach to life now is at complete variance with the earlier tenor of your life. Ganesha walks with you. Of course, I don't have to add that this is a general reading.

6 December: Full Moon in Gemini

Mars is in your sign from 5 to 31 December. Mars is like the volcano of vitality inside you and influences endurance, persistence and discipline. Mars is named after the Roman god of war, and is also known as 'the bright and burning one'. Red is the colour of Mars and it stimulates the dynamic, potent and fertile drives that power our lives. Mars rules physical energy and action and governs energy, strength, courage, life force and expansion. Well-placed Mars endows powerful energy and an indomitable will to succeed. Mars propels us like an ignited rocket. It is an important energy since it determines how we pursue what we want to achieve in life. In short, Mars represents energy, force, violence, aggression, sports, combat, wars, battles, accidents and operations. You are moving in different directions and with considerable aggression too. You toy with a million ideas and move in a zillion directions. You subscribe to the new theory of evolution, which clearly states that when Gaia doesn't need a species, it simply dies out and a new species takes its place. You are wearing new plumage and are ready for the multiple relocations of Kali yuga and the Aquarian age. Ganesha is with you.

14 December: Last Quarter in Virgo

You are filled with dynamism and energy and move about with a rare frenzy. You may think of climbing the Everest or scaling the Alps or walking across the Niagara on a tightrope. Your ideas are crazy and there are few takers. Close friends, loved ones and your family think you have lost it. Those in the media and in academia dazzle. Their genius doesn't go unnoticed. There is applause and accolades, rewards and awards. You reinvent yourself as you break self-imposed boundaries. Your evolution, considered as eccentric by some, doesn't go unnoticed. Those in public life may receive the highest awards. As a communicator, you are par excellence. Ganesha is pleased. So am I. It is people like you who break the status quo, who make change happen. You are in the firing line and the bullets that hit you are blanks!

22 December: New Moon in Capricorn

It is party time and everyone wants you. There is work to be done and lots of unfinished business. But you want to let your hair down and swing with the chic set. They want you too. You are 'happening', to quote generation next. There is money and honey, love and passion, income and expenses, multiple partners and commitment, indulgence and good health, vices and wisdom, luxury and austerity. Your plate is full and overflowing with goodies and contradictions. Children are a source of joy and there could be an addition to the family or a marriage or some such festive event. The party mood is doubly delightful. Ganesha is pleased. Laugh and the world laughs with you, and we are talking in a much larger and more profound context than a neighbourhood laughter yoga class. Your life has been a smorgasbord of colours. The year 2015 is different, and right now you have no time for it. Why, they even said that the world would end in 2012! So much for false prophets!

28 December: First Quarter in Aries

There is dynamism in your efforts. Your work sphere increases dramatically as you make waves. People want to be with you. This is a good time for counsellors and those involved in social work. You help out with neighbourhood issues. There is also time spent with the family and deep bonding. Children bring joy. It may be a good time to change your erratic lifestyle and pick up healthy habits. Watch your health. It is better to take precautions than be sorry later. Ganesha is with you.

Key Dates

January

1, 5–6, 9*–15, 18*–19, 22*–24, 27*–28.
Ganesha says that a house move, office expenses, spirituality, parents and family nursing/caring keep you even more busy this month than you were ever before. You handle it all well.

February

1*–2, 6*–11, 15*–16, 19*–20, 23*–25, 28–29.
Ganesha says that the month of February will be a launching pad to fame and fortune. Your own hard work, efforts, success, charisma, leadership ensure that favours will be granted.

March

1, 4*–10, 13–14, 17–18, 22*–23, 27*–28.
Food, family, finance—the three Fs—as well as buying and selling, new projects for you, says Ganesha! These cover a whole gamut of activities.

April

1*–9 (important), 13*–15, 18*–19, 23*–24, 28*–29.
Travel, neighbours, fine communication and reaching

out. You will be loved and respected, and that makes for a wonderful feeling.

May

2*–3, 6*–7, 11*–17, 20*–22, 25*–27, 30–31.
Renovation, decoration, buying and selling (of property and assets), parents and in-laws, achievements. Home and family matters become good only after a struggle, says Ganesha, but it is still the main focus.

June

3*–4, 7*–13, 16*–18, 21*–23, 26*–27, 30*.
A wish fulfilment for you, says Ganesha! That says it all. The exact nature of your wishes cannot be forecast, so no more details!

July

1, 4–5, 9–10, 14*–16, 19*–25, 28*–29.
Loans, income, pets, projects are highlighted. Therefore, finances are exhausted! Extra pressures in your work could cause bad health and low vitality. Health care is, therefore, important this month, says Ganesha!

August

1*–7, 10*–11, 15*–16, 20*–21, 24–25, 28–29.
Success, partnerships, opposition, marriage, journey with a stopover. Lots of activity this month, says Ganesha! Take care to avoid overstraining yourself.

September

1–3, 6–8, 11*–17, 20–21, 24*–26, 29*–30.
Funds, buying, selling, property, investment, passion in an intoxicating mix of activity, says Ganesha! Money and honey—the story has a new twist!

October

4*–5, 9*–14, 17*–18, 22*–23, 26*–27, 31*.
Contacts, contracts, children, joy, romance are all there for you Aquarians. Go out and win on all these counts now, says Ganesha! The timing is right.

November

1, 5*–11, 14*–15, 18–19, 22–24, 27–29.
Profession, money from the family and father, progress as well as competition. The health of parents, in-laws may not be up to the mark. You're more than busy, once again!

December

2*–8, 11*–12, 15*–16, 20*–21, 24*–26, 30*–31.
Ganesha says this is one of the best months of 2014. Entertainment, socializing, group activities, hobbies and functions make you happy and keep you busy too, once again. You enjoy it and are full of hope! Success is yours!

Pisces

YEARLY FORECAST

> She walks in beauty, like the night
> Of cloudless climes and starry skies;
> And all that's best of dark and bright
> Meet in her aspect and her eyes.
>
> *– Lord Byron*
>
> In fine frenzy
> The fire fantasizes me
> We two are Radha-Krishna
>
> *– Bejan Daruwalla*

Till 16 July 2014
Summary and Guidance

The above two poems speak about romance, love and beauty. The reason is very simple. It is that Jupiter, the planet of prosperity and spirituality, will be in your fifth angle of creativity, joy, happiness, love, songs, laughter, fun and frolic in life. In other words, Jupiter will make you dance with joy and delight. For artists, actors, astrologers, singers, musicians, dancers, and research scholars, this is a truly wonderful time. Pisceans are very creative and human. The finest examples are Einstein and Steve Jobs. I have no need to say more.

17 July 2014 to 11 August 2015

Jupiter will be in your sixth house of work, rewards, employment, pets, colleagues, servants, health and hygiene, loans and funds, debts and thefts. It would be wonderful if you start exercising and taking good care of your health. You will be fit and trim and feel good about it. On the practical side it means better health, therefore more efficiency, better rewards. A change of job, a promotion, perks, bonus are strong possibilities. In short, this is a time to work hard and get excellent results. I am sure you understand it very clearly.

Main Trend

There are two main trends. Till 16 July 2014 the focus will be on creative activities, hobbies, children, sports, prayers, good deeds, knowledge, vedas, spirituality, religious ceremony, authorship, mantras and karmas. In short, it is a long and wonderful list.

The other main trend is from 17 July 2014 to 11 August 2015. Health and wealth will be interconnected. You must learn to take care of your servants, pets and those who depend upon you in one way or the other. Nurses, doctors, publishers, industrialists, psychiatrists and sportspeople will do excellent and noble work. If you are connected in any way with social welfare, you will do much for others. In other words, this is the time to show the world your abilities and efficiency. Group activities will make you not only satisfied but deliriously happy. Happiness lies in making others happy. This is the simple truth.

Journey and Communication

Saturn will be in your house of journey and communication. For short journeys, Venus will be active and lucky.

Combining the effects of both Saturn and Venus, Ganesha says the months of May, July, September, January and, to some extent, February will be very important. Mercury, the winged messenger, will be in and out of your sign between 1 February and 17 April which is a good period for you.

Health

As said earlier, health will improve drastically between 17 July 2014 and 11 August 2015. Try to be fit and healthy as I have pointed out earlier. Exercise, yoga and meditation will certainly help. You Pisceans, are very sensitive. For you it will be mind over matter. Relationships with colleagues, partners, friends and servants will set you off in a good mood. And that will lead to good health. Now you know the reason why you should have sweet relationships with one and all. Please read your happiness quota given later.

Love/Marriage

The two poems at the beginning and the big paragraph about summary and guidance till 16 July 2014 clearly show the importance of love and marriage in your life. I say, once again, that you will dance to the tune of love and marriage. Venus is the planet of both. The months for it are September, July, May, October and January. Let music guide your footsteps. Love is the fabric of life.

Property

Strictly speaking, this may not be the year of great property unless the trend has started in the two years prior to this, i.e., 2012 and 2013. Mercury is the symbol of property. Mercury will be in and out of your sign between

1 February and 17 April. Again it will help you in June and September. In property we include house, office, land, real estate, godown, shop, warehouse, garage and so on. I want to be very clear about it.

Job/Business/Loans/Funds/Investments

As said earlier, your best bet is in jobs and investments. These will be particularly so from 17 July 2014 to 11 August 2015. But life is not made of watertight compartments. In real life, one trend flows into the next. In other words, it is a continuation. The months for it will be August, April, December, May and March.

Children/Entertainment

I have clearly pointed out that children and entertainment will give great delight at least till 16 July 2014. This does not mean that children and entertainment will not give great delight after that. It only means that till 16 July 2014 the seeds, the creative juices, will be in full flow. In entertainment, I certainly include hobbies, films, arts, festivals, weddings, sports and all fun games including, obviously, comedies. My suggestion is: Life is short. Make it sweet.

Trips and Ties

Please read the paragraph on journey and communication. Ties include relationships. For you, very specially, the months of May, July, September, November, January and February will show the way.

Publicity/Projects/Performance

You, Pisceans, are very subtle and artistic. Also, you are the escape specialists of the entire zodiac. You can slip away and also give the slip anytime and in all possible ways. Therefore your publicity and performance will be smooth, effective, lasting, powerful. Believe me. I have used my words wisely and well for you.

Happiness Quota

You, Pisceans, are oversensitive, artistic, easily hurt, and given to great mood swings. Also, I am taking into consideration that Mars will be in your 8th angle of upsets and possibly unpleasant surprises till 25 July 2014. I have to weigh all the planets in the balance. Jupiter and Neptune work hard and long for you. They are your great friends. They will defend you against the attack or onslaught of Mars. For you Mars represents, to some extent, operations and accidents. But please do not get nervous. I am not God. I do go wrong at times.

This is not a horoscopic reading. It is only a reading based upon the position of the sun. By prayers and charity the effects of Mars can be lessened. If you believe in mantras, I have two for you. The first mantra is '*Om gun ganpataye namah.*' The second mantra is '*Om kraam kreem krom sa bhowmaya namah.*' Take care of food poisoning, allergy, colds, bronchitis and asthma. The marks I give you are 85 per cent.

Monthly Round-up

January: You will be off and away to a really flying start, says Ganesha, and as you know, well begun is half done; February and March: expensive but also progress, therefore, mixed results; April: excellent for finances and family affairs and earned income; May: reaching out to people and places by all means of transport and communication; June: important for peace, buying/selling/renovating/decorating, a home away from home; July: love, romance, the luck of the draw, creativity and children, family and fun and fortune; August: health, employment, pets, servants and colleagues and a few problems connected with these; September: love and hate, marriage and making merry, but paradoxically, in a few cases, separation and legal cases, and that is why life is so complex, uncertain, full of contradictions and surprises; October: funds, loans, capital formation, money matters, shopping; November: inspiration, journey, name and fame, good luck; December: power, prestige, parents, profession, awards and rewards, money, home, house and office.

Summary

The word 'joy' best sums up the celebration of life; of daring and caring despite odds, for you, Pisceans. Ganesha says, home, house, work, status, prestige, parents, in-laws and travel will keep you on your 'twinkling toes' in 2014.

Outer Planets

URANUS: Uranus in your angle of finance, speech, food, drugs, drinks, family, could bring about sudden changes for both good and bad. Life is a mix of good and bad. Astrology is a mirror to life. Therefore expect the good and the bad and be prepared for it. That is what astrology is all about. Ganesha blesses you.

NEPTUNE: By modern astrology, Neptune is your main planet. By ancient astrology, Jupiter is your main planet.

We have spoken about Jupiter. Neptune makes you creative, artistic, clever, sensitive, ever-changing and possibly, slippery and not able to face facts. You may be a dreamer. It is both good and bad.

PLUTO: Pluto in your eleventh angle of friendship, group activities, gains and joy works very powerfully in these directions for you. Pluto will be a blessing for you. My suggestion is to drink the cup of life to the dregs.

Month by Month
January

You busy yourself with bills, business expansion, family affairs and a whole set of sundry issues. You may use work as a sort of escape from the realities and pressures of the mundane world. You are torching the stage with your hard work and genius. There is fire in your belly and also a boost in willpower, optimism and vision. By mid-month there are many emotional moments. There are domestic issues to handle. Travel, new associations and many indulgences keep you occupied. There is love and lust. Those in the media and artistic fields do exceptionally well. By the month-end there could be moments of distress in your personal life. There could be depression and maudlin moments. Ganesha is with you.

February

You prosper and make big bucks. You are also busy with different fiscal instruments and investments. Your emotions have stabilized and your focus on work is without distractions. All your plans bear fruit. There are awards and rewards, accolades and applause. You make huge investments in new projects. There are lucky breaks, new opportunities, and the universe smiles on you. Ganesha is pleased.

March

It is your birth month. Make the most of the energies that are at your beck and call. You use all the networking tools and social sites with great strategy. There is love and bonding, lust and raw passion. Mercury is in Pisces from 18 March to 17 April. This is a great period and you must make the most of it. Media folk, writers, painters and those in the film and television industry, do exceptionally well. There is increased prestige, recognition, popularity, awards, rewards, money and honey. Ganesha is with you.

April

All the energies of the cosmos are working in your favour. Venus is in Pisces from 6 April to 2 May. There could be marriages, engagements, births, anniversaries, birthdays and every other excuse to celebrate. There is money and honey, love and bonding, and great times to be had. You are sitting on a sea of possibilities. The single have a field day and those in committed relationships are torn asunder by the various temptations on offer. There are new properties purchased, international travel, rewards, awards, accolades and applause. Ganesha is happy for you.

May

There are big deals, wise investments, lending, borrowing, funds, capital-raising, buying, selling, expenses and indulgences. Many of you will be seeking out yoga, meditation, alternative therapies, mantra, yantra and tantra. There are new ties, bonds, partnerships, associations and collaborations. You may also spend on charities. You are drawn to religion, spirituality, prayer, meditation, rituals, esoteric sciences, gods and godmen. Ganesha is with you.

June

You are back to the grind and working hard. There are medical emergencies, and children and the spouse need attention. You are filled with passion and this can lead to indiscriminate displays of affection. This is an excellent time for all personal contact and private talks. You are filled with new awareness and sensitivity to others and their needs. You could be a riot of emotions, hypersensitive and overemotional. As the month ends there are happy moments in the family. Ganesha is pleased.

July

The tempo is brisk and thoughts flash through your head at amazing speed. Those in the media, sales and in the legal profession have a great run. Your energies are robust. You are filled with generosity and happiness and share it with others. You are in an indulgent mood. You are at your creative best and see love, beauty, joy and hope in the smallest of things. By the month-end you are in a communicative mood and want to discuss your relationships, love affairs and platonic friendships with others. There is money and honey, the work front is good and you are ambitious, energetic and determined to make it all happen. Ganesha is pleased.

August

With the death of old patterns in your life, a new phase begins. You are in the throes of change. You meet different kinds of people and new vistas open. People support you, miracles happen, and the magic of life unfolds. By mid-month there is stability and work and money to be made. The health of elders, sibling rivalry, emotional discord with children are in focus. As the month ends you are fascinated by every new phenomenon that you encounter. There is also new love and bonding. Ganesha is with you.

September

There are new and fruitful contacts. There could be international travel too. Work areas are well defined, but your aspirations are all about gaining a higher consciousness. This is a great period for healthcare providers and those in social work. Your popularity zooms through the stratosphere. There is money and honey, awards and rewards, applause and accolades. The month-end sees you capable of precision and concentrated effort. You are relentless in your efforts and there could be lasting accomplishments. This is a great period for those in showbiz. Ganesha is pleased.

October

You continue to slog. You lock yourself at your work station and go hammer and tongs at new assignments. There is frenzied action and high-octane energy powering you. You look at formulating long-term plans. You also look at personal change. You are fuelled by a philanthropic bent of mind. There are new realizations as you grow as a person. Mid-month sees love and longing. There are also great times with friends. The month-end sees great intensity in all that you do. There is a lot on your plate and you have your hands full. The month-end sees you take risks in business. On the other hand, you also display a strong evangelistic streak. Ganesha is with you.

November

You work hard and make money through sheer talent and the sweat of your brow. There are domestic issues that need your attention. You live large and make grand plans. Even better, you are able to execute your plans perfectly. There is applause and money. You conquer new peaks and touch delirious heights of excellence. There is travel, visits to shrines, serious networking, new insights, feelings, longings, friendships, hopes and desires. The month-end sees love, longing, bonding, loss, separation, fear, hope, joy, sorrow, marriages, celebrations and divorces. It is all happening for you as the year ends. Creative folk will do wonderfully well. Ganesha blesses you.

December

You look for distractions. You immerse yourself in escapist fantasies. You look for freedom from bondage. Mid-month sees more stability. Those in stocks, insurance and realty do well. There is love and bonding as you meet up with old friends. There are new collaborations. You may spend the last week in contemplation and work, in domestic chores and intimate fellowship. As the year ends, you spend happy days with close friends and family. There is clarity and determination. There is incision, direction, thrust and parry as you mow down the opposition. There is also love and bonding. Ganesha wishes you well.

Month at a Glance

January

You will be off and away to a really flying start, says Ganesha, and as you know, well begun is half done.

February and March

Expensive but also progress, therefore, mixed results.

April

Excellent for finances and family affairs and earned income.

May

Reaching out to people and places by all means of transport and communication.

June

Important for peace, buying/selling/renovating/decorating, a home away from home.

July

Love, romance, the luck of the draw, creativity and children, family and fun and fortune.

August

Health, employment, pets, servants and colleagues and a few problems connected with these.

September

Love and hate, marriage and merry making, but paradoxically, in a few cases, separation and legal cases, and that is why life is so complex, uncertain, full of contradictions and surprises.

October

Funds, loans, capital formation, money matters, shopping.

November

Inspiration, journey, name and fame, good luck.

December

Power, prestige, parents, profession, awards and rewards, money, home, house and office.

Weekly Review (By the phases of the moon)

1 January: New Moon in Capricorn

You are in great company, quite like all the other signs. Every zodiac sign has giants in its bosom. You share your birthday with Anais Nin, Gabriel Garcia Marquez, Henrik Ibsen, George Washington, Albert Einstein, Constantine The Great, Cindy Crawford, Alexander Graham Bell, Gloria Vanderbilt, Rupert Murdoch, Steve Jobs, Bruce Willis, Farrah Fawcett and several other celebrities. Pisces is a water sign and can be careless, indecisive, melancholy, impractical, indolent, compassionate, charming, emotional, intuitive and artistic. They generally hate altercations and disagreements. They don't like hurting others and so they suffer fools and get into relationships from which an exit is difficult. They are masters of disguise and have an amazing capacity to slip into anyone's shoes. They are filled with empathy and sympathy. The new moon is in Capricorn now and you are hard at work. You busy yourself with bills, business expansion, family affairs and a whole set of sundry issues. You may use work as a sort of escape from the realities and pressures of the mundane world. Whenever there is a domestic upheaval or a relationship you can't handle, work is a good excuse. But, in the bargain, thanks to all the time spent in the office, you make the big bucks. Ganesha blesses you.

8 January: First Quarter in Aries

You go all out like Lionel Messi on a goal-scoring spree. You turn and twist past the opposition and score goals from every conceivable angle. You are torching the stage with your hard work and genius. You have spread yourself too thin and you have to streamline now. There are many demands on your time and space. There is fire in your belly and also a boost in willpower, optimism and vision. There are many secret rendezvous, clandestine love affairs, journeys and out-of-the-box experiences. There is never a dull moment. Life doesn't surprise you. It is the other way round—you surprise life! This is a good period and the year has begun with money and honey. Ganesha is with you.

16 January: Full Moon in Cancer

The full moon is in Cancer and there are many emotional moments. There are domestic issues to handle. Elders at home need medical care; children and spouse need attention; you may also have to wrestle with the demons residing in your subconscious. You are torn apart by many emotions. There could be indiscreet affairs and subsequent domestic unrest. You are a people's person and love gatherings, associations and alumni meetings. You will be invited everywhere and you feel happy. You like to be wanted. You like the boost in self-esteem.

Ganesha watches over you as you wade through murky waters like a shark seeking out a seal.

24 January: Last Quarter in Scorpio

There is new intensity in all your dealings. Travel, new associations and many indulgences are on the cards. There is love and lust. Passion takes you by the throat. You cannot let it go. It seeps through you like the poison of a venomous snake and you are at its mercy. Youngsters will be lost in the throes of passion. Nothing else in life will make sense. You have to go through with the journey and emerge from the tunnel at your own speed. All Ganesha can do now is wish you well. We have to find our path irrespective of the boulders along the way. There could also be ego battles at work. You may want your way in all dealings but it may also be prudent to give in. Those in the media and artistic fields do exceptionally well. You are crowned with success.

30 January: New Moon in Aquarius

You flirt with new ideas. Work will take on many new dimensions and you will be adequately rewarded. There could be moments of distress in your personal life as you go through the ebb and flow of contrasting thoughts. You want to change tack and are looking for a better deal both in your personal and professional life but you don't know how to go about it. There could be depression and maudlin moments. Hang on and let it pass. Life has its seasons, and this too shall pass. It is not that there is anything specifically wrong in your life. It is just that your inner demons are playing havoc with you. There are pulls and pressures and you have to sort them out before moving to the next level. Ganesha is with you and that is all that matters.

6 February: First Quarter in Taurus

There is greater stability in all your undertakings. You prosper and make huge bucks. You are also busy with different fiscal instruments and investments. Your emotions have stabilized and your focus on work is without distractions. Ganesha is pleased. I must add here that I am not God and these are mere indications. I mean well for all humanity. Astrology impels and never compels, though personal readings can be quite accurate. Many factors influence a person's life and the idea is to make the most of a given situation. No human being can be completely happy or fulfilled. As Osho said, only the idiot is truly happy. Ignorance is bliss. But with greater stimuli all around, every iota of bliss is being robbed from our lives. Work is a great panacea. You realize this and submerge yourself in it.

14 February: Full Moon in Leo

You are living it up. You are like an African lion in the rutting season. Nothing can deter you from your avowed goals. You run through the opposition. All your plans bear fruit. There are awards and rewards, accolades and applause. You also sow your wild oats like confetti. There are expenses, luxury purchases and grand living. The single have a field day. Those who are married may throw caution to the wind. I am sure you know what I mean. I don't have to explain further. There may be travel, and you party with friends till the cows come home. Ganesha is with you on this upward swing. You live large and in abundance.

22 February: Last Quarter in Sagittarius

There is a lot of movement now. Those in the media do exceptionally well. You make huge investments in new projects, hoping they will do well. You tread into the darkness without a flashlight. There is no fear as you take huge business risks. Somehow, you know that it will all work out well for you. Ganesha ensures that. There are lucky breaks, new opportunities, and the universe smiles on you, showering you with its abundance. Gaia is pleased. Mother earth rocks you in her bosom.

1 March: New Moon in Pisces

This is a period of powerful energy flow. It is your birth month and also the new moon is in your sign. Make the most of the energies that are at your beck and call. You use all the networking tools and social sites with great strategy. People flock around you. Your charm oozes from every pore. The opposite sex finds you irresistible. There is love and bonding, lust and raw passion. Youngsters, smitten by first love, see nothing else. So a word of caution for parents. There could be domestic upheavals as a consequence. These are indicators, says Ganesha, as he helps you through troubled waters.

8 March: First Quarter in Gemini

Your mind is here, there and everywhere. You think of a million things and don't know where to begin. The start is vital in any venture and this dithering may cost you valuable time and money. You may also be set upon by emotional leeches and it won't be easy to get rid of them. You are emotional and sensitive and make time for tears. So people flock to you and there is no escape. I am old and emotional too, and have spent a lot of time with people who have taken my time. So I know what I am talking about. Experience pays. I hang my emotions on my sleeve but I am not, in any way, recommending that. Ganesha watches over you with affection.

16 March: Full Moon in Virgo

Mercury is in Pisces from 18 March to 17 April (Mercury shifts between Aquarius and Pisces because of retrograde or reverse motion). Mercury, the mighty, all-powerful planet, is in your sign now. It favours travels, meetings, conferences, interviews, trips, more brain power, contacts, communication, correspondence and contracts. Mercury has a special connection with the circuits of the brain. Chess, crossword and other such games belong to Mercury. Also, short-distance runners and spin bowlers are controlled by Mercury. Mercury, in short, is the ambassador and salesman of the zodiac. It is the symbol of news, views, messages, interviews, contacts, communications, travel and transport. Mercury gives an impetus to all of the above in the sun sign where it is located. You are moving ahead at a frenetic pace. There is success. This is a great period and you must make the most of it. As I always paraphrase the Bard, take the tide at the flood. It will lead to fame and fortune. Media folk, writers, painters and those in the film and television industry, do exceptionally well. The energy inherent in this period is powerful. Ganesha is happy and urges you to make the most of it.

24 March: Last Quarter in Capricorn

There is hard work ahead. You have set your sights high and made the necessary investments. This is a particularly lucky phase and whatever you touch turns to gold. There is increased prestige, recognition, popularity, awards, rewards, money and honey. You are able to sort your mind out and plunge into work as the dividends are so alluring. There is domestic peace and nothing disturbs your focus. Life is beautiful and you are waltzing with it. This is a great time to be. Life is filled with innumerable facets and when the going is in your favour, Ganesha suggests you entrap it in your fist.

30 March: New Moon in Aries

You are propelled to make miracles happen. The new moon is in Aries and the profitable run continues unabated. You have the Midas touch. You may distance yourself from the family in this quest for gold and glory. You have little time for the spouse, parents, in-laws and siblings. There is resentment but you are unperturbed. 'Show me a sane man and I will cure him,' said Albert Camus. How true! Despite all your sensitivities and kind and caring nature, you show little time for the people who really matter in your life. In the process, you get alienated. It could be the shadow side or the blind spot making its presence felt. In a way, you are trapped, like all of us are, by the various slices of our personalities. Ganesha is with you and that is what matters.

7 April: First Quarter in Cancer

The streak of good fortune continues. This is a dream run. All the energies of the cosmos are working in your favour. Venus is in Pisces from 6 April to 2 May. Venus is another important planet and is of great significance. This is an important phase. As often discussed, Venus is the planet for love, romance, sex, beauty and the good life.

This is the planet of attraction, love, wealth, knowledge and prosperity. The compatibility of partners and also the type of life the individual will lead is also judged from the placement of Venus in the horoscope. As a planet, Venus is considered to be beneficial, feminine and gentle. It symbolizes the force of attraction in the universe. In human beings this attractive force manifests as love and beauty. When Venus is well placed in the chart, there is love, art, beauty and all the goodies of life that make life worth living. Venus rules Libra and Taurus though its role in every sign is important. Like other planets, it also has its transits. In Libra, Venus is aesthetic and cultured. In Taurus it is more earthy, materialistic and sensual. Venus rules the venous system, kidneys, urinary tract, throat, larynx, and is responsible for good looks. In short, Venus in Western astrology stands for comforts, arts, wealth, relationships, sex, decorations, luxuries and wealth. There are several domestic issues that need attention. There could be marriages, engagements, births, anniversaries, birthdays and every other excuse to celebrate. Children will be a source of joy. There could be family holidays at exotic locales. There is money and honey, love and bonding, and great times to be had. Ganesha is happy for you.

15 April: Full Moon in Libra

You are sitting on a sea of possibilities. It is as though you are on the ocean bed and wondering which coral to pick. You are dazzled by everything. You have to make a choice and move on but you don't know what to do. There is deep bonding too. There are reunions and an old love may walk out of thin air into your arms. Seize the moment and mint it. The single have a field day and those in committed relationships are torn apart by the various temptations on offer. Ganesha guides you along the stormy paths of life. Money runs through your fingers as you make priceless purchases.

22 April: Last Quarter in Aquarius

There are maudlin moments. You step back from it all and wonder if it is worth it. Finally, you leave this body with nothing; you take nothing with you. So why the fuss? Such thoughts cripple your mind and you hesitate in enjoying the splendours of life so bountifully thrust into your palms. 'We are what we think. We make the world with our thoughts,' said the Buddha, and he couldn't have been more right. But all this doesn't linger for too long and you snap out of the reverie. You could be particularly concerned about the health of a parent. There are medical emergencies and if you happen to be the favourite child or the son or daughter at the spot, there will be many anxious moments when the entire responsibility falls on you. There is continued success on the work front. Ganesha is with you all the way.

29 April: New Moon in Taurus

You are batting on the front foot and carting every ball over the boundary as though it were the last over of the last match in the IPL and you carry the success of not only your team but the entire tournament on your shoulders. You have not only mastered the *doosra* of Harbhajan Singh but are well prepared for the *teesra* and *chautha* as well. You also mock the sway, carry, speed and drift of raw pace. I am an old, corpulent man now, but I was also young once and an athlete and sportsman of prominence. So I know my cricket well. You display the power of Afridi, the staying power of Tendulkar, the irreverence of Sehwag, the cunning of Steve Waugh, the quirky genius of Dhoni, the elan of Yuvraj, the swagger of Viv Richards, the style of Brian Lara and the technical completeness of Gavaskar. You are all this rolled into one. Need I say more? Your performance is stunning, to say the least. There are new properties purchased, international travel, rewards, awards, accolades and applause. The din is overwhelming. Ganesha is happy as you bask in the afterglow of hard-fought victories.

7 May: First Quarter in Leo

According to Shankara, *turiya* is the fourth or superconscious state which is beyond the three ordinary states of consciousness—waking, dreaming and dreamless sleep. It is the state of unitary consciousness or pure bliss. This, he says, is not a state but the 'atman'. You are in that state now. Those seeking spiritual gurus and deliverance meet with success. The universe sends the right energy and you grab it. We are all interconnected and we send different energies into the cosmos. There are big deals, wise investments, lending, borrowing, funds, capital-raising, buying, selling, expenses and indulgences. Many of you will be seeking out yoga, meditation, alternative therapies, mantra, yantra and tantra. You have got worldly success and now you want to go beyond that. Ganesha helps you on the journey.

14 May: Full Moon in Scorpio

There is powerful intensity propelling you. You are like a speedboat slicing the water with a scythe. Albert

Einstein said, 'Reality is merely an illusion, albeit a very persistent one.' Despite the many shades and nuances of the parchments of life dangling before you, you are in touch with reality. Your feet are on the ground and there is fire in your belly and a gleam in your eyes. Along with your empathy for life and empirical knowledge, you make grand plans, and execute them too. There are new ties, bonds, partnerships, associations and collaborations. Ganesha is happy for you. I must add here that there is also new love and bonding. You are irresistible.

21 May: Last Quarter in Pisces

There is time spent at home. You may also spend on charities. You want to help the downtrodden and will find the time to work in old people's homes, hospices for the underprivileged and in teaching children. You could also look at mantra, tantra and yantra with new eyes. You will look to overhaul your life right from your diet to a new exercise regimen and a completely different wardrobe. There have been new revelations and you may want to reinvent yourself. You are at your creative best and may write a book, a screenplay, take to offbeat roles if you are an actor, make out-of-the-box films and do something wild and crazy. As you can see, this old babaji, your favourite astrologer for decades, is heavily influenced by the next generation. Finally, it is they who will inherit the earth. Ganesha is with you.

28 May: New Moon in Gemini

There are new thoughts playing with you. You are inundated by them. You cannot think straight. You wander in circles and nothing is achieved. You try to please everybody and this takes a toll on you. Unless you are a politician standing for elections, there is no need for this. 'Progress is impossible without change, and those who cannot change their minds cannot change anything,' said George Bernard Shaw, the Irish playwright. Darwin also said that the species that adapts, survives. You are also looking at new ways of living. You want to break free, move on from the clutter of your everyday life and seek new vistas. You feel trapped. You are drawn to religion, spirituality, prayer, meditation, rituals, esoteric sciences, gods and godmen. Beware of conmen and charlatans. The mood you are in, you could be taken for a ride. Ganesha is with you.

5 June: First Quarter in Virgo

There is a modicum of stability. You are back to the grind and working hard. The mind is a monkey and it happens to all of us. Sometimes, we just fly off the handle. We are filled with millions of emotions and need to allow the hovering clouds to pass before we can settle down. You have let that happen and now get down to the task of shouldering your domestic responsibilities. There are medical emergencies, and children and the spouse need attention. Ganesha ensures that you work hard and solve everything that is thrown at you like darts.

13 June: Full Moon in Sagittarius

The god of love looks hard at you and the influence is destabilizing. You are filled with passion and this can lead to indiscriminate displays of affection because your desire to love overrules discretion. You are in the mood for love and it may be unwise to make a permanent commitment to a love affair now. You are not objective about your feelings, and extreme emotionalism is dangerous. It will be best to look at the situation objectively, particularly if you are seriously courting someone. I would suggest a calm, rational and reasonable approach devoid of the frills of proclamations of undying love. The work front is good and you touch new frontiers. This is an excellent time for all personal contact and private talks. Ganesha is with you as you network furiously and make many new associations.

19 June: Last Quarter in Pisces

There is confusion and uncertainty in the air. You are filled with new awareness and sensitivity towards others and their needs. Your encounters with others may be confusing as your energy may be low and you are not in a self-assertive mood. You look to avoid confrontations, as you want peace and harmony and not ill will and tempers running riot. Domestic issues take your time and there is family bonding. You could be a riot of emotions, hypersensitive and overemotional and could take offence at the slightest of slights. There is love and profound bonding. Work is good. Ganesha blesses you.

27 June: New Moon in Cancer

You seek excitement and stimulation through your love relationships. You are impatient with loved ones, resulting in altercations and misunderstandings. The idea is to be flexible and learn to compromise. You cannot have your way all the time. Every relationship is about sharing, giving and taking. You either cower and behave like a slave or you are domineering. Both approaches won't help. Go out of your way to make allowances for the other person and you can have a beautiful relationship without needless disruptions. There are happy moments in the family with all sorts of celebrations. Children may be returning home after a long time and the air is filled with festivities. There could be indulgences and you will fill your glass to the brim with bubbly over and over again. Ganesha is happy for you as you bask in the warm afterglow of domestic bliss.

5 July: First Quarter in Libra

Your intellectual faculties are stimulated. You are fascinated by every new phenomenon that you encounter. You want intellectual challenges and excitement. You get bored with routine and set about looking for unusual experiences. This is a great propellant for growth of all kinds but it will be wise not to go overboard. The tempo is brisk and thoughts flash through your head at amazing speed. Those in the media, sales and in the legal profession have a great run. Pisces is an enigmatic sign. You are like a duck in water. On the surface you are calm and composed but are being torn apart by a million contrary thoughts. You are the master of disguise. Often, you imprison yourself without even knowing what you are doing. In a sense, you are your prisoner. I am just stating how it is and not being judgemental. Every sign has its peculiarities and you have yours. The key is in understanding yourself and being liberated from it all. Ganesha is with you.

12 July: Full Moon in Capricorn

Your energies are robust and you are energetic and want to accomplish a lot. There is hard work ahead and you are ready for it. But different areas of your life are not in harmony and you will have to work on developing a synergy between your home and professional life. Your emotions are in control but you could get into bouts of depression. You think of the past and weep. We all have failures and you are no exception. There is no point in rewinding your life and highlighting the sorry, desperate times. Discordant moods get the better of you and you are like a fish out of water as you struggle with your emotions. This phase will also pass. Ganesha wishes you well.

19 July: Last Quarter in Aries

You are in a happy state. The storm clouds have rolled by and you are not in the war room. There are pleasant feelings between you and everyone around you. You want to be with friends and just hang out having chai and gossiping. You are filled with generosity and happiness and share it with others. You are in an indulgent mood and may not be working in a crazed manner as you are wont to do sometimes. This is a good time to love, and beautify and redecorate your home. You are at your creative best and see love, beauty, joy and hope in the smallest of things. You are in love with love and will enter into a relationship at the slightest provocation. Like fire in a barn, your emotions can engulf you. There is new work, but for now you prefer the land of dreams. You don't want to roll your sleeves and dirty your hands. I had also been young once and understand the power of romance. Go for it if it pushes you so hard. Your favourite astrologer has a confession to make here: I have also loved and lost. And, let me add with some certainty, it is much better than never to have loved at all! You give free rein to many layers of emotion and passion as they bubble forth from your breast like Mount Vesuvius. Ganesha quietly chuckles.

26 July: New Moon in Leo

You live large. Every emotion and action of yours is exaggerated. You are in a communicative mood and want to discuss your relationships, love affairs and platonic friendships with others. You share pleasant moments with your beloved and discuss the situation as objectively and rationally as an oncologist viewing a new case. This is an intense phase. There is money and honey, the work front is good and you are ambitious, energetic and determined to make it all happen for you. Ganesha is pleased. You could be spending more than you are earning as there are unexpected expenses added to the indulgent mood. You want to live in style and will buy new goodies, a country home, fancy gadgets, maybe the most coveted sports car. You are surfing the Niagara Falls. Wow!

4 August: First Quarter in Scorpio

Carlos Castaneda said, 'Things don't change, only the way you look at them.' In this phase, your perspective changes. The same things mean different things to you now. What you hated once is likeable now. There are endings and new beginnings. There could be crises too if your life has been built around inappropriate activities. With the death of old patterns in your life, a new phase begins. You may junk old patterns of behaviour and adopt an entirely new lifestyle. You are in the throes of change. Ganesha wishes you well.

10 August: Full Moon in Aquarius

There are many changes taking place in your life. Consciously or unconsciously, you are pruning your life. Many patterns of behaviour come to an automatic end. Like a boa constrictor shedding its skin, you too make way for the new. These are all vital changes and necessary to clear the decks for the ensuing period of action on an entirely new tack. You may change residence, type of work, even your partner. You meet different kinds of people and new vistas open. There is excitement and energy as you prepare to face new challenges. People support you, miracles happen, and the magic of life unfolds. Ganesha is with you all the way, guiding you and often even carrying you along.

17 August: Last Quarter in Taurus

There are many changes in your life now. A major cycle of experience is closing. There is stability and work, and money to be made. There could also be an unusual person who suddenly enters your life now. This person could be from another culture altogether and distant from all the other associations that you have had. It could be platonic or sexual love, I don't know. Like I always say, these are mere indications and a more accurate reading will depend on the personal horoscope. I am not God and these are mere gentle prods. Astrology never compels, it just impels. If you have been living away from home, there could be a return. The health of elders, sibling rivalry, emotional discord with children and some fissures at work are the highlights of the package this week. Ganesha wishes you well.

25 August: New Moon in Virgo

You are in the throes of all types of stimulation. You are fascinated by every new phenomenon that you encounter. You want desperately to pack off routine and ride the tallest wave. The Mother of Puducherry said, 'We must aspire to conquer all mistakes, all obscurities, all ignorances.' You are flexible now and are ready for a type of spiritual explosion in your life. There are all types of surprises as you embark on this journey. There are new conditions in your life, and different challenges. You are compelled to cope as you seek a release from restrictions and obligations. There is also new love and bonding. I have to repeat this here but Pisceans are silent romantics, and there could be many affairs of the heart. Piscean women, in particular, are simply enticing. I have said this before but I am sorry, I have to repeat it. If you at times wonder at my eloquence and erudition, I must add here that I have been a professor of English! Ganesha is with you and that is what is important.

2 September: First Quarter in Sagittarius

This is a deeply satisfying and liberating period when you enjoy life with more gusto and freedom. There are new and fruitful contacts and there could be new love brewing like Indian coffee. You are networking furiously and there could be international travel too. You get in touch with many facets of your personality and get to understand yourself better. Many encounters now are profound and meaningful and you may be forced to act out of character and acknowledge your injuries or sensitivities to total strangers which you would normally never have done. You generally fear rejection and keep secrets close to your bosom. But in this phase you just blindly trust and spill it all out. Ganesha watches over you. The work areas are well defined but your aspirations are all about gaining in higher consciousness. You feel good about yourself and project positive energies. Personal and professional transactions are smooth.

9 September: Full Moon in Pisces

You are in a happy phase. Your relationship with others is congenial. Even your enemies have softened their stance towards you. You are ready to make peace and compromise. You want harmony at all costs. As a result, you are much sought after. People feel good around you. You are eager to help and are keen to listen to everyone's problems. This is a great period for health care providers and those in social work. You are filled with good cheer and positivity. Your kind words are like healing balms. You have a natural empathy for suffering. People flock to you with their problems and you are the person of the moment. You could win a Gallup poll hands down. Your popularity zooms through the stratosphere. Ganesha is delighted.

16 September: Last Quarter in Gemini

'That sorrow which is the harbinger of joy is preferable to the joy which is followed by sorrow,' said Saadi, the great poet. How true, says Ganesha. You have been through trials and tribulations and they have been the harbinger of joy. There are happy moments now as you embark on hard work. There is money and honey, awards and rewards, applause and accolades. Nothing stops you as you put your heart and soul into your work. Nothing is too small for you. Your energies are powerful and you express them in a controlled manner. Your diligence and perseverance are rewarded and you are smiling all the way to the bank. There is a new you facing the world as you not only play with ideas but also how to execute them well.

24 September: New Moon in Libra

Your work is going great guns. You are capable of precision and concentrated effort. You are good with detail as you patiently work towards your objectives. In this period, you are capable of selfless work without bothering about the results. You are a formidable opponent and a great ally to have as you choose your options carefully and methodically. You are relentless in your efforts and there could be lasting accomplishments. Along with the work swinging your way, there is also love and bonding. You are the cynosure of all eyes and are oozing charm. This is a great period for those in showbiz. Ganesha is pleased.

1 October: First Quarter in Capricorn

The hard slog continues. You are like the latest model of Ferrari, zooming away at top speed. You enter new frontiers of excellence. On the personal side, you are filled with sensitivity and feelings and are able to appeal to the deepest emotional concerns of your peer group. You do not feel vulnerable and exposed and your immediate psychological needs, though paramount normally, take a back seat now. There are maudlin moments in the privacy of the soul when you think of the foolish mistakes of the past. But you have to let it go. Hard work is a good escape and you do just that. You lock yourself at your work station and go hammer and tongs at new assignments. Your brain is stilled; you have no time for the playful antics of the mind. Ganesha walks with you.

8 October: Full Moon in Aries

There is frenzied action and high-octane energy powering you. You look at formulating long-term plans. You think far ahead, beyond immediate needs, and plan for a distant future. You also look at personal change that can help your plans happen. There is success at work. The employed see promotions and better pay packets and the self-employed branch out in several areas and reach new heights of excellence. You are also fuelled by a philanthropic bent of mind and find the time to work for social good. You may help out with an NGO, or volunteer with shelters for old people and the less privileged. There are new realizations and understandings as you grow as a person. Ganesha is pleased. There will also be journeys, ceremonies, publicity, meetings, collaborations, new associations, interviews and conferences.

15 October: Last Quarter in Cancer

There is love staring you in the face and you cannot avoid it. You could be in a dreamy and romantic mood. Your passions are aroused and you could be wildly erotic. In the mood you are in, even Osho, can take a leaf out of your book. It is not that you will be sowing your seed. It just means that you will bond powerfully with one partner. There are also great times with friends as you jog down memory lane and share the past. You may also spend time at home with the spouse and children, with parents and relatives. There is housework to be done and you plunge into domestic demands. There are spiralling expenses but you are in an indulgent mood and spend lavishly on the family. You are loving, exuberant and happy. Ganesha is pleased.

23 October: New Moon in Scorpio

There is great intensity in all that you do. You are normally a team player but now you want to lead from the front. You want independence. You are also filled with impatience for laggards and slow coaches. You are aggressive and assertive and safeguard your turf. You are able to tell others where to get off. There are emotional leeches, rivals, opportunists, charlatans and hustlers who want your time. You tell them in no uncertain terms to leave you alone lest they experience the power of your fist. You do not want a fight. But you also do not want to be taken for granted. You are able to communicate that quite effectively. There is a lot on your plate and you have your hands full. Ganesha is with you. You could be tempted by underhand deals and quick-buck schemes. You may also try every trick to dupe the taxman. Watch your step is all I can say.

31 October: First Quarter in Aquarius

You are in dreamland. Your mind is packed with Ponzi schemes. You want to make more money and look at short cuts. There could be problems with the law. You look at ways for slipping out of the dragnet but it would be much easier to handle your greed for more. There is no use in being devious. You have the ability to sell anything to anybody. You can lie with a straight face. It is a skill, and very helpful if your profession demands it. Lawyers get a lot of bad press for twisting and turning the truth. Piscean lawyers can be extremely successful in this phase. Of course, these are gentle prods and I could be wrong; a lot depends on your personal horoscope. On the other hand, you also display a strong evangelistic streak. As we all know, a human being is a bundle of contradictions and inclinations. Circumstances allow different facets to explode. There are maudlin moments and periods of depression. Hang in there and before long, Ganesha says, you will snap out of it.

6 November: Full Moon in Taurus

There is more stability now. You work hard and make money through sheer talent and the sweat of your brow. There are domestic issues that need your attention. The spouse, children, in-laws and elders take your time. There is big money coming your way; you are in line for a windfall. There is also new love and great bonding. Like they say, when it rains, it pours. Life has several shades and the idea is to lie low when the going gets tough. The clouds always part and the sun will come shining through. Make the most of this period. Ganesha is with you.

14 November: Last Quarter in Leo

As the winter chill tweaks the bones, you are making hay even without the sun! This is a great phase. You live large and make grand plans. Even better, you are able to execute your plans perfectly. There is applause and money. Media folk are crowned with success. Family life can either be excellent or awry. You are filled with temptation and there are many opportunities to stray. It all depends on your free will and the bonding you share with your current partner. There could also be ego issues and altercations. Watch your tongue and your fist. Ganesha is with you as you take risks and experiment with life. You conquer new peaks and touch delirious heights of excellence.

22 November: New Moon in Sagittarius

You are moving in many directions. The world is filled with new gizmos and I can see that a new generation is optimizing its uses. Wherever I go, people are in communication mode. You too are. Travel, visits to shrines, serious networking on the net, new insights, feelings, longings, friendships, hopes and desires will keep you busy. You are looking for more meaning. There may not be any more to your life than what it is now but there is no harm at all in looking. You also look for gods and godmen and may join some spiritual organization or at least take up a short programme to understand it better. You use this period to get to know yourself. You are also busy with domestic chores. Through it all you are able to come to grips with inner demons, feelings that embarrass you, weaknesses and vulnerabilities that shadow you. There are times when you could feel lonely despite having it all. You should be living with gratitude, but that learning will come only once you have understood yourself. The journey is on and Ganesha is with you.

29 November: First Quarter in Pisces

It is party time and your emotions are heightened. There is love, longing, bonding, loss, separation, fear, hope, joy, sorrow, marriages, celebrations and divorces. It is all happening for you as the year ends. This is an excellent time for all personal contact as you relate with the heart. Creative folk will do wonderfully well and will be in great demand. Actors, singers, painters, and writers are in their element. Ganesha is happy as you find your inner core, slowly but steadily. Let me add here, there are no quick fixes. The learning process is lifelong. The moment you feel that you have reached some sort of destination, another journey begins. Each challenge that confronts you helps in your evolution and the final surge forward of the human race as a whole.

6 December: Full Moon in Gemini

The inexplicable feelings of loss and loneliness continue. You have to come to grips with it. No one else can. It is your private misery. Everyone has it. You feel unloved despite all the power, pelf and prosperity crowning you. You are not able to put your finger on this mood but it is there and sometimes even demonic in its incarnation. You look for distractions. You look for new partners and some may even immerse themselves in work or drugs and booze and escapist fantasies. Some methods may be ruinous and the execution of your inclinations will depend on free will and your personal chart. These are indicators. You look for freedom from bondage. That will entail hurt. Others will be involved as we are all connected. Ganesha holds your hand.

14 December: Last Quarter in Virgo

There is more stability now and you grow as a person. You meet someone who acts like a mentor and answers all the troubling questions. In the midst of it all, you also need money and its trappings. You know that work may provide it if there is no inheritance or windfall coming your way. So you get down to the straight and narrow. Those in stocks, insurance and realty do well. You are preparing hard to make progress and take the coming year by the scruff of its neck. Ganesha wishes you well.

22 December: New Moon in Capricorn

There is increased stability thanks to the moon in Capricorn. There is love and bonding as you meet old friends. There are new collaborations and many dreams. You may spend the last week in contemplation, work, in domestic chores and intimate fellowship. You have looked hard for greener grass on every bank and somehow realized that it is within you and that there is nowhere else to seek it. Ganesha is delighted and wishes you a very happy new year! You may not realize it now, but this knowledge will hold you in good stead in the coming years.

28 December: First Quarter in Aries

As the year ends, your melancholy times, if any, are over. You spend happy days with close friends and family, but a new energy is growing within you. There is clarity and determination in whatever you do. You move ahead like a German panzer division during the World wars. There is incision, direction, thrust and parry as you mow down the opposition not with the rapier but with natural charm and skill. It is a long way to go, says Ganesha. There is also love and bonding and party times to go with the mood of the day!

Key Dates
January
1*–7, 10–11, 14–15, 18*–20, 23*–25, 28–30.
Ganesha says, January is for connectivity, contacts, conferences, contracts, calls, communication, romance, marriage, also court cases, lots of Cs there for you. And you will start the year very well, chuckles Ganesha.

February
2–3, 6–7, 10*–16, 20–21, 25–26.
Inheritance, joint finance, passion, litigation, buying and selling, loans, also sudden help from Ganesha. The focus is on money matters this month, anyway you care to look at it.

March
1*–2, 5*–7, 10*–17, 19*–20, 24*–25, 28–30.
Pilgrimages, ceremony, name and fame, foreign connections—all spell out victory for you. Inspiration and intuition will guide you perfectly towards the right choice. And that's what astrology gives you: being on the right track.

April
2–3, 6*–12, 15–17, 20*–22, 23–25–26, 29–*30.
You will be recognized, appreciated and rewarded, says Ganesha. And that's what we all want, but the good thing is that it's due to your own effort, and so it's well deserved.

May
3–9 13–14, 18*–19, 22*–23, 26–27, 30–31.

May will be one of the finest months of the year. You will be at your best. Love, money, attention and praise should all make you happy. You will socialize most happily too.

June

1*, 4–5, 9–10, 14*–20, 23–24, 27–28.
June will lay the foundation for a great July and August. Secret work, meets, conferences and travel should keep you on your toes. Be positive. Tremendous expenses, visits to holy places are both likely.

July

1*–3, 6–8, 11*–17, 20*–21, 24*–25, 28–30.
July brings you the horn of plenty. Both power and pelf, which means money, will be yours. You will be amused, entertained, delighted and in a fine position to afford it all. That's important.

August

2–3, 7*–13, 17–18, 21*–22, 25*–26, 30*–31.
Insurance, heavy expenses, taxes, gifts, wining and dining, buying and selling. Lots of fun and frolic will make you happy. This is just what you like best!

September

4*–10, 13–14, 17*–19, 22*–23, 26–28.
A great reaching out to people and places. Your work will be done and your dreams will be realized. Friends and well-wishers make you happy, and you are proud to be a success.

October

1*–7, 11*–12, 15*–16, 19–20, 24*–25, 29–30.
You focus on home, house, renovation and decoration.
Good news, domestic happiness, joy, harmony and
merrymaking for you, so says Ganesha.

November

2*–3, 5–6, 11*–16, 20*–21, 25–26, 29–30
The trend continues. Home, house, renovation,
decoration, good news, domestic happiness, joy, harmony
and merrymaking. The focus will be home, family life,
the social scene.

December

1, 4–5, 8–9, 12*–14, 17*–18, 22*–28, 31.
You will get your just and due awards, promotions
and inspiration. Health will improve. Funds and loans
will be available. Colleagues will love and respect you!
You feel good about yourself and face the future with
confidence.

Section II

Articles

All about You

(Ganesha says this is very comprehensive, all-inclusive information about each and every sign of the zodiac in Western astrology. Yes, your astrologer openly admits that the material is collected from various sources. I am sure you will relish it. Enjoy!)

ARIES
(21 March 21–19 April)

GENDER: Masculine

ELEMENT: Fire

QUALITIES: Cardinal. Aries is raw, primitive energy; a courageous, assertive, passionate, headstrong, pioneering spirit; full of physical strength.

RULING PLANET: Mars, ancient god of war, aggression, conflict. In astrology, Mars's influence creates tension and accidents; it rules over fire and danger.

SYMBOLIC INTERPRETATION: The Ram represents the horns and nose of the Ram. It also pictures the eyebrows and nose of man (the head is the part ruled by Aries). Combative, obviously, the horns go with the head and the face in any animal.

OPPOSITE NUMBER: Libra (the seventh sign from yours is your opposite number).

BODY PART RULED BY ARIES: The head. Aries people are prone to headaches and facial injuries.

ANIMALS RULED BY ARIES: Sheep and, especially, rams.

HAZARDS: Fire, war and injury from sharp instruments. They may suffer from accidents in sports; surgical operations, especially on the head and face.

Traditional associations of Aries

GEMSTONE: Diamond

METAL: Iron

COLOURS: Red, scarlet and carmine

CITIES: Florence, Verona, Naples and Marseilles

COUNTRIES: France, Germany, Poland, England and Denmark

Lucky for Aries

DAY: Tuesday

NUMBER: Nine

FLOWERS: Anemone, honeysuckle, thistle, mint

TREES: Hawthorn, evergreen thorn, spruce, all thorny trees

FOODS: Most strong-tasting foods such as onions, leeks, garlic. Hot spices associated with Aries are mustard and cayenne pepper.

ALPHABETS (that vibrate to Aries): A, L, E

TAURUS

(20 April–20 May)

GENDER: Feminine

ELEMENT: Earth

QUALITIES: Fixed. Taurus is quiet, affectionate, patient, stable, determined and practical, stubborn, and resistant to change.

RULING PLANET: Venus. In astrology, Venus's influence inclines towards a love of luxury, beauty, artistic pursuits and love.

SYMBOLIC INTERPRETATION: The Bull. Strong, stubborn, plodding; can be both fierce and gentle. The symbol represents the horns and head of the Bull. It also outlines the chin and Adam's apple of the human throat (the part of the anatomy that Taurus rules).

OPPOSITE NUMBER: Scorpio (the seventh sign from yours is your opposite number). Taurus is the sign of property, money and possessions; and Taureans are known to cling to what is theirs. Scorpio, Taurus's opposite sign, is the sign of legacies and shared wealth. The wealth of Scorpio people tends to be spiritual rather than material, which they give to others in the form of teaching, writing, and the healing arts.

BODY PARTS RULED BY TAURUS: Neck and throat. Many Taurus people have beautiful speaking and singing voices, but they are vulnerable to colds and thyroid problems, laryngitis, and sore throats.

ANIMALS RULED BY TAURUS: Cattle, especially the bull.

HAZARDS: Taurus people often antagonize others over love and money. They are famous for their stubbornness and possessiveness.

Traditional associations of Taurus

METAL: Copper

COLOURS: Pale blue, yellow, pink and pale green

CITIES: Palermo and St. Louis

COUNTRIES: Ireland, Switzerland, Cyprus and the Greek Islands

Lucky for Taureans

DAY: Friday

NUMBER: Six

FLOWERS: Narcissus, lily of the valley, foxglove, rose, poppy

TREES: Fig, vine, apple

FOODS: Wheat and most other cereals, grapes, apples, pears, artichokes, asparagus and most spices are associated with Taurus.

ALPHABETS (that vibrate to Taurus): B, V, U, O

GEMINI

(21 May–20 June)

GENDER: Masculine

ELEMENT: Air

QUALITIES: Mutable. Gemini is lively, energetic, versatile, and intellectual; lives primarily in the mind rather than the emotions; is extremely adaptable to new situations.

RULING PLANET: Mercury. In astrology, Mercury rules communication and travel; its influence emphasizes a nervous temperament.

SYMBOLIC INTERPRETATION: Sagittarius (the seventh sign from yours is your opposite number). Gemini is the sign of thought, self-expression and communication on a personal level. Natives of Gemini strive for, and try to impose, their point of view on others. Sagittarius people tend to shrink from close personal involvement and, unlike Gemini, are shaped by what others think of them.

BODY PARTS RULED BY GEMINI: Hands, arms, shoulders and lungs. Geminis are susceptible to sprains and accidents involving arms and hands; also prone to bronchitis and respiratory ailments.

ANIMALS RULED BY GEMINI: Parrots and other brightly colored birds, monkeys and butterflies.

HAZARDS: Gemini people are susceptible to accidents while travelling, especially by air. Their changeability and fickle nature also tend to irritate others.

Traditional associations of Gemini

GEMSTONE: Agate

METALS: Quicksilver/mercury

COLOURS: Yellow, slate grey and spotted mixtures

CITIES: London, San Francisco, Cordoba and Bruges

COUNTRIES: Belgium, USA, Sardinia and Armenia

Lucky for Gemini

DAY: Wednesday

NUMBER: Five

Flowers and Trees

FLOWERS: Lavender, blue violet, lily-of-the-valley, ferns

TREES: Hazel, chestnut, and all nut-bearing trees

FOODS: Nuts and all vegetables grown above the ground, except cabbage, are foods associated with Gemini, as are such herbs and spices as marjoram, caraway and aniseed.

ALPHABETS (that vibrates to Gemini): K, GH, Q

CANCER

(21 June–22 July)

GENDER: Feminine

ELEMENT: Water

QUALITIES: Cardinal. Cancer is emotional, and possesses an active, shrewd, and intuitive mind. Cancerians are sensitive, kind, often sympathetic, and receptive to change.

RULING PLANET: The Moon. In astrology, the Moon governs the emotions and intuitive behaviour.

SYMBOLIC INTERPRETATION: The Crab, possessing a hard, and crusty exterior, covering soft flesh underneath. The symbol represents the claws of the Crab.

OPPOSITE NUMBER: Capricorn (the seventh sign from yours is your opposite number). Cancer is the sign of home and family life, and personal relationships. Capricorn, Cancer's opposite sign, is the sign of reputation and public standing, even advancement of self.

BODY PARTS RULED BY CANCER: The breasts and stomach. Cancerians love to eat and have to fight overweight in later years, and also digestive ailments.

ANIMALS RULED BY CANCER: Crab and other shell-covered animals, all crustaceans.

HAZARDS: Cancer people are susceptible to theft, losses and accidents in the home.

Traditional associations of Cancer

GEMSTONES: Moonstone and pearl

METAL: Silver

COLOURS: White, opal, iridescent silvery hues, smoky grey, sea green and blue

CITIES: Amsterdam, New York, Istanbul, Tokyo, Algiers

COUNTRIES: Scotland, Holland, New Zealand and Paraguay

Lucky for Cancer

DAY: Monday

NUMBER: Two

FLOWERS: White lily, acanthus, white rose, larkspur, convolvulus, water lily, all white flowers

TREES: All trees, particularly those rich in sap

FOODS: Milk, fish, fruits and vegetables with a high water content, white and red cabbage, and herbs such as verbena and tarragon are all linked with Cancer.

ALPHABETS (that vibrate to Cancer): H, D

LEO

(23 July–22 August)

GENDER: Masculine

ELEMENT: Fire

QUALITIES: Fixed. Leo is dogmatic and fixed in opinion; large-hearted, creative, self-willed, powerful; full of generosity and extravagance.

RULING PLANET: The Sun. In astrology, the Sun is the most powerful planetary influence, bestowing vitality and authority.

SYMBOLIC INTERPRETATION: The Lion. Regal, brave, dominating, sometimes indolent; possessing nobility and pride. It represents two valves of the human heart (a part of the anatomy that Leo rules). It is also the Greek symbol for the first letter of Leo. In symbolic terms, it is two incomplete circles of the Sun, joined by a crescent Moon, symbolizing power derived from both the intellect and the emotions.

OPPOSITE NUMBER: Aquarius (the seventh sign from yours is your opposite number). Leo is the sign that governs pleasure and creativity, domination and ego. Aquarius, Leo's opposite sign, is the sign of hopes and wishes, and the higher ideals of mankind.

BODY PARTS RULED BY LEO: Back, spine, and the heart. Back and spinal ailments are common in Leo people.

ANIMALS RULED BY LEO: Lion and all felines (i.e., the entire cat family)

HAZARDS: Leo people tend to be challenging and boastful. They are also prone towards being victims of slander and violence, since they are impulsive and often domineering.

Traditional associations of Leo

GEMSTONE: Ruby

METAL: Gold

COLOURS: Orange, gold, rich shades of yellow, brown

CITIES: Rome, Madrid, Damascus, Mumbai and Hollywood

COUNTRIES: Italy, Sicily, southern Iraq, Romania and Lebanon

Lucky for Leo

DAY: Sunday

NUMBER: One

FLOWERS: Sunflower, marigold, celandine, passion flower

TREES: Laurel, bay tree, palm, walnut

FOOD: Honey, rice and green vegetables with a high iron content, such as spinach, kale and watercress, are typically Leonine foodstuffs. These also include meat and the herbs rosemary, rue and saffron.

ALPHABETS (that vibrate to Leo): M

VIRGO

(23 August–23 September)

GENDER: Feminine

ELEMENT: Earth

QUALITIES: Mutable. Virgo is reserved, modest, practical, discriminating and industrious, analytical and painstaking, seeking to know and understand.

RULING PLANET: Mercury. In astrology, Mercury rules intelligence and reason, and bestows a highly strung temperament.

SYMBOLIC INTERPRETATION: The Virgin represents purity, modesty, industriousness and service to fellow workers. The symbol represents a Virgin.

OPPOSITE NUMBER: Pisces (the seventh sign from yours is your opposite number). Virgo is the sign of work, perfectionism and self-improvement. Pisces, Virgo's opposite sign, is the sign of illusion, dreaminess, self-delusion and escapism.

BODY PARTS RULED BY VIRGO: The nervous system and the intestines. Virgos are particularly susceptible to ulcers, nervous disorders, and stress-related illnesses.

ANIMALS RULED BY VIRGO: Small domestic pets, cats and bees.

HAZARDS: Virgos have critical and sharp tongues, a tendency to interfere and are not very emotional. They can easily offend others. They are hypochondriacs.

Traditional associations of Virgo

GEMSTONE: Sardonyx

METAL: Quicksilver/mercury

COLOURS: Shades of green, dark brown, slate and spotted patterns

CITIES: Boston, Heidelberg, Paris, Strasbourg, Corinth

COUNTRIES: Greece, Turkey, Crete and Lower Silesia, West Indies

Lucky for Virgo

DAY: Wednesday

NUMBER: Five

FLOWERS: Buttercup, pansy, forget-me-not, morning glory, aster, mimosa

TREES: Hazel, horse chestnut, and all nut-bearing trees

FOODS: Potatoes, carrots, turnips, swedes and all vegetables grown under the earth; also nuts of all varieties.

ALPHABETS (that vibrates to Virgo): P, TH, AN

LIBRA

(23 September–22 October)

GENDER: Masculine

ELEMENT: Air

QUALITIES: Cardinal. Libra is diplomatic, polished, and very socially inclined; very charming too.

RULING PLANET: Venus. In astrology, Venus rules pleasure and luxury, social pursuits, art, and adornment.

SYMBOLIC INTERPRETATION: The Scales, signifying balance, equilibrium, order, and justice. The symbol represents the scale which is in perfect equilibrium.

OPPOSITE NUMBER: Aries (the seventh sign from yours is your opposite number). Libra is the sign of marriage, union and partnership. Aries, Libra's opposite sign, is the sign of ego, personality and self.

BODY PARTS RULED BY LIBRA: The lower back, kidneys, hips. Librans are prone to kidney infections, lower back strain and problems in the lumbar region.

ANIMALS RULED BY LIBRA: Snakes, lizards and other small reptiles.

HAZARDS: Libra people are indecisive and sometimes make a declaration of love too easily, and can hurt and disappoint people who care for them.

Traditional associations of Libra

GEMSTONE: Opal

METAL: Copper

CITIES: Copenhagen, Vienna, Lisbon, Charleston, Frankfurt and Nottingham

COUNTRIES: Austria, Burma, Argentina, Tibet, China and Japan

Lucky for Libra

DAY: Friday

NUMBER: Six

FLOWERS: Dahlia, cosmos, daisy, lilac (purple), cabbage rose, bluebell, hydrangeas

TREES: Ash, poplar, both black and white

FOODS: Berry fruits, apples, pears, grapes, wheat, barley and other cereals, artichokes, asparagus and almost all spices.

ALPHABETS (that vibrate to Libra): R, T

SCORPIO

(23 October–23 November)

GENDER: Feminine

ELEMENT: Water

QUALITIES: Fixed. Scorpio is intense, obstinate and unyielding, but can be passionate and emotional as well. They can be both tenacious and carping, but also very subtle and caring.

RULING PLANET: Pluto. In astrology, Pluto rules regenerative forces, and the beginnings and ends of phases in life.

SYMBOLIC INTERPRETATION: The Scorpion, Secretive, often fatal. The symbol depicts the stinger of the Scorpion and is connected to a representation of the human reproductive organs.

OPPOSITE NUMBER: Taurus (the seventh sign from yours is your opposite number). Scorpio is the sign of inheritance. They have a sense of purpose and destiny. Taurus is the sign of possession, ownership.

BODY PART RULED BY SCORPIO: The genitals. Scorpios

are susceptible to exhaustion and ill-health, infections of the urinary tract and sexually transmitted diseases.

ANIMALS RULED BY SCORPIO: Snakes, insects and other invertebrates.

HAZARDS: Scorpios are secretive and jealous. Their sharp tempers and harsh tongue can cause others' anger.

Traditional associations of Scorpio

GEMSTONES: Topaz and malachite

METAL: Plutonium

COLOURS: Dark red, maroon, crimson and the colours of smoky cloud formations

CITIES: New Orleans, Cincinnati, Washington D.C., Newcastle, Valencia and Liverpool

COUNTRIES: Morocco, Norway, Uruguay, Syria, Tahiti, Algeria

Lucky for Scorpio

DAY: Tuesday

NUMBER: Nine

FLOWERS: Red chrysanthemum, red carnation, rhododendron, honeysuckle, gentian

TREES: Blackthorn, thorn apple, hawthorn, branches with thorn

FOODS: Strong tasting foods, onions, hops, leeks and shallots. Most of the pungent, sharp tasting foods are attributable to Mars and Aries

ALPHABETS (that vibrate to Scorpio): N, YU, Y

SAGITTARIUS

(22 November–21 December)

GENDER: Masculine

ELEMENT: Fire

QUALITIES: Mutable. Sagittarians are ambitious, even driven, generous, focused, freedom-loving, and a seeker of challenge, open to new ideas, innovation and exploration.

RULING PLANET: Jupiter. In astrology, Jupiter is the planet of good fortune, optimism, expansion, abundance.

SYMBOLIC INTERPRETATION: The Archer. He is the symbol of directness, high aims, a lover of outdoor activity and the chase. The free-ranging, pointed arrow of the archer is represented. It is also a picture of the human leg from thigh to knee (the part of the anatomy that Sagittarius rules).

OPPOSITE NUMBER: Gemini (the seventh sign from yours is your opposite number). Sagittarius is the sign of broad concepts, philosophy, higher learning, exploration. Gemini is the sign of personal expression and 'one-to-one' communication.

BODY PARTS RULED BY SAGITTARIUS: The liver, the hips, and the thighs. Sagittarians have a sensitive liver and need lots of outdoor exercise to stay healthy and fit.

ANIMALS RULED BY SAGITTARIUS: Horses, and those which are hunted – deer, etc.

HAZARDS: Sagittarians can be hurt by fire and explosion, especially while travelling. Their freedom-loving nature can make them loners, and make other people either jealous or insecure.

Traditional associations of Sagittarians

GEMSTONE: Turquoise

METAL: Tin

COLOURS: Rich purple, violet, red and indigo

CITIES: Toledo, Budapest, Sheffield, Toronto, Cologne and Acapulco

COUNTRIES: Spain, Australia, South Africa, Arabia and Hungary

Lucky for Sagittarians

DAY: Thursday

NUMBER: Three

FLOWERS: Narcissus, golden rod, pinks, pink carnation, dandelions

TREES: Oak, ash, birch, mulberry, chestnut

FOODS: Bulb vegetables such as onions, leeks and celery. Currants, sultans, mulberries and bilberries. Grapefruit is also attributed to Sagittarius.

ALPHABETS (that vibrate to Sagittarius): F, DH

CAPRICORN

(22 December–19 January)

GENDER: Feminine

ELEMENT: Earth

QUALITIES: Cardinal. Capricorn is patient, disciplined, determined, and quick to seize opportunity. Capricorns seek security, want acquisitions, and rely on cunning rather than brute force. They are reserved, prudent and sometimes aloof and withdrawn.

RULING PLANET: Saturn. In astrology, Saturn represents obstacles, limitation, restriction, discipline.

SYMBOLIC INTERPRETATION: The Goat, who is able to ascend the heights because of its nimble surefootedness. The goat butts its way through obstructions. The symbol represents the V-shaped beard of the goat and the curved tail of the fish (the sea goat, which was the ancient symbol for Capricorn). It also pictures the human knee and circular kneecap.

OPPOSITE NUMBER: Cancer (the seventh sign from yours is your opposite number). Capricorn is the sign governing reputation, career, standing in the community, honour, praise, and approval of the world at large. Cancer, Capricorn's opposite sign, is the sign of domesticity and home life.

BODY PARTS RULED BY CAPRICORN: The bones, joints, and knees. Capricorns may suffer from stiff joints, rheumatism and orthopaedic problems.

ANIMALS RULED BY CAPRICORN: Goats, all animals with cloven hoofs.

HAZARDS: Capricorns can be aloof, uncaring, reserved and unemotional, and may thus seem to be intentionally hurtful.

Traditional associations of Capricorn

GEMSTONE: Garnet

METAL: Lead

COLOURS: Dark grey, dark green, black, dark brown and indigo

CITIES: Delhi, Mexico City, Ghent, Brussels, Oxford, Chicago and Montreal

COUNTRIES: India, Mexico, Macedonia, Orkney and Shetland

Lucky for Capricorn

DAY: Saturday

NUMBERS: Eight and Two

FLOWERS: Red poppy, amaranthus, pansy, red carnation, ivy

TREES: Elm, pine, aspen, poplar, holly, weeping willow

FOODS: Potatoes, beets, barley and malt are attributed to Capricorn; also starchy foods, onions, spinach and quinces.

ALPHABETS (that vibrate to Capricorn): J, KH, X

AQUARIUS

(20 January–18 February)

GENDER: Masculine

ELEMENT: Air

QUALITIES: Fixed. Aquarius is original and inventive, has strong dislikes and firm opinions. Aquarians can be very progressive, strong-willed and assertive. They are independent and analytical and are born leaders and free thinkers.

RULING PLANET: Uranus. In astrology, Uranus is the planet of change and the unexpected, invention and modern science

SYMBOLIC INTERPRETATION: The Waterbearer, bearing the gift that gives life. The symbol represents the water which flows from the vessel of the waterbearer. It is also a picture of the human ankle in motion.

OPPOSITE NUMBER: Leo (The seventh sign from yours is your opposite number). Aquarius is the sign of idealistic humanitarians who often remain personally detached in their own relationships. Leo, Aquarius's opposite sign, is the sign of pleasure, affection, love, close ties, fun and good times.

BODY PARTS RULED BY AQUARIUS: the circulatory system, shins and ankles. Aquarians may suffer from varicose veins and hardening of the arteries, fractures and sprains.

ANIMALS RULED BY AQUARIANS: Large, far-flying birds

HAZARDS: Aquarians are often eccentric, usually innovative, and unconventional. Their 'way out' bohemian attitudes can also cause trouble.

Traditional associations of Aquarius

GEMSTONE: Aquamarine

METALS: Uranium and aluminium

COLOURS: Aquamarine, turquoise and electric blue

CITIES: Moscow, St. Petersburg, Buenos Aires, Hamburg and Salzburg

COUNTRIES: Russia, Sweden, Ethiopia and Poland

Lucky for Aquarius

DAY: Saturday

NUMBER: Four, one and seven

FLOWERS: Apple blossom, peach blossom, elder flowers, orchid

TREES: Cherry, plum, fig, and all fruit trees

FOODS: Zestful citrus fruits, such as lemon and lime, peppers, chillies, herbs and spices with sharp, distinctive flavours.

ALPHABETS (that vibrate to Aquarius): G, S, SH

PISCES

(19 February–20 March)

GENDER: Feminine

ELEMENT: Water

QUALITIES: Mutable. Pisces is very changeable, impressionable and mystical, and adaptable. Pisceans are usually romantics, who are both kind and receptive, and are strong on both intuition and emotion.

RULING PLANET: Neptune. In astrology, Neptune is the planet of illusion, glamour, mystery, deception, and was discovered in 1846.

SYMBOLIC INTERPRETATION: Two Fishes tied to one another in opposite directions, signifying hidden depths, shifting emotional currents. The symbol represents two fishes tied together. It is also a picture of the human feet (the part of the anatomy that Pisces rules.)

OPPOSITE NUMBER: Virgo. Pisces is the sign of dreams, intuitions, psychism and mysticism, spiritual values in life. Virgo, Pisces's opposite sign, is the sign of work and service.

BODY PARTS RULED BY PISCES: The feet. All foot ailments from corns to sprains and aches.

ANIMALS RULED BY PISCES: Sea-loving mammals and all fish.

HAZARDS: Pisceans can be unpredictable, vacillating and indecisive. They can be unbalanced, and prone to addictions.

Traditional associations of Pisces

GEMSTONE: Amethyst

METALS: Germanium and strontium

COLOURS: Mauve, purple, violet, sea green, silver

CITIES: Hollywood, Alexandria, Lisbon, Seville, Dublin, Warsaw and Jerusalem

COUNTRIES: Portugal, many small Mediterranean islands, the Gobi and Sahara deserts, and Scandinavia

Lucky for Pisces

DAY: Thursday

NUMBER: Seven, two and six

FLOWERS: White poppy, iris, orchid, water lily, angelica, violet, jonquil

TREES: Weeping willow, all trees growing by water, fig

FOODS: Foods with a high water content, such as cucumber, watermelon, lettuce, and the gourd family.

ALPHABETS (that vibrate to Pisces): Z, CH, D, X

Note: *Strictly speaking the alphabets given here in all the signs really go with the Indian Moon signs. However, only as an experiment, I have incorporated them here and placed them with the Western sun signs. You can take it or leave it.*

Can We Stop Time?

Ganesha says, 'Only change is constant'. We all know, 'time changes everything'. Can we stop the constant change in this world? Can we halt time? Can we push or shove time in a different direction altogether?

Yes, I admit that far superior minds have been baffled by the above questions. I am no rocket scientist. I am not a genius. Ganesha has given me intuition, inspiration and imagination. I know that it is my dharma to go to the end of the line – and even beyond. In simple English, I want to give it a shot, try to solve the impossible. So what if I fail? As Shakespeare had said, 'The readiness is all.'

In astrology, Saturn represents time. In fact, Saturn is Father Time. Therefore, to this astrologer at least, Saturn is of the essence in all questions and issues related to time and change.

Perhaps, I say perhaps, with the help of a Saturn mantra in Vedic astrology for example, *Om Praam Preem Proum Sa Sanaye Namah* we may understand time better, and thus be able to deal with time more efficiently.

Together with that, I combine Western Astrology, I Ching, Tarot Cards, Hebrew Kabala of Numbers, Palmistry, dice and colours for my predictions.

Yes, I have read *The Grand Design* by Stephen Hawking. Science connects time, gravity, space, atoms, pulsars, electrical solar system, electricity, magnetism, solar flares, black hole, Milky Way, galaxies, helium, hydrogen, lithium – all for a 'unified theory of everything'. It is the goal of physics.

PREDICTION

I see a sphere/a rocket/a ball of fire of a rare unknown metal being created. This object zooms through the cosmos at unimaginable speed and breaks what I call frequencies, velocities, more dark unknown spaces than the black hole and punches or penetrates right through the galaxies. Thereby, it sets the cosmos on a different frequency, velocity, gravity. It alters the course, the very axis of the universe.

Let me put it in a different way. The top is spinning one way. It stops spinning, does not fall down, but rests on its needle. Then the top starts circling in the opposite direction. By starting to circle in the opposite direction, it not only stops the change but makes the world, that is, time and space and energy, move in a totally different direction. You have every right to call it stupid, nonsense and fool's gold. I also see technology using the power of the Collective Unconscious of human beings. This Collective Unconscious is stored energy in space and time. It can be used creatively and constructively in the adventure that is time and space.

Through technology or meditation, or very possibly a grand fusion of psychology, technology, biology, the willpower and imagination of human beings, and also, according to me, by the grace of gods (I call God Ganesha but you are most welcome to call God by any other name, for example: Allah, Supreme Energy, Christ, Zoroaster, Buddha, Shiva and so on), time and space can change.

Given the assumption that this may be possible (I know the chances are totally against me), when can this happen by astrology? My forte is only astrology and I know that astrology has its limitations. Still, my Ganesha says around 2056 change might come to a stop; halt as if with the screeching of tyres when brakes are applied.

In 2056, by Western Astrology, Saturn, Father Time, will be in the powerful enemy sign Aries;[1] Jupiter, the prosperity planet, in earthy cardinal sign; Capricorn and yes Uranus, the rebel, the awakener, (the electrical planet), in the sign of balance, Libra. Uranus the rebel, the upstart, the acrobat, 'the enfant terrible' (completely unruly and rough, and smasher of rules and regulations) can contribute to the change by violating time, space, and gravity. As I have said in my poem, 'the balance of things could be in their imbalance.' It could mean changing the change.

Let me make it simple. It will be the combined efforts of Saturn, Father Time, Jupiter, old solid order, and Uranus, the revolutionary and the terrorist, along with technology and the collective unconscious and the will of God which could perhaps bring about a change in change itself.

---

[1] Saturn in his enemy sign, Aries, is weak. Therefore, it is easier to change Saturn. I take my work very seriously. But I do not take myself seriously. Therefore, in a light-hearted manner I say, even if by pure chance, or fluke or coincidence I come right about the year 2056, I will be hugely happy. I am not important. My theories are not important. Only the good of mankind is important.

Time, space and change could be in a different direction, or they could stop momentarily or for a long time. Also, I could fall on my face and break my nose. These are the possibilities I place before you on a platter, my dear readers. Wish me a slice of heaven.

Special Note: *We Indians have stories and legends regarding Shiva and Saturn, Ravana and Saturn, Krishna and the Syamantaka Gem. In conclusion, Saturn has said, 'This is the way I aggravated even Sri Krishna; if I did not spare Him, who will I spare?' So now you know, dear readers, the terrible power of Saturn, and the sheer impossibility of halting time and changing history and destiny. Still, this Ganesha devotee is willing to try. Let us wait for 2056.*

Fate, Chance, Coincidence, Serendipity, or What?

M.S. Dhoni, born: 7 July; Sourav Ganguly, born: 8 July; Sunil Gavaskar, born: 10 July. Ganesha says, my devotee Bejan is not out to prove a point, convert anybody into belief in astrology, or push for victory. He is just interested in presenting facts to the best of his limited ability. He just wants you to keep an open mind and decide for yourself. Bejan was born on 11 July 1931! He jokingly says that's an undeniable fact! He adds, you are free to dispute that too! This is being open-minded, tolerant!

Ganesha says India's three cricket captains Dhoni, Gavaskar and Ganguly were born on 7 July, 10 July and 8 July. In other words, three Cancerians born within four days of each other. But the similarity or the coincidence doesn't end there. *The Times of India*, 18 June 2013 says 'There are other similarities between the Dhoni era and the Ganguly one. Fighting to have a team of his choice, backing his youngsters, putting immense trust in their abilities and not thinking twice in letting a player know if he's not in the scheme of things are the aspects that allowed Ganguly to build Team India into quite a force. Dhoni has been swimming in similar waters for the past year.'

Finally, here is another quote from the same paper: 'Like Ganguly, Dhoni too seems to have given his least possible followers no choice but to admire him. The team that Ganguly built lasted well for close to 10 years, finally working its way to the top of the Test-rankings and finishing with a World Cup win. The team Dhoni is building has potential to repeat that kind of performance.'

Dear readers, may I remind you that Dhoni was born on 7 July and Ganguly on 8 July. Is this similarity fate, chance, coincidence, serendipity, or what? I leave it to you.

One illustration/example is worth a thousand words. Aavi Doctor, a gracious Parsee lady, lives in Pune. I wrote a poem about her emerging like an angel out of the fire. We Parsees worship fire and that is why our place of worship is called Fire Temple. On 19 June 2013, Aavi reported that people had trespassed into her house and felled or cut down the sandalwood trees in her garden. Parsees use only sandalwood in their fire rituals. Therefore, taking away the sandalwood hurt and shocked Aavi. She did not report it to the police. She said, maybe these people needed the sandalwood more. That reminded me of Tagore who said, 'The sandalwood, as if to prove, how sweet to conquer hate by love, perfumes the axe that lays it low.' This whole incident came to me in a single blinding flash. How come? I leave it to you to judge.

Let me tell you about Shruti, a fine healer from Baroda, who meets me from time to time. I am a devotee of Ganesha as I am sure you know. Many times as Shruti is talking to me, photos of Ganesha and my Zoraster and Fire come in quick succession. This happens with unimaginable frequency. Both of us have observed it. We have often gone together for the worship of Hanuman and Ganesha. The why of it Ganesha and Hanuman know best.

Lastly, and most importantly, let me tell about my wife Gooli, psychic and tarot reader. I am happy to say that she is the astrologer of the astrologer. In other words, she is my astrologer. When I am in doubt I go to her for guidance. Believe it or not, not once has she failed me. I may go wrong, being human, in my predictions, and I admit it openly. With me she has never gone wrong. Always optimistic and always correct. She is infallible, always right. In other words, with me she always scores a century. How is that possible? Frankly I have no answer to it. You readers decide.

The Scintillating and Luminous Power of Jupiter

All my life I have been fascinated by the powers of Jupiter as Jupiter is fat and roly-poly like I am! Also, it is a planet of good luck and I call it the Santa Claus of the zodiac. I look like a Santa Claus!

In addition, Jupiter is the planet of wisdom, knowledge and, surprisingly enough, luxury, riches, beautiful items of art and paintings. Let me introduce you to Prince Lakshyaraj Singh Mewar, my son. He exemplifies the power of Jupiter. One illustration is worth a thousand words. Prince Lakshyaraj Singh Mewar of Udaipur has Jupiter in his 7th house in his Indian horoscope and the 7th house stands for inheritance of intelligence, innovative ideas and aptitude to perform the duties soulfully and diligently to keep Mewar's living heritage alive.

Prince Lakshyaraj has Pluto, the atom bomb power planet, in Scorpio by Western astrology. This gives him magnetism, dynamism and brilliant ideas. From July 2013 to July 2014 Jupiter will be in the sign Cancer as per Western astrology. Jupiter will make a fine trine or powerful formation with Pluto. Ganesha says *it will be a grand time for the dashing and kind Prince Lakshyaraj Singh and his majestic palace which gives livelihood to so many people and that gives me great happiness.*

Please wait. I have reserved the final stroke of grandeur for the end. Venus, the planet of beauty, arts, weddings, birthdays, celebrations, rituals, in short hope and happiness, is in Pisces by Western astrology. Venus in Pisces is at peerless perfection and opulence and magnificence. Yes, Venus gives the finishing touch to both Prince Lakshyaraj Singh Mewar and the palace. That is the real reason why the palace in Udaipur is truly world famous.

For you dear readers, I have two mighty mantras for Jupiter/Guru. They are: 1) Om guruvey namah, and 2) Om jhram jhreem sa guruvey namah. For Venus/Shukra the mantra will be Om dhram dhreem dhroom sa sukraya namah. These mantras will help you in life.

On a strictly personal note, I must say that I was thrilled to be the chief guest at the annual prize-giving ceremony of the Maharana Mewar Educational Institution, Udaipur. As a former professor of English, a host of memories swelled in me and I was for once overwhelmed with the response of the students. The students of India represent the mighty destiny of Bharat Mata. Yes, that is my deep and abiding conviction and faith.

All of it was a truly memorable occasion for me. To me the Maharana Mewar Educational Institution is most meaningful as it shows the generosity and philanthropy of Prince Lakshyaraj Singh Mewar. He is both a good man and a noble son. May Ganesha always be with Prince Lakshyaraj Singh Mewar and his royal and divine family by the grace of the planet Jupiter which is the planet of wisdom. May they carry the royal tradition of Mewar flying high with pride and honour.

Prime Ministers, the General, and I

Ganesha says my devotee Bejan has been up close and personal with two prime ministers and a general, and of course Narendra Modi. I met both A.B. Vajpayee and Morarji Desai by pure chance or serendipity. I have also noticed that Nawaz Sharif, the present PM of Pakistan, and Vajpayee are both born on 25 December. Nawaz Sharif has Venus and Jupiter in the objective and very humane sign Aquarius, by Western astrology. Both Ganesha and Allah bless him. Dhirubhai Ambani and Ratan Tata were born on 28 December. All these four are Capricornians and, by Western astrology. Capricorn is the ruling or dominant sign of India. Great writing and good astrology depend upon the mantra 'observe, observe, observe'. Believe me, at eighty-three, I should know what I am talking about.

I am yet to see a more affable, genuine human being than Vajpayee. Let me quote from my 2001 book: 'A smiling spectacled Buddha, in a white kurta, exceptionally comfortable white slippers, and looking you directly in the eye, was my first impression of our prime minister. Yes, our prime minister was very much there in the Tarot. He was represented by Card no. 5, Jupiter, with a crown on his head. It means power through peace and prosperity.'

'Sir, you are an Avtar!' I said. As I write this piece on 20 June 2013, I can say that my remark was not mere flattery. I distinctly remember asking him point blank, 'Sahab, it is not fair for the BJP to be aggressive towards the Muslims and the Christians.' With a smile and a wave of the hand Vajpayee made it very clear that he agreed with me. Fine lines of head, life and heart showed that he had both integrity and balance. To me that is the hallmark of a statesman. I remember that when the astro-numero session with Vajpayee was over, I said to him, 'Thank you for inviting me.' He said softly, 'No, thank you for coming.'

It was Mr Joshi, the Managing Director of India International Centre, Delhi, who took me to Vajpayee. Just like that. His suggestion and his very gracious action. In the same way it was Shantibhai Shah, editor of *Gujarat Samachar*, who took me to see Morarji Desai who had been axed under the Kamraj Plan. Ruddy, broad shoulders, paws rather than hands, and looking me straight in the eye, he said, 'Here is my horoscope. What do you have to say?' I looked at the horoscope, fused it with lines on the hands and tried the dice test, my own invention, on Morarji. He threw the number 6. He was out of power then. The number 6 in my single dice was the maximum number. Therefore, he was at his ebb.

Morarji was a Piscean. Unlike most Pisceans, he was rigid and very firm. I almost blurted out, 'Sahab, you will first become the deputy PM and later on the PM.' I may be right or wrong but I do go in a slight trance when I predict. I openly admit I was amazed at my own prediction because I really don't know what happened inside me. People say Gujaratis are misers. I must contradict them by admitting that Shantibhai Shah presented me with a Standard Herald convertible when Morarji became PM.

Yes, I know you are looking forward to what I have to say about Narendra Modi. Maharaj Kunwar Lakshyaraj Singh Mewar of Udaipur wanted to meet Narendra Modi. My great friend Behram Mehta knew Narendra Modi. Therefore, I merely tagged along with these two just out of pure curiosity. The moment I saw Modi I said, 'My son you are handsome.' Without blinking an eye he said, 'We must learn to have fun from the Parsees.' Later on, he called me inside for a private astro-numero session.

How did I find this man? Very sharp but not aggressive. Open to reason. He knows how to protect himself from the onslaught of enemies but he never speaks a word against any person. Shrewd but not hostile is my reading of this Virgo man. What passed between us will remain between us till I die or till he gives me permission to tell the world. But this I can say with a straight face. At the end of the session, I requested him to inaugurate my book *End of the World* at a big gathering. He immediately caught my wrist and said, 'Pakoo.' It means deal done. I am happy to say he kept his word. I am also happy to say that I had a ball during the launch of the book, Parsee style. To me Parsee style is pure, wholesome fun with loads of laughter at oneself.

What do I make of him? Complex character, likes to streamline everything (the hallmark of the Virgo), wants everything perfect, plans meticulously. Now we come to Indian astrology. Narendra Modi, the chief minister of Gujarat, has Mars and Moon in the shrewd, combative, expressive sign Scorpio in the second house. In simple language, the second house stands for oratory. Mars is energy. The moon represents the masses. No wonder he can rouse the masses and win them over to his side. Technically, the Moon-Mars combination is called the *Laxmi Yog*. Jupiter, the planet of prosperity, is superbly placed. This makes him a natural born leader and an entertainer. Saturn in the house of gains makes him a fine and an able administrator. A man with a vision. Please do not misunderstand me. No man is perfect. We all have our faults including your Ganesha devotee. Narendra is human (yes I call him Narendra because I am his senior by 23 years). Yes, my Ganesha says, Narendra has the makings of a great leader. My Scorpio son Nastur has a strong gut feeling that he will become the prime minister. I do not impose. I do not compel or impel. I let people be. I give them the air and water to grow and be whatever they want to be. I am a gardener.

I met Field Marshal Manekshaw at a party. It was hilarious. Parsee to Parsee he turned towards me and with mock seriousness said, 'Tell me, O mighty astrologer of India, whether I am the real Manekshaw or his duplicate?' With equal mock seriousness, I replied, 'Both of us know that you are only a duplicate.' Loud laughter boomed for quite some time. Manekshaw was a typical Arien, a great soldier. Master of strategy. In Western astrology, Aries is the sign of war. In a split second I had observed that Manekshaw has a straight, strong, even line of fate and powerful mounts of Mars, both negative and positive (two mounts). This is the only secret I can reveal.

Finally, let me say on a winning note, India will be a superpower and share good fortune with the world. Happiness shared is happiness doubled. I had said it as early as 1990 in the *Eve's Weekly* of 20 January 1990.

Saturn in Scorpio

(5 October 2012 to 23 December 2014)

In my 2010 annual book, I had said, 'In this piece "World Horoscope", which I am writing on 3 June 2009, I have observed that Saturn will be in Libra, Western astrology, from 13 October 2009 to 5 October 2012. We may expect the following happy results for the world: 1) The poor, the downtrodden, the weak will find prosperity and peace. Justice will be done to them and that, to me, is of vital importance. 2) A New World Order: Ganesha claims there will be a new and certainly more just, fair and equitable world order replacing our present state of affairs. Why? Saturn in Libra will be in square or bad and ugly formation with Pluto in Capricorn. The main result of this will be the end of tyranny and brute force all over the world.'

We have seen the rebellion and the awakening in Syria, Egypt, Yemen and all over the Middle East. I find sweet satisfaction in my predictions. And please remember that the 2010 book came out in September 2009.

Encouraged by my fantastic predictions about Saturn in Libra, I am now making my predictions on Saturn in Scorpio, Western Astrology. Here goes:

Your Ganesha devotee is obsessed, wildly excited, about world peace. I am thrilled to predict that a most forward and positive step towards a better, brighter future will be taken when Saturn will be in Scorpio from 5 October 2012 to 23 December 2014.

Astro reason why?

Simply put, all the three watery signs Cancer (Jupiter), Scorpio (Saturn), Pisces (Neptune) will have a sweet and strong relationship between 5 October 2012 and 23 December 2014. In simple terms, it means inspiration, imagination, intuition, emotion; god's light, benevolence and blessing will be on common humanity, that is, all of us. It will make us kind, considerate, and understanding of the sorrows and sufferings of others. Human beings are more psychological than logical; this is my finding and experience from sixty years of actual astrology. Also, it will raise our level of consciousness to a different high. It will be a huge leap forward for mankind.

What will it be in easy-to-understand, practical terms?

The sea, the lakes, the rivers of India and the world will provide new and varied seafood, oil, products, minerals and matters as well as particles from outer space. Let me also be very frank with you. This will be a universal phenomenon, and not restricted only to India, though India will certainly go in for a powerful navy with more warships and submarines. Indian divers and deep-sea discoverers, scientists, engineers will help the world in research.

Fisheries, aquariums, new and better swimming, diving and surfing techniques will lead to benefits. In short, the treasures of the sea, including big and bountiful ships sunk years ago, will yield booty and riches. New systems of navigation will be discovered. In one single sentence, everything pertaining to the sea, rivers, lakes and water bodies will surface to the top and yield many surprises. We will be on a voyage of discovery. Yes, something will be done for the whales, dolphins, sharks and all marine life. I promise you all this in the name of Ganesha.

New Fuel Time, Chemical Time, Water Time, Liquid Time

I am eighty-three years old. I know I will not be there to see it but I can certainly promise revolutionary new techniques and even a new way of looking at the sea. It is quite possible that the sea will somehow find a way in space stations. Underground waterways will be feasible. From 5 October 2012 we have a tryst, or a meeting with the waters of the world. It is possible that ships, steamers, rafts and canoes of infinite size and possibilities will be built. Who knows, the seas will ride us, instead of us riding the seas! In a nutshell, it will be 'water time', liquid time. Obviously, this too will be universal. India cannot live in a vacuum.

Let me also quote from my 2012 book on Saturn in Scorpio, Western astrology. 'What does this imply for India and the World? Our army will specialize in the 4Cs, namely, command, control, communication and computers.' I have taken the 4Cs from *The Sunday Times* dated 1 May 2011. Scorpio is an aggressive, war-like, military sign. Saturn gives Scorpio structure, method and management. Therefore, for India, especially, Saturn in Scorpio from 6 October 2012 to 23 December 2014 will give these results.

Lakes, rivers, seas, water, and most certainly chemicals, DNA, drugs, medicines, surgery, private parts of the body, the back, mental anxiety and phobias, paranoid conditions and fear complexes, lunacy, sexual aberrations and deviations, all sorts of water therapy and mud packs, loss of limbs, anus trouble and surgeries come under Saturn in Scorpio. So does life-death-regeneration. That means karma and dharma, reincarnation, tantra and mantra come under the influence and impact of Saturn in Scorpio. Longevity may go up to 125 years or so. The mysteries of the sea and the ocean, the fish, the whale and the shark, the submarines will be fathomed, shown and revealed.

Scorpio is a powerful water sign. Ganesha has asked me to go a step further and predict that between 27 June 2013 and 16 July 2014, the above predictions will come true. It is like a long jumper who springs ahead. I am writing this now, to the chanting of mantras in the Shiva temple, which is in the same compound as my building. It is a good and lucky omen. It is a sign from God. It is between 27 June 2013 and 16 July 2014 that results will be obtained and targets achieved; technology will reach out to common humanity. Why common humanity? Appliances for homemakers, new and better fuel, oil, gas, gadgets for cookery, laundry, better washing soap, injections, drugs, soft and alcoholic drinks will be introduced. In other words, household amenities will be in plenty.

Why have I emphasized the period from 27 June 2013 to 16 July 2014? Jupiter will be in the watery sign Cancer during this period and will be making an excellent formation to Saturn in Scorpio and Neptune in Pisces. In other words, all the three watery signs will be in fusion, or exceptionally powerful and lucky in bonding.

Negative Impact

In life, we have sun and shadow, positive and negative, upside and downside. What will be the downside of Saturn in Scorpio? Scorpio is a very powerful money sign. Saturn is not happy in Scorpio. Therefore, on the financial frontier there will be tremendous highs and lows, conning and scams and bribery, and scandals. It will be a tsunami of frauds and deceits because Scorpio is capable of it. Mighty financial fluctuations are certain. In all fairness, I admit most happily and openly that Scorpio can be the yogi and the guru, adept in spiritual practices.

But Saturn in Scorpio has a cunning and shrewd side which cannot be neglected. Saturn in Scorpio is determined, but rather cruel, tyrannical and sometimes brutal. Secondly, Scorpio is about regimentation and control, and total power. The government may have extra surveillance, close observation and strict watch over the movements and even the aspirations, hopes and desires of the people. I also admit that I could be wrong, or I might have overemphasized or exaggerated it. There is a real and horrible danger of biological warfare, the use of virus, bacteria, nerve gas, bird flu, swine flu, viral epidemics, influenza, Spanish flu and other such ghastly and terrible threats to humanity.

We cannot forget that Scorpio is a warlike, powerful, solid, fixed, combative sign. As Saturn is unhappy in it, these negative impacts cannot be ruled out. The astrologer should be as impartial and objective as possible in his predictions. But as a human being he should be kind, considerate, understanding and forgiving of human foibles, weaknesses and shortcomings. That's my viewpoint. Readers are free to agree or disagree. I keep an open mind.

Drugs, earthquakes, tsunami, water-borne diseases and bacteria are the other awful possibilities.

Ganesha and the Energies proclaim that, despite difficulties and calamities, Saturn in Scorpio will be a mighty leap forward at all levels for all of us. Through determination and God's grace, waterways of universal prosperity will open out.

Secrets of Human Nature by Astrology

My Lord and Master Ganesha says human beings are a bundle of contradictions. We keep on changing. A husband can live with his wife for twenty years and yet the wife may not really know him. Murderers and rapists can be very kind to pets. Sometimes cool and calculating persons can suddenly go berserk, wild, angry, irrational, eccentric and completely mad with rage and anger. How come this sudden, different changes in the same person?

When we say that you are a Cancerian or a Leo or a Libran it only means that your sun is in Cancer or Leo or Libra by Western astrology. But other planets, example Mercury, Saturn, Jupiter, Venus, Uranus also have their influence, effect and say. It is the great and mighty possible combinations of all these planets at a given time which will decide your character and your human nature. When the planets change, when the combinations alter, human nature also alters. Also, it is fact that we want different things at different times. In other words, our motivations, our targets, our purpose, our goals also go on changing. Change is the only real guarantee in our life. Nothing else is final.

Here is a short exciting list of the characteristics of some celestial bodies:

JUPITER: Wisdom, religion, expansion at all levels including becoming fat, prosperous, egoistic, loves flattery, very social. Attracts money and fame.

MERCURY: Communication, contacts, correspondence, travel, trade, gossip, quick-witted, versatile. Often changes work and pleasure.

SATURN: Very responsible, duty conscious, stingy, hard working, organized, uses people. Surprisingly, very spiritual. I cannot explain this contradiction.

VENUS: Fond of harmony, food, flowers, decoration, luxury, fashions, beauty, sex, creativity. Charming, great lover, very vain and needs praise all the time. Can love and be loved.

SUN: Glory, good looking, lover of life, arts, governmental position, born leader. Also selfish and lazy. Attracts success and people like a magnet.

MARS: Energy, combative, assertive, born fighter, courageous, very physical, sexual. Difficult to deal with but frank, warm, open, generous. A paradox. Good friend, bad enemy.

URANUS: Science, technology, all things new and strange and mysterious, computers, aviation. Uranus can turn the world on its head.

NEPTUNE: Inspiration, intuition, perfume, narcotics, drugs, fishing, dreaming, hallucinations, psychic, prophetic, visionary of the future. Swindling, cheating, smuggling, deceiving. Many mixed characteristics of Neptune.

PLUTO: Power of the atom bomb, very mysterious, life-death-regeneration comes under Pluto. Gases, common people, revolution. Pluto is all about power.

MOON: Changeable, impressionable, inspirational, kind, sympathetic, caring, tender, loving, moody. Also divine, gracious, uncertain, forgiving. Like the ebb and rise of the tide.

Now, dear readers, you can understand that human nature is the sum total or compost of all the planets. These planets often pull in different directions. That makes life interesting, exciting, complex, but unpredictable. Twelve months therefore twelve signs. Each planet shows different characteristics in each and every sign. Now you can understand the complexity, complications and the changing kaleidoscope of human nature.

Also, I must admit that psychology, psychiatry, hypnotism, biology, genetics, scientific methodology, have their influence and importance. I may be right or wrong but I believe that if there is no God we will discover or invent God. The need and demand for God is there. In addition, technology also has a part to play, for example the lie detector test. Your Ganesha devotee loves to explore human nature in all its diversity and ramifications. I also admit that my reach is limited. I try to go to the end of the line – and beyond.

World Horoscope 2014

Here
   wild roses laugh
   mocking the cruelty
   of their thorns,
Here
   there are no heroes of humanity
   only common people
   who live and love and laugh.

From Bejan's book, *I Am the Sky*

Ganesha says this poem speaks about: a) Courage and determination of Nature. b) Mankind's determination and guts to go right ahead and win the game of life. I have begun with this poem because it is the essence of the world in 2014. In short, we shall prevail. How and why?

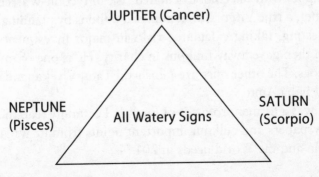

Ganesha says you can see from the illustration of the triangle that Jupiter, signifying growth, is right at the top. The simple reason is that from 27 June 2013 Jupiter will be at maximum strength and power in the sign Cancer by Western astrology. Jupiter simply put means growth, prosperity, plenty, good luck. Jupiter will be in Cancer till 16 July 2014. During this period, Saturn will be in Scorpio and Neptune in Pisces.

Here is the clincher. Jupiter, Neptune and Saturn will all be in watery signs. In other words, a triangle or trine of watery signs. Water is life. Water is hope. Water is any shape or form you can conceive of. Water is the juice of creation. Water is the essence of nature itself. Therefore, your Ganesha devotee, who believes in all religions, says very humbly but firmly, 'The period between 27 June 2013 to 16 July 2014 will lay the foundation stone or seeds of peace, prosperity and progress for mankind.' Yes. I am laying myself on the line because, right or wrong, all the energies force me to take a strong, positive, final decision. Remember the lines, 'Heard are the voices, the saints and the sages, say, hope and despair not.'

To me, astrology fuses the inspiration and intuition of the poet with the cold, calculated risk of tycoon Warren Buffet, a true Virgo. Buffet amassed billions by planning, investing, taking calculated risks in major investments and then gave away millions in charity. He is one of my heroes. The other ones are Jamshedji Tata, Vivekananda and Baba Amte.

I was a former professor of English. I certainly read the newspapers and cull out important points from it. What India and the World needs in 2014 is:

1) Infrastructure
2) No prejudice
3) Less corruption
4) Better health and hygiene
5) Less is more
6) Systematizing LIFE itself
7) Performance orientation
8) Technology, rationality are kings
9) Methodology and perfection
10) Managing men and matters better
11) The best way to get things done
12) Precision and Perfection
13) Health, Hygiene, Welfare
14) Canned packaged spirituality, salvation.
15) Contacts and Communication
16) Open mind and fair play
17) Resourcefulness (key to everything in life)

I admit openly that I am not quite sure of the canned and packaged spirituality. Meditation and Yoga take time and patience. Spirituality is not a magic wand.

Numerology

I follow the Hebrew Kabala of numbers. Adding the year 2014 we get 2 + 0 + 1 + 4 = 7. The number 7 vibrates to the planet Neptune. It means imagination and inspiration and intuition and a leap from the known to the unknown which will lead to joy and happiness. In other words, take risks. Also, Neptune stands for drugs and drinks and corruption. Avoid these three. By the Tarot, card number 7 stands for the Chariot. A young man is riding it. Chariot means progress. The young man means the future of the world is not with the old but with the young. To me this is as simple as daylight. In other words, it means the reins of power will shift to the young, the brave, the active, the agile who can implement new ideas and innovations and inventions for the future of all of us. I am sure it is all absolutely clear to you.

Ganesha says my devotee Bejan goes with the flow. That is the secret of his success. Right now he is the river, changing into a sea, becoming the ocean and gushing again. Yes, today, 30 June 2013, I am with Nelson Mandela and Obama in spirit but not in flesh. Mandela was born on 18 July 1918. He is a Cancerian. Jupiter entered the sign Cancer on 26 June 2013. Both Jupiter for luck and Sun for power are in the sign Cancer by Western astrology. Double power, double compassion, double caring, double generosity. Therefore, double joy for the world starts. By Hebrew Kabala of numbers Mandela comes to 23: M(4), A(1), N(5), D(4), E(5), L(3), A(1). I have said about number 23: 'Fortune's favourite. Communication with others will be vibrant and richly rewarding. Your talents will be recognized. What more do you want?'

Number 23 is called Star of Lion. (Ratan Tata, the philanthropic tycoon, is also the number 23 by Hebrew Kabala.) The paradox is Mandela has two 8s in his complete birth date. That means Saturn. Saturn is duty. Saturn is voice of God. But if we add his personal birth date 18 we get number 9. Number 9 means energy, power, bravery. Combining 8 and 9 we get the real Mandela. Strong, caring, doing duty, surviving everything. Loving everybody. Finally, winning the game.

This also means that Africa, Cancerian continent, will come into its own between July 2013 and July 2014. But what is the final forensic match? Many times Cancerians live in the past. That is their speciality. Today 30 June 2013, *The Times of India* says, 'Last week, thousands of Greeks took part in the Prometheia festival, celebrating the Titan Prometheus, who, according to legend, stole fire from the Gods and gave it to humans. The Prometheia festival involves prayers, marriages and even a naming ceremony where adherents give up their Christian names and take up a Hellenic name, usually out of myth and literature.' This is the clincher, the final evidence, of Jupiter in Cancer, Western astrology. I combine facts, reality and actual happening of events. Not mere theory.

Thanks to Jupiter in Cancer, Neptune in Pisces, Saturn in Scorpio, anything connected with liquids, for example, 'Water Monitor', water therapy will rescue us all. I repeat once again growth and resourcefulness, the two basic water qualities, will lead India and the world to fame, fortune, fun. Amen. So be it.

Nastur, Bejan's Hanuman

A word about the Uttarakhand tragedy. My son Nastur says, 'Bapuji, you must speak about this great horrible human tragedy.' Yes, he is right. Before such suffering and misery, I kneel in prayer and utter humiliation to Ganesha, Christ, Allah and the Zoroastrian Holy Fire. It is not a time to predict why it happened, though I can do so. This is just a time for all of us to be human and humane (kind). I will put it very simply. We cannot be happy till all are happy. By sharing the misery of others, misery becomes less and perhaps bearable. Humanity is God. We must do our very best to make others happy. This is very simple. To me this is the greatest mantra. Believe me or not – it is up to you. I openly admit that my son Nastur is my Hanuman. I am sure this says it all.

Vision of the Future

Ganesha commands me to have a world view, a real spectrum of things to come. Ganesha says that in prediction the placing of planets is important. What is more important is the VISION combining planetary positions with whatever ESP, intuition, inspiration I do have, I am humbly marking out the predictions for the world.

1) 2021, watermark for technology
2) 2033, important for technology and genetics
3) 2035-2037, crucial for chemicals and experiments about life and living, Jupiter in Cancer, Saturn in Virgo
4) 2040, relationships taken to the next level, Jupiter and Saturn in Libra
5) 2040, the year marks justice for the whole world. Yes, Ganesha says this is my devotee's mighty prediction
6) 2045, another unimaginable breakthrough in technology, space travel, brain mapping, time-warp galaxies, Jupiter in Aquarius, Saturn in Sagittarius
7) 2047, all of the above will be superbly analysed, organized, methodized, mapped out in complete detail and, most importantly, put and harnessed to the greatest use for the greatest number of people. It

is the high point or the tipping point for the service to the wide cosmos.

Special note

Putting on a 'thinking cap' to increase brain power is also another wondrous and awesome technological possibility of our Aquarian age. (I am writing this on 7 July 2013 under the auspicious conjunction of Moon and Jupiter in Cancer, Western astrology.)

Mars, Planet of War

Till 25 July 2014 Mars, planet of war, revolution, assassination, violence, riots, could play havoc with leaders and even tear apart the fabric of a country. I know these are strong words. I hope I go wrong, but pre-warned is pre-armed. This applies not only to India but to the world. Yes, so many goodies, but still upsets and violence. It breaks my heart. But I have tried to develop the vision of seeing the world complete and seeing the world whole, warts and all. I bleed. I am sticking my neck out and further saying that in 2014 the months of January, April, July, October could cause havoc. Could means only a mere possibility. Not to panic.

Difficulties and Mishaps

Your Ganesha devotee is a born optimist. For him, the bottle is always half full. He is positive. Therefore, for him to predict mishaps and accidents is like cutting away or amputating his own arm. But astrology deals with reality, facts, figures. In other words, the astrologer cannot afford to blink at the cruelty and mighty tragedies of life.

I hope I go wrong but this is what may happen (not must).

The assassination of world leaders, tsunamis, earthquakes is a possibility. Let me quote about the previous tsunami from my 2004 book, page 33. I am quoting word for word. You are most welcome to check it out. 'The bugbear could well be typhoons, tidal waves, pollution of rivers and waters, earthquakes, as Uranus, planet of sudden and sharp reversal and even calamities, will be in Pisces, a great water sign. The death and destruction, pollution of water life everywhere in the world, terrifies me, gives me nightmares. Astro-reason? Saturn, the tough one, will be in Cancer, a water sign, till 16 July 2005, and will be actively cooperating, colluding, conspiring with Uranus in Pisces, another water sign.'

There is a somewhat parallel to it from 26 June 2013 when Jupiter enters Cancer and will be in power position with Saturn in Scorpio and Uranus in Pisces, all three overflowing water signs. This overflow, this huge bubbling water energy, could result in floods, tsunami, typhoons, hurricanes, storms and the horrendous destruction which can go with it. I repeat. This is a mere possibility. We should be prepared for it. But it does not mean that the world will end. No way. I say with the blessings of all the 'ENERGIES', the best is yet to be.

Now I am eighty-three. Time to live for others. It is in the time of real crisis that we human beings show our resourcefulness, ingenuity and daring. It will be so during 2013 and 2014 also. I live by this principle. The courage to go to the end of the line and even beyond. It is a line from the ancient hero Boewulf. Yes, time to open out my heart to you. Who knows, I may not be there! I know, dear readers, you are hoping for predictions about countries.

INDIA: Capricornian India marches along bravely. Despite economic crises, corruption, pollution, sheer chicanery, deception, trickery and cheating, India will prosper and progress. Pluto in India's own sign by Western astrology has the power of the atom bomb.

IRAN: Iran has a new leader in Hussain Rohan. There is a possibility that he will turn Iran around to a peace settlement. I know it is easy to say it. But I have his birth particulars: 12 November 1948. Hussain has his Venus, the planet of peace and balance in Libra, the sign of harmony and balance. Therefore this man is reasonable and the world can consequently deal with him, come to a sort of understanding. That's the main reason for hope.

AMERICA, RUSSIA, BRAZIL AND AFRICA: Cancerian country America (Born July 4) will have sinew and muscle power. China will not be able to get the better of America. Leo Obama will prove his mettle. For America, I take three signs: Cancer, Gemini and Sagittarius. The actual mix is my very own. America will lead. That says it all. Obama is a Leo. Jupiter will be in Leo from July 17, 2014 to August 11, 2015. Ganesha says this will be a great and glorious period for Obama and America.

Russia under Putin comes under Gemini, Aquarius and Scorpio. Not a very easy time for it. Weather conditions and strong disciplinary action will take a huge toll. I report it as I see it. Like my great Hanuman, I too am humble and submissive. No pretentions to greatness.

Brazil and Africa are the surprise packages, not China. Yes, strange as it may seem, there is a possibility of a compromise between Afghanistan, USA, Pakistan and India. This may seem like a pipedream. But given time and the right climate, the impossible can be made possible. Time and again, I have noticed this, and remember I am now eighty-three and still feeling good about the future of the world.

JERUSALEM: I openly admit that Jerusalem shakes my heart and I am transported to this mighty city. It is one of the most sacred and unique and magical hubs of the world. It is most unfortunate, ironic and truly tragic that these two Semitic races fight each other to the death. The Jews and the Arabs are both descended from Shem. I quote from my 2012 book *End of the world*: 'The final countdown for a lasting peace could, however, well be 2018 when Jupiter will be in Capricorn, an earth sign. Ganesha gives the final nod to Jerusalem which is only 125 sq km of land but PURE GOLD ALL THE WAY! Ganesha says it could well be around 2015 also.'

CHINA: I acknowledge the great civilization of China and its massive economic power and clout. Here China is superior to my beloved India. But China has crushed Tibet and discarded HH the 14th Dalai Lama. I may be right or wrong but my gut feeling is China will have to pay dearly for it. The Dalai Lama is a Cancerian, a cardinal water sign. To deny the Dalai Lama is to deny life itself. China comes under the signs of Libra and Cancer by my theory. Mars will be in Libra for half the year and Mars in Libra is very miserable and could (not must) cause havoc in every which way. No country is my enemy. I wish China all the best. I am only predicting what I see with my very limited powers. I wish the whole world well, as the mystics say.

Lastly, the gene responsible for the elixir of youth is PHA-4. Virgo is the sign of youth. Jupiter will be in Virgo from 12 August 2015 to 9 September 2016. No wrinkles. No crinkles. No rough spots. Clean glistening skin and body. Please expect this. And now, I jokingly predict that all the women of the world will kiss my soft rosy cheeks with passion unlimited! Ha! Ha!

What Is So Special about Dhoni?

- Helicopter shot
- Captain cool
- Explosive Force

Ganesha says the whole cricketing world knows and acknowledges that Dhoni has attained the Number 1 position. Where does Dhoni go from here? (I am writing this piece on 21 July 2013.) The numerologist in me is excited by the undeniable fact that three Cancerians Sunil Gavaskar, (10 July), Saurav Ganguly (8 July), Dhoni (7 July) have made it big. Who knows, the cricketer with the missing birth date 9 July is on his way! Please, I am half-kidding!

Dhoni was born on 7/7/1981. There are two 7s in his birth date, and he wears a shirt No 7. No. 7 vibrates to Neptune, mysterious, restless, unknown depths of reserve and energy, an appeal to the sentiments of people, matched only by film stars. Why film stars? Because Neptune is the key planet for film stars! Now you know the magnitude and power of Dhoni's appeal. Interesting, eh?

The distinguishing quality of Dhoni is his ability to smash the bowlers for huge sixes and, also, to play quietly and slowly with a straight bat when the team requires him to do so. The astro reason is Jupiter, planet of good luck, and Saturn, planet of determination and tenacity, are in the cool, balanced, objective sign, Libra. When Jupiter (good luck) combines with Saturn (willpower) it results in:

a) calculated risks
b) intuitive tactics
c) the law of chance working in favour
d) tremendous self-confidence.

Gemini is the sign of quicksilver reflexes, movement, hawk's eye, versatility of strokes. In Gemini, Dhoni has Mars, the planet of force and tremendous striking power. Therefore, Dhoni is able to hit towering sixes in all directions. Dhoni also has Mercury in Gemini. *Mercury means speed and instant decisions. In other words, even as the ball is in the air, Dhoni can change his strokes instantly. This is the hallmark of a great batsman.* Rahu is associated with explosive force. Leo indicates tremendous power. Therefore, Rahu in Leo in Dhoni's horoscope clearly shows the sledgehammer might of his strokes. This mighty force is responsible for his helicopter shot and his unorthodox, inventive, square-cut and cover drive.

Thanks to Mercury (versatility and great repertoire of strokes), Sun in Cancer (fixity and fortitude), Uranus in Scorpio (tremendous ability to change the entire complexion and nature of a game), he will continue to entertain and enthrall. That to me at least is worth a thousand centuries! That's what cricket is all about.

I keep an open mind. Therefore, you have a right to believe or not believe in astrology. Your choice. But just for the record I have to state that in July 2013 Dhoni had been praised to the sky. He deserves his accolades.

But why was he so openly and universally applauded and given accolades around July 2013? The astro reason is Dhoni is a Cancerian, and in July 2013 Jupiter, the planet of good luck, was also in the sign Cancer. Jupiter will be there in Cancer till 16 July 2014. Therefore, he will continue at the apex of power at least till 16 July 2014. Let me add, Dhoni is there to stay for quite a few more years. I am now eighty-three and like all old people I love to ramble. It is the curse of old age. Therefore bear with me when I say I was born on 11 July. Ha! Ha! Ha!

I am now giving out a few invaluable astrological secrets. My father Jehangir was the weaving superintendent of seven mills in the good old days when Ahmedabad was the Manchester of India. I was the neighbour of Sir Udain Chinubhai (Baronet). Udain had specially called old stalwarts like Vinoo Mankad, Kishenchand, Salim Durrani, Umrigar to Ahmedabad. Therefore, I too had the benefit of being coached by Vinoo Mankad and specially Kishenchand. Like Vinoo I too was a left-hander. This has enabled me to relate cricket and planets. Here is exactly what I have to say:

Cricket	Planets
Majestic cover drive	Jupiter
Swing, googly, flipper, off-break, leg-break	Mercury and Neptune
Timing of strokes and style	Venus
Sixers and helicopter shot	Rahu, Sun, Mars
Wristy glance and drives	Combo of Mercury, Venus, Neptune

Dhoni has two 7s in his birth data. By the tarot card, the number 7 shows a young, dashing, charioteer. This fits in wonderfully well with our Dhoni. Ganesha calls him the Prince of Cricket.

Ganesha has the last word.

Match Fixing

Ganesha says match fixing is horrendous and is a slur, a smudge, a curse on the fair name of cricket, the game of true sportsmanship. It is a crying shame. The most horrible part of it is that the offenders are not needy but plain and simple greedy. In short, it is unforgivable.

Astrology alone does not have all the answers. No discipline – be it psychology, technology, biology and so on – has all the answers. But astrologically I do say that Neptune, the planet of both imagination and deceit, in the secret sign Pisces is mainly responsible for it. Neptune will be in Pisces till 30 March 2025. Obviously, this does not mean that cheating and match fixing will continue till then.

I am an astrologer. I deal in real life, facts, things as they are, not things as we would wish them to be. Life is cruel. Life can hurt and cripple even a great and good man. This I know well. I am writing this on 21 July 2013 when Jupiter is in Cancer. Jupiter in Cancer favours honesty, integrity and uprightness. Therefore, the howl of protest against match fixing. Jupiter will be in Cancer till 16 July 2014. During this period match fixing will be less and the offenders will be meted out due punishment.

Virgo is the sign of the Virgin, that is, absolute purity and goodness. Jupiter, the planet of goodness, will be in Virgo, the sign of purity, in 2015-2016. Ganesha says it should almost eliminate match fixing then.

Jimmy Mistry: Vibrant, Versatile Gemini

~~~

Ganesha says versatility is the first, middle and last name of the Geminis. Yes, versatility fits them like the proverbial glove, a cliché, but very apt. A case in point, to use an old English expression, is Gemini Jimmy Mistry who has realized his dream of Della Adventure, India's Largest Adventure Park, Lonavala.

Della Adventure has it all – spa, saloon, gym, pool lounge, yoga centre, training room, boardroom, archery, rappelling, rope challenge courses, barrel crawl, mini flying fox, Tarzan jump, balance beam, wheelbarrow race, running bungee, vertical climb, slippery slope, kayaking, and so much more ... Wow! A typical Gemini list.

Jimmy was born on 12 June 1971. He has the Sun and Mercury in versatile Gemini, the Moon and Mars in original and exceptionally creative Aquarius, the sign of our New Age, and Saturn and Venus in Taurus, the sign of hotel, food, spa and all sorts of entertainment. It is the combination of all these planets which have made him a leader in his chosen field. In addition, Jimmy has a passion for speed, stunts, good design, great food, excellent music. He was in Italy working with the Italians and the Italians know how to enjoy. To me the most important fact about Jimmy is his love for goodness in all its forms, namely thought, word and deed. Yes, Jimmy will do India proud in the years to come. It all comes together from around July to October 2013. All the energies bless Jimmy.

The Mystery and Secret of
Narendra Modi

Ganesha points out that be it a safe deposit vault or a human being, there is a master key to open it. What is the master key which will open the personality of Narendra Modi? I am now eighty-three. For the first time I am revealing the inner workings of the horoscope. Narendra was born on 17 September 1950. Therefore the degree of his Sun is 23 degrees, as per Western astrology. This is fine tuning. The 23rd degree of Narendra shows 'an animal trainer, harnessing energies'. In other words, he is born to crack the whip in the circus of politics. It is in his genes. I do not judge people. That's not my job. My job is to find out what makes them tick and report it to the best of my ability. In other words, if Narendra, whom I have met twice, can control politicians and organize successfully, he will be a winner. Whether he will be the prime minister or not is a different issue. We all have warts and defects. I neither excuse nor accuse. My final comment is he is a good politician.

As per palmistry it is the absence of lines on his palm which makes Narendra unique. He has a strong mount of Jupiter. In the dice test, my secret research, tried out before on Morarji Desai and Vajpayee, Narendra threw the dice numbers 3 and 5. 3 means luck. 5 means intelligence. Therefore, by this method Narendra = luck + intelligence. For the first time I am revealing how I actually predict. I am after all only mortal and I have enjoyed my innings thoroughly. I specialize in laughing at myself!

By the tarot card the number 17 is named 'L'ETOILE'. A lady is pouring a pitcher of water. Above her are the stars. It shows nourishment. This also applies to Narendra. Therefore, the basic quest of Narendra is to tame the politicians, organize efficiently and also nourish the poor and the weak. It is quite a poser. To me that is his real challenge. May Ganesha bless him. According to me, and I may be wrong, the number 17 of the tarot card has a connection with our Aquarian Age. That's a very big deal.

Experiments in Verse

Holy Fire

(The Holy Fire is sacred, both to the Hindus and the Parsis. This is a paean of praise to the Holy Fire)

The world is a rosebud
Smiling in the heart of your flame
Oh Divine Fire, holiest of the holy,
Oh Fire, most High, sacrosanct
Favour me with a sip of light, and
Love and laughter
Shall hug the cosmos
In boundless generosity.
Joy will be the Bird of Paradise
Winging the galaxies and the Milky Way.
Magic and melody
Will dance in eternity of ecstasy.

***

Woman

(For my wife Gooli)

You are more
Much, much more
than full, fertile, flowing over...
cornucopia

You are light and darkness
Everything in between
And beyond.

Important Announcement

Our Ganesha devotee Bejan Daruwalla has moved from Mumbai to Ahmedabad. His Ahmedabad address is:

Bejan Daruwalla
Astrologer and Columnist
C/o Nastur Daruwalla,
A-5, Spectrum Towers,
Opposite Police Stadium,
Shahibag
Ahmedabad 380004
India.

Telephone: (079) 32954387
Nastur's telephone: 09825470377
Meetu's telephone: 09974031159

Email:
info@bejandaruwalla.com
bejandaruwalla@rediffmail.com
Website: www.bejandaruwalla.com